The Welcome Business

The Welcome Business

Glenn Mehta

Gill & Macmillan

Gill & Macmillan Ltd
Hume Avenue
Park West
Dublin 12
with associated companies throughout the world
www.gillmacmillan.ie

© Glenn Mehta 2007

978 07171 42620

Index compiled by Helen Litton
Print origination in Ireland by TypeIT, Dublin

The paper used in this book is made from the wood pulp of managed forests. For every
tree felled, at least one tree is planted, thereby renewing natural resources.

Acknowledgments

This book is dedicated to Eileen, Lex and Shawn, with heart-felt thanks for all their love and support – always.

Thanks also to Emma-May Thunder for her contribution to Chapter 11 – Tourism Law.

Finally, I would like to acknowledge the contributions and support from my fellow lecturers and management at ITT Dublin.

Additional Resources for *The Welcome Business:*

Easy to use online support material for this book is available at

www.gillmacmillan.ie/lecturers.

To access lecturer support material on our secure website:

1. Go to www.gillmacmillan.ie/lecturers

2. Log on using your username and password. If you don't have a password, register online and we will e-mail your password to you.

Contents

Preface

Tourism in Ireland is at a crossroads. After a decade of unprecedented growth, external factors are impacting on growth patterns. World terror alerts, wars, economic crises, currency and oil price fluctuations and a myriad of other factors impact on most industries, but particularly the tourism industry, given the international nature of tourism. These factors are mainly out of the control of the Irish government, which relies on tourism as a crucial indigenous industry, supporting one in every eight members of Ireland's workforce, and is of particular importance in regional economies.

Internal challenges come from Ireland's growing economy. Obviously of benefit to all industries (including tourism), the booming economy of the 1990s and the (slower) growing economic situation since has resulted in several challenges. Irish people often turn their back on home-grown/domestic tourism offerings, choosing instead to spend their high levels of disposable income on foreign travel. Increasing home-purchase prices, interest rates and general inflation put a demand on the levels of disposable income traditionally spent on luxury items such as travel and tourism. The growing economy has created the need for immigration in Ireland, and a challenge facing tourism organisations and private product and service providers alike is how to continue to offer a unique Irish welcome when a large proportion of the staff actually doing the welcoming are non-Irish nationals themselves, some with a poor command of the English language. This trend is set to continue as Ireland's economy grows, leading to further demands for immigrant workers from all over the world.

Even with the many challenges facing the industry, Irish and world tourism is continuing to grow. New markets are opening up as both tourism-generating regions and tourism destinations. Ireland's position in the near-future tourism world order is uncertain, as traditional destinations struggle to hold their market share of international tourist arrivals. Further, newly emerging generating markets that were previously isolated by political or economic factors (Eastern Europe, China, India) pose a major opportunity that Irish tourism will wish to exploit at the expense of many competitors.

This book introduces the reader to the area of tourism and travel. It looks at world and Irish tourism patterns and shows how mass tourism has evolved since its humble beginnings to become a major force in international trade. The structure of world and Irish tourism (Republic of Ireland and Northern Ireland) is highlighted and the organisations (public and private) with a voice in Irish tourism are presented. Tourism's importance to the economy of any particular country or region is also discussed in detail before focusing in particular on how tourism impacts the Irish economy in terms of taxation and other income for the government, employment in the industry, regional economic factors, balance of payments and investment in tourism. The aim is to contextualise the economic importance of tourism, first globally, then nationally (in the case of Ireland) and finally regionally.

The book then moves on to focus on the various elements of the tourism product – the unique collection of products, services, events and attractions that actually make up the experience of the tourist to the island of Ireland, helping them to realise their own 'Island of Memories', as Tourism Ireland (the all-Ireland agency that markets Ireland) describes the destination. Once the general area of the tourism product has been discussed, the book presents what the author believes to be the three most important elements of the tourism product: accommodation, transport and visitor attractions. Each of these areas will be comprehensively discussed in their own respective chapters.

The travel industry is analysed and critiqued, with particular emphasis on competitive pressures facing tour operators and travel retailers alike. The process of disintermediation (cutting out the intermediary) and the growing impact of technology and e-commerce in travel and tourism are given their own dedicated chapter.

Towards the end of the book, business tourism is contrasted to leisure tourism, and the different forms of business tourism precede the evolution of the sector in Ireland, including the provision for a National Conference Centre in Dublin.

The final chapter of the book presents some of the Irish and EU legal issues that any student, researcher or employee in the area of travel, tourism and hospitality should be aware of.

Appendices in this book include a complete glossary of tourism and travel terms used in the book, as well as comprehensive website resources for further reading and research. An up-to-date contacts directory for hundreds of public and private travel and tourism organisations on the entire island of Ireland is also presented. Finally, tables of tourism and travel statistics for Ireland and world tourism patterns are presented.

Each chapter begins with a summary of the key points of the chapter, followed by the expected learning outcomes of the chapter. After a brief introduction to the topic, the major points of the topic are discussed in detail. Relevant case studies appear throughout each chapter. URL addresses as a link to web resources for further reading or research are provided where appropriate. Each chapter concludes with basic revision questions, exam-type essay questions, tasks and assignments. The basic revision questions require short answers, while the exam-type essay questions look for a more detailed analysis of the topic, encouraging the reader to illustrate a deeper understanding and to demonstrate their ability to contextualise an issue or solve a problem from a tourism management point of view. Many tasks include topics for debate relevant to the chapter and suggested assignments are presented which can be used as gradable assessments.

As tourism is a living and rapidly changing discipline, this book discusses the situation with regard to the specific topic up to summer 2006. Several chapters conclude with speeches and press releases by the Irish government minister with responsibility for tourism, in most cases illustrating the current and future plans relevant to the chapter, as announced by the government of Ireland. Further updates are available from the relevant websites highlighted throughout the book.

The Welcome Business

'Hospitality skills must include the ability to offer visitors the traditional Irish welcome, which is the centrepiece of our branding as a holiday destination...as leaders of those troops, I would appeal to you to make sure that every one of them – no matter where they come from, no matter what their job is – knows they are all in the welcome business... If we should ever lose that simplicity, that humanity or that naturalness, then we can literally shut down our tills and go home.' – Gillian Bowler, Chairperson of Fáilte Ireland

Source: Connolly, N., 'Irish tourism to rely more on foreign staff', *The Sunday Business Post*, 7 March 2004.

Chapter 1

The Concept of Tourism

SUMMARY

In this, the opening chapter, the reader is introduced to the concept of tourism. The chapter brings together various definitions of the terms 'tourism' and 'tourist' as well as the different forms of tourism. Some of the travel motivators are presented and discussed. It also provides an introduction to the massive growth of tourism over the last century throughout the world. Barriers to travel are highlighted, as are the growing number of career opportunities in the industry.

LEARNING OUTCOMES

Having completed this chapter, the reader should be able to:
- Understand the concept of tourism and travel.
- Define the terms 'tourism' and 'tourist'.
- Understand the motivators for travel.
- Understand the reasons for worldwide tourism growth.
- Appreciate the various barriers to tourism.
- Research the career paths relating to tourism.

INTRODUCTION TO TOURISM

'Tourism: The sum of processes, activities and outcomes arising from the interactions among tourists, tourism suppliers, host governments, host communities, origin governments, universities, community colleges and non-governmental organisations in the process of attracting, transporting, hosting and managing tourists and other visitors.'

This is the definition of tourism offered by Weaver and Lawton (2006). Indeed, several authors offer various definitions of tourism. The world organisation charged with the responsibility of research and development of tourism, the United Nations World Tourism Organization (UNWTO or WTO) defines tourism as comprising 'the activities of persons travelling to and staying in places outside their usual environment for not more than one consecutive year for leisure, business and other purposes.'

The UNWTO further divides the term 'tourism' into three concepts, depending on whether a person is travelling to, from or within a certain country.
- **Inbound tourism** involves non-residents received by a destination country from the point of view of that destination.

- **Outbound tourism** involves residents travelling to another country from the point of view of the country of origin.
- **Domestic tourism** involves residents of a given country travelling within that country.

All types of travellers who engage in tourism are termed visitors. This can further be divided between same-day visitors (day-trippers) or overnight visitors (tourists).

Ireland is quite unique when it comes to defining the type of visitor coming to the Republic. International inbound tourism includes all foreign arrivals to the Republic of Ireland from every destination outside the island of Ireland (visitors coming to Ireland are termed arrivals). Arrivals from within the twenty-six counties of the Republic of Ireland visiting any part of the Republic are termed domestic tourists for the Republic. This leaves arrivals from Northern Ireland fitting into neither the international inbound sector nor the domestic tourist sector. Irish tourism statistics have a third unique sector – Northern Ireland arrivals. Therefore, the three categories of arrivals in the Republic are as follows:

- International arrivals.
- Domestic arrivals.
- Northern Ireland arrivals.

Tourism may also be defined as the ability of people to escape from familiar surroundings and everyday routine, and centres around travel and the industry that has developed to service it.

From the various definitions, we can note that there are three fundamental components in the definition of tourism, as follows:

1. Movement away from a place of habitual residence…
2. …for a particular period of time of less than one year but more than one night, and
3. for a particular purpose, e.g. business, leisure.

Some definitions of tourism involve staying at least one night in another country. However, it is this author's opinion that such a definition fails to take account of domestic tourism, and so the term 'place of habitual residence' serves better to include domestic tourists.

FORMS OF TOURISM

There are several possibilities for dividing tourism into various forms. The following is one such division.

Visiting Friends and Relatives (VFR)

The VFR section involves people travelling to a destination to visit family, relatives and friends. The people travelling could be guests in their destination country, or they could originally be from such a country, for example, an Irish-American family living in New York travelling to Kerry to visit their family. A sizeable proportion of Ireland's tourists belong to this category. Around three-quarters of Ireland's tourist arrivals come from Britain and the US, many of whom are originally Irish or are Irish by ancestry. This is a major source of visitors for Ireland's VFR segment. From a tourism economic point of view, those who travel to visit friends and relatives often do not spend money on accommodation or food and beverage, compared to visitors who do not have friends and relatives in a destination and so are forced to engage accommodation and eat in restaurants.

Business

Business tourism is an extremely lucrative form of tourism, as it generally brings large amounts of income to a destination. The varying forms of business tourism are discussed in detail in Chapter 10 and include incentive travel, conferences, congresses and business meetings.

Leisure

A sizeable majority of world tourism is devoted to the pursuit of leisure activities. There are countless sub-categories; what constitutes leisure for one tourist may not for another. Leisure holidays may include city breaks, seaside holidays, skiing holidays, etc.

Special Interest

There has been a growth in recent years in alternative forms of tourism, focused on specific segments of the population. The list is once again endless, and so the following is simply a small sample of such special-interest holidays:

- Religious tourism.
- Health and medical tourism.
- Green tourism.
- Sports tourism.
- Gay and lesbian tourism.
- Seniors tourism.
- Singles tourism.
- Arts and cultural tourism.
- Heritage tourism.
- Smoking breaks (destinations where there is no smoking ban).

MOTIVATION FOR TRAVEL

Wright and Linehan (2004: 2) note that 'people's desire for travel is related to their immediate socio-physical environments and the appeal of what lies beyond.' Humans are natural explorers, and travel feeds this appetite for exploration. Weaver and Lawton (2006) define motivation for travel as follows:

> *Travel motivation is different from travel purpose in that it indicates the intrinsic reasons the individual is embarking on a particular trip. Thus, a person may be travelling for VFR purposes, but the underlying motivation is to resolve a dispute with a parent, or to renew a relationship with a former partner. A pleasure or leisure purpose may indicate a deeper need to escape routine. In all these cases, the apparent motivation may itself have some even more fundamental psychological basis, such as the need for emotional satisfaction.*

The American Traveller Survey asked over 10,000 households in the US what motivated them to travel the last time they did so, and offers the following four categories:
1. Relaxation.
2. Desire to learn.
3. Adventure.
4. Social contact.

A more psychological approach for studying motivation for travel can be linked to Maslow's Hierarchy of Needs, beginning with basic physiological needs (food, water, sex) and climbing through safety needs, acceptance needs, esteem needs and finally self-actualisation/fulfilment needs, in that order from basic needs for survival to self-fulfilment. The first three needs are termed deficiency needs, as they must be satisfied for basic human comfort. The last two are termed growth needs, as they focus on growth and development.

Maslow's hierarchy is based on the premise that individuals move up the hierarchy, from satisfaction of basic physiological needs right up towards self-actualisation. Once a lower-order (deficiency) need has been satisfied, it is no longer a motivating factor. Some analysts in the area of motivation for travel believe that in regions of the world (and indeed of a country) where lower-order needs have been satisfied, travel becomes a motivator for self-esteem. Other authors (such as Weaver and Lawton 2006) do not believe this to be the case, as travel may be a motivator to satisfy some of the lower-order needs, e.g. for health (basic physiological needs), to a perceived safe destination (safety needs) or to make new acquaintances or find a new partner (acceptance needs).

Some of the factors which motivate people to travel are listed below.

Safe Destinations

Many people wish to visit destinations perceived as safe, i.e. those not involved in international conflicts. Such destinations can attract many safety-sensitive tourists, many of whom are willing to pay a premium for the peace of mind of being in a perceived safe destination.

Economic Prosperity

There is a correlation between levels of disposable income and an increased demand for travel products. In countries where there is economic prosperity and rapid growth (such as Ireland in the late 1990s), people are motivated to spend some of their excess income on travel, believing that the economy will continue growing (economic factors impacting on global, national and regional tourism are discussed in detail in Chapter 3).

Transport

A reduction in transport costs, larger jets, more routes and fierce competition all serve to motivate people to travel more (transport is discussed in detail in Chapter 6).

Annual Leave

Many people take statutory annual leave for granted. However, it was not always a right. Being paid while you are on holidays is a motivator to take a break and perhaps travel during this time.

Government Policy

Policies of national and international regional governments (such as the EU) encourage their people to travel and embrace different cultures. Irish and EU policies provide funding for students who wish to travel to other countries to complete part of their studies under such programmes as the Erasmus and Socrates programmes.

Education Levels

A higher level of education motivates people to wish to explore more in the quest to increase their knowledge and awareness of different peoples, cultures and languages.

Marketing

Increased marketing by national tourism organisations motivates people to consider the destination in question. Ireland makes use of excellent marketing techniques in an effort to motivate potential tourists to find out more information and consider Ireland as a destination for a holiday or short break.

The Internet

The internet is an excellent source of information for potential tourists wishing to search for details on any destination or attraction, often from the comfort and safety of their own home.

Goeldner and Ritchie (2006) conclude that

> Travel motivation studies can be the basis of many consumer analyses in tourism. A good motivational profile of visitors should be of assistance in understanding how well the destination characteristics fit the needs of the travellers. The key to linking travel motivation studies to other tourism studies such as destination choice lies in analysing the activities offered by the destination and the activities that fulfil the travellers' motives. Thus if visitors strongly motivated by the need to enhance their understanding of art and history visit well-managed, quality cultural attractions, then satisfaction is likely.

DEVELOPMENT OF MASS TOURISM

The concept of mass tourism is a relatively new phenomenon. While there is evidence of tourism of varying forms stretching back millennia throughout the planet, mass tourism is only about a century old. Improvements in transport, such

(1) as larger and faster ships, the motor car and eventually the aircraft, were all catalysts for rapid international tourism growth, in many cases at the expense of domestic tourism. On the other hand, world wars, international economic instability and terrorism are negative contributors to the growth of international tourism.

(2) Over the decades we have seen further major advancements in transport technology, including faster and even larger ships and ferries, rapid rail transport and improvements in the world's road networks. However, by far the biggest contributing factor to transport advancements was the development of the jet engine and its use in passenger travel. The size of aircraft, their speed and range have all increased over the decades. Competing manufacturers such as Europe's Airbus and America's Boeing have presented various aircraft types to suit the demands of airlines and their customers. Advancement in aircraft technology will inevitably benefit world tourism. It is worth noting that larger jets (such as the new Airbus A380 double-decker jet) that carry more passengers can offer a lower cost per passenger for the airline, a saving which may be passed on to the passenger, which drives down the cost of travel. Nowadays, we see air travel at its lowest-ever price, especially since the development of the concept of no-frills, low-cost airlines such as Southwest Airlines in the US and Ryanair in Europe.

(3) The development of mass tourism was and still is encouraged by world governments and world agencies (such as the UNWTO). In the absence of world war, global co-operation can flourish in the area of tourism amongst others. One (4) such development which was a major catalyst for world tourism growth was the development of the package holiday concept, where flights and accommodation were bundled together in a generally affordable package.

Legal and regulatory changes introduced by governments and economic blocs (such as the present-day EU) have also provided a business climate that is conducive to the growth of tourism. Shortly after the US government liberalised its airline sector, Europe followed suit and moved towards a pro-competition European Open Skies policy. Even enlargement of the EU in successive stages has a positive impact on tourism growth, especially between new accession states and the regions of Europe with the highest levels of employment. Harmonisation of consumer regulations, common excise duties, the dropping of internal borders and the euro single currency are further examples of how the EU has helped mass tourism to grow.

(5) DEREGULATION

WORLD TOURISM ORGANIZATION

The UNWTO is the United Nation's branch dealing with world tourism. The organisation provides support and facilitates world tourism co-operation, as well as researching and publishing comprehensive, up-to-date information and statistics on the global industry which can be used by industry and national tourism organisations to aid the planning and development of their own tourism product. Given the international nature of tourism, a global organisation such as the UNWTO is a vital link for the industry. It's not just a source of information, but also a support and voice to the decision-makers of the world.

The World Tourism Organization (UNWTO/OMT), a specialised agency of the United Nations, is the leading international organisation in the field of tourism. It serves as a global forum for tourism policy issues and practical source of tourism know-how.

With its headquarters in Madrid, Spain, the UNWTO plays a central and decisive role in promoting the development of responsible, sustainable and universally accessible tourism, with the aim of contributing to economic development, international understanding, peace, prosperity and universal respect for, and observance of, human rights and fundamental freedoms. In pursuing this aim, the organisation pays particular attention to the interests of developing countries in the field of tourism.

The UNWTO plays a catalytic role in promoting technology transfers and international co-operation, in stimulating and developing public-private sector partnerships and in encouraging the implementation of the Global Code of Ethics for Tourism, with a view to ensuring that member countries, tourist destinations and businesses maximise the positive economic, social and cultural effects of tourism and fully reap its benefits, while minimising its negative social and environmental impacts.

In 2006, the UNWTO's membership is comprised of 150 countries, seven territories and more than 300 Affiliate Members representing the private sector, educational institutions, tourism associations and local tourism authorities.

At the start of the new millennium, tourism is firmly established as the number one industry in many countries and the fastest-growing economic sector in terms of foreign exchange earnings and job creation.

International tourism is the world's largest export earner and an important factor in the balance of payments of most nations.

Tourism has become one of the world's most important sources of employment. It stimulates enormous investment in infrastructure, most of which also helps to improve the living conditions of local people. It provides governments with substantial tax revenues. Most new tourism jobs and businesses are created in developing countries, helping to equalise economic opportunities and keep rural residents from moving to overcrowded cities.

Intercultural awareness and personal friendships fostered through tourism are powerful forces for improving international understanding and contributing to peace among all the nations of the world.

The UNWTO recognises that tourism can have a negative cultural, environmental and social impact if it is not responsibly planned, managed and monitored. The UNWTO thus encourages governments to play a vital role in tourism in partnership with the private sector, local authorities and non-governmental organisations.

In its belief that tourism can be effectively used to address the problems of poverty, UNWTO made a commitment to contribute to the United Nations Millennium Development Goals through a new initiative to develop sustainable tourism as a force for poverty elimination. The programme, known as ST-EP (Sustainable Tourism-Eliminating Poverty), focuses the long-standing work of both organisations on encouraging sustainable tourism with a view to alleviating poverty and was implemented in 2003.

The World Tourism Organization had its beginnings as the International Congress of Official Tourist Traffic Associations, set up in 1925 in The Hague. It was renamed the International Union of Official Travel Organizations (IUOTO) after World War II and moved to Geneva. IUOTO was a technical, non-governmental organisation, whose membership at its peak included 109 national tourist organisations (NTOs) and 88 associate members, among them private and public groups.

As tourism grew and became an integral part of the fabric of modern life, its international dimension increased and national governments started to play an increasingly important role, their activities covering the whole spectrum from infrastructure to regulations. By the mid-1960s, it became clear that there was a need for more effective tools to keep developments under review and to provide tourism with inter-governmental machinery especially equipped to deal with the movement of persons, tourism policies and tourism's impacts.

In 1967, the members of IUOTO called for its transformation into an inter-governmental body empowered to deal on a worldwide basis with all matters concerning tourism and to co-operate with other competent organisations, particularly those of the United Nations' system, such as the World Health Organization (WHO), UNESCO and the International Civil Aviation Organization (ICAO).

A resolution to the same effect was passed in December 1969 by the UN General Assembly, which recognised the decisive and central role the transformed IUOTO should play in the field of world tourism in co-operation with the existing machinery within the UN. Following this resolution, the UNWTO's statutes were ratified in 1974 by the states whose official tourist organisations were members of IUOTO.

Thus IUOTO became the World Tourism Organization (UNWTO) and its first General Assembly was held in Madrid in May 1975. The Secretariat was installed in Madrid early the following year at the invitation of the Spanish government, which provides a building for the headquarters.

In 1976, UNWTO became an executing agency of the United Nations Development Programme (UNDP), and in 1977 a formal co-operation agreement was signed with the United Nations itself. In 2003, the UNWTO was converted into a specialised agency of the United Nations and reaffirmed its leading role in international tourism.

Since its early years, UNWTO's membership and influence in world tourism have continued to grow. By 2005, its membership included 145 countries, seven territories and some 350 Affiliate Members, representing the private sector, educational institutions, tourism associations and local tourism authorities.

Source: UNWTO.

The UNWTO divides the world geographically into the following regions and sub-regions.

Table 1.1: World Tourism Regions

Region	Sub-region	Countries
Africa	North Africa	Algeria, Morocco, Sudan, Tunisia
	West Africa	Benin, Burkina Faso, Cape Verde, Côte d'Ivoire, Gambia, Ghana, Guinea, Guinea-Bissau, Mali, Mauritania, Niger, Nigeria, Senegal, Sierra Leone, Togo
	Central Africa	Angola, Cameroon, Central African Republic, Chad, Congo, Democratic Republic of Congo, Equatorial Guinea, Gabon, Sao Tomé e Principe
	East Africa	Burundi, Comoros, Djibouti, Eritrea, Ethiopia, Kenya, Madagascar, Malawi, Mauritius, Mozambique, Reunion, Rwanda, Seychelles, Tanzania, Uganda, Zambia, Zimbabwe
	Southern Africa	Botswana, Lesotho, Namibia, South Africa, Swaziland
Americas	North America	Canada, Mexico, United States
	Caribbean	Anguilla, Antigua, Barbuda, Aruba, Bahamas, Barbados, Bermuda, Bonaire, British Virgin Islands, Cayman Islands, Cuba, Curaçao, Dominica, Dominican Republic, Grenada, Guadeloupe, Haiti, Jamaica, Martinique, Montserrat, Puerto Rico, Saba, St Eustatiuis, St Kitts-Nevis, St Lucia, St Maarten, St Vincent, Grenadines, Trinidad and Tobago, Turks and Caicos, US Virgin Islands
	Central America	Belize, Costa Rica, El Salvador, Guatemala, Honduras, Nicaragua, Panama
	South America	Argentina, Bolivia, Brazil, Chile, Colombia, Ecuador, French Guyana, Guyana, Paraguay, Peru, Suriname, Uruguay, Venezuela
Asia	North-east Asia	China, Democratic People's Republic of Korea, Hong Kong (China), Japan, Republic of Korea, Macao (China), Mongolia, Taiwan (PR of China)
	South-east Asia	Brunei Darussalam, Cambodia, Indonesia, Lao PDR, Malaysia, Myanmar, Philippines, Singapore, Thailand, Vietnam
	South Asia	Afghanistan, Bangladesh, Bhutan, India, Iran (Islamic Republic of), Maldives, Nepal, Pakistan, Sri Lanka

Table 1.1: World Tourism Regions (contd.)

Region	Sub-region	Countries
	Oceania	American Samoa, Australia, Cook Islands, Fiji, French Polynesia, Guam, Kiribati, Marshall Islands, Micronesia (Federated States of), North Mariana Islands, New Caledonia, New Zealand, Niue, Palau, Papua New Guinea, Samoa, Solomon Islands, Tonga, Tuvalu, Vanuatu
Europe	Northern Europe	Denmark, Finland, Iceland, Ireland, Norway, Sweden, United Kingdom
	Western Europe	Austria, Belgium, France, Germany, Liechtenstein, Luxembourg, Monaco, Netherlands, Switzerland
	Central and Eastern Europe	Armenia, Azerbaijan, Belarus, Bulgaria, Czech Republic, Estonia, Former USSR, Georgia, Hungary, Kazakhstan, Kyrgyzstan, Latvia, Lithuania, Poland, Rep Moldova, Romania, Russian Federation, Slovakia, Tajikistan, Turkmenistan, Ukraine, Uzbekistan
	Southern Europe	Albania, Andorra, Bosnia Herzegovina, Croatia, Former Yugoslav Republic of Macedonia, Greece, Italy, Malta, Portugal, San Marino, Serbia and Montenegro, Slovenia, Spain
	East Mediterranean Europe	Cyprus, Israel, Turkey
Middle East		Bahrain, Egypt, Iraq, Jordan, Kuwait, Lebanon, Libyan Arab Jamahiriya, Oman, Palestine, Qatar, Saudi Arabia, Syrian Arab Republic, United Arab Emirates, Yemen

Source: UNWTO.

CHANGING TOURISM PATTERNS

Tourism patterns have changed significantly over the period 1990 to 2004. At the beginning of the period, there were 441 million arrivals, compared to 763 million just fourteen years later. The total number engaging in tourism for the purposes of leisure, recreation and holiday has declined from a total 55.4 per cent share in 1990 to a 51.8 per cent share in 2004, while there was an increase in both business and professional tourism (up from 13.7 per cent to a 15.7 per cent share) and in visiting friends and relatives, health and religious tourism (up from 19.7 per cent to 24.2 per cent). The changing patterns are illustrated in Table 1.2. Recently released updated figures report world tourism arrivals of 808 million in 2005 (UNWTO estimates).

Table 1.2: World Arrivals by Purpose of Visit

	International Tourist Arrivals				Share			Average Annual Growth
	Millions				%			%
	1990	1995	2000	2004	1990	1995	2004	1990–2000
Total	441.0	538.1	680.6	763.2	100	100	100	4.4
Leisure, recreation and holidays	244.3	289.7	356.7	395.2	55.4	53.8	51.8	3.9
Business and professional	60.4	81.6	111.9	119.9	13.7	15.2	15.7	6.4
VFR, health, religion, other	86.9	115.3	152.6	185.0	19.7	21.4	24.2	5.8
Not specified	49.5	51.5	59.4	63.2	11.2	9.6	8.3	

Source: UNWTO, November 2005. The UNWTO has used estimations for countries with missing data.

World's Top Destinations

France is the world's top destination in terms of tourist arrivals (defined as the number of tourists visiting the country), although only third in terms of revenue spent by tourists. The United States is the top destination in terms of tourism spending, although third in terms of arrivals. Spain is second on both counts. Italy ranks fourth in terms of revenue and fifth on arrivals, and China is fourth in arrivals and sixth in receipts. The UK, Germany, Turkey and Austria rank in positions five, seven, eight and nine, respectively, in terms of receipts and one place lower, i.e. six, eight, nine and ten, respectively, in arrivals. Mexico features in the top ten in terms of arrivals only. Similarly, Australia features in terms of revenue only. The main reasons for the difference between rankings for arrivals and revenue are that each destination has a different visitor profile, including levels of expenditure, costs of living, length of stay and type of accommodation, e.g. staying with relatives rather than in a hotel. World tourism revenue is illustrated and discussed in more detail in Chapter 3.

Table 1.3 illustrates the top ten destinations in the world in terms of tourist arrivals. As we can see, the traditional destinations such as France and Spain have had modest growth, while there has been rapid growth from emerging destinations such as China and Turkey.

Ireland ranks in 25th position in terms of tourist arrivals. As well as the top ten destinations listed above, 2004 figures list Hong Kong, Canada, Malaysia, Ukraine, Poland, Greece, Hungary, Thailand, Portugal, the Netherlands, Russian Federation, Saudi Arabia, Macao (China) and Croatia ahead of Ireland.

Table 1.3: The World's Top Ten Tourism Destinations (in terms of arrivals)

World Ranking	Country	2002	2003	2004	2005	Previous (2004)
		(in millions of arrivals)				Ranking
	World	700	690	763	Unspecified	
1	France	77.0	75.0	75.1	76.0	1
2	Spain	52.3	51.8	53.6	55.6	2
3	United States	43.6	41.2	46.1	49.4	3
4	China	36.8	33.0	41.8	46.8	4
5	Italy	39.8	39.6	37.1	36.5	5
6	United Kingdom	24.2	24.7	27.8	30.0	6
7	Mexico	19.7	18.7	20.6	21.9	8
8	Germany	18.0	18.4	20.1	21.5	9
9	Turkey	12.8	13.3	16.8	20.3	12
10	Austria	18.6	19.1	19.4	20	10

Source: UNWTO, May 2005.

Table 1.4: Ireland's World Ranking (in terms of arrivals)

World Ranking	Country	2002	2003	2004
		(in million of arrivals)		
25	Ireland	6.5	6.8	7.0

World's Top Emerging Tourism Destinations

The UNWTO lists the following countries as the top emerging destinations between 1995 and 2002, with growth of at least double the world average and an increase of at least 100,000 arrivals. The countries are presented in order of highest to lowest growth within their respective regions.

Table 1.5: UNWTO Top Emerging Tourism Destinations (1995–2002)

Africa	Zambia, Botswana, Malawi, Tanzania, Algeria, Namibia, Ghana
Americas	El Salvador, Cuba, Honduras, Peru, Nicaragua, Dominican Republic
Asia and Pacific	Cambodia, Iran, Malaysia, China, Maldives, Lao People's Democratic Republic
Europe	Armenia, Azerbaijan, Croatia, Georgia, Iceland, Estonia, Lithuania, Serbia and Montenegro, Slovenia, Turkey, Ukraine, Latvia
Middle East	Oman, Syrian Arab Republic, United Arab Emirates, Saudi Arabia, Bahrain, Lebanon, Egypt

Source: UNWTO.

BARRIERS TO TRAVEL

There are several reasons why people cannot or do not travel. However, some of the factors may be overcome when the motivation is strong enough. Further, some of the factors are stronger barriers at certain times, e.g. at times of certain international events.

According to Goeldner and Ritchie (2006), studies have shown that barriers to travel may fall into the following six broad categories.

1. **Cost:** Travel is often considered a luxury expense, and nowadays travel often competes with many other demands on disposable income. In some countries, there is an extreme shortage of employment and thus income, and travel may not even be a consideration, primarily for those who have difficulty meeting their basic needs. Further, those who do travel may be put off by perceived high-cost or 'rip-off' destinations.

> Tourists put off by pricing and airport standards
>
> Opportunistic pricing, inadequate cultural facilities and the sub-standard condition of Dublin Airport are deterring visitors, according to a major report on Irish tourism.
>
> The third and final report by the Tourism Action Plan Implementation Group, published yesterday, highlighted a number of key barriers to the government's aim of increasing visitor numbers to 10 million annually.
>
> Of most concern is the loss of competitiveness by the tourism sector in recent years, which the report attributes to high wage costs and high charges for services.
>
> The report adds that the 'sometimes opportunistic pricing by certain operators and the comparatively low productivity in the services sector do not help either'. The group warns that the services sector must make the necessary adjustments to survive in the new economic environment.
>
> Facilities at Dublin Airport are also criticised in the report, which finds that the airport does not meet the expectations of visitors to a modern, highly developed country. While acknowledging that the basic decisions needed to provide the required infrastructure at the airport have now been made, the report states it is frustrating for the tourism industry that delays in taking these decisions will ensure that it will take years for changes to occur.
>
> Meanwhile, Ireland as a tourist destination was found to have become 'tired' and 'lacking in verve' at a time when visitors are seeking authentic experiences.
>
> 'A fundamental weakness is that much of the existing product, in both public and private ownership, is not packaged, presented, made accessible or marketed to best effect either internationally or domestically,' the report stated.
>
> Dublin is classed as being 'inadequately served with cultural facilities', due to the lack of attractions.
>
> This absence represents a barrier to attracting key segments of the

international tourism market to Ireland, according to the report.

Although the number of holiday makers in Dublin has increased by more than 3 million to almost 7.5 million in recent years, areas outside the capital have had 2.5 million fewer tourists.

The group warns that this trend is likely to continue because of the increasing popularity of short breaks, which a city such as Dublin will benefit from at the expense of regional centres.

Yesterday, Minister for Arts, Sport and Tourism John O'Donoghue welcomed the group's contention that the tourism strategy is in many ways doing better than anticipated.

'We cannot afford to be complacent about our tourism revenue, however, with competition from new tourism destinations ever increasing.

'The falling numbers of visitors to rural areas is also a worrying trend that needs to be tackled,' he said.

The group concluded that competitiveness, product development, access and marketing and the regional spread of tourism should be prioritised.

Tourism report: Key findings
Areas of good progress
- Industry commitment to responding and repositioning for tourism growth.
- Government commitment to the implementation of the tourism strategy.
- The additional resources allocated to tourism marketing by the government and state tourism agencies.
- Significant increases in air access.
- Commitment to upgrading transportation infrastructure and services.
- Decision to provide a National Conference Centre in Dublin.
- New capital investment programme for the Abbey Theatre, the National Concert Hall, the Gaiety Theatre and Theatre Royal in Wexford.

Areas of slow progress
- Deterioration in competitiveness.
- Less than satisfactory experiences of passengers in Dublin Airport.
- Full VAT is chargeable on conference business in Ireland, in contrast to Britain.
- Tourism products lack 'bounce' for many tourists.
- Regional spread of tourism is in decline, with 2.5 million fewer visitors travelling outside Dublin between 1999 and 2004.
- Signposting on national, regional and local routes is inadequate.

Source: Kerr, A., 'Tourists put off by pricing and airport standards', *The Irish Times*, 14 March 2006.

2. **Lack of time:** Although most industrialised countries have statutory paid holidays (some more than others), many individuals find it difficult to take a break from their position to consider travelling, even for a short break. Stereotypically relaxed and laid-back countries such as Ireland even see a social change with people

working longer hours and taking fewer holidays. Further, for many, time taken from annual leave is often used for catching up on chores, e.g. home maintenance.

3. **Health limitations:** Given the many health crises experienced in the world in recent years (SARS, bird flu, etc.), as well as a general fear of contracting any of a myriad of diseases, people are often reluctant to travel to certain regions.

4. **Family and life stage:** Depending on the stage in the traditional life cycle, people may feel a barrier to travel. For example, couples with young children may not want the hassle of travelling, and older generations may also consider travel to be physically draining. Levels of disposable income at each stage may also become a barrier.

5. **Lack of interest:** Many individuals are unaware of the array of destinations available to choose from. Further, many people are happy and comfortable in their own surroundings and are unwilling to try new experiences, new cultures, new foods, etc.

6. **Fear and safety:** This is a widely discussed barrier to tourism, especially since 2001. War, terrorism, political and civil unrest as well as natural disasters have all taken their toll on travel and tourism. The attacks on the US on 11 September 2001, as well as subsequent bombings in Bali, Madrid and London, coupled with continued terrorism, war on Iraq and Afghanistan, Middle East tensions and natural disasters such as the Asian tsunami on 26 December 2004 all resulted in a downturn in tourism, and not just in the region affected, but in the whole world. Many people even have a fear of flying on the airlines of certain countries as they may be perceived as a terrorist target.

Press release by Minister for Tourism at beginning of US-Led war on Iraq, 20 March 2003

Minister for Arts, Sport and Tourism, John O'Donoghue, today expressed his regret at the outbreak of hostilities in the Gulf. 'With global economic slowdown, foot and mouth and September 11th, this is the fourth major challenge experienced by the tourism industry in the past two years,' said O'Donoghue.

'This is a time for cool heads and measured responses. The key to tackling the situation is to closely monitor evolving consumer reactions in key marketplaces and to develop appropriate and balanced responses, in particular in the area of marketing and promotion,' the Minister said.

O'Donoghue said that he had already met with the CEOs of the main tourism agencies – Tourism Ireland Ltd and Bord Fáilte [now Fáilte Ireland] – to put plans for a response to the current scenario in place.

The Minister outlined the key elements of that response:

- 'We have put in place excellent communications from our key markets (Tourism Ireland has an overseas staff of about 100, located in nineteen countries) to provide best intelligence driven by the marketplace, the reactions of consumers and the overseas trade.'

- 'We have put in place excellent communications with the tourism trade here (through the setting up of a Tourism Industry Response Group utilising Tourism Marketing Partnership structures, adjusted as appropriate, and also through regular communications bulletins, including e-zines. The Group held its inaugural meeting yesterday to review developments, and will meet again next week).'
- 'I will continue to liaise with representatives of the Irish Tourism Industry Confederation and the CEOs of the state tourism agencies as matters develop.'
- 'Internal response teams have already been established within Tourism Ireland Ltd and Bord Fáilte to deal with operational marketing and promotion issues.'
- 'Marketing and promotional campaigns will be adjusted in 2003 as appropriate, using the substantial level of funding provided in the Estimates. The location, nature and extent of these will be determined by the intelligence flowing from the marketplace on consumer and trade behaviour. Further details will be provided over coming weeks by the state tourism agencies.'

O'Donoghue said that experience with foot and mouth and the aftermath of September 11th showed that the Irish tourism industry was resilient and had the capacity to overcome great challenges. He was confident that it would face and overcome this latest challenge.

Source: Department of Arts, Sport and Tourism.

CAREER OPPORTUNITIES

One in every twelve workers on the planet is employed in a tourism-related position. In Ireland, this figure is significantly higher, as circa one in every eight workers is employed in the tourism and hospitality industry. These figures are rising globally and in Ireland as tourism expands internationally at a rapid rate, making tourism the world's largest industry (see 'Tourism and Employment' in Chapter 3).

Employment opportunities available in the tourism and hospitality sector include jobs in the following types of organisations (this list is non-exhaustive):

- Accommodation providers.
- Transport operators.
- Visitor attractions.
- Food and beverage service providers.
- Leisure and recreation business.
- Amenities and tourist services.

Careers in any of these organisations may begin with part-time or seasonal employment and often progress to permanent positions. As the industry expands, hard-working individuals who start at the bottom often find themselves working their way up towards management positions. Many individuals branch out and set up their own tourism enterprise.

In Ireland, more than a quarter (27 per cent) of workers in the tourism and

Tourism has a multiplier effect in an economy as regards to employment creation.

hospitality sector are non-Irish nationals. This is testament to the rising demand for employees in the sector, much of which cannot be met from within the Irish employment pool.

There is a downside to careers in the sector – tourism and thus tourism employment is heavily dependent on international stability. Travel and tourism suffer at times of international conflict, and this often causes employers in the sector to cut staff costs. However, in Ireland's case, an employee with a good command of the English language who has good customer service skills and the ability to give a traditional Irish *fáilte* should be the last person on the list to be considered for staff cuts.

Fáilte Ireland is the state agency charged with promoting and developing careers in the Irish tourism and hospitality sector. Their website, www.failteireland.ie, lists various opportunities for college and industry-based training courses, as well as placements and research opportunities, at locations all throughout Ireland. The provision of this service is in line with Irish governmental policy to encourage (primarily) young people to consider a career in the sector.

The Irish Hotels Federation publishes a magazine entitled *Get a Life...in Tourism* profiling careers in the industry as well as people in those careers. It also provides information on training courses and college-based tourism education as well as general tourism information.

Making reservations for your career in tourism

Careers in tourism and hospitality are attractive at the moment, with more than fifty new hotels due to open in 2006, bringing an additional 5,000 rooms to the industry.

While access to a management career in hotel and catering can be gained through several channels, the most popular among today's employers is the recruitment of college graduates with degrees in hotel and catering management or a related discipline.

Institutes of technology throughout the state as well as some universities offer these degree programmes, and entry is through the CAO applications procedure.

DIT, Galway Mayo Institute of Technology (GMIT), Waterford IT and IT Tralee as well as the specialist Shannon College of Hotel Management offer Level 8 degree courses in hospitality management (DIT, Waterford and Tralee), culinary arts (DIT), hotel and catering management (GMIT), tourism marketing (DIT) and event management (DIT). Shannon College offers a business studies degree in international hotel management and a commerce degree in which students spend the fourth year at NUI Galway.

Entry to Shannon is, however, through a combination of CAO points and an interview.

The points requirements for Level 8 courses in 2005 (first round) ranged from 230 for hospitality management at Tralee to 590 for the Shannon commerce degree.

Level 7/6 courses are widely available from ITs including Athlone, Cork, Dublin, Dundalk, Galway-Mayo, Letterkenny, Sligo, Tralee and Waterford.

Degree courses on offer include hotel and catering management, tourism, hotel and catering supervision, hotel and restaurant management, leisure management, international bar and food service management, culinary arts, hospitality management, event management, hospitality information technology, bar management, front office management, sports and recreation and business studies.

DIT provides the widest range of these courses. Three courses offered by Letterkenny IT are delivered at the specialist Tourism College in Killybegs. Points requirements in the first round of 2005 ranged from 145 for hotel and catering management at Athlone and business studies (tourism) at Tralee to 265 for business studies (recreation and leisure) at Waterford IT.

For those who want to pursue a career in tourism but do not wish to go through the CAO system, courses leading to internationally recognised qualifications are available through Fáilte Ireland.

Fáilte Ireland offers courses in four categories – skills training, craft certificate, advanced and higher certificate, and degree programmes. Most courses are full time, but some offer part-time options or on-the-job training. All courses provide an opportunity for professional, supervised work experience.

All courses lead to qualifications awarded by the Further Education and Training Awards Council (FETAC) or the Higher Education Training Awards Council (HETAC), which are recognised internationally. The majority of the courses are grant aided and 99 per cent of trainees find employment within the tourism industry.

The first category, skills training courses, are held in Fáilte Ireland training centres throughout the state. They take place over thirteen weeks and lead to a national skills certificate. On completion, trainees can go directly into employment or apply for further full-time college-based training. They can also opt for on-the-job training through the Industry Qualification Scheme or apply for the National Apprenticeship Scheme.

The second category, craft certificate courses, are held at institutes of technology. These full-time programmes run for one or two years and lead to a national certificate. Graduates can then go into employment, take short professional development courses or apply to take an advanced or higher certificate degree course.

Institutes of technology also deliver advanced and higher certificate courses. These run on a full-time or day release basis over varying periods, depending on the course. Graduates receive an advanced national certificate or higher certificate and can then gain further training at work, take short professional development courses or apply to study for a degree.

Of course, careers in tourism are not confined to hotels, restaurants and bars – they can also be found in many visitor attractions, sports and activity centres, tourism information offices, tour operators and travel agencies.

Fáilte Ireland can facilitate all entrants to the industry by helping them choose an appropriate course and career path, and by monitoring and encouraging their professional development. There is even a scheme that enables those working in the industry to gain formal recognition for their experience and achievements.

With 6,000 new jobs coming on stream every year and many enterprises opening or expanding their operations, career prospects are bright.

Contact Fáilte Ireland at 1850 256 256 or visit their website.

Source: Mooney, B., 'Making reservations for your career in tourism', *The Irish Times*, 18 January 2006.

Speech by John O'Donoghue, TD, Minister for Arts, Sport and Tourism, at the launch of Fáilte Ireland Go Places in Tourism Roadshow and *Get a Life in Tourism* magazine Fáilte Ireland, Amiens Street, 9 October 2003 at 3:00 p.m.

Good afternoon, ladies and gentlemen. I am delighted to have this opportunity to say a few words to you about the tourism industry and to officially launch this National Tourism Careers Roadshow and the *Get a Life in Tourism* magazine.

The overall purpose of the events here today is to promote job and training opportunities in the hospitality and tourism industry to school leavers around the country. The roadshow will travel the length and breadth of the country over the next two months and will give those who wish to make a career in the industry an idea of what it has to offer. It will highlight the huge variety of careers available and, crucially, the excellent and flexible training options provided by Fáilte Ireland.

We have an excellent tourism product here in Ireland and we need talented young people like yourselves to help ensure that we maintain and improve the high standards that have so far been achieved. You can be assured that there are excellent prospects, identifiable and attractive career paths and exciting opportunities available in Irish tourism.

So why tourism? Well, it generates €4 billion in foreign earnings each year as well as €1 billion in domestic expenditure. It contributes €2.2 billion in tax receipts and employs over 140,000 staff. Despite the growing challenges and some uncertainty in the last two years in particular, it has demonstrated remarkable resilience in the way it has rallied and is clearly still a key player in the Irish economy.

Another reason to choose tourism is the diversity of jobs on offer. The variety is incredible, ranging from chefs, tour guides, gardeners and receptionists through to marketing, finance, IT, management and leisure centre positions.

A further motivation is the substantially improved commitment to training and career development. Training is the basis for success in the tourism and hospitality industry and the industry needs the support of skilled staff to ensure that it maintains the high international standards it has achieved to date. I can confidently say that pursuing a recognised training course is a passport to success in an industry where there continues to be a high demand for trained staff in all sectors.

Tourism employers, some of whom are represented here today, are well aware of the need to keep upgrading the skills of their employees. This is also why Fáilte Ireland offers such a range of courses, not just in its own centres and in third-level colleges, but also through on-the-job training and development.

Successful completion of a Fáilte Ireland course leads to EU-recognised qualifications from the Further Education Training Awards Council (FETAC) and, if you progress to a very advanced training, the Higher Education Training Awards Council (HETAC). In fact, there are distinct career paths on offer throughout the industry with qualifications to match.

I have no doubt that if you put in the effort and avail of the appropriate training, there is no reason why you cannot become the Jamie Oliver or Nigella Lawson of the future. There is also no reason why you cannot go on to create your own business, for example as a publican, restauranteur or a hotelier, where you can do well and reap the rewards of your success.

I have only outlined some of the reasons why you might consider tourism as your career of choice. You will get a better flavour of what you might like to do in the industry from the roadshow itself and from the *Get a Life in Tourism* magazine, which features many of the young people who are enjoying rewarding and fulfilling careers in the industry…

In conclusion, can I urge you all to consider joining our vibrant tourism industry. As this roadshow presentation has highlighted, career prospects in tourism have never been better, and you will have the opportunity to be part of the success story that is Irish tourism.

Source: Department of Arts, Sport and Tourism Speech Archives, 9 October 2003.

REVISION QUESTIONS

1. Define the terms 'tourism' and 'tourist'.
2. What is the distinction between inbound, outbound and domestic tourism?
3. List and define the various forms of tourism.
4. What motivates people to travel?
5. What is the UNWTO and what are its functions?
6. How has mass tourism developed internationally?
7. How are tourism patterns changing globally?
8. List the newly emerging destinations. Where do you think the emerging destinations of the next decades will be? Why?
9. In your opinion, why are Northern Ireland visitors not classed as domestic or international arrivals?

ESSAY QUESTIONS

1. List and briefly discuss the world's top tourism destinations. What makes them so popular? Use examples to illustrate your answer.
2. 'In today's globalised economies, there are no barriers to tourism.' Discuss

whether you agree or disagree with this statement, giving reasons for your answer.

TASKS

Task 1
The class is to be divided into groups. Each group is required to collect newsworthy tourism articles for a designated week and present them to the class the following week. Students should gather at least ten news articles from newspapers, the internet, journals, magazines, etc.

Task 2
Divide the class into two roughly equal groups. Each group should be given ten to fifteen minutes to develop opposing points on the following statement, followed by a forty to forty-five minute debate.

Statement: Tourism growth is inevitable.

Statement: Promoting special-interest tourism is a waste of resources that could be redirected to generic marketing strategies.

Task 3
Conduct a survey of 100 students to ascertain what motivated them to travel the last time they took a trip.

ASSIGNMENTS

1. Compose a report on the newly emerging destinations that are competing with traditional destinations. Analyse what these new destinations have to offer. Comment on the strategies traditional destinations should employ to maintain their market share.
2. Consult the list of what motivates people to travel presented in this chapter. Expand and update this list. Compile your newly expanded list into a report entitled *Why People Travel*.

Chapter 2

The History and Structure of Tourism in Ireland

SUMMARY

Chapter 2 begins with a timeline of the previous century of tourism in Ireland, presenting a growing industry from its modern beginnings to the complex organisations that exist today. In particular, this chapter focuses on the developments and changes in the structure of tourism since the 1990s, including North-South co-operation on the island of Ireland, as well as individual public organisations that promote and develop the Irish and Northern Irish tourism product, respectively. The reader is introduced to the importance of national tourism organisations such as Fáilte Ireland, Tourism Ireland and the Northern Ireland Tourism Board. The chapter also focuses on tourism at a regional level in the Republic and on the government departments that regulate the various facets of the industry and set policy nationally and locally. The conclusion to the chapter presents a synopsis of tourism strategy review groups in place since 2002 as well as the implementation plans for these strategies.

LEARNING OUTCOMES

Having completed this chapter, the reader should be able to:
- Comprehend the historical development of tourism.
- Understand the structure of Irish tourism.
- Appreciate the complexity of the Irish tourism structure.
- Understand the role played by the Irish government in tourism.
- Understand the role of public and private tourism organisations.
- Appreciate the importance of recent structural changes.
- Understand the nature of regional tourism authorities.
- Comprehend the importance of implementation of tourism strategy.

INTRODUCTION

Tourism accounts for approximately 5 per cent of Ireland's GDP (gross domestic product) and approximately 60 per cent of all service exports. It is Ireland's second-biggest exchequer earner.

Wright and Linehan (2004: Preface) note:

> *Over the decades, tourism has endured the influence of many diverse factors. World economic factors, together with adversities such as natural disasters, terrorist attacks and, in particular, world wars, have adversely affected tourism since it was first recognised as an industry. The Irish tourism industry has suffered greatly from many such factors, particularly, in the recent past, because of the political unrest in Northern Ireland. However, government policies, including the deregulation of airlines, have greatly supported the industry.*

It is evident that Irish tourism has grown from humble beginnings to become an extremely important contributor to the national economy. More tourists visit the Republic of Ireland annually than there are people living on the entire island! In this chapter, we will look at a timeline of the last century of growth in Irish tourism, including the turbulent times. We will also introduce the major public and private organisations that together form the backbone of the entire tourism industry, north and south. It is worth noting with regard to the second half of this chapter (and as evidenced by the first) that the structure of Irish tourism has regularly changed in the recent past, and may continue to do so. For this reason, any book aiming to present a definitive structure of the public and private organisations representing tourism or with an interest in it – in both the Republic of Ireland and Northern Ireland – often becomes out of date as soon as it is published. Any changes to the structures of Irish tourism shall be updated accordingly in subsequent editions of this book. In the meantime, the reader should consult the web resources provided for updated information.

A BRIEF JOURNEY THROUGH HISTORY...

> The substantial growth of the tourism activity clearly marks tourism as one of the most remarkable economic and social phenomena of the past century. The number of international arrivals shows an evolution from a mere 25 million international arrivals in 1950 to an estimated 763 million in 2004, corresponding to an average annual growth rate of 6.5 per cent.
>
> Source: UNWTO.

Several authors have presented comprehensive timelines of the history of tourism, both worldwide and in an Irish context. Wright and Linehan's (2004) history is extremely comprehensive, and this section is partly drawn from their timeline. Further, in order that the importance of transport to tourism is highlighted, the particular entries in the following chronology relevant to the origins and development of access transport and internal transport are highlighted by the relevant year appearing in bold.

The origins of tourism lay in the necessity of the people of the ancient world to travel, whether for business or leisure, as well as military reasons. The history of the ancient world has left behind clues from the past world of tourism and points to the fact that travel and tourism existed in many of the ancient empires (Egyptian,

Roman and Greek, to name but a few). However, the age of mass tourism is relatively new, coinciding with advancements in transport technologies such as the development of large ocean liners, railways, the motor car, aircraft and eventually jet engines.

Early 1800s	Charles Bianconi, based in Clonmel, sets up a network of horse-drawn carriages (over 100 coaches), linking many towns in the south and mid-west, and links up hotels for stopovers.
1800s	The era of the railway begins. Resorts begin to grow along coastal towns (including Bray in Co. Wicklow). Many hotel chains develop around the main railway stations.
1836	The steamer ferry service between Dublin and Holyhead links up with the railways at both ports for onward travel.
1893	The Irish Tourism Association (ITA) is established by F.W. Crossley.
1899	ITA invites British parliamentarians and journalists to visit Ireland. The journalists are wined and dined and return to write very positive accounts of Ireland.
1909	ITA sets up an Irish Tourism office in London.
1914–18	World War I leads to a reduction in the expansion of tourism worldwide.
1916–22	Easter Rising and War of Independence lead to a reduction in demand from Britain – closure of the ITA.
1919	International Air Traffic Association established, based in The Hague.
1923	Re-establishment of the ITA by J.C. Foley, although the new agency has no connection with the older one. It produces the first-ever accommodation guide, entitled *Tourists Guide to Ireland*, listing 300 hotels. The ITA is funded by its members, with no government support, making survival extremely difficult.
1935	**October:** The Irish government appoints the Civil Aviation Section of the Department of Industry to carry out a survey for a potential base for sea planes and land planes serving a new transatlantic route.
1935	**November:** Sites in the west of Ireland are surveyed for the establishment of a sea plane base. Sites included the Shannon just below Limerick, Lough Derg, Lough Corrib, Tralee Bay, Kenmare Bay, Lough Ree and Valentia. Foynes, near the mouth of the Fergus River, is finally selected. Its good sheltered anchorage and its proximity to long, open stretches of water convinced the surveyors that Foynes was the best choice.

1935	**December:** Colonel Charles E. Lindbergh of the US airline Pan Am surveys the Foynes site by air and land to find a European base for the airline's transatlantic operations, and finds the site suitable.
1936	**May 27:** Aer Lingus is established. First commercial flight on *The Iolar* (a five-seater De Havilland DH84) from Baldonnel in Co. Dublin to Whitechurch airfield near Bristol.
1937	Aer Rianta established to manage Irish airports and aviation.
1937	Irish Hotels Federation (IHF) established.
1939	As Minister for Industry and Commerce, Seán Lemass introduces the Tourist Traffic Act, which establishes the Irish Tourist Board (ITB) under J.P. O'Brien's leadership. It also mandates that all establishments wishing to be classed as a hotel must register with the ITB.
1939	Taoiseach Éamon De Valera and Minister Seán Lemass improve the facilities at the Shannon estuary at Foynes, which is used for flying boats to land. In preparation for the expected demand to land the newly developed aircraft, the government decides to move the facility from Foynes to Rineanna, which is the current site of Shannon Airport.
1939–45	World War II, little or no tourism activities. The war eventually contributed greatly to aviation, but delays the development of the new Shannon Airport.
1940	**January:** Dublin Airport officially opens when an Aer Lingus Lockheed 14 aircraft departed Dublin for Liverpool.
Early 1940s	Imperial Airways (the forerunner of BOAC, now British Airways) operates routes from Bristol to Shannon to coincide with the flying boats operating to and from Foynes.
1945	Tourism promotion resumes and there is an increase in British visitors.
1945	TWA (Trans World Airways) and Pan Am (Pan American Airways) begin flights to Shannon.
1945	International Air Transport Association (IATA) founded in Havana, Cuba in 1945 as a successor to the International Air Traffic Association, which was established in 1919.
1946	Decline in the use of commercial flying boats. Foynes airboat facility closes.
1946	**October 24:** First scheduled commercial flight arrives in Shannon from the US, an American Overseas Airlines DC4.

Late 1940s	Given the limited range of many aircraft, Shannon's importance as a hub airport on transatlantic routes between many European and North American cities grows. Shannon provides food, drink and accommodation as well as refuelling facilities.
1947	Shannon Airport initial construction completed.
1947	Government passes the Customs Free Airport Act, exempting passengers and aircraft from customs duties (even if they are not disembarking the aircraft). This establishes Shannon as an International Industrial and Distribution Centre and stimulates further traffic growth.
1947	Dutch airline KLM begins the first continental service to Dublin.
1947	First airport shop opens, selling gifts and souvenirs. Shannon Sales and Catering Organisation receives permission from Department of Transport to conduct commercial and catering activities at the airport. Becomes part of Aer Rianta in 1974.
1948	Dublin Airport gets its first concrete runways.
1950s	Europe leads the way in the field of business tourism, as approximately 80 per cent of congresses (international meetings) are held in Europe.
1951	Wexford Opera Festival established.
1951	World's first airport duty free opens in Shannon Airport, selling liquor and eventually tobacco products.
1952	Fógra Fáilte (Welcome Advertisements) established, with a remit to promote Ireland for tourism purposes. Bord Fáilte (Welcome Board) also established to develop domestic tourism.
1952	The movie The Quiet Man wins two Oscars and is a vital promotional tool for Ireland in America. Later movies (such as Ryan's Daughter and Michael Collins) also prove to be an important promotional tool for Ireland.
1952	An Tóstal spring national festival initiated by Bord Fáilte to extend the tourist season in every part of Ireland.
1955	Merger of Fógra Fáilte with Bord Fáilte to form Bord Fáilte Éireann (The Irish Welcome Board), to be funded by the Irish exchequer.
1956	Appointment of Dr Timothy O'Driscoll as the first Director General of Bord Fáilte Éireann, who introduces modern marketing methods and obtains US Marshall Aid funding to finance a study into the tourism industry. The market is segmented to target the groups most likely to visit Ireland.

1956	Grant schemes are introduced to encourage upgrading of accommodation.
1956	Intercontinental Hotels (a large chain) builds three new hotels in Dublin, Cork and Limerick.
1956	Dublin Theatre Festival established.
1958	National Tidy Towns competition established by Bord Fáilte.
1958	First Programme for Economic Expansion is published and encourages foreign trade and investment as well as developing new tourism products and upgrading existing ones.
1958	Restaurant guide *Where to Eat in Ireland* is published.
1959	Shannon Development is established to develop the region around the Shannon River and Shannon Airport.
1960s	Rose of Tralee, Festival of Kerry, Galway Oyster Festival and Cork International Film Festival established.
1960s	Boeing, McDonnell Douglas and Lockheed develop super-large jets, including the famous Boeing 747 'jumbo' jet.
1961	Shannon Airport commissions new runway to take larger jets.
1961	The European Confederation of Travel Agents' Associations (ECTAA) is founded in Germany (headquarters are now located in Brussels), representing twenty-four of the twenty-six national associations of travel agents and tour operators of the EU's twenty-five states in 2006.
1966	Shannon Airport's main runway extended to its present length (3,200 metres).
1969	Emergence of The Troubles in Northern Ireland, with negative British and worldwide media coverage damaging Irish tourism. This forces Bord Fáilte to market the Republic as a distinct area from Northern Ireland.
1969	Introduction to service of the Boeing 747 jumbo jet, drastically improving capacity on routes serving Ireland.
1970s	World economic recessions, oil crises, massive inflation.
1970s	Continuation of The Troubles in Northern Ireland, capturing world headlines.
1971	May: New, larger terminal opens at Shannon Airport to handle large amounts of passenger numbers from larger aircraft.
1971	Construction of new larger terminal begins at Dublin Airport to handle an estimated 6 million passengers per year.
1977	Tourism recovery begins.

1977	First-ever Irish Minister for Tourism and Transport is appointed: Pádraig Faulkner.
1978	US airline market is deregulated. Europe begins process of liberalisation soon after.
1980s	Continued world economic hardship, particularly in the key markets of the US and UK.
1980s	Continuation of The Troubles, receiving heightened world media attention in 1981 at the time of the H Block hunger strikes.
1984	Improvement in tourism growth and Irish economy.
1984	Ryanair established.
1986	Slowdown in tourism growth.
1987	Bord Fáilte initiates a four-part strategy for Irish tourism, consisting of targeted promotion, competitiveness, improved distribution and product investment.
1988	The Programme for National Recovery is published, containing key tourism elements. These include the doubling of visitor numbers to 4.2 million, increasing foreign revenue to IR£500 million (€635 million) and creating 25,000 jobs over a five-year period. The government and industry work closely together and schemes such as the Business Expansion Scheme and EU funding aid the task.
1989	Shannon Development takes over the regional tourism role of the Mid-West Regional Tourism Authority.
1990s	Further liberalisation of air routes, especially between Britain and Ireland, allow for a reduction in airfares, primarily provided by growing airline Ryanair.
1990s	The 1990s in general sees unprecedented tourism growth, the rival of most European and international destinations.
1990s	Europe's share of international business tourism falls from a high of 80 per cent in the 1950s to 60 per cent in the 1990s.
1990	Tourism plans seem to be working, as 1990 becomes a boom year for Irish tourism.
1991	The Gulliver national tourism information and central reservations system set up in conjunction with the Northern Ireland Tourism Board.
1993	Tourism revenue from overseas breaks the IR£1 billion (€1.27 billion) mark for the first time, and total revenue (overseas, domestic and Northern Ireland) breaks the IR£2 billion (€2.6 billion) mark, representing a five-year increase of 52 per cent.

1993	Tourism Task Force established by the government to examine tourism in anticipation of the five-year strategy for 1994–99. Recommendations implemented by government include further liberalisation of air transport, easing compulsory Shannon stopover on transatlantic routes and establishing a National Tourism Council.
1994	First IRA ceasefire in Northern Ireland begins the stabilisation of The Troubles.
1995	Little Report is published by government-appointed consultant Arthur D. Little and recommends that Bord Fáilte should divest of all activities except for marketing Ireland. The government subsequently restructures Bord Fáilte into three divisions: international marketing, corporate affairs and secretariat.
1995	The Tourism Brand Ireland (TBI) concept is developed jointly by Bord Fáilte's international marketing division and the Northern Ireland Tourism Board to brand and market Ireland together as a single destination.
1996	TBI is launched in November. Enda Kenny is the Republic's Minister for Tourism and Trade at the time.
1997	Gulliver becomes Gulliver InfoRes, a partnership between Bord Fáilte, the Northern Ireland Tourism Board and private Kerry-based company Fexco.
1998	The Good Friday Belfast Agreement is signed in Belfast, promising a lasting resolution to the Northern Ireland Troubles.
2000s	At the dawn of the new millennium, the Republic's tourism is worth a total of €4.8 billion per annum, of which approximately €2 billion ends up with the government in taxation. There are roughly 145,000 people employed in the industry.
2000	December sees the establishment of Tourism Ireland Limited (TIL), a product of the 1998 Good Friday Belfast Agreement, with an estimated budget of €28 million. TIL takes over all international marketing functions for the entire island of Ireland as a single destination.
2001	Major setbacks for Irish tourism come in the form of the foot and mouth disease (FMD) crisis and the terrorist attacks in the US on 11 September.
2001	Belgian flag-carrier airline Sabena goes into bankruptcy shortly after the 9/11 attacks on the US. Aer Lingus is accruing over €2 million per day in losses.
2002	The TIL's first marketing campaign is launched on 1 January, ending fifty years of Bord Fáilte's international marketing of the Republic.

2002	John O'Donoghue is appointed minister at the newly created Department of Arts, Sport and Tourism (DAST) and sets up the Tourism Strategy Review Group, chaired by John Travers.
2003	**May:** Fáilte Ireland (also known as the National Tourism Development Authority) is formed by the merger of Bord Fáilte and the Council for Education Recruitment and Training (CERT).
2003	**June:** Government announces plans for a National Conference Centre (NCC).
2003	Aer Rianta's three state-run airports are divided into three competing entities: Dublin Airport Authority, Cork Airport Authority and Shannon Airport Authority.
2003	**September:** Tourism Strategy Review Group publishes its report: *New Horizons for Irish Tourism: An Agenda for Action.*
2004	Shannon Airport rebrands as a 'low-fares' airport.
2004	**January:** Tourism Action Plan Implementation Group established to put the recommendations of the *New Horizons* report into practice.
2004	Singapore Airlines offers the world's longest non-stop flight between Singapore and Los Angeles on the ultra long-haul Airbus A340. Later the same year, Singapore Airlines breaks its own record by using the A340 on an even longer route, from Singapore to New York-Newark.
2005	European aircraft manufacturer Airbus launches the world's first fully double-decker super-jumbo jet, the Airbus A380, with a capacity for up to 853 economy-class passengers or around 555 passengers in mixed classes, which can fly non-stop for 8,000 nautical miles.
2005	Willie Walsh resigns as CEO of Aer Lingus and takes up a position as CEO of British Airways. Dermot Mannion (formerly of Emirates Airlines) is named his successor at Aer Lingus.
2005	**November:** DAST announces Spencer Dock International Conference Centre Consortium as Provisional Preferred Tenderer for Dublin's National Conference Centre.
2006	Aer Lingus's first non-European/non-American route is launched to Dubai, in the United Arab Emirates, as the company begins the process of privatising.
2006	**May:** Tourism Strategy Implementation Group established to advise Minister on the implementation of the remaining recommendations of the *New Horizons* report.

World tourism – 2005

In 2005 international tourism sustained the sharp upturn that began in 2004 in spite of the various tragic events it had to contend with. According to preliminary results presented today by the United Nations specialised agency, the World Tourism Organization (UNWTO), the number of international tourist arrivals recorded worldwide grew by 5.5 per cent and exceeded 800 million for the first time ever.

Although 2005 was certainly a tumultuous year, international tourism has fared amazingly well. Despite various terrorist attacks and natural disasters, such as the aftermath of the Indian Ocean tsunami and an extraordinarily long and strong hurricane season, the recovery, which started in 2004, continued firmly through 2005. Even though the disruptions experienced definitely left traces locally in the short term, they did not substantially alter the global or regional traffic flows. Based on detailed results for a large number of destinations included in the January issue of the *UNWTO World Tourism Barometer*, the number of international tourist arrivals in 2005 is estimated at 808 million, up from 766 million in 2004. This corresponds not only to an increase of 5.5 per cent, but also means a consolidation of the bumper growth achieved in 2004 (+10 per cent). Although growth was more moderate, it is still almost 1.5 percentage points above the long-term average annual growth rate of 4.1 per cent.

UNWTO Secretary-General Francesco Frangialli commented, 'The tourism sector has gained substantially in resilience over the past years. In spite of the turbulent environment we live in nowadays, destinations worldwide added some 100 million international arrivals between 2002 and 2005.'

Results by region

Africa led the way in 2005, with growth estimated at 10 per cent. Growth was stronger in Sub-Saharan Africa (+13 per cent), with particularly remarkable results for Kenya (+26 per cent between January and October compared with the same period of the previous year) following an already buoyant 2004, and Mozambique (+37 per cent Jan–Sep). South Africa (+11 per cent Jan–Aug) as well as the island destinations of Seychelles (+7 per cent) and Mauritius (+6 per cent) all improved on their 2004 results. In North Africa growth continued but at a more moderate pace, with Tunisia recording an increase of 8 per cent between January and November and Morocco 5 per cent for the full year.

Growth in Asia and the Pacific averaged 7 per cent following the exceptional post-SARS rebound in 2004 (+27 per cent). North-East Asia (+10 per cent) emerged as the most dynamic sub-region, with the strongest performers being Taiwan (PR of China) (+15 per cent Jan–Oct), China (+13 per cent Jan–Nov) and Japan (+9 per cent Jan–Nov). In South-East Asia (+4 per cent), Oceania (+4 per cent) and South Asia (+4 per cent), results overall were more modest and above all rather mixed. Cambodia (+35 per cent

Jan–Nov), Lao PDR (+27 per cent Jan–Sep), Vietnam (+18 per cent), the Philippines (+14 per cent Jan–Oct) and India (+13 per cent) nevertheless managed to report remarkable growth. Among the countries affected by the December 2004 tsunami tragedy, the Maldives reported a 39 per cent decrease up to November, although the rate of decline has eased in the last months. Arrivals to Indonesia were down by nearly 9 per cent, as the country also suffered from the October Bali bombing. Sri Lanka reported only a slight 0.4 per cent drop, although this result may in part be attributed to the large number of Sri Lankan expatriates who visited the country in the aftermath of the tsunami and to the flow of aid workers. As for Thailand, although overall data up to June shows a 6 per cent decline, arrivals at the Bangkok airport registered 4 per cent growth in the period through October.

In the Americas, growth reached 6 per cent, with North America (+4 per cent) and the Caribbean (+5 per cent) slightly below the regional average. Of the major destinations, the United States continued the recovery started in 2004 (+8 per cent Jan–Sep), while Mexico (+8 per cent Jan–Nov) and Cuba (+13 per cent Jan–Nov) still showed above-average increases, even after having suffered the impact of last year's devastating hurricanes. Destinations in Central America (+14 per cent) and South America (+13 per cent), on the other hand, can look back on a very positive year. The strongest growth was reported by Venezuela (+23 per cent) and Colombia (+22 per cent), while Argentina, Brazil, Chile, Paraguay, Peru, Costa Rica, El Salvador, Guatemala, Honduras and Nicaragua all recorded, or were on their way to record, growth rates of between 10 and 20 per cent.

Following the very strong performance over the past couple of years, the Middle East seems to have entered a more moderate phase of growth, with the increase for 2005 estimated at 7 per cent. Egypt (+6 per cent), Dubai (United Arab Emirates) (+7 per cent Jan–Sep) and Jordan (+5 per cent) are all close to the regional average, while Bahrain (+11 per cent Jan–Sep), Saudi Arabia (+21 per cent Jan–Jun) and Palestine (+45 per cent Jan–Sep, albeit from a small base) are on their way to exceeding it. Available data, however, is rather limited and the picture could certainly still change.

Europe recorded relatively modest growth of 4 per cent, which is still one percentage point above the long-term trend of the region. This result can be considered very encouraging given the rather weak economy in some of its major intra-regional source markets. Moreover, due to Europe's already very large base of over 400 million arrivals, in absolute terms it recorded the largest increase, corresponding to some 18 million arrivals. Growth was strongest in Northern Europe (+7 per cent), boosted by the United Kingdom (+10 per cent Jan–Nov), which was seemingly not notably affected by the London bomb attacks. International tourist arrivals in Southern and Mediterranean Europe increased by 6 per cent. Turkey was the star performer in this sub-region, with an increase of 20 per cent, adding 3.4 million arrivals and passing the 20 million mark. Furthermore, Spain (+6 per cent), Croatia (+7 per cent Jan–Nov), Israel (+26 per cent Jan–Oct) and

Serbia and Montenegro (+27 per cent Jan–Oct) also recorded respectable results. Western Europe and Central and Eastern Europe grew by 2 per cent and 4 per cent, respectively. In Central and Eastern Europe, the Baltic states, Latvia (+20 per cent), Lithuania (+15 per cent Jan–Sep) and Estonia (+7 per cent Jan–Nov) stood out, while in Western Europe, the best results came from Germany (+6 per cent Jan–Nov) and Switzerland (+6 per cent Jan–Nov).

Prospects for 2006
For 2006 the current pattern of gradually slowing growth is expected to continue. In co-operation with the Fundación Premio Arce of the Universidad Politécnica de Madrid, a short-term forecast has been elaborated, according to which international tourist arrivals worldwide are expected to grow between 4 and 5 per cent in 2006. Growth is projected to be around one percentage point lower than in 2005 but still somewhat above the forecast long-term annual growth rate of 4.1 per cent. This outlook is supported by the continued good shape of the world economy in most parts of the world and the improved prospects for the eurozone economies, in particular its most important source market, Germany.

Three major uncertainties remain for 2006. First, it is likely that terrorism will continue to be present. However, experience shows that its impact lately has been rather limited and short lived. Travellers overall have assumed the risk and have been undeterred by external threats. Secondly, rising energy prices, inflation and interest rates might finally change the economic scenario. This has not been much of a problem until now, as the price hike has mostly been an expression of the strong economic growth and the corresponding demand for energy. Should this situation continue and affect economic growth in Asia, the tourism industry could start feeling the impact.

Finally, the further spread of avian flu could be a serious threat for the tourism sector. Avian flu has been present in the world for several years now and it is currently limited to birds and isolated cases of people living in very close contact with infected animals. As yet no transmission of the virus between humans has been detected and it is hard to say whether, when and where such a mutation will occur. For the moment there is no reason to change travel plans as long as recommendations issued by national and local health and veterinary authorities are respected.

'Panic is always a bad advisor,' says Mr Frangialli. 'What we can do is to monitor the situation closely and prepare for it, should it happen. In spite of the current uncertainties I am confident that world tourism and all its stakeholders will weather the storm – if it does come – in the best way possible.'

Source: UNWTO, January 2006.

THE STRUCTURE OF IRISH TOURISM: GOVERNMENT DEPARTMENTS

The Irish government has a vested interest in the marketing, development and administration of tourism in the state. As we shall see, this interest has extended beyond the boundaries of the state to encompass an all-Ireland approach to reaping the rewards of tourism.

The first time tourism appeared in a department was in 1977 as part of the Department of Tourism and Transport. This was the first time that the area of tourism was deemed worthy of becoming a part of a government department, and so marked a crossroads for government involvement in the industry.

In the 1997–2002 Dáil led by Taoiseach Bertie Ahern (Fianna Fáil) and Tánaiste Mary Harney (Progressive Democrats) in coalition, the **Department of Tourism, Sport and Recreation** was formed, led by Minister Jim McDaid, TD. This changed once again at the beginning of the 2002–2007 Dáil (under the same leadership and same coalition) to the **Department of Arts, Sport and Tourism**. The Minister in charge at the time of writing is John O'Donoghue, TD.

See www.arts-sport-tourism.gov.ie/ for a direct link to the department. The website of the Irish government (www.irlgov.ie) provides a full link to all government departments and agencies. Appendix B of this book is a comprehensive listing of web resources relevant to the study of tourism and contains the web addresses for direct links to press releases and speeches made by the Minister for Tourism, as well as the full text of Dáil debates relating to tourism. Appendix C of this book provides a detailed database of contact details for tourism organisations in Ireland (including Northern Ireland), both public and private, to enable the reader to research in further detail. The contact details of all the organisations discussed below are contained in Appendix C.

The department has the responsibility of formulating national tourism policies in conjunction with the government's overall developmental policies, as well as providing a funding, regulatory and supervisory role. According to the Minister's welcome on the department website, its function is to

contribute to the economic, social and cultural progress of Irish society and the enrichment of its quality of life through promoting sustainable tourism; encouraging excellence in sporting and artistic achievement; facilitating greater access to sport and the arts; and preservation of our cultural inheritance.

O'Donoghue signs Cultural Agreement with India
At a ceremony today in New Delhi, the Cultural Co-operation Agreement between the Government of Ireland and the Government of the Republic of India was signed. The Minister for Arts, Sport and Tourism, John O'Donoghue, TD, signed on behalf of Ireland. Minister for Culture, Mr Jaipal Reddy, signed on behalf of the Republic of India.
    Under the terms of the agreement, closer relations and understanding

between both countries will be promoted and developed in the fields of art, culture, archaeology, education, including activity in the fields of science and technology, public health, mass media, tourism and sports.

'There are already well-developed links between Ireland and India,' Minister O'Donoghue said. 'For example, there are already strong educational links between the two countries. This agreement will now provide the basis for a new and deeper level of cultural co-operation and exchange between our countries and will also create a context in which to enrich the co-operation and understanding between the cultures and peoples of Ireland and India,' the Minister added.

The agreement also offers a new impetus for the thriving Indian film industry to consider Ireland as a film-making location. Ireland's spectacular landscape, scenery and our film-making skills base make it one of the finest locations for filming in the world.

Source: Department of Arts, Sport and Tourism press release, 19 January 2006.

In the 1997–2002 Dáil, the following departments also had a role to play in relation to tourism policy.

Department of Arts, Heritage, Gaeltacht and the Islands:
- Responsibility for Office of Public Works (OPW) Parks and Wildlife Service.

Department of Public Enterprise:
- Policies on transport.
- Development of infrastructure.
- Licensing airlines, ferry operators, travel agents and tour operators.

These two departments were changed in the new Dáil in 2002. What remained were the:
- Department of Community, Rural and Gaeltacht Affairs.
- Department of Transport.
- Department of Communications, Marine and Natural Resources.

Naturally, the Department of Transport (see www.transport.ie) is the most relevant of the above three in tourism terms.

The Department of the Environment, Heritage and Local Government (DEHLG) also has a tourism responsibility in their management of the National Parks and Wildlife Service (see www.npws.ie), formerly known as Dúchas – The Heritage Service until March 2003. It is also responsible for national monuments, historical properties and parks and gardens (under the Office of Public Works, see below).

The Department of Finance and the Department of Enterprise, Trade and Employment also have a role to play in tourism, and have done so for the last number of Dáils.

Department of Finance
The Department of Finance has overall budgetary control for the Irish economy. It allocates the budgets to other government departments and agencies and collects

revenues on behalf of the state. The tourism marketing, development and administrative support budgets allocated to tourism agencies via the Department of Arts, Sport and Tourism are dependant on the allocation from the Department of Finance. Tourism is a net contributor to the Department of Finance and thus to the Irish economy, i.e. it brings in more than it costs.

The Department of Finance also manages and sets policies for the Office of Public Works.

Department of Enterprise, Trade and Employment

A growing economy is dependent on availability of labour and an entrepreneurial spirit of investment. The Department of Enterprise, Trade and Employment aims to foster such a climate. This department's labour role has changed markedly since the early 1990s, when its function was to find employment for countless unemployed Irish people. Its current task is more focused on satisfying employers' demands for highly skilled and reasonably priced labour, including for the tourism sector.

This department also operates the local and county Enterprise Boards, which give enterprise start-ups in all sectors (including tourism and tourism-related services) practical support.

O'Donoghue launches tourism industry 2004 First Annual Forum
The Minister for Arts, Sport and Tourism, Mr John O'Donoghue, TD, today [17 November 2004] welcomed the convening of the first National Tourism Forum, which was held in the Royal Hospital in Kilmainham.

'This forum will play a key role in helping us refocus and redouble our efforts one year on from the publication of the Report of the Tourism Policy Review Group, *New Horizons for Irish Tourism: An Agenda for Action*, which is the blueprint for the future development of the industry. It should also help to identify the actions that require prioritisation by both the industry and the government in order to underpin the development of an industry which is a major sector of enterprise, employment and wealth creation for Ireland and its regions.'

The forum was convened by the Tourism Action Plan Implementation Group, in conjunction with the Department of Arts, Sport and Tourism and the tourism state agencies, and reported in-depth on the progress of the implementation of the new tourism strategy as well as providing representatives of the tourism industry in Ireland with the opportunity to advise the Implementation Group and the government, through the Minister for Arts, Sport and Tourism, of their views on the current status of the industry and the implementation of the strategy.

The Minister again highlighted the need for all sectors of the tourism industry to ensure that the quality and level of service they are offering is in accordance with what the customer wants and consistent with what the customer has been led to expect.

'I am already on public record as saying that much of the public debate this year on tourism prices and competitiveness has been ill informed and unfair. We must draw a distinction between the vitally important need to deliver good value for money to our visitors – which I have constantly highlighted since becoming Minister – and a growing domestic obsession about an alleged widespread rip-off culture in Ireland. "Rip-off" is defined in the *Oxford English Dictionary* as "cheating someone, especially financially". Are we seriously saying that this is the case in Ireland? It is a fact of life that modern Ireland is a high-cost and price location and that is, in part, a reflection of our high income and low personal tax levels. But that is not to say that we cannot, and do not, deliver a high-quality, value-for-money holiday experience to the vast majority of our visitors. It is potentially very damaging and destructive to our tourism industry and our international marketing effort to have constant references to an alleged rip-off culture in Ireland. I suspect that no other country runs down its tourism industry in such a way.'

The key issue now is 'collectively to get the industry back on a sustained course of renewed growth to achieve the ambitious targets which have been set by the Review Group', the Minister said. In this context, he noted the important role of air access and expressed the view that 'there is considerable potential for the development of new air services from America'. He also emphasised the government's continuing commitment to the tourism sector and noted that the department's provision for tourism services in the Estimates, which are due to be published tomorrow, 'will increase considerably in real terms on last year, with a particular emphasis on the Tourism Marketing Fund'.

Minister O'Donoghue thanked Mr John Travers, chairman, and the other members of the Implementation Group for their work in pushing forward the tourism agenda in conjunction with his department and the tourism state agencies, expressing the view that those attending would 'leave with renewed confidence and commitment to take the steps necessary to further develop the sector and to address the challenges that lie ahead'.

Source: Department of Arts, Sport and Tourism press release, 17 November 2004.

FÁILTE IRELAND

Fáilte Ireland (FI), also known as the National Tourism Development Authority (NTDA), encompasses the range of tourism support functions previously carried out by Bord Fáilte and CERT, and as such is the Republic of Ireland's NTO (national tourism organisation). These two organisations were merged on 28 May 2003, with businesswoman Gillian Bowler as chairperson and former CERT CEO Shaun Quinn as chief executive officer (see www.failteireland.ie for corporate information, or www.ireland.ie for tourist information for those prospective tourists to Ireland).

Figure 2.1: The Fáilte Ireland Brand

Source: Fáilte Ireland.

> In their own words...
>
> The key role of Fáilte Ireland is to support and help the industry to meet the challenges facing the entire global tourism market and to sustain, or increase, the level of activity in the sector.
>
> We are primarily a catalyst of other people's activity. We support the industry in its efforts to be more competitive and more profitable. As the state's tourism development authority, we are well placed to address some of the broader issues that need to be tackled if the industry is to grow and develop.
>
> Our emphasis is on strategic partnership, with all the interests in Irish tourism at national, local and regional levels working together towards a common goal.
>
> Fáilte Ireland's range of supports and services provides those involved in, or considering becoming involved in, Irish tourism with a one-stop shop to meet their business or professional needs. Working in partnership with the industry, Fáilte Ireland will meet the industry's needs, leading and supporting Irish tourism in its next phase of development.
>
> Source: Fáilte Ireland.

FI is responsible for tourism development in the twenty-six counties of the Republic of Ireland at a national, regional and local level. It works in strategic partnership with various organisations (public and private) involved in the Irish tourism industry. Its aim also includes helping the industry to be 'more competitive and more profitable and to help individual enterprises to enhance their performance'. According to the FI website, it carries this out under the following four headings.

Marketing Services

FI provides marketing support and promotional opportunities for Irish product providers, marketing groups, tour operators, handling agents and visitor services to the consumer.

Training Services

FI provides training and advice for businesses and people working in the industry, career development and promotion for school leavers, skills training for unemployed adults and those returning to work.

Product Development

FI administers grant aid and tax incentive schemes, accommodation quality assurance and information as well as a business advisory service.

Research and Statistics

A key responsibility of FI is to provide comprehensive information gathered via the Central Statistics Office, as well as surveys and research specifically carried out by FI (such as the Survey of Overseas Travellers – SOT). This includes an overview of tourism performance in Ireland and a profile of overseas visitors to Ireland as well as strategic research on all aspects of development and training.

The members of the National Tourism Development Authority have remained unchanged (apart from one member) since May 2003. As of May 2006, the members are as follows:

Gillian Bowler (Chair)	Businesswoman
Maureen Cairnduff	Journalist and Writer
Dominic Dillane	Lecturer in Hospitality Management, DIT
Brian Dowling	Managing Director, CIE Tours International
John McDonnell	Former General Secretary, SIPTU
Noel McGinley	Businessman
Noel O'Callaghan	O'Callaghan Hotels
Richard Bourke	Deputy Chairperson of the ITIC
An tUasal Pádraig Ó Céidigh	Managing Director, Aer Arann
Patrick O'Donoghue	Gleneagles Hotel
An tUasal Páidí Ó Sé	Publican
Catherine Reilly	Tour Operator
Eithne Scott-Lennon	Fitzpatrick Hotel Group

O'Donoghue appoints Gillian Bowler as chair of Fáilte Ireland – the new National Tourism Development Authority

John O'Donoghue, TD, Minister for Arts, Sport and Tourism, today [21 May 2003] announced the board members of Fáilte Ireland, the new National Tourism Development Authority, at a function in the National Gallery of Ireland.

Fáilte Ireland will be formally established on Wednesday, 28 May 2003. On that date, Bord Fáilte Éireann and CERT will be dissolved and their functions transferred to the new authority. The membership includes a broad representation of industry interests and business experience.

The Minister expressed his particular satisfaction that Ms Gillian Bowler had agreed to be the Chair of Fáilte Ireland. 'Irish tourism is facing an increasingly competitive international environment. Gillian has extensive knowledge of international travel and tourism. She has wide business experience through a number of directorships of state, public and private companies. Her knowledge of the tourism and travel trade and her involvement in reviews of Irish tourism give her an incisive and objective insight into the challenges facing the sector and its need to be internationally competitive and to respond to changing customer needs.

'Fáilte Ireland will focus on the experience of visitors when they get here, by working closely with the tourism industry to provide a one-stop shop for strategic and practical support to develop and sustain Ireland as a high-quality and competitive tourist destination. Tourism Ireland Ltd, which has responsibility for the international tourism marketing of the island of Ireland, will continue its focus on getting people here,' said Minister O'Donoghue. Mr Shaun Quinn, formerly chief executive of CERT, has already been appointed chief executive designate of Fáilte Ireland.

'In view of the challenging times facing the tourism industry, it is vital to have Fáilte Ireland up and running as soon as possible. For that reason I intend to formally establish Fáilte Ireland with effect from 28 May 2003. The establishment of the authority has been one of my main tourism priorities since I took up office. I undertook to secure early passage of the necessary backing legislation and I am pleased that I have been able to deliver on that commitment. With the establishment of the new body, one of the key tourism commitments in the Agreed Programme for Government has now been met,' Minister O'Donoghue added.

The establishment of Fáilte Ireland will mean the passing of two organisations that have made an enormous contribution to Irish tourism. Bord Fáilte succeeded, from extremely small beginnings, in building up a product and a marketing strategy that has become the envy of many countries across the globe. CERT has played a vitally important role, since its inception in the early 1960s, in helping to upskill the industry and has worked ceaselessly to stimulate it to raise its standards. It has been particularly successful in attracting and developing young people who have provided vibrancy, growth and resilience within the sector.

'Together, Bord Fáilte and CERT have played a key role in growing the tourism industry into one of the biggest economic sectors in the state. The women and men who have served on the board of Bord Fáilte and the council of CERT and all the members of staff who have worked for these organisations over the years with such commitment, creativity and diligence have played a key role in achieving this success. On behalf of the government, I would like to take this opportunity to express my sincere thanks to them for their commitment and their valuable contribution,' said Minister O'Donoghue.

In December 2002, the Minister appointed a high-powered Strategic Review Group to review tourism policy in the state. This group is currently finalising its interim report, which it will present to the Minister shortly. Its recommendations are expected to form the template for a revised strategy for the further successful development of tourism throughout the country.

'The tourism industry in Ireland is at a pivotal point in its development. The factors central to our success to date are not necessarily the ones to carry us forward into the future. With the establishment of Fáilte Ireland we will have, for the first time, an organisation dedicated to excellence in both product and service, the twin experiences of the tourist visitor to Ireland,' said the Minister.

An interim board, appointed by the Minister shortly after he came into office last summer, has progressed preparatory arrangements for the establishment of the new authority. The Minister thanked the members of the interim board, and, in particular, its chairman, John Travers, for their work in preparing the ground for a new dynamic in the development of the Irish tourism industry.

Source: Department of Arts, Sport and Tourism press release, 21 May 2003.

Originally, Bord Fáilte (Welcome Board) was established in 1952 and merged with Fógra Fáilte (Welcome Adverts) in 1955 to form Bord Fáilte Éireann (Irish Welcome Board). This is the agency that had overall responsibility for the Republic's tourism sector from this time until it merged with CERT in 2003.

Its functions included:

* Marketing Ireland as a destination, both at home and abroad, for all forms of tourism, e.g. leisure, business.
* Development of Irish tourism products.
* Enforcing regulations.
* Administration of public tourism sector, including RTAs (see below).
* Funding support.
* Providing information and statistics for public and private tourism marketers, managers and researchers.

The Council for Education Recruitment and Training (CERT) was established in 1963 to provide industry as well as college-based training for students in the tourism and hospitality industry. Students attended lectures and/or block release programmes at several centres around the country.

FI also has responsibility for regional tourism and provides links to tourist information on all regions as well as research and statistics on regional tourism patterns. In addition, it provides links to external travel and tourism resources, such as Tourism Ireland (the all-Ireland tourism marketing agency) and Ireland Inspires (from the Business Tourism Forum).

Specialist tourism products are marketed and developed by Fáilte Ireland. The organisation takes part in trade fairs and promotions for such products and liaises with private sector organisations dealing with such niche products. It also hosts individual websites for the following niche market products:

Golf in Ireland	www.golf.ireland.ie
Walking in Ireland	www.walking.ireland.ie
Angling in Ireland	www.angling.ireland.ie
Cycling in Ireland	www.cycling.ireland.ie
Water-based activities in Ireland	www.waterbased.ireland.ie
Equestrian in Ireland	www.equestrian.ireland.ie
Heritage in Ireland	www.heritage.ireland.ie
Genealogy in Ireland	www.genealogy.ireland.ie

Festivals and events in Ireland   www.festivals.ireland.ie
Learning English in Ireland   www.learnenglish.ireland.ie

NORTHERN IRELAND TOURIST BOARD

The Northern Ireland Tourist Board (NITB) represents tourism in the six counties of Northern Ireland and performs much of the same functions in its jurisdiction as Fáilte Ireland does in the Republic. Its corporate website is www.nitb.com, while its commercial tourist website is www.discovernorthernireland.com.

The NITB chairman is Tom McGrath, OBE and its CEO is Alan Clarke, supported by a director of marketing, a director of industry development, a director of finance and business planning and a director of special projects. The NITB is responsible to Northern Ireland's Minister with responsibility for Enterprise, Trade and Investment.

Figure 2.2: The NITB Brand

Source: NITB.

Tourism is worth around €600 million to Northern Ireland, with more than two-thirds of this coming from visitors outside Northern Ireland. Tourism accounts for around 2 per cent of Northern Ireland's GDP and supports around 20,000 jobs.

Northern Ireland's tourism regions are as follows.

Causeway Coast and
Glens of Antrim (North-east)   www.causewaycoastandglens.com

Belfast City   www.gotobelfast.com

City of Derry   www.derryvisitor.com

The Sperrins – Mountains
and Moorland (North-west)   www.sperrinstourism.com

Fermanagh Lakeland
and South Tyrone (South-west)   www.fermanaghlakelands.com

The Mourne Mountains
and St Patrick's Country (South-east)   www.visitarmagh.com
www.kingdomsofdown.com

The NITB's self-professed challenge is:

for tourism in Northern Ireland to attract more visitors and then make their stay memorable so that they are encouraged to return and to recommend Northern

Ireland. It is also important to encourage people from Northern Ireland to take leisure breaks and holidays at home.

Northern Ireland's strategic objectives for the coming years include the following.
* Increase Northern Ireland's share of visitors to the island of Ireland.
* Increase visitor tourism revenue by 9 per cent per annum.
* Increase visitor numbers by 7 per cent per annum.

These challenges and strategic objectives form part of the NITB-commissioned report entitled *A Strategic Framework for Action 2004–2007*, available from the Strategy menu on www.nitb.com.

The NITB aims to achieve these objectives through the key goals of attracting visitors, business enhancement and communicating effectively.

Attracting visitors:
* Know the visitor market intelligence.
* Develop a compelling proposition.
* Reach the consumer.
* Take care of the visitor every step of the way (first and lasting impressions).

Business enhancement:
* Develop signature projects – deliver international 'stand out' for Northern Ireland.
* Focus on winning themes – deliver a competitive advantage for Northern Ireland.
* Develop internationally competitive enterprise – focus on quality.
* Deliver memorable experiences – the less tangible side of tourism.

Communicating effectively:
* Share information – tell others about successes.
* Strengthen effective relationships for delivery – work together.

The way forward
NITB is starting a new phase in its development. The strategic framework is seen as a significant step forward by the majority of stakeholders and there is an overwhelming wish to see NITB succeed in delivering it. Stakeholders feel that the organisation has been through a hard time in its recent history, with the establishment of TIL and the Public Accounts Committee investigation in particular, and it is recognised that these changes may have taken its toll on staff and management morale.

There is, however, a strong feeling that tourism is a major untapped area of economic growth for Northern Ireland and a sense of impatience exists with regard to moving ahead and making the most of it, before other countries (particularly Eastern Europe) do so instead.

Responsibility for tourism in Northern Ireland is complicated and not for the faint hearted. Awareness is growing with regard to tourism roles and responsibilities, although confusion still exists. The majority of stakeholders feel that significant concentration on communicating detailed accounts of who is responsible for what is a waste of money. What is felt to be important is that NITB takes responsibility for facilitating results/actions through others, as well as themselves. NITB is perceived to either be or should be the strategic leader of tourism in Northern Ireland. Where they are not directly responsible, they are seen to have an automatic role facilitating others to achieve results on their behalf. There is a growing impatience at strategic stakeholder level of the debate and a sense that NITB should assume the role and formulate the delivery of results either through their own resources or those of others.

There are six areas of work needed to provide evidence to stakeholders that NITB is moving forward on its strategic framework. These are the areas which need to be prioritised and structured to ensure that effective delivery takes place. The six themes are:

- Improving communication and engagement with the tourism sectors.
- Developing staff in line with the needs of the strategic framework.
- Developing NITB culture to deliver a responsive and accountable organisation.
- Showing delivery success on the strategic framework, based on priority needs.
- Influencing others, particularly within government, to increase awareness of the importance of tourism to Northern Ireland and achieve results.
- Providing more timely research and market intelligence to the industry.

Source: Tourism Industry Stakeholder Satisfaction Survey and Action Plan, NITB.

TOURISM IRELAND LIMITED

As we can see, various tourism agencies have played a role in attracting foreign tourists to Ireland. Up until the 1990s, Bord Fáilte Éireann was the main tourism representative agency for the Republic of Ireland in all foreign markets. Similarly, the Northern Ireland Tourist Board (NITB) was the main agency in Northern Ireland. The 1990s saw an era of much cross-border co-operation between both administrations on the island of Ireland. In the mid-1990s, plans were put in place for a co-operative tourism promotion to attract foreign tourists to all parts of Ireland. This became known as Tourism Brand Ireland (TBI). This venture was short lived, as it soon became part of a broader cross-border project.

Figure 2.3: The Tourism Ireland Limited Brand

Source: TIL.

As part of the Good Friday Belfast Agreement, a North–South ministerial council was established for the tourism sector. Minister Jim McDaid represented the Republic and Sir Reg Empey represented Northern Ireland at its inaugural sessions. Both representatives agreed that the way forward for all-Ireland tourism was to market Ireland as a single destination around the world. Therefore, a new body was set up and launched its marketing campaign on 1 January 2002.

Tourism Ireland Limited (TIL, see www.discoverireland.com for tourist information and www.tourismireland.com/ corporate for corporate information) was commissioned to represent the whole island of Ireland as a single destination in all foreign markets (including Great Britain, which had previously been a domestic market for the NITB). The pre-existing bodies (Bord Fáilte – now Fáilte Ireland – and the NITB) remain in existence, but have different roles (product development and internal promotion).

TIL took over the remit of TBI, as well as the tourism promotional ads that were in the process of being developed for TBI. A new campaign of television and print ads, as well as comprehensive travel brochures, was unveiled in January 2002 in the world's media. Further, a revamped website (in various languages) and promotional CD-ROMs were also launched.

TIL spends considerable resources in the major tourism-generating countries. Television ads are relatively expensive, as is the production of glossy, full-colour travel-planner brochures, print ads, websites and CD-ROMs. The marketing campaign was produced by McCann-Erickson London (one of the world's best-known marketing agencies).

Minister opens Tourism Ireland office in Shanghai

Minister for Enterprise, Trade and Employment, Micheál Martin, opened Tourism Ireland's first office in China today. The office is based in Shanghai and it represents continuing expansion in Asia and recognition of the growing importance of the significance of the Chinese tourism market for Ireland. The World Tourism Organization (UNWTO) recognises that China will have the greatest outbound tourism market in the world by 2020. Last year saw the granting of Approved Destination Status (ADS) for Ireland and the UK. Over 5,000 Chinese visitors came to the island of Ireland in 2005.

Source: *Kildare Times*, 12 July 2006.

Ireland's tourism message 'confused'

Tourism Ireland is failing to market Ireland Inc. to overseas visitors, according to leading Irish hoteliers. They claimed Tourism Ireland's marketing message to overseas visitors was diluted by an over-emphasis on diverse products. 'We are marketing everything from horse-riding to golf, but have missed the bigger picture of selling Ireland Inc.,' said the marketing manager of one five-star hotel, who did not want to be identified.

'We need a review of the Irish product. The Aran jumper of Irish tourism is gone and we need to refocus.' This was reiterated by Niall Rochford, general manager of the exclusive Ashford Castle in Mayo. Rochford said it had been 'a difficult season' for the tourist industry. 'We need to be marketed as a quality destination. There is no brand image for Ireland and the message has become confused.'

While budget airlines and an increase in mid-range hotels have attracted budget business to Ireland, hoteliers voiced concern about an over-reliance on the lower end of the market. 'We can only get a bad name if we attract a budget business to a high-cost destination,' said one hotelier.

'Ireland's cost base is a lot higher than other European countries.' He said that advertising slogans such as Aer Lingus's 'Ireland for the price of a pint' were sending out the wrong message to holidaymakers. Last year, when inflation was taken into account, individual visitors to Ireland spent less than in 2003. The overall number of tourists rose by 2.6 per cent, but this growth reflected short-stay visitors to Dublin and masked a sharp fall in numbers to traditional locations.

For the first time in decades, the number of British tourists actually fell. The fall in tourist numbers has particularly affected the Border, Midlands and West regions. Rochford said improved infrastructure was needed to mitigate against this trend.

Source: Mitchell, S., 'Ireland's tourism message "confused"', *The Sunday Business Post*, 14 August 2005.

REGIONAL TOURISM AUTHORITIES (RTAs)

The Regional Tourism Authorities (RTAs) administer, promote and develop the tourism sectors in each of their respective regions. There are seven defined tourism regions in the Republic, which are structured on the basis of EU planning areas. The RTAs are funded by Fáilte Ireland, members' fees and commercial activities (such as visitor services). Their functions are to provide guest service through tourist information offices (TIOs) located at major tourist points around the country. They also encourage local organisations, businesses and individuals to get involved in tourism development.

Six of the seven tourism regions are administered by RTAs, and one is administered by Shannon Development. The regions are divided as follows.

Table 2.1: RTA Regions

Dublin	Dublin City	www.visitdublin.com
	Dublin County	
East Coast and Midlands	Kildare	www.eastcoastmidlands.ie
	Laois	
	Longford	
	Louth	
	Meath	
	North Offaly	
	Westmeath	
	Wicklow	
South East	Carlow	www.southeastireland.com
	Kilkenny	
	South Tipperary	

Table 2.1: RTA Regions (contd.)

South East	Waterford Wexford	
Cork-Kerry	Cork Kerry (North Kerry was part of Shannon Development until January 2005)	www.corkkerry.ie
Ireland West	Galway Mayo Roscommon	www.irelandwest.ie
Ireland North West	Cavan Donegal Leitrim Monaghan Sligo	www.irelandnorthwest.ie
Shannon Development	Clare Limerick North Tipperary South Offaly	www.shannonregiontourism.ie

Kerry to be unified for regional tourism marketing and development

The Minister for Arts, Sport and Tourism, John O'Donoghue, TD, has decided that Kerry should be unified, at regional level, for tourism marketing and development purposes. With effect from the beginning of next year, all of County Kerry will be included under the remit of Cork-Kerry Tourism – the South West Regional Tourism Authority.

At present North Kerry is part of the Mid-West region, which is administered by Shannon Development, while South Kerry is part of Cork-Kerry Tourism.

'I am pleased that there is broad agreement at industry and political level that Kerry should be reunited for tourism marketing and development purposes at regional level,' Minister O'Donoghue said.

'In 1989 Shannon Development was tasked by the then government to strengthen the tourism product base of North Kerry. Now, fifteen years on, the tourism product offering is far stronger as a result of their efforts. The main emphasis now has to be on marketing and promotion in what are increasingly competitive times for the tourism sector. Therefore, at this stage, I believe that it makes sense that Kerry be promoted in its totality and under the Regional Tourism Authority that carries "Kerry" in its name – Cork-Kerry Tourism.'

The appropriate state tourism agencies, Fáilte Ireland, Shannon Development and Cork-Kerry Tourism, will now work through the implications of the decision as regards resourcing, board representation, necessary legal changes and operational issues with a view to the new arrangements coming into effect from the beginning of next year.

Source: Department of Arts, Sport and Tourism press release, 15 September 2004.

As of 2005, the RTAs work under the auspices of Fáilte Ireland (except Dublin Tourism) in order to integrate regional and national tourism policy, as was the recommendation of a tourism strategy review conducted by consultants to the Department of Arts, Sport and Tourism (PricewaterhouseCoopers) as well as a strategy recommended by the Tourism Policy Review Group.

O'Donoghue meets with Regional Tourism Authority on proposed reform of regional tourism structures

John O'Donoghue, TD, Minister for Arts, Sport and Tourism, met [on 19 July 2005] the chairpersons and chief executives of the Regional Tourism Authorities to ascertain their response to the PricewaterhouseCoopers (PWC) proposals on regional tourism structures. 'Overall I was very pleased with the positive response the proposals received.'

The proposals are the outcome of a major consultancy study of the roles and functions of the Regional Tourism Authorities commissioned by Fáilte Ireland in response to a recommendation of the Tourism Policy Review Group. The consultants' report, which is available on Fáilte Ireland's website, highlights the need for regional tourism to play a strategic rather than administrative role and to input more directly into national policy. It also recommends that the regions should greatly increase their emphasis on targeted marketing, product development and enterprise support. To achieve this substantially revised brief, the PWC report recommends that an integrated linkage between regional tourism strategy and national policy should be reflected in revised structures.

'My key concern is to ensure that whatever changes are made result in more efficient and effective regional structures to service the needs of the visitor and the needs of the industry,' said the Minister. 'The background work towards achieving this objective has been substantially completed and I expect to be in a position to make a final decision in the near future.'

Source: Department of Arts, Sport and Tourism press release, 19 July 2005.

Tourism: The game has changed

The government's response to the problems facing the tourism industry has been all too predictable. Shuffle the deckchairs. Tourism promotion outside Dublin is to be centrally integrated under Fáilte Ireland, while Dublin Tourism will continue to do its own thing. The move results from a consultant's report that was commissioned to examine how to tackle the fall-off in tourist numbers outside Dublin.

It would be cynical to dismiss the new initiative. It is important that the promotion of tourism be properly organised and co-ordinated. Competition between regions to attract tourists can be fruitful but, equally, it is important that a coherent message is delivered across international markets. Last week's announcement would appear to be a step towards doing this in a more efficient way.

However, it is folly to pretend that an institutional reorganisation can address the core problems of Irish tourism. The key issue is the product on offer – in many cases it simply does not come up to scratch. Too often, the experience of tourists is that staying or eating out in Ireland is overpriced or substandard, or both.

Ireland is now, of course, a high-income, high-cost country, meaning that we can no longer compete purely on cost with other international locations, where prices are low and the cost of access has tumbled due to low-cost airlines. But, equally, the cost of getting here is cheaper, and we should be able to take advantage of that. A 14 per cent fall in tourist numbers outside Dublin between 1999 and 2003 suggests that we still need to do a lot better.

We have seen the same predictable government response to other 'crises' over the years – most notably the various changes in the industrial promotion agencies, which have gone through a bewildering number of identities.

Fortunately, the rate of inflation here has now fallen into line with our international partners – even if higher oil prices are causing it to edge upwards.

Unfortunately, the long period when we had a higher rate has left Ireland with a level of prices at the top of the euro league. Holding down the rate of price increase remains central to stemming further losses in competitiveness in tourism and other areas. The whole issue of access transport and infrastructure also remains crucial – perhaps tourism to the west will pick up again when the various bypasses are completed and it does not take six or seven hours to drive from one side of the country to the other. Much responsibility lies with the regions themselves and the tourist interests there. Investment is needed, and a realisation that the game has changed in terms of attracting tourists.

Fáilte Ireland and the new infrastructure may get people to visit once – but it is the quality of the product and its cost that will determine whether they come back.

Source: 'Tourism: The game has changed', *The Sunday Business Post*, 14 August 2005.

SHANNON DEVELOPMENT

Shannon Development (www.shannondev.ie) was established in 1959 to develop Shannon Airport and the surrounding areas. In 1989 it was given the task of developing tourism in what was then called the Mid-West RTA. The region includes counties Limerick, Clare, North Tipperary and South Offaly. North Kerry was part of Shannon Development for tourism purposes until January 2005, when it became part of Cork-Kerry Tourism (the South West RTA). Shannon Development is responsible for industrial as well as tourism development in the region. According to the organisation, their main tourism role is to 'initiate and support tourism development as a key element in the achievement of overall economic growth throughout the Shannon region'. Shannon Development operates twelve tourist information offices (TIOs) throughout the region and manages (in conjunction with Fáilte Ireland) the tourist website www.shannonregiontourism.ie, providing up-to-date information and offers for visitors. Its Tourism Product Promotion unit works with the tourism trade in the region to jointly promote the region on a year-round basis. Shannon Heritage Ltd (established in 1986) develops and runs heritage attractions in the region, including the world-famous Bunratty Castle.

O'Donoghue confirms future tourism role for Shannon Development

John O'Donoghue, TD, Minister for Arts, Sport and Tourism, today [10 November 2005] met the chairman, Liam McElligott, the chief executive, Kevin Thompstone, and other representatives of Shannon Development to discuss a range of issues relating to the operation of the company and its future tourism remit.

The Minister confirmed to Shannon Development that in the light of the continuation of an overall regional development role, the company could continue to exercise a strong regional tourism remit. The Minister stressed the need for the new tourism arrangements in the Mid-West to mirror the new vision for regional tourism structures set out in the PricewaterhouseCoopers and Travers report commissioned by Fáilte Ireland, which is currently being put in place, with the support of an Implementation Group chaired by Finbarr Flood. The Implementation Group has already commenced its work and will consult with Shannon Development in the process of drawing up its implementation plan. This consultation phase will provide Shannon Development with a platform to influence the development of future strategy for the regions and to set out the nature of the linkages that might exist between itself and Fáilte Ireland.

Shannon Development outlined their future plans for the support and development of tourism in the Mid-West region, stressing the role of the sector in driving the overall economic development of the region through domestic and international tourism marketing, product development and innovation and enhancing the less-developed areas in the region. The company's role in supporting the evolution of the region in light of the impact of a possible EU/US Open Skies arrangement was also set out.

'I am very impressed with Shannon Development's achievements and history in tourism innovation and development in the Mid-West. Following a process of consultation with local political representatives, I was happy, given present circumstances, to confirm a strong regional tourism remit for the company in the future. This, I believe, will be consistent with the new policy development and institutional structural arrangements arising from the *New Horizons* tourism development strategy,' the Minister concluded.

Source: Department of Arts, Sport and Tourism press release, 10 November 2005.

Minister for Tourism's reply to James Deenihan, TD's question in Dáil Éireann on 1 March 2006 regarding a review of the RTAs

As I previously advised the House in response to similar questions on 26 January 2006, individual actions and measures relating to tourism promotion or development at regional level are day-to-day functions of the state tourism agencies. To this end, Fáilte Ireland commissioned PricewaterhouseCoopers just over a year ago to conduct a major study of regional tourism structures. The report was published last year and is available on the Fáilte Ireland website. This work was supplemented by a short engagement facilitated by a small independent group, chaired by Mr John Travers, with the relevant parties to satisfy interests in the Dublin region that the mechanisms of consultation were complete.

The PWC report highlights the need for a much wider brief for regional tourism, with more emphasis on its strategic rather than administrative role and contributing more directly to national policy. It recommends a greatly increased emphasis on targeted marketing, product development and enterprise support. It suggests establishing an integrated linkage between regional tourism strategy and national policy and exploiting avenues to leverage increased resources.

At the end of July last, I authorised Fáilte Ireland to proceed with the proposed revision of regional tourism structures on the basis of the PWC and Travers reports. To assist this process, Fáilte Ireland set up an Implementation Group under the chairmanship of Mr Finbarr Flood. The group has completed an extensive process of engagement with relevant parties, including the existing regional tourism authorities and industry representative groups, to smooth the process of implementation, and I understand that it will report shortly to Fáilte Ireland.

In tandem with this, Fáilte Ireland has begun the process of gearing up its internal structures. A new senior management position of director of regional development has been created and applications to fill the post have been invited in the national press. A due diligence process will commence shortly with each of the regional tourism authorities. Fáilte Ireland expects that the impact of these changes will be experienced in the regions by the middle of the year.

This year Fáilte Ireland will invest more than €60 million in supporting regional tourism, from local festivals to building capability and strengthening the tourism product. The authority will channel in the region of €10 million of this sum directly into the regional tourism companies to strengthen and enhance their operational and marketing capabilities this year. This investment is designed to ensure both high-quality visitor servicing at key tourist information offices and also a strong overseas promotional effort.

Both Tourism Ireland and Fáilte Ireland will continue to roll out a number of very innovative schemes in 2006 which should heighten the regional impact of Ireland's marketing activities both nationally and overseas. [Additional information not given on the floor of the House.] The super-regions initiative launched last month is one of these.

The agencies will also maintain an opportunities fund of €1 million to allow them to respond to regional opportunities which may arise during the course of the year and are not anticipated in current programmes. Fáilte Ireland has also announced a new €1 million local area marketing fund to support the industry in generating additional business in 2006 and 2007. In addition, it has an innovation fund of about €1 million, the immediate priority of which is to encourage innovation and investment across a range of new products with a strong emphasis on products designed to attract and hold visitors outside the mature urban tourism areas.

Recognising the importance of home holidays at regional level, Fáilte Ireland will invest €4 million to sustain the recent remarkable growth in the home market. It also plans to advertise domestic holidays and short breaks forty-four weeks a year to reach and stimulate the impulse market. Fáilte Ireland's website, www.ireland.ie, generated 500,000 direct sales leads to the tourism industry during 2005. On the basis that activities and attractions – things to do and see – are central to increasing spend per visitor, Fáilte Ireland will continue to assist in product development, including developing and promoting looped walks, angling, festivals, cycling routes, equestrian, golfing and water-based activities.

Tourism Ireland, for its part, will invest an estimated €5 million in 2006 specifically to support promotion of the regions of Ireland overseas and will engage in additional co-operative marketing with all regions. Key activities include presenting and promoting a series of all-island tourist theme trails or 'rainbow routes' to help tourists get the most out of their visit. Themes will include music, gourmet, literature, history, Christian heritage and houses and gardens. It will be cross-regional, thus further promoting and supporting regional access development as well as reinvigorating the car touring sector.

THE OFFICE OF PUBLIC WORKS (OPW)

The Office of Public Works (OPW, see www.opw.ie) was established in August 1831 from the merger of three existing organisations (dating back to the 1670s) which had responsibility for all public buildings and works (civil and military). Today, it is one of the oldest organisations in the state, with headquarters on St Stephen's Green. Its early remit included contracts for many government 'civil works, including roads, bridges, canals, the early railways, piers and harbours and river and field drainage' (OPW 2006). In the twentieth century, the OPW even designed and constructed the first runways and airports at Dublin and Shannon.

Many of the light railways, which flourished at the beginning of the 20th century, were provided by or under the aegis of the OPW. The OPW ran steamer and coach services on the Shannon between Killaloe and Rooskey during the tourist season in the late 19th century. It appears that the attractions of the Shannon region were being realised long before the potential for tourism as a national industry was considered.

The OPW is headed by a minister of state from the Department of Finance (Tom Parlon, TD between 2002 and 2007).

Today, the OPW has the following main responsibilities relevant to tourism, in conjunction with the Department of the Environment, Heritage and Local Government (see www.heritageireland.ie):

- National monuments/historical properties.
- Parks and gardens.

Ireland's National Parks and Wildlife Service (www.npws.ie, also a part of the Department of the Environment, Heritage and Local Government) now looks after these types of attractions since the abolition of Dúchas – The Heritage Service in March 2003.

Examples of Nineteenth- and Early Twentieth-Century Work of the OPW

1880s:
- National Museum, Dublin.
- National Library Dublin.
- Custom House, Belfast.

1900s:
- University Buildings at Earlsfort Terrace, Dublin.
- Department of Agriculture, Merrion Square, Dublin.

1960s:
- Refurbishment of Kilkenny Castle.
- Development of Killarney National Park.

1980s and 1990s:
- Reconstruction of Dublin Castle.
- Restoration of the Royal Hospital (Dublin).
- Restoration of the Custom House (Dublin).
- Development of Government Buildings, Merrion Street (Dublin).

The OPW's current role is highlighted in the following extract from their functions on the website www.opw.ie:

> The OPW was established to carry out a wide variety of public works, such as the construction of public buildings, roads, bridges and harbours. These projects not only increased economic development during the nineteenth and early twentieth centuries, but also provided much needed employment. The present day OPW has retained many of its original functions and has acquired new roles. It is responsible for the restoration and preservation of many prestigious state buildings, the acquisition and fitting out of office accommodation for Government Departments, the construction and maintenance of Garda stations and prisons and the arterial drainage and flood relief programme.

The OPW and Irish Art

The OPW has the responsibility of managing the 6,000 works of art (by more than 1,250 artists) which comprise the state art collection. These are located in state buildings throughout Ireland. The OPW sets aside 1 per cent of most construction budgets for artistic features in the completed construction.

Since 1990, the OPW also maintains the government art asset register on behalf of the Department of Finance and promotes state art to the public. The OPW has the final say on granting loans of state-owned art to foreign museums, as well as accepting loans from foreign museums. A three-volume catalogue entitled *Art in State Buildings* has been published by the OPW, illustrating all artwork acquired by the OPW for state buildings between 1922 and 1995.

'Currents' – Art of the State 2004 Exhibition

'Currents' is an exhibition of some of the art works acquired by the Department of Finance and Personnel and the Office of Public Works (OPW) in the new millennium. The works included in this exhibition have been purchased for public buildings located throughout Ireland, north and south. It is the seventh such joint exhibition organised by the two departments, and builds upon the experience gained in the prior six OPW touring Art of the State series.

The title of the exhibition refers to the type of works 'currently' being purchased by both departments and also to the 'current' practices of the included artists who work mainly in two-dimensional media. It features art works that have been purchased since 2000 covering a wide range of styles and media, including landscape, figurative and abstract paintings, graphics and contemporary photography. A fully illustrated catalogue accompanies the exhibition.

Source: www.opw.ie.

AIRPORT AUTHORITIES (FORMERLY AER RIANTA)

Until recently, the three large state airports – Dublin, Shannon and Cork – were part of an umbrella company called Aer Rianta, whose responsibilities included managing the airports as well as the development of Irish aviation. Its business also included duty free sales (though not on intra-EU travel since 1 January 1999). In fact, Shannon Airport was the world's first duty free airport, selling liquor to passengers at prices excluding tax and duty since 1951 (and later tobacco).

Aer Rianta was abolished in 2003 in favour of the competing Dublin Airport Authority (DAA, see www.dublinairport.com), Shannon Airport Authority (SAA, see www.shannonairport.com) and Cork Airport Authority (CAA, see www.corkairport.com). Shannon Airport has since rebranded itself as a low-cost, low-fares airport and has encouraged low-cost carriers to establish routes to and from Shannon.

Dublin Airport is Ireland's busiest airport – and the fourteenth busiest in Europe (by passenger numbers) – with more than 66,000 passengers per day travelling on eighty airlines serving more than 150 international destinations (as of 2006). The estimated passenger numbers for 2006 are more than 20 million. There are 186,000 airline movements per year (take-offs and landings), of which 86 per cent are by scheduled airlines, and only 14 per cent are charter flights, parking at the airport's seventy-three aircraft stands. The airport boasts 18,000 long-term and 4,000 short-term parking spaces. Dublin Airport has three runways and one terminal (142 check-in desks), although the second terminal is set to be open by 2009.

The Capital Development Programme at Dublin Airport is one of the largest infrastructural programmes in the state and the €1.2 billion construction programme will transform Dublin Airport over the next ten years beginning in 2006.

Passenger numbers are expected to reach 20 million in 2006 and the recent upward trend in demand at Dublin Airport is projected to continue into the future, necessitating the development of new facilities to meet this growth. The development programme includes the construction of a new passenger terminal, Terminal 2, two new piers, D and E, and an extension to the existing Pier A.

Other developments include a new ground floor check-in area (Area 14) in Terminal 1 (in addition to several other significant improvements to the terminal). The programme will also involve apron and apron-related development, new rapid exit taxiways and aircraft stands. A new road infrastructure and new car parks will also be constructed.

The Dublin Airport Authority's project team is being led by Mark Foley, the DAA's Director of Capital Programmes. The strategic management of the capital development programme is being managed by Turner & Townsend, an internationally recognised firm of project managers.

The UK-based construction company Laing O'Rourke will be responsible for the building of Pier D while the highly experienced international consultants, Ove Arup, in conjunction with architects Pascall & Watson, will be responsible for the design of Terminal 2. The development programme will roll out to a carefully scheduled timeline in order to minimise any inconvenience to the day-to-day operations of Dublin Airport.

Source: Dublin Airport Authority.

The top ten international destinations from Dublin Airport (2006) are as follows:
1. London
2. Paris
3. Manchester
4. New York
5. Birmingham
6. Amsterdam
7. Frankfurt
8. Glasgow
9. Malaga
10. Edinburgh

Since the split, two companies remain from the former Aer Rianta umbrella: Aer Rianta International and Great Southern Hotels.

Aer Rianta International (www.ari.ie) manages or co-operates several airports in Europe, North America and the Middle East. Aer Rianta International was formed in 1988 as an international division of the former Irish airport operator bearing the same name. It won the tender to establish the first international duty free in the former Soviet Union. Bahrain Duty Free (operated by Aer Rianta International) won the Frontier Award for 'Airport/Land-Based Retailer of the Year' in 2005, as well as the 'Best Marketing Retailer of the Year' in 2004. The operator also won the 'Best New Shop Opening' in the Raven Fox Awards 2005 for its Kievrianta operation at Kiev (Kyiv) Airport in the Ukraine.

Table 2.2: Airports Operated by Aer Rianta International (2006)

Europe	Moscow (Sheremetyevo Airport)	Russian Federation
	St Petersburg (Pulokova Airport)	Russian Federation
	Kyiv (Kiev)	Ukraine
	Hamburg	Germany
	Düsseldorf	Germany
	Birmingham	UK
North America	New York	US
	Montreal	Canada
	Winnipeg	Canada
	Edmonton	Canada
	Ottawa	Canada
	Halifax	Canada
Middle East	Bahrain	Kingdom of Bahrain
	Kuwait	Kuwait
	Damascus	Syrian Arab Republic
	Beirut	Republic of Lebanon
	Muscat	Sultanate of Oman

Source: Aer Rianta International.

Until 2006, Great Southern Hotels (www.greatsouthernhotels.com) was a wholly owned subsidiary of the DAA and operates nine hotels – some dating back to 1845 – in Galway, Corrib, Killarney, Rosslare, Parknasilla, Derry, Shannon Airport, Dublin Airport and Cork Airport. The group employed 700 people. The hotels were sold in 2006.

John O'Donoghue, TD, Minister for Arts, Sport and Tourism, today [11 July 2003] welcomed the government decision to establish Shannon, Cork and Dublin airports as fully independent and autonomous authorities under state ownership. He believes that this initiative will help to deliver a new competitive dynamic into the aviation sector and has the potential to expand air services to the benefit of Irish tourism.

'The government decision provides the opportunity for new independent airports at Cork and Shannon to pursue business opportunities which will help to achieve greater numbers and broader regional balance in the distribution of international visitors,' Minister O'Donoghue said.

'The low-cost airline model is now growing at a fast pace within Europe and is on course to become increasingly significant. With as yet untapped potential in several European markets, the share of low-cost airlines within

Europe on short- to medium-haul "point-to-point" routes is forecast to reach at least 25 per cent in the coming years, from its current base of 14 per cent. The challenge for Ireland will be to position itself to secure a significant share of this growth. That is why I fully support the enhancement of competition in the delivery of airport infrastructure through additional fast turnaround facilities at Dublin Airport and greater autonomy for Cork and Shannon.'

The recently published interim report of the Tourism Policy Review Group highlighted the World Tourism Organization projections that, despite recent difficulties, world tourism arrivals will more than double over the next twenty years. The recent government decision, in conjunction with other proposed aviation initiatives being pursued by the Minister for Transport...will position all three airports to capture an increased share of this growing market for Ireland.

Source: Department of Arts, Sport and Tourism press release, 11 July 2003.

Shannon Airport is unique both in its location and its place in the history of world aviation. Of all European airports it is situated at the most western point, making it the ideal stepping stone between the old world and the new. Chosen for its geographical position as the transatlantic gateway between Europe and America, Shannon was designated as Ireland's Transatlantic Airport at its inception by the Irish government.

Shannon Airport Authority is the company which manages the airport on behalf of the Minister for Transport. From the airport has grown a vast infrastructure of enormous importance to Ireland's Mid-West region, which includes an attractive and growing tourism enterprise as well as the world's first duty free industrial zone.

The airport itself covers about 2,000 acres in County Clare on the north bank of the Shannon Estuary and is located approximately 24 kilometres (15 miles) west of Limerick City and a similar distance south of Ennis.

Shannon Airport meets all the requirements of a first-class international airport and much more. Runway (06–24) is capable of taking the largest type of aircraft now in operation. This facility is used by scheduled and non-scheduled carriers. Together with Shannon's temperate and varied weather conditions, it makes the airport an ideal location for flight training.

There are almost 2,000 people employed at the airport (not counting the nearby industrial estate), of which the airport itself employs about 500. The remainder are employed by a number of state services including air traffic control, state radio, the meteorological service, immigration, customs, agriculture, public health and telecoms as well as commercial services such as airlines, aircraft handling agencies, car hire, tourism interests, taxi hire and fuel companies. In addition, some 1,000 temporary staff are recruited during the peak summer season.

Annually, Shannon handles a passenger throughput of approximately 3 million people and nearly 50,000 metric tons of freight is transported through its cargo area.

Well over half a million passengers who travel through Shannon do so as transit passengers, breaking their journey at Shannon while travelling between Europe and North America.

The airport is used by around 20,000 scheduled commercial aircraft and nearly 8,500 non-scheduled commercial aircraft. In all, there are around 26,000 aircraft movements at Shannon every year.

Source: Shannon Airport Authority.

Innovations at Shannon Airport

In 1978, Aer Rianta approached Aeroflot Moscow with a proposal to store Soviet aviation fuel at Shannon for use on the Soviet airline's transatlantic services. On 6 July 1979, a formal agreement was signed in Moscow between Aer Rianta and the USSR's Ministry of Civil Aviation. By June 1980, Aer Rianta had constructed a dedicated fuel farm at Shannon for the storage of Soviet-origin fuel.

The first Aeroflot flight to uplift this fuel landed at Shannon on 3 July 1980. From a total Aeroflot landings of 240 in 1980, the airline in 1991 operated 2,000 aircraft through Shannon using their own fuel stocks. Aeroflot operated flights from Moscow, St Petersburg, Kiev and Minsk to various cities in the USA as well as Central and South America. The airline had traffic rights from Shannon to all their Central and South American destinations as well as Miami, Chicago, Washington, DC and Gander, Newfoundland.

In 1983 a unique barter fuel agreement was negotiated between Aer Rianta and the USSR's Ministry of Civil Aviation. This enabled Aer Rianta to sell Soviet aviation fuel to other airlines, which in turn offset Aeroflot's hard currency operating costs at Shannon.

Later, in 1987, Aer Rianta would also become involved in the repainting and refurbishment of Aeroflot aircraft at Shannon when a dedicated painting hangar and refurbishing facility was constructed at Shannon and officially opened in August 1988.

With a view to the promotion of technical transit traffic at Shannon, Aer Rianta approached the US federal authorities in the late 1970s to establish United States pre-clearance for passengers at Shannon. It was intended to follow on the lines of such facilities at Canadian airports. Following various negotiations which culminated in an inter-governmental agreement between Ireland and the United States, the US Immigration Pre-Inspection facility was set up on a trial basis in 1986. This proved successful, and a permanent facility was constructed and opened in 1989. It has proven very popular with both terminal and transit passengers. It is the first of its kind in Europe and represents another innovation at Shannon Airport.

Having achieved so much at Shannon, the airport team set their sights higher and sought to use the hard-earned reputation to create commercial opportunities abroad.

The company achieved great success with commercial ventures in the Middle East and in former Soviet states. Duty free shops modelled on Shannon have been established at Sheremetyevo Airport in Moscow, Pulokova Airport in St Petersburg and Kiev Airport. Further shopping facilities were subsequently established in downtown locations in these cities. This was to lead directly to the founding of a subsidiary company, Aer Rianta International (ARI), based at Shannon Airport.

Source: Shannon Airport, part of the Dublin Airport Authority plc

THE IRISH TOURIST INDUSTRY CONFEDERATION (ITIC)

The Irish Tourist Industry Confederation (ITIC, www.itic.ie) represents all major commercial tourism interests. The organisation acts as a voice for the industry and is essentially a lobbying group. It encourages the development of legislation and deals with the Irish government in areas of tourism policy and performance as well as funding and investment, particularly in the areas of marketing and product development. It does this through research, making cases on specific relevant issues and endeavouring to influence policies.

The ITIC works with several government agencies, including tourist boards, in both jurisdictions on the island of Ireland as well as at EU level. It also makes submissions to government on issues such as VAT rates, corporation tax, long-term finance, etc. The aim of the ITIC is to provide a single voice for the tourism industry to government, Fáilte Ireland and to the public. It also provides information for the industry as well as to the media and its members.

The council of the ITIC is made up of a cross-section of representatives from all areas of the tourism industry, including representatives from local and regional authorities, transport providers, ports, restaurants and public houses.

PRIVATE ORGANISATIONS

The majority of the agencies and organisations discussed in this chapter are public organisations, with the last one being a notable exception. However, there are several small and large private organisations that work independently of the government, as well as co-operating with state agencies at times. Some of them are mentioned below.

Irish Hotels Federation (IHF)

The IHF is a privately run organisation representing its members to the government and the public. It provides research and reports on various aspects of tourism and hospitality.

The organisation's corporate website (www.ihf.ie) provides comprehensive information on its work. The reports section (www.ihf.ie/reports/) lists several reports which may prove useful to industry members, researchers and students.

The IHF also publishes the *InnSight Magazine*, which is available via their website, or directly at www.ihf.ie/news/innsight/. Online archives go back as far as 1998 and provide a comprehensive reference and study resource.

The IHF composes a pre-budget submission and presents to the Minister for Finance (as well as Irish media) calling for various support measures, including a reduction in the VAT rate applied to hotels. These are also available in the online reports section.

The IHF recently launched a commercial tourist website, www.irelandhotels.ie, to provide information and a booking engine for tourists wishing to make reservations at member hotels.

Town & Country Homes

The Town & Country Homes Association (www.townandcountry.ie) is the largest representative body for the B&B sector on the island of Ireland, as it represents 1,500 homes that offer accommodation to tourists in what is becoming a very difficult market, partly due to lower-cost hotel accommodation. Its website provides a booking facility for all members, as well as links to almost half of their members who have their own websites.

Irish Farmhouse Holidays

Irish Farmhouse Holidays (www.irishfarmholidays.com) was formed in the 1970s to promote and market member farmhouses offering accommodation. Members must be registered and approved establishments of Fáilte Ireland. This organisation represent an alternative form of accommodation in Ireland, serving the desires of visitors who want to stay on real Irish farms, some located beside towns and villages and others in the most rural of landscapes. Home cooking is a focus of the guest experience in such an establishment.

Houses, Castles and Gardens of Ireland

The Houses, Castles and Gardens of Ireland organisation (www.castlesireland.com) is a group representing 'some of Ireland's finest architectural gems and horticultural delights', according to the organisation. It is a co-operative marketing organisation, whose publications and website feature information on twenty-four houses and castles dotted around Ireland, as well as thirty-five gardens of great beauty.

Restaurant Association of Ireland (RAI)

Formed in 1970 to lobby government on behalf of the industry, the RAI (www.rai.ie) has more than 600 members throughout Ireland, representing all forms of dining, including fine cuisine, pub grub, hotel restaurants, cafés, ethnic and family restaurants. The organisation also provides practical industry support, including a recruitment and human resources service.

An Taisce

An Taisce (translates as 'the store house' or 'treasury' in English; www.antaisce.org) is 'The National Trust for Ireland'. It is an independent, voluntary body established in 1948 whose task is to assist in the conservation of Irish heritage and has expertise in Ireland's natural, built and social heritage. The roles of the organisation are as follows:

- Publishing and promoting coherent environmental policies and reports to guide and encourage public dialogue and key decision makers.
- Co-ordinating education programmes (including Blue Flag and National Spring Clean) as well as lecture series, conferences and seminars.
- Monitoring planning applications and taking action when necessary.
- Providing local and national planning advice.
- Holding and managing sixteen heritage properties on behalf of the state.
- Collaborating with public and private organisations with similar goals.

An Taisce provides representation on several state panels and boards and is the only non-governmental organisation to be classed as a Prescribed Body, meaning that local authorities are obliged by law to consult them on various development proposals. An Taisce's headquarters are in Tailor's Hall, Dublin.

TOURISM STRATEGY: REPORTS, REVIEW GROUPS AND IMPLEMENTATION

According to Wright and Linehan (2004):

> The destination marketing of Ireland has experienced many changes in its operational structures in the past and has evolved within these structures to develop completely new platforms on which to base its future path. The complexities of marketing Ireland abroad are multifaceted and always challenging. This is mainly due to adverse and unforeseen circumstances that are continually presenting themselves to those charged with the responsibility of advancing Ireland's tourist industry.

Those charged with this marketing as well as developmental responsibility have a very important role to perform. Ireland's tourist industry has grown phenomenally over the last 100 years, but particularly since the beginning of the 1990s. This coincides with the era of Ireland's economic miracle, with phenomenal growth also recorded in the nation's wealth. Such growth leads to higher levels of disposable income, much of which is spent on luxury goods and services. Tourism is a large recipient of such disposable income.

This economic growth in Ireland has a positive and negative impact on tourism. The positive impacts include more money in one form or another for tourism (discussed in the next chapter), including higher tourist tax revenue, higher employment in tourism, more investment and positive contributions to the balance of payments. However, the negative side of Ireland's economic boom is that many Irish people choose to spend their disposable income on foreign holidays rather than domestic ones. Many Irish cite the high cost of taking a break in Ireland as a reason for forsaking Ireland in favour of a foreign holiday, as inflation (due to the economic boom) prices Ireland out of the domestic market. Indeed, it is perhaps more likely that foreign economic growth has been feeding Irish tourism growth in recent years.

Tourism organisations in Ireland cannot become complacent. New threats and substitutes to traditional products are continuing to emerge. This chapter takes us from where Irish tourism had its beginnings to the modern-day structure of Irish tourism, north and south. All of the organisations discussed, both public and private, must continue to co-operatively develop and market the island of Ireland and face the competitive challenges of newly emerging destinations, as well as international events that shape global travel patterns and spending.

In an effort to push forward Ireland's future tourism strategies, the Irish government has put continual strategic review and Implementation Groups in place. The Department of Arts, Sport and Tourism has taken on board the recommendations of these groups (amongst other reports) and has made it clear to the industry that there is government commitment to the recommendations of the reports. The following press releases and articles highlight the major announcements in recent years in regard to these reports.

Shortly after taking office as Minister for Arts, Sport and Tourism in 2002, John O'Donoghue established a **Tourism Strategy Review Group** for the sector, which produced a comprehensive tourism review entitled *New Horizons for Irish Tourism: An Agenda for Action* in September 2003 (the full text of the report is available on the Department website at www.arts-sport-tourism.gov.ie and directly on www.tourismreview.ie). As many previously produced similar reports on tourism were criticised in many quarters as being a report without action and the finance to ensure action, the Minister promised that government financial commitment would be forthcoming to meet the report's recommendations. Shortly after the publication of the report, the Minister put a **Tourism Action Plan Implementation Group** in place to put the recommendations of the *New Horizons* report into practice. It published three implementation reports in its lifetime (January 2004 to March 2006) which were well received by the Minister. Finally, in May 2006, the Minister announced the creation of a **Tourism Strategy Implementation Group** to advise him on the implementation of the remaining recommendations of the *New Horizons* report. All three groups were chaired by John Travers, the former chief executive of Forfás.

O'Donoghue welcomes *New Horizons for Irish Tourism: An Agenda for Action*, the report of the Tourism Policy Review Group
'**Double overseas visitor spending by 2012**' – Key Target set by Review Group
The Minister for Arts, Sport and Tourism, John O'Donoghue, TD, was today [30 September 2003] presented with the final report of the Tourism Policy Review Group entitled *New Horizons for Irish Tourism: An Agenda for Action*, by the chairman of the group, John Travers.

The report is a comprehensive assessment of the economic importance of the tourism industry, detailing the significant growth experienced in the sector throughout the 1990s and the challenges facing it today. It sets clear targets for growth over the next ten years, including a doubling of revenue from overseas visitors to €6 billion annually and a commensurate increase in visitor numbers from 6 million to 10 million. The report presents a clear strategy, with specific recommendations to help achieve these targets. After receiving the report, the Minister announced the establishment of a high-level Implementation Group to drive forward and monitor the plan.

Commenting on the report, Minister O'Donoghue said: 'The report is the most important and authoritative document on tourism policy and performance in over a decade. It includes an overview of tourism worldwide, an assessment of the economic contribution of the tourism sector to the Irish economy, an analysis of recent tourism performance, a detailed assessment of tourism in Ireland today and an outline of the challenges and opportunities facing the industry. But, more importantly, it proposes a coherent and integrated strategy for Irish tourism for the next ten years and a series of recommended actions to implement the strategy.

'When I took over responsibility for the tourism portfolio some fifteen months ago, I was conscious that the industry was at a turning point after a prolonged period of significant growth. I recognised that the tourism business was undergoing fundamental changes internationally and that changes in the domestic economy were also bringing about a new series of challenges that threatened to undermine the future of the industry here. It was time to take stock and chart a new direction for the sector.

'The agenda for action, which is included in the report, is a very ambitious and challenging one, involving over seventy individual recommended actions. These are directed not only to my own department, the tourism state agencies and other departments, but perhaps more importantly, to representatives of the tourism industry and individual tourism enterprises.

'Tourism occupies a unique and pivotal place in Irish society. It has grown in the past fifteen years from being a small underperforming sector to being one of the strongest revenue generators in our economy. It is our most successful sector of Irish-owned enterprise. Our promotional agencies have helped to place Ireland on the map internationally and the commitment from industry itself has meant the promise that comes with the Irish experience has always been met with flair. The challenge for the next ten years is to build on these foundations and deliver real measurable growth which will aid the industry but also the country as a whole.

'The report highlights the number of different stakeholders that influence tourism development and the need for co-ordinated and integrated action to influence the wider agenda that impacts on Irish tourism. I know that the report has been eagerly awaited by all interested parties and I am confident that it will be very carefully considered,' the Minister said.

'I agree with the Review Group's conclusion that the "ultimate determinant of success in Irish tourism will be an energetic, innovative and profitable private sector operating within a domestic environment where government policies and actions are supportive of business investment in tourism". One of the key messages in the report is that restoring competitiveness – which is not just a pricing issue – is a major challenge for Irish tourism and that primary responsibility for restoring it rests with the industry itself. Setting a target to double overseas visitor spend, to €6 billion by 2012, is a challenging one but, as suggested in the report, the full potential of the tourism industry can be realised through shared understanding and partnership between key decision-makers in both the public and private sectors.

'I welcome the significant contribution to the development of policy represented by the report of the Review Group and I will ensure that the recommended actions will be pursued, not only within my own department and the state agencies under my remit, but also with industry representative bodies and my ministerial colleagues as appropriate. In order to ensure that the implementation of the action plan is given the priority recommended by the Review Group, I will be establishing a high-level Implementation Group to drive forward and monitor the plan.'

The Minister expressed his gratitude to the chairman, John Travers, and the other members of the Review Group for agreeing to undertake the work. He welcomed the wide consultation process engaged in by the group and said that the body of oral and written submissions was a testament to the widespread interest in the exercise. The membership of the group was unique, including not only public and private representatives of the tourism industry but also independent businesspeople and other experts who brought a broader, more critical and independent assessment of the sector.

Minister O'Donoghue concluded: 'I believe that the report of the Review Group will do much to heighten awareness of the importance of the tourism sector to economic development and wealth creation in Ireland. There is little doubt that the sector has been undervalued in the past. It is clear from the analysis that the future prospects for the sector are good and that there are major opportunities for future growth provided that the quality and competitiveness of the Irish tourism experience can be restored.'

Source: Department of Arts, Sport and Tourism press release, 30 September 2003.

O'Donoghue announces membership of the Tourism Action Plan 2003–2005 Implementation Group

Group working to targets set by Tourism Policy Review Report Implementation Group to report to Minister every six months

John O'Donoghue, TD, Minister for Arts, Sport and Tourism, today [14 January 2004] announced the membership of a high-level group to oversee the implementation of the initial two-year Action Plan for Irish Tourism, recommended by the Tourism Policy Review Group in its recent report, *New Horizons for Irish Tourism: An Agenda for Action*.

Mr John Travers, who chaired the Tourism Policy Review Group, will chair the Implementation Group. Mr Travers, former chief executive of Forfás, also chaired the interim board of the National Tourism Development Authority, which brought together the two tourism agencies, Bord Fáilte and CERT, and led to the setting up of Fáilte Ireland.

The full membership of the Implementation Group is as follows:

John Travers (Chairman). Philip Furlong, Secretary General, Department of Arts, Sport and Tourism. Jim Murphy, President, Irish Hotels Federation. Michael O'Donoghue, Managing Director, O'Donoghue/Ring Hotels. Eileen O'Mara Walsh, O'Mara Travel and former Chairperson of the Irish Tourist Industry Confederation. Raymond Rooney, businessman. Paul Tansey, economist.

The Minister has appointed this group for a two-year period to advise him on the implementation of the first two-year rolling action plan set out in the Tourism Policy Review. It will work with the tourism industry, state agencies including Fáilte Ireland and Tourism Ireland, and various government departments to act upon the strategic recommendations set out in the report.

'The initial action plan is a very ambitious and challenging one – involving over seventy individual recommendations. These are addressed not only to my own department, the tourism state agencies and other departments, but also to representatives of the tourism industry and individual tourism enterprises. Work is already underway on a number of the key issues but it will fall to the group to ensure that the plan is implemented in an integrated manner and that a partnership approach is adopted by the many actors whose co-ordinated efforts are required if the full potential of the industry is to be realised,' said Minister O'Donoghue.

The Implementation Group will be supported by a secretariat drawn from the Department of Arts, Sport and Tourism, the tourism state agencies and industry representative organisations, where appropriate. It will report directly to Minister O'Donoghue and will provide six-monthly reports on its work, results and deliberations.

Commenting on the membership of the Implementation Group, Minister O'Donoghue said, 'I am very pleased the report of the Tourism Policy Review Group has been received so positively by all those who wish to see sustained growth in the tourism industry. I am delighted that such an eminent group of people, under the energetic chairmanship of John Travers, have agreed to help drive forward the initial action plan and I am confident that they will play a key role in ensuring that the new tourism strategy is successfully rolled out in the years ahead.'

The report of the Tourism Policy Review Group was presented to the Minister on 30 September 2003. Hailed as the most important and authoritative document on tourism policy and performance in over a decade, it has presented a blueprint for the growth and development of the tourism industry over the next ten years. Among the targets it has set are the doubling of overseas visitor spend to €6 billion and a corresponding increase in the number of annual overseas visitors from 6 million to 10 million.

The report found that the economic importance of tourism is often underestimated and calls for greater recognition of the central role that the tourism industry plays as a major instrument of national and regional

development. It outlines the major success of the industry and suggests tourism may be the most successful sector of Irish-owned enterprise since the foundation of the state. It highlights that tourism:
* Employment has increased at a faster rate than the economy generally.
* Employs more people than either Irish-owned or foreign-owned manufacturing industry.
* Is by far the largest Irish-owned internationally traded services sector.
* Is a major source of foreign earnings with low import content.

Among its seventy key recommendations are specific actions, which impact on competitiveness and value for money, access transport, nurturing of the tourism business environment, product development and innovation, marketing and promotion.

Source: Department of Arts, Sport and Tourism press release, 14 January 2004.

OECD Tourism Committee endorses Irish tourism strategy

The Organisation for Economic Co-operation and Development (OECD), the world's leading public policy forum, has reviewed Ireland's tourism policy, performance, strategy, programmes and actions at the 75th annual meeting of its Tourism Committee, which was recently held in Paris.

In general, the OECD had a positive view of Irish tourism policy. It concluded that the Action Plan for Irish Tourism 2003–2005, which was included in a major report on Irish tourism policy presented to Minister for Arts, Sport and Tourism, John O'Donoghue, TD, last September, was well designed with a long-term vision and strategy.

Minister O'Donoghue welcomed the endorsement of Ireland's tourism development strategy by the OECD Tourism Committee. 'Tourism is an important economic activity for most OECD countries and a key area of public policy making. The OECD Tourism Committee is a useful forum for monitoring international tourism development and for exchanging ideas and sharing best practice in promoting sustainable economic growth of tourism,' he said.

The Minister noted that the committee highlighted a number of factors which it considered to have contributed to Ireland's successful tourism performance, including:
* The significant efforts by the Irish government to support further sustainable growth in the tourism industry.
* The streamlining of the state's support services to tourism – seen as providing an additional coherence and focus for successful implementation of the new strategy.
* Ireland's emphasis on the importance of the 'tourism experience' for the customer.
* The significant improvements in the range, quality and competitiveness of sea and air access.

The priorities identified by the OECD Tourism Committee for the future were:

- Recovery of the competitiveness of Irish tourism.
- Development of professional career paths and the improvement of the attractiveness of careers in tourism.
- A new information system on the economic impact of tourism and the tourism market.
- The building of competitive advantage through networks/clusters of enterprises.

Minister O'Donoghue said, 'All of the issues identified by the OECD Tourism Committee feature in the Action Plan for Irish Tourism 2003–2005. I will seek to ensure that the priorities identified by the committee are acted on to best effect.'

Source: Department of Arts, Sport and Tourism press release, 2 August 2004.

Second progress report published on government's new tourism strategy
Ireland on track to meet ambitious tourism targets by 2012
Positive developments including increased air access to Ireland, the opening up of new overseas markets and innovative industry development strategies at home mean Ireland is on track to meet the ambitious targets set for tourism by 2012, according to the second progress report of the high-level Implementation Group established by the Minister for Arts, Sport and Tourism, John O'Donoghue, TD. However, it has also identified a number of significant barriers to progress which must be removed if these targets are to be realised.

The Minister has received and has arranged for the publication, today, of the second report of the independent group he established in January 2004 to oversee progress on the strategy which was set out in the Report of the Tourism Policy Review Group, *New Horizons for Irish Tourism: An Agenda for Action*, published in September 2003.

The strategy document laid out ambitious development targets for the tourism industry by 2012, including the doubling of overseas revenue earnings to €6 billion, the increase in visitor numbers to 10 million annually and over seventy key action points. The progress report covers the six-month period to the end of March 2005 and indicates that overall the Implementation Group is satisfied that the strategy is being well advanced – both by the industry itself and by government.

'Many of the key actions recommended in *New Horizons* are being progressed – if not in all cases with the speed and urgency envisaged,' according to the group's chairman, John Travers.

The group identifies the areas where good progress has been made. These include increased air access to Ireland in 2005, the opening up of some new markets, the implementation of well-resourced marketing and development programmes by the tourism state agencies in 2005, the launch of new marketing strategies by Tourism Ireland for the British and mainland Europe markets, the preparation of a new human resource strategy by Fáilte Ireland, the establishment of a business tourism forum, the funding of a significant number of new tourism development projects and the launch of a range of programmes and incentives to address business competitiveness among tourism enterprises.

Commenting on the progress report, Minister O'Donoghue welcomed the conclusion of the Implementation Group that Ireland's tourism performance in 2004, with 6.6 million overseas visitors and €4.1 billion in foreign exchange earnings, was broadly consistent with the targets set and that the ambitious target to double revenue earnings over the ten-year period to 2012 continues to be attainable if the tourism action plan is implemented effectively.

The progress report highlights a number of key barriers to tourism development. These include concerns about the competitiveness and value for money of Ireland's tourism product against a background of tight margins and enhanced competition, slow progress in the negotiation on an EU-US 'Open Skies' arrangement that would open up the prospect of new gateways for air services from the US, the need to progress the provision of additional pier and terminal facilities at Dublin Airport, the need to restore growth from the British market, the absence of a National Conference Centre, continuing uncertainty about access to the countryside and significant gaps in Dublin's cultural infrastructure.

The progress report also includes:
- An up-to-date overview of developments since the last progress report, an outline of tourism's contribution to the Irish economy, 2004 performance and 2005 outlook, changing consumer trends and Ireland's best prospects for 2005.
- A commentary on policy and operational areas requiring further progress, including product development and innovation, regional support structures, roads and signposting, e-marketing, taxation of business expenses for international conferences/meetings and quality issues.

'This is a critical time for the tourism industry throughout Ireland. While recently released CSO statistics for 2004 reveal a healthy tourism sector overall, we all share concerns in relation to the performance of some sectors and markets last year. The trend towards shorter holidays and lower expenditure levels is depressing tourism revenue, in particular outside Dublin and other urban areas. The second progress report from the Implementation Group is timely and useful in identifying what needs to be done to build on recent progress and to highlight the continuing barriers that need to be addressed by the industry and the government to help sustain future growth,' Minister O'Donoghue said.

The Implementation Group will continue its activities over the remainder of the period of the initial two-year action plan set out in the report of the Tourism Policy Review Group. It will also continue its valuable consultation and engagement process with the industry, the tourism state agencies and other government departments whose policies impact on tourism, with a view to achieving the *New Horizons* agenda.

Later this year, the group will convene, in partnership with the Minister for Arts, Sport and Tourism, the second Forum of the Tourism Industry. The purpose of the forum will be to take feedback from the industry on the progress reported and on the future priority issues for the industry. The Implementation Group will incorporate this into its third and final report to the Minister for Arts, Sport and Tourism at the end of the year.

The Minister thanked the chairman, John Travers, and the other members of the Implementation Group for their commitment and work to date and for the comprehensive progress report that had been produced.

Source: Department of Arts, Sport and Tourism press release, 5 May 2005.

O'Donoghue publishes progress report on government's tourism strategy
John O'Donoghue, TD, Minister for Arts, Sport and Tourism, has received and has arranged for the publication, today, of the third and final report of the independent group he established in January 2004 to implement the strategy which was set out in the Report of the Tourism Policy Review Group, *New Horizons for Irish Tourism: An Agenda for Action*, published in September 2003.

The report restates the importance of tourism to the Irish economy, providing employment for 150,000 people, generating €4.3 billion in foreign revenue and a further €1 billion in domestic activity in 2005.

The strategy document laid out ambitious development targets for the tourism industry by 2012, including the doubling of overseas revenue earnings to €6 billion, the increase in visitor numbers to 10 million annually and over seventy key action points to underpin the achievement of these ambitious targets. The final progress report covers the period to the end of December 2005 and indicates that overall the Implementation Group is satisfied that the strategy is being well advanced, both by the industry itself and by government.

The group's chairman, Mr John Travers, expressed his satisfaction with the progress made in implementing the strategy, which he described as 'in many ways better than what was anticipated by the Implementation Group when it first met almost two years ago'.

The group highlighted the areas where good progress has been made. These include the decision to select a provisional preferred tenderer for the National Conference Centre, a significant increase in air access from Europe, Britain and North America, the announcement of a proposed bilateral air agreement with the US and the commitment by the industry itself in responding to the changed tourism environment. The government's commitment to tourism is evidenced in Budget 2006, which included the provision of significant new resources for investment in regional airports and the commitment to a major new capital investment programme in cultural infrastructure to encompass the Abbey Theatre, the National Concert Hall, the Gaiety Theatre and the Wexford Theatre Royal. The government has also allocated additional resources to tourism marketing, initiated a multi-annual investment plan, Transport 21, to upgrade internal transportation infrastructure and services and has decided to provide significant funding for the development of the Lansdowne Road stadium project.

The report also points to a number of key barriers to tourism development and areas where progress has been limited. These include:

- The loss of competitiveness by the tourism sector in recent years.
- Countryside access where the closure of areas which enjoyed traditional long-term public access has not been helpful to tourism.
- The divergence in the numbers of overseas visitors to urban and rural areas, with the numbers of these visitors to rural areas falling while those to urban areas are rising.
- The less than satisfactory experiences of visitors at Dublin Airport.
- The disadvantage in attracting conference business because of the differences in application of the Irish VAT regime compared to that of other EU countries.
- The need for constant innovation and product development in the sector.

'The importance of tourism to the Irish economy cannot be understated. The overall growth target in visitor numbers for 2006 is 5 per cent, which would see Ireland attracting over 7 million visitors for the first time. We cannot afford to be complacent about our tourism revenue, however, with competition from ever-increasing new tourism destinations. The falling numbers of visitors to rural areas is also a worrying trend that needs to be tackled. The work of the Implementation Group has proved invaluable in highlighting both the advances and barriers to achieving Ireland's full tourism potential,' Minister O'Donoghue said.

With the presentation of this third and final report, the Implementation Group established by the Minister for Arts, Sport and Tourism in January 2004 has completed the two-year task assigned to it, in line with the recommendations of the Tourism Policy Review Group in the *New Horizons for Irish Tourism* strategy and the agenda for action that accompanied it.

The implementation process has made a significant contribution to the progress that has been made in implementing the new strategy. The Minister proposes to appoint, in the near future, a similar high-level Implementation Group to monitor and to shape, on a partnership basis, the next stages in the evolution and implementation of the *New Horizons* strategy.

The Minister thanked the chairman, John Travers, and the other members of the Implementation Group for their commitment and work and for the comprehensive set of progress reports produced.

The progress report is available on the department's website at www.dast.gov.ie/publications/list_publications.html.

Source: Department of Arts, Sport and Tourism press release, 13 March 2006.

O'Donoghue announces members of new tourism strategy Implementation Group

The Minister for Arts, Sport and Tourism, John O'Donoghue, TD, today [28 May 2006] announced the membership of the Tourism Strategy Implementation Group, a new high-level group to continue the important work of the Tourism Action Plan Implementation Group which completed its two-year term in March. It will be chaired by Mr John Travers, former chief executive of Forfás. Mr Travers also chaired the Tourism Action Plan Implementation Group and the Tourism Strategy Review Group, which produced the well-received blueprint for Irish tourism development – *New Horizons for Irish Tourism: An Agenda for Action*.

The full membership of the Implementation Group is as follows:

* John Travers (Chairman).
* Paul Tansey, Economist.
* Margaret Jeffares, Managing Director, Les Routiers, Ireland.
* Dan Flinter, ex-Chief Executive, Enterprise Ireland.
* Nancy Moran, Moran's Seaside Farmhouse.
* Luke Moriarty, Chairman of the Moriarty Group.
* Philip Furlong, Secretary General, Department of Arts, Sport and Tourism.
* Shaun Quinn, Chief Executive, Fáilte Ireland.
* Paul O'Toole, Chief Executive, Tourism Ireland.

The group will advise the Minister on the implementation of the outstanding recommendations of the *New Horizons* report and will respond to evolving issues as they arise in the course of the development of the tourism industry in a dynamic international context. It will work with the tourism industry and other government departments and agencies to address a number of key areas. These include:

* Competitiveness, productivity and skills.
* Product development and innovation.
* Access and marketing.
* Sustainability and regional spread.
* The strategy implementation process.

The group will also be charged with making recommendations on a mid-term review of the strategy to be carried out in 2008.

Commenting on the establishment of the group, Minister O'Donoghue said, 'I am delighted that John Travers has agreed to chair the Tourism Strategy Implementation Group and that he is being joined by colleagues from within the industry and state sector and from business generally. The tourism industry is vital to the Irish economy, providing direct employment of 150,000 people and generating €4.3 billion in foreign revenue earnings. What is sometimes overlooked is tourism's very effective role in regional development. We cannot afford to be complacent about our tourism prospects, however, with competition from ever-increasing new tourism destinations. I am confident that the new group will play a key role in realising Ireland's full tourism potential by addressing the critical factors and drivers of industry growth.

The group, which will have its first meeting in June, will be supported by a secretariat drawn from the Department of Arts, Sport and Tourism, the tourism state agencies and the Irish Tourist Industry Confederation, as appropriate. It will report directly to the Minister.

The *New Horizons* report was presented to Minister O'Donoghue in September 2003 by the Tourism Policy Review Group. It was hailed as the most important and authoritative document on Irish tourism policy and it presented a blueprint for the growth and development of the tourism industry up to 2012. The Minister appointed the Tourism Action Plan Implementation Group for a two-year period, which ended earlier this year, to commence the implementation of the seventy-six recommendations made in the *New Horizons* report. In its final report, that group reported that by the end of 2005, good progress has been made on sixty-three (82 per cent) of those seventy-six recommendations. The new group has also been appointed for a two-year period and will take up where it left off.

Source: Department of Arts, Sport and Tourism press release, 28 May 2006.

REVISION QUESTIONS

1. List and briefly outline each of the state agencies and government departments that are involved in Irish tourism, north and south.
2. Describe the functions of the Regional Tourism Authorities.
3. List and briefly outline some private organisations that are involved in Irish tourism.
4. Who is the current Minister for Tourism in the Republic of Ireland?
5. Who were the previous Ministers for Tourism in the Republic?
6. What is the name of the current/last Minister in the Northern Ireland Executive responsible for tourism?
7. What is the name of the ministry responsible for tourism in Northern Ireland?
8. What is the full name of the government department responsible for tourism in the Republic?
9. Name any other government departments in the Republic that have an input into tourism.
10. What is the full name of the organisation representing all-Ireland tourism around the world?
11. What was the full name of the brand concept for all-Ireland tourism that existed before this new all-Ireland agency?
12. In what year was Bord Fáilte established?
13. What is the name of the body created in May 2003 to take over the functions of Bord Fáilte?
14. What organisation did Bord Fáilte merge with to form this new body?
15. Name the six Regional Tourism Authorities in the state (not including Shannon Development).

ESSAY QUESTIONS

1. Outline the structure of tourism in Ireland. In your answer, concentrate on both public and private agencies relevant to the tourism sector.
2. The structure of Irish tourism is a function of cross-border political agreements, EU planning and the needs of the industry. Discuss.
3. Discuss the challenges that the Irish tourism industry has faced since the year 2000.
4. The Irish government invests heavily in marketing and developing Irish tourism products. How does Ireland benefit from tourism?
5. Discuss the changes in the Irish tourism industry since the year 2000.
6. How does the Irish government help to rejuvenate the industry after a crisis?
7. Outline the key current affairs issues which have an impact on (a) the Irish and (b) the world tourism industry. Highlight specific examples.
8. 'The Irish government plays a very active role in tourism development, training and promotion.' Discuss this statement.
9. Discuss how the NITB aims to achieve its objectives in the report entitled *A Strategic Framework for Action 2004–2007*.

TASKS

Divide the class into two roughly equal groups. Each group should be given ten to fifteen minutes to develop opposing points on the following statements, followed by a forty to forty-five minute debate.

Statement: The structure of tourism development and marketing on the island of Ireland is bureaucratic and farcical.

Statement: Tourism success in any country and/or region is dependent on government commitment and funding.

Statement: Privately funded tourism organisations are key to the survival of the Irish industry.

ASSIGNMENTS

1. You are contracted as a tourism consultant to *one* of the defined tourism regions on the island of Ireland, as follows:
   (a) Dublin
   (b) Midlands East
   (c) South East
   (d) South West
   (e) West
   (f) North West
   (g) Shannon Development
   (h) Northern Ireland (Note: Not under the jurisdiction of Fáilte Ireland)
   You are required to prepare a broadly based inventory of what your region has to offer from a tourism perspective. Identify deficiencies and suggest appropriate methods to remedy such deficiencies.

2. 'Shannon did have one enormous drawback. For all its efforts to maintain the latest technological achievements, it was technology itself which was the greatest threat. The jet engine, with its capacity to reach well into Europe from the Americas, seemed to threaten obsolescence for Shannon. What was the necessity for an airport with a very small catchment area on the north-western end of the European seaboard, if aircraft could reach the main centre of Europe without technical stopovers?'

   Write a report on how Shannon Airport has adapted to the changing trends in international aviation over the decades. In your report, highlight how the Irish government has influenced the function and role of Shannon Airport.

3. Research and write a report on the tourism policy and strategy reviews conducted between 2002 and 2006. In your report, discuss how the key recommendations are being implemented. Further, you are required to present the key points of your report to an audience, e.g. your class.

Chapter 3

Tourism and the Economy: Global, National and Regional Factors

SUMMARY

Chapter 3 opens with a discussion of world tourism growth since the 1950s. It outlines the importance of tourism to global economies and illustrates the world tourism spending patterns over the previous fifty years. The major tourism-generating regions are also highlighted.

An understanding of the patterns of and reasons for Irish tourism growth is vital for the study of tourism, and Chapter 3 elaborates on these topics in great detail. The result of increasing tourist arrivals and tourism receipts is analysed, with a focus on the Irish example, and is rationalised by financial statistics of revenue earned by the Irish government over the previous years from tourism business and tax revenue. Regional tourism income and the tourism income multiplier are also presented. The rapid growth of Irish tourism from the 1990s and its contribution to various areas of the economy are analysed, including employment in tourism, the balance of payments and tourism investment. The chapter concludes by projecting future tourism growth, illustrating the UN World Tourism Organization's *Tourism 2020 Vision* forecast.

LEARNING OUTCOMES

Having completed this chapter, the reader should be able to:
* Demonstrate an understanding of patterns and reasons for growth in world tourism arrivals and revenue since the 1950s.
* Understand arrivals and revenue growth in an Irish context.
* Contextualise Irish growth patterns since the 1990s.
* Appreciate the importance of tourism to regional economies.
* Understand the contribution made by tourism to employment, investment and international trade.
* Explain the UNWTO's future tourism forecast.

INTRODUCTION: WORLD TOURISM GROWTH

Tourism is one of the world's most important industries and has continued to grow over the last century. Tourist arrivals (the amount of people visiting a destination for leisure or business tourism) have grown at an average annual rate of 6.5 per cent between 1950 and 2004, and there are an estimated 763 million annual international arrivals per annum (as of 2004), up from just 25 million in 1950. Despite setbacks such as worldwide natural disasters, war and terrorism, world tourism constantly resurges to continue its growth. As the world's population grows in number as well as lives longer, tourism will continue to flourish. Further, newly developing countries, some with massive populations (China and India), will inevitably feed international tourism growth in the twenty-first century.

Because of its continuing growth, tourism has become an economic necessity for many destinations. For most destinations, tourism serves to augment national income and provides a positive contribution to the country's balance of payments. For some countries and regions within countries, tourism is the largest industry, providing the majority of revenue and employment for a locality.

Tourism revenue is routinely calculated in the billions of euro. It is no wonder, therefore, that there is fierce competition between countries and regions for a share in the economic benefits tourism can bring. Such competition can range from local government organisations competing for tourism arrivals in any particular country, e.g. North West Tourism competing with Dublin Tourism in Ireland's case, to large countries competing with each other for the location of large-scale attractions (France and Spain competing for the location of the Euro Disney resort).

The United Nations World Tourism Organization (UNWTO or WTO, www.unwto.org) estimates that tourism accounts for approximately 6 per cent of all worldwide exports. However, if we were to consider service exports exclusively, tourism exports account for almost 30 per cent.

Worldwide tourism demand is highly dependent on the economic conditions prevalent in the major tourism-generating markets. Levels of disposable income in these markets rise as their economies grow. In such growing and emerging economies, a large part of disposable income is spent on tourism. On the other hand, at times when growth is slower or non-existent, tourism spend inevitably decreases. According to the UNWTO:

> ... the growth of international tourism arrivals significantly outpaces growth of economic output as measured in gross domestic product (GDP). In years when world economic growth exceeds 4 per cent, the growth of tourism volume tends to be higher. When GDP growth falls below 2 per cent, tourism growth tends to be even lower. In the period 1975–2000 tourism increased at an average rate of 4.6 per cent a year and GDP at 3.5 per cent, i.e. tourism grew on average 1.3 times faster than GDP.

The major growth between 1950 and 2004 has come from newer destinations, with slower growth coming from more mature regions such as the Americas and Europe, with an average annual growth rate of just 5 per cent and 6 per cent, respectively. New destinations such as Asia Pacific have seen an average growth rate of 13 per cent per year, while the Middle East has seen a 10 per cent growth rate. Indeed, Europe's global share of tourism has declined by almost 10 per cent over the same period, while the Americas' share has declined by more than 13 per cent. The Americas' performance is not solely a recent phenomenon from events such as terrorist attacks. The annual average growth rate of the region in the last fifty years of the twentieth century was only 5.8 per cent compared to a global average of 7 per cent.

Table 3.1: International Tourist Arrivals in Millions, 1950–2004

Year	World	Africa	Americas	Asia Pacific	Europe	Middle East
1950	25.3	0.5	7.5	0.2	16.8	0.2
1960	69.3	0.8	16.7	0.9	50.4	0.6
1965	112.9	1.4	23.2	2.1	83.7	2.4
1970	165.8	2.4	42.3	6.2	113.0	1.9
1975	222.3	4.7	50.0	10.2	153.9	3.5
1980	278.2	7.3	62.3	23.6	177.5	7.5
1981	278.6	8.1	62.5	25.4	174.6	8.0
1982	277.1	7.5	59.7	26.6	174.8	8.5
1983	282.1	8.2	59.9	27.1	179.1	7.8
1984	306.9	8.8	67.4	30.1	192.6	8.1
1985	320.2	9.6	65.1	33.6	203.4	8.5
1986	330.5	9.3	70.9	37.6	205.3	7.4
1987	359.8	9.8	76.6	43.1	222.7	7.5
1988	385.5	12.5	83.0	50.1	230.5	9.4
1989	410.2	13.8	86.9	50.8	249.2	9.5
1990	441.0	15.2	92.8	57.7	265.3	10.0
1991	441.0	15.2	92.8	57.7	265.3	10.0
1992	481.4	18.3	102.2	67.8	281.4	11.8
1993	494.7	18.7	102.2	74.5	287.4	11.9
1994	519.5	19.1	105.1	82.2	300.4	12.7
1995	538.1	20.4	109.0	85.0	309.3	14.3
1996	569.6	22.1	114.5	94.0	323.0	16.0
1997	592.5	23.0	116.2	93.0	343.3	17.0
1998	611.6	25.5	119.2	92.4	355.7	18.9
1999	634.1	26.9	121.9	102.3	360.5	22.5
2000	680.6	28.2	128.2	114.9	384.1	25.2
2001	680.4	28.9	122.1	120.7	383.8	25.0
2002	700.4	29.5	116.6	131.1	394.0	29.2
2003	689.7	30.8	113.1	119.3	396.6	30.0
2004	763.2	33.2	125.8	152.5	416.4	35.4

Source: UNWTO, November 2005.

Table 3.2: Average Annual Growth (%), 1950–2004

Year	World	Africa	Americas	Asia Pacific	Europe	Middle East
1950–2000	6.8	8.3	5.8	13.2	6.5	10.2
1950–2003	6.4	8.0	5.3	12.5	6.1	9.9
1950–1960	10.6	3.7	8.4	14.1	11.6	12.3
1960–1970	9.1	12.4	9.7	21.6	8.4	11.5
1970–1980	5.3	11.7	4.0	14.2	4.6	14.9
1980–1990	4.7	7.6	4.1	9.4	4.1	3.0
1980–1985	2.9	5.7	0.9	7.3	2.8	2.5
1985–1990	6.6	9.6	7.3	11.5	5.5	3.5
1990–2000	4.4	6.4	3.3	7.1	3.8	9.7
1990–1995	4.1	6.2	3.3	8.0	3.1	7.3
1995–2000	4.8	6.6	3.3	6.2	4.4	12.0
2000–2004	2.9	4.2	-0.5	7.3	2.0	8.8

Source: UNWTO, November 2005.

Table 3.3: Europe and the Americas' Joint Share of Tourist Arrivals, 1950–2000

1950	95% of global arrivals
1990	82% of global arrivals
2000	76% of global arrivals

Source: UNWTO.

WORLD TOURISM SPENDING PATTERNS

The last fifty to sixty years have seen a massive increase in tourism spending. As Table 3.4 below shows, tourism receipts have grown from circa €2 billion in 1950 to over €548 billion in 2005. Growth in revenue has been constant, with predictable drops in 1986 (terrorism, Chernobyl disaster) as well in 2002–2003 (aftermath of 2001 terrorism, further terrorism and war).

The largest tourism-generating countries (countries where the tourist comes from) are the countries that are classed as the world's most developed and most industrialised. These include Europe, North America, Japan and Australia.

The most important destinations in terms of tourism revenue are depicted below. China and Turkey have seen massive increases in tourism revenue. Turkey posted a 20 per cent increase in 2005 on 2004 figures, on top of a 26 per cent rise the previous year, allowing it to enter the world's top ten. China's growth was 13 per cent in 2005 on the previous year, overtaking Germany for the sixth position.

Table 3.4: International Tourism Receipts in Billions of Euro, 1950–2005

Year	World	Africa	Americas	Asia Pacific	Europe	Middle East
1950*	2.1	0.1	1.1	0.04	0.9	0.03
1960*	6.9	0.2	2.5	0.2	3.9	0.1
1965*	11.6	0.3	3.4	0.5	7.2	0.3
1970*	17.9	0.5	4.8	1.2	11.0	0.4
1975	32.8	1.0	8.2	2.0	20.8	0.7
1980	76.5	2.4	17.7	8.1	45.7	2.5
1981	96.8	3.3	24.9	11.8	53.2	3.7
1982	106.5	3.5	26.2	13.6	59.2	3.9
1983	117.9	3.9	29.6	15.8	63.7	4.9
1984	144.1	4.1	40.5	19.2	74.5	5.8
1985	158.3	4.0	43.7	21.3	83.7	5.5
1986	148.9	3.6	39.1	21.3	81.5	3.4
1987	159.9	4.0	37.3	24.2	87.5	3.9
1988	177.7	4.7	43.4	31.1	94.9	3.7
1989	208.7	5.2	54.7	37.2	107.2	4.4
1990	214.5	5.0	54.4	36.6	114.4	4.0
1991	230.8	4.8	61.6	38.7	121.4	4.2
1992	253.2	5.3	64.5	43.3	134.4	5.8
1993	286.0	5.9	76.2	53.0	144.1	6.8
1994	307.7	6.4	77.7	61.2	154.6	7.8
1995	314.5	6.5	75.3	62.7	162.0	8.0
1996	352.5	7.6	85.3	73.7	176.6	9.3
1997	398.9	8.4	100.9	80.1	198.2	11.3
1998	400.4	9.2	102.8	68.3	208.8	11.2
1999	433.5	10.4	112.6	78.6	218.7	13.2
2000	518.8	11.5	141.8	97.9	250.8	16.9
2001	521.4	12.8	133.7	104.4	253.1	17.3
2002	509.3	12.5	120.3	104.8	255.1	16.6
2003	463.4	13.7	100.9	83.9	250.1	14.9
2004	500.6	14.7	105.9	100.5	262.6	16.9
2005	547.8	17.1	116.8	111.6	279.3	23.0

Source: UNWTO, November 2005 and World Tourism Barometer, June 2006. Note: Certain euro rates are based on a fluctuation with the currency of the data collection, the US dollar.

* The figures representing 1950, 1960, 1965 and 1970 are represented in US dollars only, and no conversion of these is offered in the UNWTO data.

Table 3.5: World's Top Tourism Earners (2005)

World Ranking	Country	Earnings (in billion of euro)	
		2004	2005
1	United States	58.5	64.1
2	Spain	35.5	37.6
3	France	32.0	33.2
4	Italy	28.0	27.8
5	United Kingdom	22.1	23.9
6	China	20.2	23.0
7	Germany	21.8	22.9
8	Turkey	12.5	14.3
9	Austria	12.0	12.2
10	Australia	10.7	11.7

Source: UNWTO Tourism Barometer, June 2006.
(US dollar converted to euro at the rate of US$1 = €0.785 or €1= $1.27)

International tourism spending passes US$2 billion a day

Global spend up US$49 billion in 2005

Africa has fastest growth at 7.8 per cent

Boost to services exports

An estimated US$682 billion was spent abroad by tourists in 2005 – up $49 billion, or 3.4 per cent, on the previous year.

If spending on foreign passenger transport of $130 billion is added, the total export spend is more than $800 billion. This represents some 6 per cent of global export of all goods and services.

'Visitor spending continues its strong overall growth,' said UNWTO Secretary General Francesco Frangialli, 'contributing substantially to global services exports and particularly to the overall trade balances of developing economies. Africa's 7.8 per cent increase is a significant success story.'

- In absolute terms, all regions shared in the increase on visitor spending.
- Europe up US$19 billion to US$347 billion (51 per cent of the world total).
- The Americas up US$13 billion to US$145 billion (21 per cent).
- Asia and the Pacific, US$11 billion higher at US$139 billion (20 per cent).
- The Middle East up US$3 billion to US$29 billion (4 per cent).
- Africa up US$2 billion to US$21 billion.

In growth terms, the order reverses:

- Africa (up 7.8 per cent).
- The Middle East (5.8 per cent).
- Asia and the Pacific (4.5 per cent).
- Americas (4.3 per cent).
- Europe (2.3 per cent).

In comparison to receipts, international tourist arrivals grew by 5.6 per cent in 2005. Again, Africa was the fastest-growing region with a 10 per cent increase, followed by the Middle East +9.5 per cent, Asia and the Pacific +7.8 per cent, Americas +6.1 per cent and Europe +4.0 per cent.

The somewhat slower pace of growth in receipts against arrivals is attributed to the fragile recovery of high-yield business tourism, a comparatively strong increase in short breaks – stimulated by low-cost airlines – and a shift towards destinations offering perceived value for money.

Tourism development in Africa has been quite successful in the past couple of years, with the number of international arrivals growing from 28.2 to 36.8 million between 2000 and 2005, in spite of the concerns about terrorism and SARS and the economic downturn of 2001–2003. In the same period, receipts even doubled from US$10.5 billion to US$21.3 billion.

Source: UNWTO, July 2006.

TOP TOURISM-GENERATING COUNTRIES

Inevitably, the most developed and industrialised countries of the world are the countries whose people have the most disposable income. For example, Scandinavians have high levels of disposable income and so spend amongst the most per capita on tourism. Large markets such as France and Japan also spend a large amount; however, few Japanese and French travel abroad for tourism.

China and India are the world's largest and second largest countries in terms of population, respectively. At circa 1.306 billion citizens, one in five people on the planet are Chinese. India is not far behind, with a population of 1.027 billion people, or one in six people in the world. These markets are both developing rapidly and are poised to become the major tourism generators of the twenty-first century. However, economic hardships hold many of their citizens back at present.

Further, government strategies in these generating markets may hinder tourism. In order for a Chinese travel agent or tour operator to organise trips to another country for local customers, the country in question must have Approved Destination Status (ADS). Ireland has recently achieved this status. The Indian government has restrictions on the purchase of foreign currency, which encourages Indians to holiday domestically rather than abroad. The rationale is that Indian-earned currency (the rupee) is not used to purchase foreign currencies such as the euro or US dollar, which has a negative impact on the rupee. The aim is to stop leakage from the Indian economy. Indians wishing to travel abroad have to apply to their local government to purchase foreign currency. Often such foreign currency is purchased on the black market in order to avoid bureaucracy.

Table 3.6 illustrates the world's top tourism spenders, ranked in order of most spent by the country as a whole. If we ranked the countries in order of expenditure per capita, the top ten spenders would be:

1. Hong Kong (China)
2. Norway
3. Austria

4. Belgium
5. Switzerland
6. Sweden
7. Netherlands
8. United Kingdom
9. Germany
10. France

However, this ranking is not truly representative, given the small numbers of tourists from some countries and large numbers from others.

Table 3.6: World's Top Tourism Spenders (2005)

Country	International Tourism Expenditure (US$, billion)			Market Share	Population (million)	Expenditure per Capita
	2002	2003	2004	2004	2004	US$
World	485	524	623	100	6,373	98
1 Germany	52.5	64.7	71.0	11.4	82	861
2 United States	58.7	57.4	65.6	10.5	293	224
3 United Kingdom	41.5	47.9	55.9	9.0	60	928
4 Japan	26.5	28.8	38.1	6.1	127	299
5 France	19.5	23.4	28.6	4.6	60	474
6 Italy	16.8	20.6	20.5	3.3	58	354
7 China	15.4	15.2	19.1	3.1	1,299	15
8 Netherlands	12.9	14.6	16.4	2.6	16	1,007
9 Canada	11.7	13.4	16.0	2.6	33	493
10 Russian Federation	11.3	12.9	15.7	2.5	144	109
11 Belgium	10.2	12.2	14.0	2.3	10	1,356
12 Hong Kong (China)	12.4	11.4	13.3	2.1	7	1,934
13 Spain	7.3	9.1	12.2	2.0	40	302
14 Austria	9.4	11.8	11.4	1.8	8	1,388
15 Sweden	7.3	8.2	10.1	1.6	9	1,126
16 Republic of Korea	9.0	8.2	9.9	1.6	48	204
17 Australia	6.1	7.3	9.4	1.5	20	472
18 Switzerland	6.6	7.5	8.8	1.4	7	1,181
19 Norway	5.1	6.7	8.4	1.4	5	1,842
20 Taiwan (PR of China)	7.0	6.5	8.2	1.3	23	359

Source: UNWTO.

Table 3.7 shows that Europe generates more than half of the share of world tourism.

Table 3.7: Outbound Tourism by Generating Region (2005)

From	1990	1995	2000	2001	2002	2003	2004	% Share (2004)
World	441.0	538.1	680.6	680.4	700.4	689.7	763.3	100
Europe	252.5	307.2	389.5	390.4	401.6	406.7	431.3	56.5
Asia Pacific	59.8	88.8	118.3	120.6	130.8	120.6	151.2	19.8
Americas	99.3	108.0	130.7	125.5	121.2	115.4	127.7	16.7
Middle East	8.5	10.4	15.2	16.3	18.3	17.9	22.0	2.9
Africa	9.9	13.0	16.5	16.5	17.6	17.6	18.2	2.4
Origin Not Specified	11.1	10.8	10.5	11.2	10.9	11.5	12.8	1.7
Same Region	351.9	430.5	537.9	546.0	566.8	560.2	617.2	80.9
Other Regions	78.0	96.8	132.2	123.3	122.7	118.0	133.2	17.5

Source: UNWTO (includes estimations for countries with missing data).

IRISH TOURISM GROWTH PATTERNS

Ireland's annual average revenue growth rate between 1990 and 1995 was 8.1 per cent, rising to 10.8 per cent in the period between 1995 and 2000. This is in comparison to an overall European revenue growth rate of 7.1 per cent and 9.1 per cent in these two five-year periods, respectively. In this context, Ireland's tourism revenue growth is the highest of any of the Western and Northern European countries in the same period, although true revenue growth is less if high inflation is taken into account. Ireland's tourism arrivals grew by 6 per cent in 2005, ahead of the UNWTO's estimates of 5.5 per cent international growth in arrivals and a European average growth in arrivals of just 4 per cent. In 2005, Ireland earned almost €4.3 billion from out-of-state tourism. This includes visitors from all world destinations, as well as Northern Ireland. The figure also includes an estimated €600 million on fares to Irish carriers. If we were to add in the €1.16 billion value of domestic tourism, then the total value of the Irish tourism industry (international, Northern Ireland and domestic) amounts to €5.4 billion. Table 3.8 illustrates the growth in Irish tourism revenue over the period 1993–2005. In Appendix D, various tables illustrate tourism numbers and tourist spending patterns per major market in each of the years between 2000 and 2005 inclusive, including the average spend per tourist.

In terms of tourist arrivals, Ireland's average annual growth rate was 5.6 per cent and 6.6 per cent for the five-year periods 1990–95 and 1995–2000, respectively. This is once again amongst Europe's highest growth, with many European countries showing actual declines in tourist arrivals, including Austria and Germany in the 1990–95 period. The average annual growth rate for all of Europe was just 3.1 per cent and 4.4 per cent for the two five-year periods, respectively. However, with overall growth of just 3 per cent in 2004, Ireland fell behind an average European growth rate of 4 per cent and an average international growth rate of 10 per cent. The lure of newer destinations, coupled with lower-cost air travel from Ireland's main market (Britain, ironically promoted effectively by an Irish-registered carrier, Ryanair) and lack of a perceived value for money by many tourists are perhaps to blame for the fall in growth. However, Irish growth resurged in 2005. Table 3.9 illustrates the growth in Irish tourism arrivals over the period 1990–2004 for all arrivals (including Northern Ireland). The news article and press release which follow indicate that the estimated figures released are often subsequently amended as newer statistics come to hand.

Table 3.8: Irish Tourism Revenue in Millions of Euro, 1993–2005

1993	1,736
1994	1,902
1995	2,132
1996	2,399
1997	2,675
1998	2,896
1999	3,115
2000	3,637
2001	3,935
2002	3,989
2003	4,057
2004	4,068
2005	4,272

Source: Fáilte Ireland.

Table 3.9: Irish Tourist Arrivals (to Nearest Thousand), 1990–2005

1990	3,666,000
1995	4,818,000
2000	6,646,000
2002	6,476,000
2003	6,764,000
2004	6,982,000
2005	7,333,000

Source: UNWTO and Fáilte Ireland.

> Visitors to Ireland in 2005 grew to 6.7 million [international arrivals] but rural tourism still in decline
>
> Visitor numbers to Ireland grew to an all-time high of 6.7 million in 2005 but rural areas lost out, according to figures released yesterday.
>
> Total earnings from tourism last year amounted to €5.3 billion, up €200 million on 2004, and the number of tourists travelling to urban centres including Dublin, Limerick, Kilkenny, Waterford and Galway increased. But

visitors to rural areas continued to decline, according to a review of the year by Fáilte Ireland.

Trips from Continental Europe increased by 16.9 per cent, particularly from the accession countries. Visitors from Britain were also up by 2.7 per cent, but numbers from North America were down.

The increase in visitors from the Continent was attributed to a larger number of direct access routes to Ireland and a growth in the trend in trips to visit friends and relations working in Ireland.

Domestic tourism continued to grow last year, with Irish people taking 3.1 million holidays in Ireland, up by 51 per cent since 2000.

Shaun Quinn, chief executive of Fáilte Ireland, said that occupancy levels in hotels were up to 64 per cent but that the international average was 70 per cent.

'It is clear that the return on assets can be improved, that capacity is likely to be at optimum level and that the removal of tax incentives for hotel construction in the 2005 Budget was timely,' he said.

Around 230,000 people were employed in the hospitality sector in 2005 and one in four hospitality workers were not Irish. Tourism was Ireland's most important indigenous industry last year, accounting for 3.7 per cent of gross national product.

But growth targets in the industry, set by the Tourism Policy Review Group, will be difficult to reach if progress on the second terminal for Dublin Airport does not move forward, according to Fáilte Ireland's chairwoman, Gillian Bowler.

'There was some important progress made in 2005, with major infrastructural projects such as the national stadium and National Conference Centre moving forward,' she said. 'But without the second terminal we will not make growth targets. T2 is crucial.'

She cited lack of progress in access for walkers and trends such as shorter breaks and shorter booking times as having negative effects on rural tourism.

'The lack of progress in areas such as access for walkers, despite two years of effort, is deeply disappointing and is greatly to the advantage of our competitors, as Ireland is effectively not a player in a growth market.'

Visitor satisfaction was high last year, with 96 per cent of people surveyed responding that their holiday in Ireland either matched or exceeded their expectations.

Some 89 per cent of respondents said that they chose to holiday in Ireland because of the 'beautiful scenery', 86 per cent were attracted by the 'friendly people' and 84 per cent said that they came for the 'natural, unspoilt environment'.

Value for money was the most criticised aspect of holidays in Ireland, but there was a slight improvement in visitor rating, with 67 per cent finding it fair, good or very good, the first improvement since 2001.

Tourism businesses are optimistic about the industry's prospects for 2006, with the exception of those in the angling sector.

The overall growth target for 2006 is 4.9 per cent, which would see Ireland attracting over 7 million visitors. Fáilte Ireland is hopeful of an 8 per cent growth in visitors from mainland Europe, North America and other areas, and a 2.2 per cent growth in visitors from Britain.

The Ryder Cup, to be held in the K Club in Kildare in September, is seen as an important opportunity for the industry. It will have a potential television audience of 1 billion, with estimated earnings in the region of €140 million. Some 40,000 people will visit the golf course daily during the tournament.

Source: Gartland, F., 'Visitors to Ireland in 2005 grew to 6.7 million but rural tourism still in decline', *The Irish Times*, 5 January 2006.

6.97 million visitors in 2005 – O'Donoghue welcomes record visitor numbers

John O'Donoghue, TD, Minister for Arts, Sport and Tourism, today [8 February 2006] welcomed the new CSO figures which show that 2005 ended on a strong note, with the country greeting a record 6.97 million visitors.

'I'm delighted that despite all of the challenges facing the industry and the volatile international climate, Ireland has managed, once again, to attract a record number of visitors. This is a great credit to the industry and the tourism agencies and is a vindication of the government's strong and continuing support for the sector.

'We will have to wait for a few months to get the full breakdown in terms of revenue and regional spread, but these figures show that Ireland is still a highly attractive proposition for visitors. The challenge for the sector is to ensure that it remains that way,' O'Donoghue said.

Source: Department of Arts, Sport and Tourism press release, 8 February 2006.

REASONS FOR IRISH TOURISM GROWTH

There are several factors we can attribute Ireland's phenomenal tourism growth to. In order for there to be tourism growth, both in terms of arrivals and revenue, affordable and comprehensive access transport options must be in place. Ireland is extremely well serviced by air routes, especially by low-cost airlines. After all, it is the birthplace of Europe's largest low-cost operator, Ryanair. The so-called flag carrier, Aer Lingus, also offers low-cost, no-frills fares on most of its routes, primarily the intra-European routes. The cost of transport to and from Ireland is perhaps one of the lowest costs for which a visitor to Ireland has to pay. This makes Ireland an attractive option. In an era when so many travellers use the internet to plan and organise their travel arrangements, it is often the case that travellers simply search websites for airlines like www.ryanair.com or www.airfrance.com for the destinations with the cheapest airfares on their chosen date. Similarly, online intermediaries such as www.expedia.com and www.lastminute.com can offer packages including flights and accommodation to tens of thousands of destinations. Given the relatively cheap cost of airfares to and from Ireland, it is often the case that Ireland is chosen. The perceived high cost of Ireland as a destination perhaps only first becomes apparent when choosing an Irish hotel. Capacity on air routes into Ireland has also increased dramatically in recent years. More aircraft arriving at more airports (including smaller regional ones) has led to a demand for more airport terminals throughout Ireland. We can also see the development of larger aircraft with the ability to carry more passengers, increasing the number of arrivals per aircraft.

Ireland, and particularly Dublin, has also become a fashionable city break destination. Mass marketing campaigns by Irish tourism agencies have succeeded in attracting millions of tourists to the destination for culture, the arts, entertainment and shopping, although recently the Irish capital has come in for criticism for not having enough cultural attractions for foreign visitors. High-profile media events have also aided this process. These include sporting events such as Ireland hosting the Special Olympics World Summer Games in 2003 and the Ryder Cup in 2006. Ireland winning the Eurovision Song Contest four out of five years in the 1990s (1992, 1993, 1994, 1996) also enabled an estimated audience of over 300 million people in Europe (and other markets such as Australia, where the contest is extremely popular) to view a showcase of what Ireland has to offer, as the sixty-second interval between each song featured elements of Ireland. Even participating in international events such as the Olympic Games, Six Nations Rugby and FIFA Soccer World Cup (1990, 1994, 2002) has put Ireland and the Irish on the world map for positive reasons.

All of these reasons and many more served to combat the many negative international impressions of Ireland over the so-called Troubles in Northern Ireland, which received prominent headlines in the world's media between 1969 and 1994. The failed 1994 ceasefire and subsequent ceasefire, leading to the 1998 Good Friday Belfast Agreement, led to further positive media coverage for Ireland. The very visible participation of US President Bill Clinton on his multiple trips to Ireland (north and south) echoed home to the US market that all-Ireland was now a safe destination. The creation of an all-Ireland marketing concept in the form of Tourism Brand Ireland and its successor, Tourism Ireland Ltd, as a follow-on from the 1998 Good Friday Belfast Agreement further enhanced the perception around the world that Ireland was at peace and united in its efforts to attract tourism.

The British market has also performed well and contributed to Irish tourism growth. The so-called peace dividend (the benefits which would accrue to all-Ireland but particularly Northern Ireland should there be a lasting peace) began to pay off, as British visitors, once fearful that they were unwelcome in Ireland, now choose the country as a holiday or short-break destination. Indeed, we can notice a marked change in this philosophy, as the number of arrivals from Britain increases dramatically at times of war, terrorism and international unrest. This is evidenced in the increase in arrivals from Britain in the months after the US and British invasion of Iraq in 2003, as many British perceived Ireland as a safe destination.

The growth from Britain was aided by the drastic reduction in airfares on routes between Britain and Ireland, as well as the opening of many new routes from British towns and cities to Irish towns and cities which had never previously been connected. This allowed many travellers to bypass large airports in the capital cities such as London-Heathrow and Dublin in their journey to other parts of either country.

Further reasons for the continued growth from Britain include the cultural, language and ancestral links that still exist between Ireland and Britain. An extremely large number of arrivals from Britain to Ireland are part of the VFR (visiting friends and relatives) market. Unfortunately for Irish accommodation providers, many of these do not engage accommodation, but rather stay with their friends or relatives. The strong performance of the British economy in the late 1990s and early 2000s also leaves the average British person with more disposable income than ever before. Travel is the most popular purchased item with disposable income, according to the UNWTO. The strength of the British pound (sterling) against the euro also continues to be a major factor for British tourists, as this often translates to a good deal when visiting a eurozone country. In Ireland's case, the perceived high cost of living, entertainment, accommodation and purchases can be offset by the relative strength of the British currency.

Ireland offers thousands of historical and heritage attractions, some of which are world famous. However, recent developments have also served to encourage visitors to Ireland, some in their own right, such as the Temple Bar Cultural Quarter, which attracts visitors from all parts of the world, most notably at weekend British stag and hen parties. Other new attractions, such as the Spire or GAA Museum in Dublin, may not attract visitors in their own right, but are nonetheless an important part of the tourist experience.

Irish tourism agencies have also increased their marketing drives and budgets in order to attract more tourists. Since the advent of the Tourism Ireland Ltd (TIL) marketing campaign launch on 1 January 2002, cross-border tourism marketing co-operation has proved beneficial for both parts of Ireland in terms of increased tourist arrivals and tourism revenue. Joint marketing with the Irish tourism industry has also been instrumental in driving strategic growth in Irish tourism. Strategic and smart marketing methods have been employed by Irish tourism agencies, such as redirecting marketing budgets away from volatile markets at times of crises when their citizens inherently reduce their travel, e.g. the US at times of terrorism and war, to markets that are more likely to choose Ireland at such times of international volatility, e.g. Britain. Given the amount of uncertainty recently in the world's tourism-generating markets, especially in Britain and the US (which together account for approximately three-quarters of Ireland's tourist arrivals), Ireland's long-term strategic marketing goals are to ensure that it does not put all of its eggs into two baskets, i.e. Britain and America, but rather concentrate on diversifying the spread of Ireland's tourism-generating nations. This strategy includes tourism marketing in several Continental European countries, which traditionally make up a small percentage of arrivals, as well as targeting long-haul markets, including newly emerging markets such as South Africa, India and China, as well as closer-to-home emerging markets such as Eastern Europe. Marketing efforts have been highly successful in most European and long-haul markets, as figures show increases from most markets in recent years. A notable decline since the 1990s is the German market, perhaps more to do with German economic problems since reunification in 1990 than a lack of Irish marketing efforts, although we can note a resurgence from Germany in recent years. Whatever approach future marketing takes, it is imperative that marketing should continue to be seen as an investment and not a cost by all the agencies concerned.

The Celtic Tiger Irish economic boom of the 1990s and continued (albeit slower) growth since then has also been a contributory factor to the growth of Irish tourism. This resulted in more money in the Irish economy, some of which has been invested in enterprises which directly or indirectly enhance the tourist's experience. Further, the increased levels of disposable income are often spent on entertainment, which provides a domestic boost to many establishments during off-peak seasons. The increased levels of Irish disposable income cause mixed fortunes for domestic tourism. Inevitably some of it is spent on taking domestic trips such as city breaks within Ireland. However, it has often caused a decline in domestic tourism, as the level of disposable income for many Irish people is spent on trips abroad. Finally, a strong economy often leads to overseas expansion of Irish companies, or conversely, expansion of foreign companies into Ireland, resulting in the need for international trade and business tourism, benefiting Ireland's tourism industry.

Another effect of a booming economy is mass immigration, which Ireland has witnessed over the last decade. Following trade and migration agreements with several countries, including China and India (the largest and second largest countries in the world in terms of population, respectively), tens of thousands of nationals from these countries have entered employment in Ireland. Following on from the accession of ten new member states to the European Union in May 2004 (most of them Eastern European states), there was a massive influx of nationals from these states into Ireland. According to the UNWTO's definition of tourism, those who stay more than one year are not classified as tourists. However, those who are here for shorter periods can be defined as economic tourists. The impact that such migration (no matter the length of time in the state) has on Ireland is that it is creating a new VFR (visiting friends and relatives) market, as the relatives and friends of non-Irish nationals living and working in Ireland come to Ireland to visit them. Further, such a large influx of migrants creates the needs for new transport routes, and Ireland has seen many new air routes open between many of its airports (including smaller ones) and new markets from regions where immigrants to Ireland come. The largest expansion in this regard is between Irish and Polish air routes. Inevitably, as further states join the European Union, such as Romania and Turkey, more links will be established. The result for general tourism is that new air routes are open, not just for immigrants and their visitors, but also for tourists to and from Ireland.

Irish tourism growth leads to more revenue for private and public organisations, including the Irish government via direct and indirect taxation. More revenue leads to business expansion, and thus more employment in the sector. Again, higher employment rates lead to higher levels of taxation collected by the government. With increased tourism numbers and increased taxation (direct and indirect), the government has more resources to reinvest in the industry (theoretically), including a larger marketing budget. More investment and more marketing results in more tourists coming to Ireland, and so the process becomes cyclical, as depicted in Figure 3.1.

Figure 3.1: Result of Continued Irish Tourism Growth

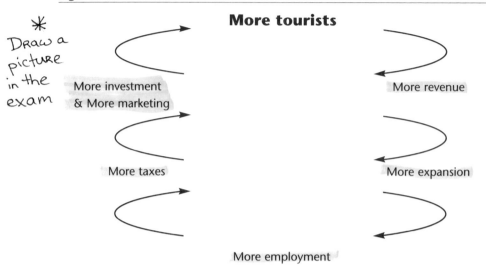

*Draw a picture in the exam

More tourists

More investment & More marketing

More revenue

More taxes

More expansion

More employment

Revenue from tourists to Ireland impacts on the Irish economy in several ways, discussed in the following sections.

IRISH GOVERNMENT INCOME FROM TOURISM

Tourism income for the government can come from direct and indirect taxation. It is estimated that over half (52 per cent) of tourism spending is directly and indirectly made up of taxes, converting to circa €2.5 billion in 2005 (of which €2.1 billion came from foreign tourism). This is an excellent return on investment, as the government estimates for 2006 allocate only €134 million to the sector. The total out-of-state tourism spend (including fares to Irish carriers) amounted to €4.3 billion. Given that Ireland's total exports amounted to €127.2 billion, tourism accounted for 3.4 per cent of the nation's exports in 2005. Further, tourism goods have low import content in comparison to other exports. According to the Central Statistics Office (CSO) in 2005 (www.cso.ie), tourism accounts for 3.8 per cent of Ireland's gross national product (GNP), down from 3.9 per cent in the previous year.

John O'Donoghue, TD, Minister for Arts, Sport and Tourism, on the 2006 estimates for tourism

Annual foreign revenue earnings from tourism have increased by over 50 per cent since 1997, from €2.7 billion to €4.1 billion.

Overseas visitor numbers have increased by 28 per cent since 1997, from 5 million to 6.4 million.

The budget for frontline tourism marketing has increased from €12 million in 1997 to €40 million in 2006 – the highest ever tourism marketing budget.

Highlights: Estimates 2006

'Increased marketing funding for both Tourism Ireland and Fáilte Ireland will enable both agencies to significantly step up their marketing activities in 2006, focusing in particular on stimulating regional dispersal of visitors and promoting greater usage of special interest products. It will also support the promotion of new air access developments and the enhancement of our e-marketing capabilities.'

- Increase of 7 per cent in tourism budget brings tourism allocation up to €134 million.
- Largest ever exchequer budget for Irish tourism promotion.
- Tourism marketing fund of €40 million in 2006 a 12 per cent increase on 2005.
- Increased funding of 8 per cent in Fáilte Ireland's core Vote.
- Clear evidence of government's strong commitment to Irish tourism.

Commenting on the tourism estimates, Minister O'Donoghue said: 'I am very pleased to have secured a level of tourism funding for 2006 that represents a considerable increase in real terms on last year's provision. This funding package will enable me to support Irish tourism in responding to the significant challenges facing the sector, as outlined in the *New Horizons* tourism strategy which is currently being energetically rolled out. It once again demonstrates the importance the government attaches to tourism and its recognition of it as a sector of major economic importance, delivering annual foreign revenue earnings of €4.1 billion and representing close to 140,000 jobs.'

Minister O'Donoghue also announced an increase of 7 per cent in funding for tourism services, bringing the total allocation to €134 million in 2006.

This increased level of funding will enable the Minister and the state tourism agencies to advance the process of implementing many of the recommendations of the Tourism Policy Review Group, which set out a new vision and strategy for Irish tourism for the ten-year period to 2012.

The increase of 12 per cent in the tourism marketing fund to €40 million builds on the increased funding provided in earlier years. This will support the marketing activities of both Tourism Ireland and Fáilte Ireland next year. It will enable both agencies to significantly step up their marketing activities in 2006, focusing in particular on stimulating regional dispersal of visitors and promoting greater usage of special interest products, including golf, building on the opportunities of the Ryder Cup 2006. It will also enable support to be provided to promote new air access developments and the enhancement of our e-marketing capabilities.

Minister O'Donoghue said: 'I know, from my involvement in tourism promotion trips abroad, that Ireland is facing intense and increasing competition in the international marketplace. This year's allocation of €40 million is the largest ever marketing budget for the promotion of Irish tourism.'

Source: Department of Arts, Sport and Tourism press release, 17 November 2005.

Direct taxation is when a tourist spends money in Ireland, and the products and services purchased have a tax component to them. Examples of these include the VAT (value added tax) on accommodation, food, drink and gifts, as well as port taxes and taxes charged by transport providers on behalf of the government. Visitors from non-EU states can claim back the VAT paid on gifts and items that leave the state (services such as hotel and food bills are excluded).

Indirect taxation revenue accrues to the government from several sources. Employees in a tourism enterprise such as a hotel, airline or visitor attraction pay income tax and social insurance on their wages, which contribute to the economy. However, most tourists use more than transport and accommodation providers and visit more than just a visitor attraction. Tourists visit restaurants, cafés, bars and nightclubs as well as shop in much the same shops as locals. The employees of these businesses also pay income tax and social insurance to the government. Indeed, some of these businesses purposefully hire extra staff for busy tourist seasons.

The businesses themselves are given a boost at peak tourist seasons. Even throughout slower off-peak and shoulder seasons, tourism contributes to the businesses' profits. Each business making a profit pays a corporation tax to the government. Higher profits from higher levels of tourism result in higher amounts of corporation tax paid to the government.

The government can accrue revenue from tourism sources other than taxation. The government and its agencies own and run many visitor attractions on behalf of the people of Ireland, including heritage sites, museums and natural attractions. Entrance fees and rent from such tourism businesses supplement the government's income from tourism. However, unlike many countries, a sizeable proportion of state-run visitor attractions in Ireland are free, such as museums and galleries. The government also provides loans and credit to many enterprises, including tourism ones. The interest paid on such loans is revenue for the government. Even if the loan comes from a privately owned financial institution, the profits of the institution are liable to corporation tax.

If we were to extrapolate further, we can see that tourism provides countless indirect economic benefits to the state. Employees in a tourism business create demand for basic domestic, personal and general products and services (such as groceries, heating bills and entertainment), which they pay for using their wages earned in a tourism enterprise. Continuing the extrapolation, the supermarket worker where the employee of the tourism enterprise buys their groceries uses his or her wages to purchase the goods and services that they need. The farmer who provides produce to restaurants or even the supermarket uses their income for similar purchases, and the cycle continues. A similar extrapolation can be envisioned for the printer of the hotels' brochures, the webmaster of the tour operator, the coach company that collect tourists at the airport, etc. As previously noted, estimates show that over half of everything spent by a tourist ends up with the government through direct and indirect taxation.

REGIONAL TOURISM INCOME

The extrapolation scenario above has an extremely important impact on rural regions of Ireland, where there may be little or no other industry apart from tourism. This effect is known as the tourism income multiplier. The theory is that the true income of any local town that attracts tourism is actually double any published figures, as at least half of the income tends to be spent locally, as per the extrapolation example depicted above. The rest of the income usually leaks out of the local economy to pay for tax to the central government or other goods and services not available locally (such as oil or wine). Leakage can also occur as foreign workers send part of their wages home, or foreign companies repatriate some or all of their profits.

According to Fáilte Ireland:

Tourism is characterised by the fact that consumption takes place where the service is available, and because tourism activity is particularly concentrated in areas which lack an intensive industry base, it is credited with having a significant regional distributive effect.

Most tourists to Ireland visit urban centres, especially larger cities such as Dublin. The Irish government's regional strategy with regard to tourism is to encourage more tourists to visit rural regions, especially regions which have been neglected in the past by tourists, and those which have a shortage of other industries.

Tourism scheme attracts 500 to North West

More than 500 British visitors arrived in Donegal town yesterday in a new tourism venture marking the North West as a popular January holiday spot.

The visitors from the north of England opted to take their chances with the Donegal weather on a four-day package costing £99 (€144.50) each.

The cross-border venture hopes to attract more than 4,000 extra visitors across the Irish Sea to the North West in the next three months – traditionally the region's worst tourism period.

It was devised by Destination North West Project, a €2 million cross-border tourism marketing initiative, and is funded by North West Tourism and local authority bodies in the North. There is an input from cross-border groups working under the umbrellas of the EU and the Belfast Agreement.

Donegal greeted yesterday's arrivals with a special welcome ceremony in the town centre.

Mostly pensioners from social clubs and day centres, they were attracted by a low-cost package which included return coach and ferry trips, four nights' bed and breakfast and evening meal in their hotels, country music evenings and tours of the surrounding countryside.

A spokesman for host-company the White Hotels Group said: 'We had one coach-load of visitors to the town this time last year. Now we're geared to greet over seventy coaches in the next three months.'

The aim is to boost tourism in what is seen as the six counties struggling most to attract visitors – Donegal, Sligo, Leitrim, Fermanagh, Derry and Tyrone.

Source: Clancy, P., 'Tourism scheme attracts 500 to North West', *The Irish Times*, 5 January 2006.

The tourism income multiplier highlights just how important tourism is to the regions of Ireland. It can be argued, for example, that the true value of tourism in the West in 2004 is actually €1.37 billion, double the €686.2 million published figures.

Table 3.10 illustrates which regions tourists visited, while Table 3.11 depicts how the regions shared the total tourism spend. Figures are divided between domestic tourism, Northern Ireland visitors and all other overseas visitors.

Table 3.10: Regions Visited by Tourists (2004)

	Overseas Tourists	Northern Ireland	Domestic	Total
	(in thousands)			
Dublin	3,680	192	976	4,848
Midlands East	777	30	873	1,680
South East	974	11	1,113	2,098
South West	1,578	51	1,428	3,057
Shannon	1,075	54	791	1,920
West	1,250	43	1,251	2,544
North West	487	234	569	1,290

Source: Fáilte Ireland.

Table 3.11: Amount Spent in the Regions by Tourists (2004)

	Overseas Tourists	Northern Ireland	Domestic	Total
	(in €, mn)			
Dublin	1,163.0	64.6	143.7	1,371.3
Midlands East	248.4	7.1	90.3	345.8
South East	267.4	2.6	150.9	420.9
South West	652.1	22.6	248.0	922.7
Shannon	281.1	14.1	111.0	406.2
West	460.4	15.7	210.1	686.2
North West	162.5	56.4	83.2	302.1
Total Revenue	3,243.9	183.1	1,037.2	4,455.2

Source: Fáilte Ireland.

Extract from Developing Regional Tourism – Fáilte Ireland 2005

The importance of tourism in contributing to regional development has been widely acknowledged. However, in recent years, the benefits of tourism have become more concentrated on Dublin and the East, due to some extent to the significant increase of those taking urban-based short breaks. The flow of visitors must be managed to ensure that the spread of tourism throughout the regions has maximum effects, thus ensuring that the industry remains sustainable.

Fáilte Ireland encourages the regional spread of tourism through a range of activities. We provide substantial funding to the regional tourist authorities which are responsible for the administration of the regional tourism marketing fund. In addition, the festivals and cultural events initiative aims to encourage the movement of visitors throughout the country. In 2005, some of the key activities will be to:

- Assist with the marketing of less-developed areas in co-operation with the RTAs and Shannon Development.
- Focus support on additional air access into regional airports.
- Address the challenges currently facing festival/event organisers identified in recent research.
- Roll out a mentoring programme for festival/event organisers.
- Target regions where in the past applications for funding have been low in order to ensure a better regional spread of tourism.
- Review the TIO [tourist information office] network and establish a 'best practice' model.
- Target, incentivise and train local labour market in skills suitable for the local tourism industry in the regions in which our permanent training centres are based.
- Create a series of highly localised partnerships, particularly in the BMW regions, between Fáilte Ireland and local community groups in order to deliver training locations, identify trainees and provide training.
- Target regions where training provision is low or non-existent and operate temporary training centres which will offer training services appropriate to local need.

The domestic holiday market is a critical contributor to the distribution of the benefits of tourism throughout the country. Effective marketing to domestic consumers in the face of increasing competition from overseas is vital to stimulating a vibrant industry, by good spatial spread and by extending the season.

In 2005, a new communications strategy will be designed which will involve a creative campaign with a regional focus. The campaign will be supported by an intensive public relations effort which will drive word of mouth, the greatest influencer of consumers' holiday choices.

Fáilte Ireland's domestic marketing strategy will focus strongly on regionality and will also concentrate more on special interest products in order to drive a more balanced regional and seasonal spread.

TOURISM AND EMPLOYMENT

The governments of the world have come to recognise the employment-generating potential of tourism. In Ireland, general employment levels have hit their highest levels ever in recent years. The tourism sector has shown significant growth as a result of the rapid growth in tourist arrivals. It is estimated that there are circa 246,000 employees working in the Irish tourism and hospitality business (of which 200,000 work all year round). The share for tourism alone is circa 150,000. This figure can rise significantly if extra seasonal and part-time workers are taken into account. Just over one-fifth of employees in the tourism sectors work in Dublin (21 per cent), while half (49 per cent) work in the remainder of the Southern and Eastern Region, and 30 per cent work in the BMW region. Considering that the total Irish workforce as of the end of 2005 was 1,989,800 according to the CSO, tourism accounts for 12.4 per cent of the total Irish workforce, or one in every eight workers. This is higher than the global average of circa one in every twelve workers on the planet.

Just less than three-quarters of people working in tourist-related services in Ireland in 2005 were Irish nationals (73 per cent), while the remaining 27 per cent were non-Irish nationals. On a national scale, there are 159,300 non-Irish national workers in Ireland (2005), or 8 per cent of the workforce. The fact that over one-quarter (27 per cent) of workers in tourism and hospitality are non-Irish nationals, compared to 8 per cent for all industries, shows that the tourism and hospitality sector is a large employer for non-Irish nationals.

In some regions of the world (and indeed some regions of Ireland), tourism can account for a much larger proportion of employment, given that such regions may be highly dependent on tourism for economic survival, perhaps due to a lack of other major industries.

Table 3.12: Number Employed by Sector in Ireland, 2001–2005

Sector/Year	2001	2002	2003	2004	2005
Hotels	54,275	54,656	54,164	53,637	54,095
Guesthouses	2,943	2,914	2,879	2,849	2,918
Self-Catering Accommodation	3,830	n/a	3,878	3,848	3,641
Restaurants	41,827	41,409	41,085	41,367	43,309
Non-Licensed Restaurants	13,849	n/a	15,642	15,407	16,589
Licensed Premises	78,225	80,121	79,319	78,803	88,986
Tourism Services and Attractions	34,568	34,852	34,749	35,016	36,421
TOTAL	229,517	n/a	231,716	230,927	245,959

Source: Fáilte Ireland.

Tourism can benefit employment in either the tourism-generating country or in the destination. In terms of the former, such jobs include travel agents, tour operators and airlines of the country in question. In terms of the latter, employment may be in hotels, restaurants, visitor attractions, entertainment and shopping establishments, to name just a few.

It must also be noted that an increase in domestic tourism as well as international tourism can also boost employment in the sector. Oftentimes a tourist attraction, venue or service developed with the attraction of foreign tourists in mind can serve to attract tourists from other parts of the same country to the destination. Further, such an attraction, venue or service may attract immediate locals, for example the bar of a hotel, a restaurant or a theme park. Tourism employment may be vital for a region. This is especially true in more rural and isolated parts of Ireland. Employment operates similar to the tourism income multiplier: as new jobs are created, it has knock-on effects for the prosperity of regions, as a large proportion of the income from tourism and tourism employment is spent locally.

Women targeted for West tourist work

Fáilte Ireland is targeting 'work-at-home mothers' in the South West in a move to encourage women back into the tourism industry in Cork and Kerry.

The move has been endorsed by Minister for Tourism John O'Donoghue, who said tourism wanted to provide 'an Irish welcome'.

Piloted last year, training programmes are under way or about to start in ten centres in west Cork and Kerry to encourage women in particular to work in the industry. Some €1.5 million of the €10 million announced for tourism by Fáilte Ireland on Thursday night is being allocated to the effort.

'We are trying to get more local people back into the industry,' Shaun Quinn, chief executive of Fáilte Ireland, said.

'We are targeting work-at-home mothers who have a fantastic Irish welcome. They are what the industry wants.'

One worker in four in the industry at the moment is non-Irish and in some establishments the ratio is far greater.

Mr Quinn was speaking at a tourism briefing in Killarney on Thursday night, where many tourism workers are foreign nationals and where non-Irish workers outnumber Irish workers in some tourism establishments. 'We are convinced there are more Irish people within the local population who can be attracted.' It was a question of 'looking hard enough' and finding them, he said.

Women who chose to work in tourism could expect flexible hours and 'reasonably paid' work.

Source: Lucey, A., 'Women targeted for West tourist work', *The Irish Times*, 16 January 2006.

Growth in tourism employment has slowed recently, as many employers cut costs in an effort to keep their offering more affordable. Even those employers who have continued to increase their staff levels seemed to have focused more on cheaper labour costs, employing non-Irish nationals to perform roles previously performed by Irish workers. However, there are still many skills shortages, especially in the pub trade, hotels and restaurants. These sectors often have difficulty attracting workers given their traditional low pay and seasonal demands, resulting in many workers being made unemployed at the end of the high season. Irish government strategy in this regard is focused on lengthening the tourist season.

Irish tourism to rely more on foreign staff

Irish tourism will rely even more on foreign workers over the coming years, according to the chairwoman of Fáilte Ireland, Gillian Bowler.

Fáilte Ireland has launched a human resources plan to address critical labour shortages in the hospitality industry. This followed a survey last year which found that half of all hotels reported staff vacancies, and that labour shortages were not expected to ease. 'Hoteliers must ensure that everyone they employ has the right skills, including the ability to speak English,' Bowler told an Irish Hotels Federation conference in Killarney last week. 'If they don't have the right skills, then you must accept the responsibility for training them.'

Hospitality skills must include the ability to offer visitors 'the traditional Irish welcome, which is the centrepiece of our branding as a holiday destination', she said. 'As leaders of those troops, I would appeal to you to make sure that every one of them – no matter where they come from, no matter what their job is – knows they are all in the welcome business,' Bowler said. 'If we should ever lose that simplicity, that humanity or that naturalness, then we can literally shut down our tills and go home.'

Bowler, the founder of Budget Travel, said that the demographic trend indicated a steady fall-off over the next decade in the number of school-leavers coming onto the labour market, and that tourism was becoming less attractive as a career choice. 'A particularly disturbing indicator is the number of trained graduates, despite having spent some years becoming qualified, who are choosing not to spend a lifetime in the business, but to seek their future in other directions,' she said.

Bowler hits out at insurance disparity
Preliminary research by Fáilte Ireland into the insurance industry shows a huge disparity between the level of premiums and claims. Figures compiled so far show that hoteliers paid €3 million in premiums, while only half a million was paid out in claims. Fáilte Ireland chairwoman Gillian Bowler said this was 'a totally indefensible charging basis'. If the eventual figures showed anything like the same discrepancy, she said, hoteliers would have 'an open-and-shut case to negotiate significantly reduced premia'.

Source: Connolly, N., 'Irish tourism to rely more on foreign staff', *The Sunday Business Post*, 7 March 2004.

Wages and working conditions in the Irish tourism sector are often not as lucrative as other sectors of the economy. The tourism and hospitality sector is also highly non-unionised. Lower pay and related factors often result in a high level of staff turnover in the sector. The costs of recruitment increases the employer's overall staffing costs. Many employers are unwilling to pay for training for their employees, as they see training as a cost and not an investment, given that there is little chance that the employee will remain in the same position for a significant period of time.

Staff costs are an extremely large proportion of costs for all tourism product and service providers. It is no wonder, therefore, that many such providers are turning to new and existing technology to lead the way to reductions in the number of staff needed, and therefore a reduction in staff costs. This is evidenced in all branches of the tourism sector, including the following:

*   Airlines encourage customers to book online and not via an agent or call centre.
*   Travel agents and tour operators are facing constant competition with the internet, resulting in their need to cut costs – resulting in less staff. The result is a conveyor belt approach in many larger agencies: a high turnover of

enquiries, resulting in each customer receiving less time from an agent, and so less customer service.

- Hotels are becoming more automated, e.g. budget hotels/motels, and are often run by the bare minimum of staff. Small and large hotels (such as 5,000-room Las Vegas hotels) use automation to encourage guests to check out via the television screen and TV remote control in their room.

The result of such cost-cutting measures may be that tourists to Ireland may feel that they have not truly experienced the Irish welcome that is so evident in the tourism marketing that first attracted them to the destination, as it becomes eroded by cheaper labour, unprofessional customer service through lack of training and more automation rather than a personal *fáilte*.

BALANCE OF PAYMENTS

The balance of payments is an analysis of the total amount of goods and services entering a country compared to the amount leaving a country. It is vitally important for any country to balance its imports and exports for economic success. No country in the world is completely self-sufficient – that is, no country can rely solely on its own produce, but rather must import some products and services which for one reason or another cannot be produced at home, or for which there is a production deficit, e.g. oil. Such imports of products and services are balanced against the surplus of products and services that a country produces and so can export, e.g. technology. In the continuing globalisation of world consumerism, world trade is growing at phenomenal rates. Since the 1990s, Ireland has had a consistent surplus of exports, which is a positive indicator of Irish economic success. Ireland exports large quantities of agricultural produce, such as dairy and beef, as well as technology products such as computer hardware and software (even if the latter is produced in Ireland by non-Irish companies). However, Ireland must rely on many imports, including oil and wine, and many other products which are not available or produced in Ireland.

Services also make up a growing proportion of world imports and exports. They are not as visible as a physical product such as oil or computer components, and so they are termed **invisible imports** and **invisible exports**. They are nonetheless extremely important, especially to service economies such as Ireland. Tourism is one such service that augments Ireland's trade surplus with the world.

One would assume that if an Irish tourist goes to Spain for two weeks' holiday that we would class that as an invisible export, and an American visiting Cork would be classed as an invisible import. This is **not** the case. We must remember that an import means that there is a leakage from the Irish economy to another world economy and that Irish-earned euro is paying for a product or service produced in another country. Therefore, an **invisible import** in tourism terms would be when an Irish tourist goes to Spain and spends Irish-earned euro on the Spanish resort and purchases Spanish goods and services, ranging from food and beverages, sightseeing and entertainment, accommodation and gifts. It is classed as an import because it results in a leakage out of the Irish economy, as the Spanish economy benefits. It has the same result as an Irish fruit wholesaler buying a large consignment of Spanish oranges – Irish-earned euro purchasing Spanish products, and so benefiting the Spanish economy. They are both classed as imports. The tourism example is classed as an **invisible import** as it is not as obvious as a container load of oranges arriving from Spain.

On the other hand, **invisible exports** are made up of foreign tourists buying Irish products and services such as hotels, transport to and within Ireland, gifts, meals, entertainment, etc. For example, if an American tourist visits Cork, they spend US-earned dollars on goods and services, and this is a boost to the local and national economy. It is classed as an export as it has the same impact on US-Irish trade as an American company buying a consignment of Irish beef. In both cases, the Irish economy benefits.

From a currency point of view, tourism to countries using the euro from any other currency creates a demand for the euro currency, making it more expensive. This results in a stronger euro relative to the other currency in question. For example, a large increase in the number of Australians visiting eurozone countries would result in a larger demand for the euro, causing its value relative to the Australian dollar to soar. This would result in the euro becoming more expensive for an Australian to purchase. On the currency markets, this would be reflected as less euro being offered for each Australian dollar. The impact of currency fluctuations was much more acutely felt within Europe in the days before the single currency, when the national currency of each state traded against all of the other national currencies. A single currency benefits tourism, as it eliminates such fluctuations within the eurozone, as well as allowing for easy price transparency.

Extract from UNWTO *World Tourism Barometer*, Vol. 4, No. 2, June 2006

Exchange rates
The first five months of 2006 were marked by a gradual appreciation of the euro against the US dollar, reversing the overall decreasing trend of 2005. In May 2006, one euro bought 5.5 per cent more dollars than in January. However, the difference was much less marked when compared with the situation a year ago. In May 2005 a euro bought US$1.27, while in May 2006, this was up to US$1.28.

A similar appreciating trend was registered in the relation of the euro with a series of Asian currencies including the Japanese yen, which is now at 143 yen per euro against 140 yen per euro in January. On the European front the picture for the period January–May 2006 is more mixed. While appreciating against some central European currencies such as the Hungarian forint (+4.7 per cent) and the Polish zloty (+2.0 per cent), the euro lost some ground against the Czech koruna (–1.6 per cent), the Croatian kuna (–1.4 per cent), the Norwegian krone (–3.0 per cent) and the British pound (–0.4 per cent).

On the other hand, besides losing to the euro (–5.2 per cent), the US dollar also depreciated between January and May 2006 against the Russian rouble (–4.6 per cent), as well as against most other European and Asian currencies. The most noteworthy change is its 3.3 per cent depreciation against the Japanese yen, which contrasts with the 1.8 per cent appreciation registered in 2005, and the slight but continued devaluation against the Chinese yuan (–0.6 per cent). In North America, the US dollar continued to depreciate against the Canadian dollar (–4.2 per cent), making it more expensive to travel from the USA to Canada. The recent series of continued significant increases of the value of the Canadian dollar have been the largest and most rapid in more than fifty years. At the end of May the Canadian dollar reached its highest level since early 1978.

Four currencies that deviate from the overall trend are the Turkish lira, the New Zealand dollar, the Mexican peso and the South African rand. All four depreciated both against euro and dollar, thus favouring traffic from almost all major outbound markets. In a way this also can be seen as a correction on a substantial appreciation – and loss of price competitiveness – in previous years. The euro gained 14.9 per cent against the New Zealand dollar, 13.9 per cent against the Turkish lira, 10.8 per cent against the Mexican peso and 9.5 per cent against the south African rand (which is not only reference for South Africa, but also for other southern African countries such as Namibia, Lesotho and Swaziland). For the US dollar the gains were some 5–6 per cent lower.

Ireland has a large tourism surplus, as more visitors come to Ireland than there are Irish people to go abroad! This brings more money into the Irish economy from tourism than is leaked out of the economy from tourism. Other countries are not so lucky. The UK, for example, has had consistent tourism deficits, as the number of Britons spending their holidays and short breaks abroad has soared. Economic success in a country inevitably leads to more disposable income, and travel and tourism is a key product when it comes to spending disposable income. Irish economic success is already having an impact on domestic tourism, as many Irish opt to travel abroad for a holiday or short break rather than staying in Ireland. This will inevitably erode Ireland's tourism balance of payments surplus.

Some world governments have come up with several approaches in an effort to limit the negative effects on the balance of payments from tourism deficits. The governments of the former Soviet-bloc countries in Eastern Europe during the Cold War required their citizens to apply for exit visas to leave the state to enter a non-allied state. Chinese travel agents and tour operators are only permitted to offer tours to Approved Destination Status (ADS) countries. Other countries such as India limit the amount of foreign currency that their citizens can buy and take abroad to an unrealistic amount. Limiting foreign currency purchase is common practice in many countries.

The most common way of influencing the tourism balance of payments is evidenced in Ireland – the government encourages domestic tourism (through Fáilte Ireland) as well as encouraging foreign tourists to come to Ireland (through Tourism Ireland Ltd). This marketing approach is practised in most destinations.

Some countries can afford to let their citizens travel abroad, as any tourism deficit is offset by surpluses in other sectors of the economy, for example Japan's large manufacturing surplus.

TOURISM INVESTMENT

Investment in tourism comes from both public and private sources. The former encompasses the range of supports, grants and loans from state agencies of the Irish and EU government, while the latter comes from private sources such as individual and group investors as well as financial institutions. Investment in Irish tourism was over €1.25 billion between 1989 and 2002. The majority of investment in Ireland has been directed at hotels, conference and leisure facilities, self-catering accommodation and tourist attractions. Public grants as investments often cover a large proportion of the cost of a project, while the owner/company is required to fund the balance. There is often fierce competition for such limited state and EU resources.

Ministers launch €2.5 million tourism initiatives

€2.5 million is to be spent on two tourism initiatives to market the North West and North East regions as vibrant tourist destinations.

Destination North West, a joint marketing campaign, aims to enhance the visitor experience to Derry, Fermanagh, Tyrone, Donegal, Sligo and Leitrim. The Glens and Lakelands project, the North East initiative, plans to increase the competitiveness and sustainability of tourism businesses in the North East of Northern Ireland and the Cavan and Monaghan area.

Minister for Arts, Sport and Tourism, John O'Donoghue, TD, and his Northern Irish counterpart, Angela Smith, MP, launched the cross-border initiatives at the Guildhall in Derry.

At the event, Minister O'Donoghue said: 'I was delighted to meet with my ministerial colleague in Northern Ireland, Angela Smith, MP, at Tourism Ireland's office in Coleraine where we launched their annual report for 2004. The report reviews a good overall performance last year and signals some key challenges ahead for tourism on the island. In Derry, I was privileged to participate in the launch of a major cross-border marketing initiative for the North West, Glens and Lakeland initiatives, which will see a significant investment – over €2.5 million – of EU and public funds over the next number of years. These initiatives will go a long way to ensuring that this region is well placed to reap the full benefits of the tourism growth enjoyed by the island as a whole.'

Minister Smith said: 'Regional tourism partnerships play an important part in developing the local economy through tourism projects such as these and I commend the Special European Union Programmes Body for funding both programmes.'

At the event, Angela Smith also spoke of the design for the planned new visitors' centre at the Giant's Causeway unveiled earlier in the day by the Secretary of State and said: 'The winning design for the new visitors' centre at the Giant's Causeway is a stunning piece of architecture that will provide a world-class facility for Northern Ireland's number one tourist attraction. With the launch of the North West and North East initiatives this region can be marketed as a seamless experience for tourists on both sides of the border.'

Minister O'Donoghue concluded: 'The unveiling of the design for the new visitors' centre at the Causeway is great news not just for tourism in Northern Ireland, but also for tourism across the island. The Causeway has always been one of the great icons of Ireland and I wish Minister Smith, her department and NITB every success in the implementation of this truly great project.'

Note: Destination North West is a joint marketing campaign between North West Tourism, Derry City Council and Fermanagh District Council. The campaign will run for two years and is receiving €1.5 million in grant aid from SEUPB. The total value of the campaign is €2 million.

The Destination North West project is an initiative aimed at developing a cross-border network to enable enhanced co-operation between tourism development and marketing agencies in the North West of Ireland. The project will create an area-based marketing initiative incorporating the development of events and gateway signage to enhance the visitor experience, focusing on the six counties of Derry, Tyrone, Fermanagh, Donegal, Sligo and Leitrim.

The Glens and Lakeland's objectives are: (1) to build strategic alliances and further develop an action plan with all partners within the region in order to build the reputation of the North East of Northern Ireland, Cavan and Monaghan region as a leading tourism destination within the island of Ireland; and (2) to identify and brand the North East of Northern Ireland, Cavan, Monaghan region as a tourism region and promote the key products of the area.

North West Tourism, based in Sligo, is receiving funding of €393,750 from INTERREGIIIA for the Glens and Lakelands project.

Source: Department of Arts, Sport and Tourism press release, 11 October 2005.

FUTURE TOURISM GROWTH

The World Tourism Organization has a long-term forecast for the world tourism industry, called the *Tourism 2020 Vision* (as discussed below). This forecast, along with many other analyses, predicts a growing dominance of technology and the emergence of new destinations, some of which are literally out of this world.

Technology

It is inevitable that technology will continue to advance, perhaps to levels that we cannot as yet imagine. If someone was to tell you in the 1990s that within a decade you would be able to conduct all business, including shopping for groceries, banking and ordering any good via a PC or laptop connected to a phone line (and later with wireless connection), you most likely would have said perhaps by 2020. If someone was to tell you that you could do all this from a hand-held communication device, at a cost much lower than the price of the 1990s, you would not have believed them. However, these are just a few of some of the impacts of the mass proliferation of new technologies like the internet, wireless communication, mobile technology, etc., and they are becoming more functional, faster and even cheaper year after year. It is inevitable, therefore, that technology will continue to advance and have a massive influence on all aspects of life, including how we find information about and buy tourism products and services.

Globalisation

Already we see the emergence of large regional organisations such as the European Union, which makes it easier for its citizens to travel within its borders, as well as harmonising external border controls. We will most likely see similar movements from other regional organisations, e.g. NAFTA, making travel easier. Globalisation will also lead to a further mixing of cultures, especially as previously closed-off markets like China and India (perhaps because of political or economic reasons) begin to open their markets and their citizens have political permission and economic wealth to travel to other destinations. This globalised effect will make more and more travellers curious about a destination and perhaps wish to explore it.

Air Travel

Air travel has become cheaper than ever before on local, regional and long-haul routes. Irish airline Ryanair is leading the way in Europe, as Southwest Airlines is in the US in terms of low-cost air travel. This is continuing to force traditional full-cost airlines to cut their fares to compete, the net benefit being felt by the customer in terms of lower fares, thus encouraging air travel. A key threat to this growth is the rising cost of fuel, although this has been offset to some degree in Europe when the euro trades strongly against the US dollar.

Space Tourism

This is not as far away from reality as some may think. As explorers, the human race is constantly looking for new and more exotic territories to explore. Space tourism obviously has such an appeal. The world has already seen some wealthy individuals who have paid large amounts of money to be taken into space on government missions, and so these are the world's first space tourists. American Dennis Tito (2001) and South African Mark Shuttleworth (2002) paid Space Adventures, based in Arlington, Virginia (US) and Moscow (Russia), to take them to the International Space Station, and Richard Branson has already discussed his plans for a *Virgin Galactic* service to satisfy the likely future demand for space tourism. Even the US$10 million X Project Prize (for the developer who can develop a shuttle that can be successfully launched to sub-orbital space and landed twice) has been won and is testament to the importance of this future growth area.

Terrorism

A key determinant of future growth is the pattern of terrorism, political stability and military action seen in the world. The first years of the new millennium have not been favourable to tourism growth based on war and terrorism. Continued terrorism and war will lead to slower levels of tourism growth.

Tourism 2020 Vision is the World Tourism Organization's long-term forecast and assessment of the development of tourism up to the first twenty years of the new millennium. An essential outcome of the *Tourism 2020 Vision* are quantitative forecasts covering a twenty-five-year period, with 1995 as the base year and forecasts for 2000, 2010 and 2020.

Although the evolution of tourism in the last few years has been irregular, UNWTO maintains its long-term forecast for the moment. The underlying structural trends of the forecast are believed not to have significantly changed. Experience shows that in the short term, periods of faster growth (1995, 1996, 2000) alternate with periods of slow growth (2001 and 2002). While the pace of growth until 2000 actually exceeded the *Tourism 2020 Vision* forecast, it is generally expected that the current slowdown will be compensated in the medium to long term.

UNWTO's *Tourism 2020 Vision* forecasts that international arrivals are expected to reach over 1.56 billion by the year 2020. Of these worldwide arrivals in 2020, 1.2 billion will be intraregional and 0.4 billion will be long-haul travellers.

The total tourist arrivals by region shows that by 2020 the top three receiving regions will be Europe (717 million tourists), East Asia and the Pacific (397 million) and the Americas (282 million), followed by Africa, the Middle East and South Asia.

East Asia and the Pacific, South Asia, the Middle East and Africa are forecasted to record growth at rates of over 5 per cent per year, compared to the world average of 4.1 per cent. The more mature regions – Europe and the Americas – are anticipated to show lower than average growth rates. Europe will maintain the highest share of world arrivals, although there will be a decline from 60 per cent in 1995 to 46 per cent in 2020.

Long-haul travel worldwide will grow faster, at 5.4 per cent per year over the period 1995–2020, than intraregional travel, at 3.8 per cent. Consequently, the ratio between intraregional and long-haul travel will shift from around 82:18 in 1995 to close to 76:24 in 2020.

Source: UNWTO.

Table 3.13: UNWTO's Tourism 2020 Vision Forecast

	Base Year	Forecasts		Market Share		Average Per Annum Growth Rate
		(millions)		(%)		(%)
	1995	2010	2020	1995	2020	1995–2020
World	565	1006	1561	100	100	4.1
Africa	20	47	77	3.6	5.0	5.5
Americas	110	190	282	19.3	18.1	3.8
East Asia and Pacific	81	195	397	14.4	25.4	6.5
Europe	336	527	717	59.8	45.9	3.1
Middle East	14	36	69	2.2	4.4	6.7
South Asia	4	11	19	0.7	1.2	6.2

Source: UNWTO.

REVISION QUESTIONS

1. What countries are the top spenders on tourism in the world?
2. How many foreign tourists did Ireland have in the most recent statistics (to the nearest million people)?
3. How much did foreign tourists spend in Ireland in the most recent statistics (to the nearest billion euro)?
4. What is the impact of higher levels of tourism tax revenue?
5. Explain the tourism income multiplier.
6. List the top tourism-generating countries.
7. How does tourism impact on a country's (a) employment and (b) balance of payments?

ESSAY QUESTIONS

1. (a) Outline the reasons for Irish tourism growth in the last twenty years.
   (b) List and briefly discuss the ways in which the Irish government benefits from tourism.
   (c) Briefly discuss the importance of tourism revenue to the regions.
2. List the areas of the Irish economy that benefit from tourism. Choose any two areas and discuss their importance to the Irish economy in detail.
3. 'The Irish government earns an excellent return on investment in tourism.' Discuss.
4. 'As visitors forsake regions and we evolve from traditional offerings, tourism in Ireland needs a new map.' Discuss.
5. 'The supply of tourism products is dependent on a range of factors, most notably those under the government's control.' Examine the validity of this statement, with particular emphasis on the situation in Ireland.

6. 'The value of tourism to the regions in Ireland is far greater than the published revenue figures.' Discuss.

TASKS

Divide the class into two roughly equal groups. Each group should be given 10 to 15 minutes to develop opposing points on the following statements, followed by a 40 to 45 minute debate.

Statement: Ireland is no longer an attractive place for tourism investment.

Statement: Tourism may bring income, but its social and environmental costs outweigh any advantages.

Statement: The Irish government purposefully exploits tourism taxation to increase exchequer revenue.

ASSIGNMENTS

1. Compile a report on why tourism has grown significantly since the 1950s. In your report, include graphs and statistics as well as specific examples.
2. Europe and America's share of world arrivals has dropped significantly over the last fifty years. Investigate why this is the case and present the findings to the class.
3. Investigate the key points of the *Tourism 2020 Vision* and analyse whether you believe them to be realistic. Compile your research and analysis into a short report.

Chapter 4

The Tourism Product: An Overview

SUMMARY

Chapter 4 gives a brief overview of the main elements of the tourism product, with specific emphasis on what tourists visiting Ireland can expect. The elements discussed briefly include:

- Accommodation.
- Transport.
- Visitor attractions.
- Food and beverage.
- Leisure and recreation.
- Amenities and tourist services.

Accommodation, transport and visitor attractions are discussed in detail in Chapter 5, Chapter 6 and Chapter 7, respectively.

LEARNING OUTCOMES

Having completed this chapter, the reader should be able to:

- Demonstrate a knowledge of what elements constitute the tourism product.
- Acquire a basic understanding of accommodation, transport and visitor attraction as an introduction to the three chapters dealing with them later in the book.
- Exhibit a better understanding of some of the other elements of the tourism product.

INTRODUCTION

'Tourism product' is the term used to describe all of the components on offer to a tourist. It includes the services and facilities which a tourist may require as part of their overall travel experience. Some of the components are necessary as part of the definition of tourism. You will recall from Chapter 1 that for tourism to take place, there must be movement away from the place of habitual residence and it must include at least one overnight stay. We can identify transport and accommodation as two components of the tourism product which satisfy each of these criteria, respectively.

The following are the key components of the tourism product. This is by no means an exhaustive list. The chapter dealing with these exclusively (if any) is shown in brackets.

- Accommodation (Chapter 5).
- Transport (Chapter 6).
- Visitor attractions (Chapter 7).
- Food and beverage.
- Leisure and recreation.
- Amenities and tourist services.

ACCOMMODATION

The concept of accommodation is dealt with in detail in Chapter 5. The primary focus of the chapter is the hotel sector. However, there are various forms of accommodation on offer in Ireland, as in any other market. The choice of accommodation is highly dependent on the guest's budget. At the low-cost end of the scale there are campsites and hostels, and at the opposite, high-cost end there are luxury hotels. There are several options in between and variations exist within each category of accommodation. This includes different grades and different costs as well as different meal options.

Caravan and Camping Sites

Ireland's climate does not lend itself well to an abundance of campsites. However, the price-conscious traveller or nature enthusiast can find campsites dotted throughout Ireland. Campsites on the continent generally have a great deal more to offer campers, including clean on-site shower and toilet facilities, cooking and laundry facilities, entertainment and a bar/restaurant, while some even have swimming pools and activity centres for children.

Many caravan sites in Ireland are populated by domestic tourists, few of which rent their caravans to foreign visitors. Most caravan owners pay an annual premium to a site manager/owner for the privilege of a space on the site. Facilities vary from site to site – some have running water and electricity, while others do not.

Hostels

An Óige is the Irish Youth Hostel Association (www.anoige.ie), listing twenty-four youth hostels located around Ireland. They offer hostel accommodation in various room types (large and small dormitories, private rooms, en-suite rooms) to backpackers, groups, families, students, school tours, sports clubs, members of Hostelling International as well as non-members. Hostel accommodation is extremely popular with predominantly young travellers, for example those inter-railing around Europe.

B&Bs, Guesthouses and Farmhouses

Like French and German *pensions*, Irish B&Bs (bed and breakfasts) and guesthouses are a popular choice for domestic and foreign travellers alike. A farmhouse B&B is a similar offering, the only difference being that the latter is located in the farmhouse of a (usually) working farm. Many are part of marketing alliances such as the Town & Country Homes Association or other co-operative organisations. Some of these establishments are simply spare bedrooms in family homes or run by parents of empty-nest homes who have turned their spare rooms into B&B rooms. The quality can vary, as can the facilities. Some are en-suite, while others have shared facilities. Many are registered with Fáilte Ireland, while those that are not make up what is known as the unapproved sector.

Apartments and Self-catering

Self-catering apartments are synonymous with package holidays, where the accommodation and transport are included in the price paid by the tourist. These are more common in sun destinations of the Mediterranean, for example, than Ireland. Self-catering accommodation in Ireland often takes the form of hiring a summer residence for a specified time (a week, two weeks), and as the name suggests, no meals are included. Generally, there is also no cleaning or linen service either.

Hotels

Hotels are perhaps the most discussed and researched element of accommodation. They can vary in size and standard, in price and in grade. Even from country to country, standards can differ immensely. What constitutes a five-star luxury hotel in South Africa, for example, is vastly different to what constitutes five-star in Ireland.

Budget Hotels

An emerging trend in the Irish hotel sector, budget hotels have been a major player in many other countries' accommodation sectors for decades. The most notable example is France, where budget hotels are an imposing force in the French accommodation sector. Budget hotels are similar in many ways to American motels (motor-hotels) and offer similar facilities as regular hotels, but without the frills.

→ Ibis, Travel Lodge

Cruises

Once only the playground of the wealthy, cruises have become much more affordable, while at the same time Irish and European levels of disposable income have increased, leaving more money to spend on luxury purchases such as a cruise holiday. Cruises are unique in tourism, as the form of transport is also the form of accommodation. New developments in cruises include the concept of low-cost cruises, pioneered by easyCruise, a company associated with easyJet airlines. Apart from large liners which provide luxury cruises around the Mediterranean or Caribbean, for example, local cruises along inland waterways such as the Shannon have also become very popular. Ireland often uses such imagery of cruising on the Shannon in its general tourism marketing to attract tourists to Ireland.

VFR

Ireland's largest single visitor group is the British. Many British tourists come to Ireland because they have family and friends living here, and many reside with them during their visit. This is termed the VFR segment – visiting friends and relatives. Unfortunately, this results in a large proportion of Ireland's inbound tourists not engaging paid accommodation at all.

TRANSPORT

Transport is a huge area of importance for Ireland, like any tourism destination. As an island, Ireland is heavily reliant on air and sea transport for inbound and outbound tourism. It cannot rely on road and rail transport for this purpose, except via Ireland's only land border – Northern Ireland. In the recent past, vast improvements to Ireland's transport infrastructure have been either completed or announced by the government. This includes:

- Upgrades and expansions at airports and ferry ports, including faster turnaround times.
- Extensions to Ireland's motorway network, including public-private partnerships and bypassing towns that were traditionally traffic bottlenecks on major national routes.
- Extensions to the existing LUAS and suburban rail lines as well as intercity rail expansion.
- Plans for Dublin underground metro lines.
- Opening of the Dublin Port Tunnel.

These have been completed under successive plans, including the National Development Plan 2000–2006, or are planned under plans such as Transport 21, announced in November 2005 by the Irish government.

Having a world-class transport network obviously benefits the inhabitants of the region. However, it is also a key driver in tourism growth. Crucially, it is of key importance for business tourism, as conference and congress organisers demand an excellent transport network before considering a destination to host an event.

Transport is discussed in detail in Chapter 6. Access transport to Ireland (including the ongoing battle between Ryanair and Aer Lingus for passengers to and from Ireland) is of key importance to Ireland as a tourism destination. The major changes that have taken place in the European and international airline industry are also discussed. Internal transport is also a key feature of the chapter, given that government and tourism agencies' strategy is to spread tourism throughout the regions, rather than focusing it on the urban centres of Ireland.

VISITOR ATTRACTIONS

The concept of visitor attractions is examined in detail in Chapter 7, as well as some of Ireland's attractions. Ireland has plenty of attractions to offer. These range from man-made cultural and heritage attractions to natural attractions. Together, they combine to present the visitor to Ireland with a unique experience, according to Tourism Ireland Ltd. Examples of Ireland's visitor attractions include galleries and museums, libraries and monuments, religious sites, heritage sites, castles and historic buildings as well as the arts.

Ireland does not have, nor does it claim to have, internationally renowned theme parks such as Disneyland or visitor attractions such as the Taj Mahal or Great Wall of China. These serve as attractions that bring tourists to them in their own right, rather than necessarily to the city that hosts them. Yet Ireland still attracts record tourist numbers who choose Ireland for whatever reason they do. Ireland's tourism agencies seem to have successfully moulded Ireland's heritage and history into a winning product offering that attracts ever-growing numbers of tourists.

FOOD AND BEVERAGE (F&B)

Ireland is not very famous for its indigenous culinary dishes, but it is becoming more famous for the high-quality food on offer as well as the fine dining experience and the high-quality chefs who have become brand names in their own right. Ireland has various categories of restaurants to offer, as well as a range of cafés, fast food and snack options. A new development is the concept of the café bars, which is part of the government's strategy to discourage binge alcohol consumption in Ireland and instead encourage continental-style café bars which sell food as well as alcoholic and non-alcoholic beverages.

The Licenced Vintners Association (LVA, www.lva.ie) promotes Dublin pubs as the best in the world, where friendly service and a delicious pub grub menu await visitors and locals alike. The organisation comprises 750 members (95 per cent of Dublin pubs) and dates back to 1817. Its main purpose it to represent Dublin pubs, their owners and their interests.

Although the Irish food and beverage trade has benefited from economic growth as well as the growth in tourism, it has suffered several setbacks recently. The smoking ban in force indoors of any public building in Ireland has led to a downturn in the pub trade, according to the LVA. Inevitably, stricter drink-driving legislation is also having an impact on pub revenue, especially in rural locations where public transport is not always available. This is coupled with massive increases in operating costs such as staff, rent, insurance, utilities, etc., which are severely impacting on profits of food and beverage providers. Prices in Irish restaurants and pubs are often perceived as extremely high, and the comparison is made easier by the euro single currency for tourists from those countries. This is despite claims from several restaurants and representative bodies that the profit margin on restaurant food is extremely low.

Customer service standards are often criticised, especially by tourists coming from a country where excellent customer service is paramount, e.g. the US. Finally, many staff members working in Irish restaurants and pubs do not always have a proficient level of English. All of these create a climate of uncertainty and volatility for Ireland's food and beverage industry.

Dublin turns from 'craic' to culture in bid to woo tourists
Dublin Tourism yesterday outlined proposals aimed at attracting more visitors to the city. Under the terms of the new plan, due to be launched in May, Dublin will be promoted as a city of culture, rather than one of just 'music, pubs and craic'.

Frank Magee, Dublin Tourism's chief executive, said that while these attributes had proved extremely attractive in bringing tourists to the city in the past, the ambition now was to embrace and build on what already exists with new ideas.

Last year [2005] the number of people visiting Dublin rose by 5 per cent, producing an 11 per cent gain in tourism revenue. Mr Magee said 2006 was also set to be a 'bumper year', with visitor numbers and revenue expected to increase by 7 and 9 per cent, respectively.

He said the ability of Dublin to attract visitors was essential to the overall Irish tourism market, as only 40 per cent of visitors actually leave the city for other parts of the country.

This is backed up by a report by the Irish Tourist Industry Confederation released at the end of last year showing that while the Dublin tourism market continued to grow last year, growth in many parts of rural Ireland was static.

As part of the new campaign, Dublin Tourism has expanded www.visitdublin.com to 5,000 pages and created downloadable podcasts, which can be used as self-guided walking tours around the city.

The majority of visitors to Dublin are expected to continue to come from Europe, though markets such as the Middle East are becoming increasingly important and the US remains a key market.

Source: 'Dublin turns from "craic" to culture in bid to woo tourists', *The Irish Times*, 17 January 2006.

LEISURE AND RECREATION

Recreation is defined as any activity carried out during free time, i.e. leisure time. Ireland has a great deal to offer in terms of leisure and recreation. This includes general entertainment, such as pubs and nightclubs, frequented by locals and visitors alike. There is also an abundance of traditional Irish entertainment such as traditional music and dancing. These all take place year round. However, there are annual festivals such as the Wexford Opera Festival, Cork Jazz Festival, Galway Races, Heineken Green Energy and the St Patrick's Festival which attract large tourist numbers from abroad as well as domestic tourists. Similarly, the many concerts (such as at Slane Castle, Croke Park, Phoenix Park), theatre festivals (Dublin International Theatre Festival) and film festivals (International Lesbian and Gay Film Festival) are just some examples of countless opportunities for recreation throughout Ireland.

Ireland also has a plethora of offerings in terms of sport, including both participative and spectator sports. The government minister in charge of tourism is also in charge of sports and arts, i.e. Minister for Arts, Sport and Tourism. Hence, there have been efforts to bring sports events to Ireland to boost tourism. Examples include the failed joint bid with Scotland to host the 2008 European Soccer Championship, as well as the successful bids to stage the 2003 Special Olympics World Summer Games and the 2006 Ryder Cup.

Apart from such internationally recognised events, there are many sporting activities available for visitors. Ireland is famous for its equestrian activities. County Kildare, for example, is known as 'The Thoroughbred County'. Race meetings that take place all over Ireland have become large festivals and are well-known by equestrian enthusiasts the world over.

Given that Ireland is an island, the Irish coastline is an attraction in its own right in terms of fishing and water sports, weather permitting. Inland waterways also offer fishing opportunities. Other sporting activities include shooting, walking and cycling to name just a few.

Finally, soccer and rugby serve to attract international tourists to Ireland's shores for international games, such as FIFA World Cup qualifier matches, as well as Six Nations and Heineken Cup rugby matches. These, together with GAA sports, also attract large numbers of domestic tourists to the event.

AMENITIES AND TOURIST SERVICES

We may forget that tourists to Ireland require many of the same day-to-day services and amenities that locals do, such as banking, post office, laundry, medical and health and beauty services. General and gift shopping are also some of the services that both tourists and locals enjoy.

Some specific services that a tourist needs include tourist information services, which are provided by tourist information offices (TIOs) located in major tourist destinations throughout Ireland. These provide accommodation reservation facilities, brochures, maps, event guides and transport listings.

Speech by John O'Donoghue, TD, Minister for Arts, Sport and Tourism, at the launch of Irish Tourist Assistance Service

Ladies and gentlemen, I am delighted to be here today to launch the Irish Tourist Assistance Service. As Minister for Tourism, I am very glad that the excellent services provided by the former Tourist Victim Support Service will now continue to be provided by the new organisation.

I believe it is fortunate that the change of name and company structure in this instance does not also mean a change in key personnel, administration staff and volunteers. Thankfully, those who contributed so much to the success of TVSS are remaining with ITAS, and this will ensure continuity and further success. The new name is most appropriate and is a reflection of the key contribution the service makes to the tourism industry.

Being a victim of crime at any time is traumatic, but being victimised while in a foreign country can be even more traumatic, especially if there are language, cultural or legal difficulties. The excellent help that the ITAS provides to victims deserves all our support. The value of the service can be seen from the fact that a large majority of tourists seen by the service continue with their holidays and go home with an overall positive image of Ireland, which from a tourism perspective is extremely important.

Tourism is at the heart of our economy and Irish tourism continues to grow. In 2005, the number of overseas visitors to Ireland reached not far off 7 million, the highest ever recorded. People increasingly choose destinations that are welcome and safe. In international terms, Ireland is a very safe destination. But, like any country, things can sometimes go wrong and if they do, it is up to the industry to try to make it right.

ITAS underpins this responsibility by providing assistance to victims of crime and support, also to visitors who require help because they may have mislaid or lost vital documents such as passports, credit cards, etc. The skill and knowledge of the staff and volunteers in helping visitors with problems, not only in Dublin, but throughout the country is something which we as a country can be justifiably proud. I understand that there is only one other country in Europe where a similar service is provided and, unlike ours, it is not a national service.

I know that ITAS works with many organisations in the tourism and hospitality industry to ensure that the best possible assistance is given to victimised tourists. It is important for the future well-being of the service that the support base is as broad as possible. I feel that the rebranding will be viewed positively within the industry and I appeal to the tourism industry to continue to support this very worthy service.

Source: Department of Arts, Sport and Tourism speeches archive, 8 March 2006.

CONCLUSIONS

The tourism product in Ireland is more than the sum of its parts – it is more than a collection of hotels and transport providers, heritage sites and festivals, pubs and clubs, theatre and nature walks. The Irish tourism product is the unique set of these variables that the tourist, whether domestic or international, combines into the set of experiences and memories they take from their holiday in Ireland. There are many challenges ahead if Ireland is to maintain its unprecedented tourism growth in revenue and tourist arrivals. There are further challenges ahead from other destinations Ireland must compete effectively with for its share of the world tourism spend. However, Ireland is well placed to meet these challenges if the industry and the government continue working together with a clear goal of being marketing orientated – that is, putting the customer (tourist) first and building all future tourism plans around the tourist.

REVISION QUESTIONS

1. (a) List the elements of the tourism product.
   (b) Can you think of any other elements that should be added?
2. What is meant by the terms 'leisure' and 'recreation'?

ESSAY QUESTIONS

1. Comment on the current competitive position of the following transport elements in Irish tourism:
   - Ferries.
   - Traditional airlines.
   - Low-cost airlines.
   - Rail.
   - Coach/bus travel.
   - Car hire.
2. 'A good tourist destination must have a wide range of food and beverage options.' Discuss.
3. 'The modern tourism product includes a range of elements and activities which are often overlooked by tourism agencies.' Discuss.

TASKS

Divide the class into two roughly equal groups. Each group should be given ten to fifteen minutes to develop opposing points on the following statements, followed by a forty to forty-five minute debate.

Statement: A tourist destination is only as good as its visitor attractions.

Statement: The amenities and services available in a destination play no role whatsoever in attracting people to a destination.

Statement: The Irish tourism product is generally a let-down to tourists.

Statement: The Irish welcome's dead and gone.

ASSIGNMENTS

1. You are a tourism management consultant and you have been contracted by a client to compile a report on the components of the Irish tourism product. The client wants the report to contain examples of specific companies offering the specific elements of the tourism product discussed in the report. Prepare the report as well as a thirty-minute multimedia presentation to include colour pictures and video clips.

Chapter 5

Accommodation

SUMMARY

Given the importance of accommodation to the tourism industry, this chapter outlines various types of accommodation, ranging from farmhouses to B&Bs, hostels to hotels. The chapter outlines the various accommodation terminologies in use worldwide and the major grading structures used, particularly for hotels. The Irish accommodation sector is discussed with relevant examples. The chapter also outlines the economics and cost structures associated with accommodation providers, especially hotels, given that more than half of Ireland's rooms offered for hire are located in hotels.

Chapter 5 presents two opposing forms of accommodation, as it compares and contrasts budget hotels to five-star hotels. Firstly, the luxury and five-star (and beyond) phenomenon is analysed. The grading criteria and standards required to be a five-star luxury hotel are illustrated. There is also a focus on service in this section. Secondly, it defines budget hotels and outlines why they have grown in popularity. It also presents the economics of budget hotels as well as the marketing and distribution strategies employed by them. The chapter concludes with future projections for the accommodation sector.

LEARNING OUTCOMES

Having completed this chapter, the reader should be able to:
- Define the basic types of accommodation.
- Illustrate an understanding of the various accommodation terminologies used in the industry.
- Describe the Irish accommodation sector.
- Understand the grading structure of accommodation.
- Appreciate economic factors impacting on the sector.
- Demonstrate an understanding of both budget and luxury offerings.
- Consider possible future projections for the industry.

INTRODUCTION

Accommodation is an integral part of the travel and tourism industry. As you will recall from our definition of tourism, tourism involves at least one overnight stay at a place away from that of habitual residence. This chapter deals with the place where the tourist may stay. In Ireland (as in most countries), there is a wide variety of accommodation options to suit all visitor tastes, demands and budgets. Since the

1990s, Irish and especially Dublin accommodation has grown significantly. There was a time in the 1990s where the number of bedrooms in Dublin accommodation could not keep up with the demand from overseas and domestic visitors.

The main developments recently have included the expansion of the luxury hotel sector. As Ireland became more of a fashionable short break and holiday destination amongst the wealthy tourists of the world, the demand for higher-priced, full-service and high-quality luxury accommodation became essential. Dublin city centre is just one of Ireland's cities that answered the call for such establishments, and the late 1990s and early 2000s saw the development of many luxury hotels in the capital, most notably around the St Stephen's Green, e.g. Fitzwilliam Hotel, Stephen's Green Hotel, and Ballsbridge areas, e.g. Four Seasons.

Budget hotels have also seen an increase in demand, as more price-sensitive domestic and international travellers seek out quality, standardised accommodation at affordable prices. These tourists forsake the opulence of the luxury city centre hotels in favour of a reasonable overnight rate in comfortable lodgings, perhaps on the periphery or suburbs of the city.

Even further down the cost ladder are the youth hostels. Hostels around Ireland's cities, towns and villages (as well as in isolated areas) have increased in popularity. This comes not only from price-sensitive travellers, but also those seeking a different holiday experience, e.g. green tourism, nature walks, etc.

ACCOMMODATION TERMS

- **B&B**: Bed and breakfast.
- **Bed nights**: Number of rooms available in a particular timeframe, e.g. 100 rooms x 365 nights in a year = 36,500 bed nights in a year for a 100-room hotel.
- **Bed stock**: Number of rooms available in a hotel/city.
- **Budget hotel**: Limited service but usually comfortable lodging accommodation.
- **Categorisation**: Refers to separation of accommodation by type.
- **Classification**: Physical features of accommodation, e.g. Georgian townhouse.
- **Full board**: Room and breakfast as well as lunch and dinner.
- **Grading**: Quality rating assigned by reputable agency.
- **Half board**: Room and breakfast, with either lunch or dinner.
- **Hotel**: A lodging accommodation offering rooms for hire for leisure or business (at least fifteen rooms under Irish law); of varying quality depending on grading.
- **Hotel chain/consortia**: Group of hotels that co-operate in key functional areas, e.g. marketing and distribution.
- **Hotelier**: Hotel manager or management company running a hotel.
- **Rack rate**: Full published rate, not discounted.

The Term 'Hotel'

Sangster (2003) defines the concept of a hotel as:

> ... *a business that, as its main activity, rents at least four bedrooms [fifteen rooms under Irish law]. The rooms need to be available to the general public who must*

be able to rent the room for a minimum of one night. Excluded are guesthouses, farmhouses, private clubs, hostels and boarding houses. Hotel groups are defined as organisations responsible for, on a continuing basis, at least one management function for more than one hotel.

According to Marvel (2004), there is a problem with endeavouring to develop a global definition of the concept of a 'hotel'. The author notes:

In some countries, such as Italy, lodging establishments that might fall into the category of inns, boarding houses ('pensions'), or guesthouses in other countries, are counted as hotels. Also, for some countries, there are no official statistics for accommodation capacity.

Hotel Chain/Consortia

It is also difficult to agree a uniform definition of the various forms of alliances and co-operative arrangements that exist internationally in the hotel sector. Sangster (2003) defines consortia as:

... loose associations of hotels that typically focus on one or two management functions such as marketing and/or distribution. The individual hotel is usually owner-operator managed although sometimes both private companies and public companies can have some or all of their hotels within a consortium.

Marvel (2004) adds that:

*For the average independent European hotel, the best affiliation solution is often to be found with a **voluntary chain** or **consortium**. These two terms are basically synonymous and refer to loosely structured hotel groupings that demand less of the individual hotelier in terms of conformity to rigidly prescribed standards, and, especially, in terms of cost. Whilst the independent hotelier will pay between 7 per cent and 10 per cent of his annual room revenues for an integrated chain brand franchise, such as Holiday Inn or Ibis, voluntary affiliations typically cost much less – between 1 per cent and 2 per cent. In fact, yearly franchise fees charged by an integrated chain often represent only the 'tip of the iceberg', as compared to the total outlays necessary to renovate and maintain a property to the chain's standards. Another advantage to the hotelier is the ease with which the affiliation can be cancelled, usually within a period of two years or less, as opposed to chain franchise or management agreements which typically stretch over a decade or more... Consortia operate by grouping together independently owned hotels and then marketing them as one single brand. The problems with the approach are in the competing demands of providing consistency to the guest and allowing the independent owners to run their businesses in the way they see fit. Consortia are not surprisingly rather weak on brand standards, generally being more of a collection of hotels than what might be considered a hard brand.*

THE ACCOMMODATION PRODUCT

In Ireland, there are 7,643 establishments registered as offering a variety of different accommodation options for visitors (2005 figures, up from 7,590 in 2004). As illustrated in Table 5.1, Ireland's bed stock is approximately 84,000 rooms, more than half of which are classed as hotel rooms.

Table 5.1: Bed stock in Ireland (2005)

	Number of Premises	Rooms (to nearest thousand)
Hotels	854	46,000
Guesthouses	448	5,000
Farmhouses and Town and Country Homes*	3,161	13,000
Self-catering	3,000	8,000
University Accommodation	13	3,000
Hostels**	167	9,000

*Includes specialist and pub accommodation.
**Two hostel beds constitute one room.
Source: Gulliver/Fáilte Ireland.

Table 5.2 depicts type of accommodation visitors to Ireland stayed in, illustrated by each of Ireland's main generating markets individually. As we can see, the largest users of hotels are the North Americans. On the lower-cost end of the scale, very few visitors stay in caravans, hostels or on campsites (5 per cent altogether). There is a balanced spread between most markets illustrated for most other forms of accommodation, with the exception of the friends/relatives segment. A large proportion (44 per cent) of Ireland's number one visitor market (Britain) stays with friends or relatives. Indeed, each of the key markets illustrated posted an increase in this segment on the previous year's figures. This has a major impact on accommodation revenue for Irish accommodation operators.

Table 5.2: Distribution of Bed Nights as Percentage (2005)

	Total	Britain	Mainland Europe	North America	Rest of World
Hotels	21	24	15	34	13
Guesthouses/B&Bs	13	10	14	17	12
Rented	20	14	27	15	18
Caravan and Camping	2	2	3	<0.5	1
Hostels	3	1	4	3	5
Friends/Relatives	32	44	24	25	42
Other	9	6	13	6	10
Million Nights	50.7	17.5	20.6	8.8	3.8

Source: Fáilte Ireland/Central Statistics Office.

B&B sector hungry for change, recovery

With 'themed B&Bs' and higher standards, we can rebuild a sector of our tourism economy which has been in steady decline, writes **Alan Hill**.

The extraordinary growth of our tourism industry over the last twenty years was built on the highly successful marketing of three important components of the Irish holiday experience – our great people, the relaxed pace of life and our beautiful, unspoiled scenery. Nowhere were all three found in greater proximity or abundance than in a bed & breakfast holiday, where visitors delighted in the expert local knowledge and warm welcome of several Irish families as they wound their way around our rural areas, soaking in the unique charms of the island.

Ireland gave the world the concept of the B&B. We defined it and were unequalled in its delivery. However, much like tourism itself, the B&B sector is now at a crossroads where the old ways no longer work as effectively, and strategic action taken in the near future will determine whether this sector can once again be elevated to its position of unequalled importance, especially in regional economies.

Town & Country Homes is the largest representative body for the registered B&B sector, with nearly 1,400 island-wide members. Over the last year we have attempted to understand this decline and, importantly, to identify strategic actions that will help sustain the sector. We have consulted our members on how we move forward and the valuable feedback can be summarised thus: we need to modernise, to improve marketing, embrace technology and consolidate the traditional welcome, which is our most unique and valuable feature.

We need to remind ourselves that a B&B holiday experience is taken in a family home of no fewer than three bedrooms and no more than six. All properties are independently approved. What makes the product so special is the access it gives to an authentic Ireland and the Irish. Millions of visitors from around the world have experienced this personal touch, which often gives them the memories that confirm Ireland as a special tourism destination. More than three-quarters of all our members have properties in non-urban areas, thus the impact on the rural economy must never be underestimated. A recent survey indicates that the average price of a B&B home in Ireland is over €500,000, with 98 per cent of all rooms in rural areas en-suite. This confirms that the sector has invested and continues to invest in upgrading its properties.

Over the last few years all has not been perfect in tourism. We have engineered an industry that is regionally imbalanced, with 80 per cent of visitors going to the east and south of this country. The phenomenal growth of the hotel sector, nurtured through tax breaks and incentives, has increased its room capacity by nearly 75 per cent in less than ten years, while we have seen an alarming decline of 26 per cent in the number of registered B&Bs over the same period. A quick scan of the back pages of our national newspapers demonstrates the glut of hotels that tend to use price and special offers to bring in business at any cost. This obviously has had a huge impact on the commercial sustainability of our sector, especially in the under-performing areas. In addition the retirement of older operators from the sector, together with the lack of new B&B entrants coming in to replace them, has been an unhealthy feature over the last number of years.

The sector's decline can also be explained by a lack of confidence and capacity within the sector to change, a more complex global market and sometimes ineffective alliances with our external partners. We acknowledge the strategic value of the recent B&B research by Fáilte Ireland, and we are keen to support the Product Development Review Group. This gives us confidence that our transformation process will be encouraged and facilitated at the highest level of national tourism development.

If we mine deeper this downturn is complex and it would be naïve to attribute it entirely to one cause. Undoubtedly, the sector generally has not kept up to speed with the demands of the global customer. Our product offering, built on a warm Irish welcome in a comfortable home, has not altered much over the last two generations. We have not kept pace with current fashions and tastes of some consumers. We must work hard to regain lost ground and reposition ourselves for the new generation. Do our tourists really seek homogeneity of experience in every country they visit? More probingly, does the personal touch and interaction of a great B&B symbolise an Ireland we would like to believe we have left behind? If so, what does this say about us?

The B&B experience, however, is not defined by the measurement of a bed or the meat content of a sausage, but by the warmth and friendliness you receive during your stay. As an experiment, visualise in detail a memorable recent holiday you have had. I suggest that what you imagine will be led by a friendly waiter, a knowledgeable guide or an extraordinary host rather than by something material. This is the essence of the Irish B&B experience and explains why so many international visitors (and agents) have found it so attractive. The greatest single contribution the sector can make to sustaining its business in the short term is to continue to refine and hone this special welcome.

Fresh thinking is needed to create a holistic and tailored approach to business support for the sector (incentives, training, product development and promotion all working in harmony). In essence, a national B&B development plan with all partners pulling together. Our vision for the Irish B&B product is built on a dynamic network of hundreds of themed B&Bs. These could vary from the mainstream examples of walking, angling and golf to niche offerings like disability holidays, genealogy, language learning (English and Irish), heritage/culture, wellness and food. All this is underpinned by an internationally respected standard of delivery and environmental good practice dovetailing with the best tourism marketing on the planet.

A tourism landscape without a dynamic B&B sector would be a cold, sterile place. The sector is hungry for change. Next Wednesday our members will be voting on a new constitution which embodies the values and aims of a modern organisation that can lead the way for the sector. By professionalising, innovating and working in partnership, the B&B sector has a vital and exciting role to play in the ongoing development of our much admired and imitated tourism economy.

Alan Hill is chief executive, Town & Country Homes.

Source: Hill, A., 'Wake-up call for B&Bs', *The Irish Times*, 26 March 2006.

THE IRISH HOTEL SECTOR

The hotel sector in Ireland is made up of Irish and international organisations. Some Irish hotels are family owned and run, while others (which perhaps began that way) are large, international players, e.g. Jurys-Doyle group. The Irish hotel sector is similar to many other countries in terms of the increasing dominance of international hotel chains. These large chains are often driven by market dominance and have the power of large, internationally recognisable brands, e.g. Hilton, Holiday Inn. Further, they are able to offer a wide range of accommodation types and prices to suit leisure and business travellers alike. Ireland's hotel chain growth rate is the highest in Europe, estimated at 135 per cent over the period 2000–2004. However, at 18 per cent, overall chain penetration in Ireland is below Europe's average of 24 per cent.

The Fitzpatrick hotel group has revamped its www.fitzpatrickhotels.com website, offering visitors 360-degree virtual tours of the hotel facilities, real-time online booking and what it claims is Ireland's first link to websites in Times Square and Fifth Avenue in New York.

Group marketing director John Costigan said the hotel industry will become e-commerce driven over the coming months, and the group's new website will be 'a major cornerstone of our future strategy'.

Visitors to the site can download recipes that use Bailey's Cream and there is information on Irish whiskey. The Fitzpatrick group, which has the Fitzpatrick Manhattan Hotel and Fitzpatrick Grand Central Hotel on the site, is also using the website to recruit staff.

Source: *The Sunday Business Post*, 6 August 2000.

Irish hotels have seen increased room capacity available after several years of under-capacity. Such under-capacity can be a major threat to a tourist destination. Increased demand with a smaller supply inevitably drives prices up and creates a perception of a high-priced destination for many tourists, given the fact that a large proportion of many tourists' spend is devoted to accommodation (this of course excludes the VFR – visiting friends and relatives – sector). Although the capacity issue is being addressed, prices are continuing to rise in Irish hotels. The average price of a hotel in Dublin is amongst the highest in the EU.

Irish hotels are represented by the Irish Hotels Federation (IHF, www.ihf.ie), which represents the industry's interests to government as well as engaging in marketing and support activities, including the Quality Employer scheme, which regulates employment practices for member hotels.

HOTEL OPERATIONS

It is common nowadays for medium and large hotels to be owned by property companies and for a hotelier to operate a management contract, franchise or lease. This implies that there are two businesses operating in different markets. Firstly, a property company actually owns the hotel land and building. They are seeking an opportunity for an investment vehicle which will provide short-term income (rent, profit sharing) as well as long-term income (capital appreciation). Secondly, the hotelier or hotel management company is operating in the welcome business – the business of hospitality. They run the hotel and often the restaurant and/or bar attached for a profit. If a rental or profit-sharing scheme is in place, the hotelier is released from finance arrangements with lenders and the cost becomes semi-variable.

Asset management structure

In general in Europe, as compared to North America, franchising is less present as brand structure. On the other hand, leasing is far more important than in other parts of the world. Accor is almost an exception amongst the largest hotel chains in the world in the sense that it still owns or leases a large proportion (over 60 per cent) of its total operated capacity, and it makes relatively little use of franchises (20 per cent of the total) in spite of a high commitment to the budget sector. In Europe, the proportion of franchises is somewhat higher at 30 per cent, but the proportion of rooms owned and leased is similar, at 63 per cent. However, the percentage of rooms under management contract is significantly lower in Europe, at 7 per cent versus 17 per cent worldwide.

Source: Marvel, M., 'European hotel chain expansion', *Travel and Tourism Analyst*, May 2004.

COST AND PRICING

In hotels, the cost structure contains a large fixed component. This includes finance charges in the case of a loan secured on the property, labour, fixtures and fittings, energy, maintenance, etc. Whether there are one or 100 guests staying on any given night, the above costs would still have to be met.

A hotelier will strive to sell all rooms at the highest published rate – the rack rate. This is the ideal scenario, but an unrealistic one. Often the hotelier must make a choice between selling fewer rooms at the full rate or more rooms at a lower rate. The decision is not always an easy one, as the following example shows.

Let's say a hotel has 100 rooms and a rack rate of €200. If all rooms were sold at rack rate, the total revenue for the night would be €20,000 – this is the theoretical maximum revenue for full occupancy at full rack rate.

If the hotel offered sixty rooms at the rack rate of €200, the total revenue would be €12,000.

However, the hotelier could decide to sell more rooms at a specially reduced rate of €150 to boost sales, e.g. ninety rooms at €150, yielding revenue of €13,500.

Selling more rooms at a reduced rate increases revenue by €1,500. However, the increase in revenue comes at the expense of opening an extra thirty rooms, all of which need to be recleaned and reserviced, not to mention the extra service the guests may require during their stay as well as an extra thirty rooms for breakfast. Therefore, the extra revenue raised through the specially reduced price may easily be swallowed up by increasing variable costs.

In reality, the cost and pricing structure of hotels is not so simple. Like airline seats, hotel rooms are sold at different rates, depending on how the guest books, e.g. internet versus travel agent versus marketing agency, as well as when the guest books. Often, hoteliers will have one price for the prospective guest who calls the hotel direct or logs on to the hotel website. This is usually the rack rate or a specially discounted rate, which can be updated frequently as required. Another rate applies to prospective guests who book through a marketing agency or consortium. The rate is agreed between the hotel and the agency/consortium, who markets the hotel along with other member hotels, and guests book directly with the agency/consortium, who in turn pay the hotel the agreed flat fee per room and mark these rooms up to make their profit. Often, such organisations have a set allocation of rooms for sale which the hotel cannot sell unless certain criteria are met, e.g. if the room remains unsold by the agency/consortium forty-eight hours before the date, then the hotel may sell it if there is a booking enquiry directly to them. Finally, different rates apply to various other distribution methods. Tour operators, travel retailers and e-tailers (online agencies) take different commission rates, depending on what the agreement is. Last-minute agencies such as accommodation desks in airports, ferry ports and train stations are often a lifeline for hoteliers who panic as a result of unsold rooms. (Remember, accommodation is a service, and as such any unsold capacity cannot be stored and resold tomorrow. If a room remains unsold on any given night, the potential revenue is lost forever.) Commission rates for last-minute agencies are also pre-agreed. Online last-minute agencies such as www.lastminute.com or www.laterooms.com often do not take a commission at source. Rather, some of them send an invoice to the hotel claiming their commission or a set annual fee for membership. An exception to this is the www.gulliver.ie reservations system (online and desk presence in many ports), who take their commission at the time of booking.

OCCUPANCY MEASUREMENT

Most types of accommodation have a fixed supply of rooms or beds for letting. A campsite or caravan site is a notable exception where the supply can be added to, but even these have finite space.

As mentioned previously, an accommodation manager such as a hotelier would like to sell their full capacity at the highest rate possible, i.e. full occupancy at rack rate.

Table 5.3: Percentage of Irish Hotel Room Occupancy by Region (2001–2004)

	2000	2001	2002	2003	2004
National	68	63	61	62	62
Dublin	76	71	68	69	70
Mid. East	60	55	56	53	51
South East	65	56	61	60	60
South West	70	65	62	63	64
Shannon	66	64	63	61	59
West	58	53	47	54	56
North West	59	57	52	56	53

Source: Fáilte Ireland.

Occupancy is a very important indicator for hoteliers. It gives an indication of profitability as well as general statistics and trends for the property. Most hotel front-desk computer packages have built-in occupancy formulae, providing the hotelier with rapidly available occupancy information. The following occupancy formulae are amongst the most common indicators used:

- **Basic occupancy rate:** Percentage of rooms used on any given night.
- **Bed occupancy rate:** Number of guests physically accommodated as a percentage of maximum capacity.
- **Revenue occupancy:** Comparison of total revenue on one particular night in comparison to maximum revenue (full occupancy at rack rate).

Example
Hotel New Ross has 100 rooms. Each room has two single zip and lock beds, whose base and mattress can be joined together to create a double bed. Therefore, each room can be a double room (one double bed) or a twin room (two single beds) as required. The rack rate is €100 per night.
    On one particular night:

- Thirty-five rooms are set as double rooms, occupied by couples at a rack rate of €100 per room.
- Twenty rooms are set as double rooms, occupied by couples at a group discount rate of €75 per room.
- Fifteen rooms are set as twin rooms, occupied by a travelling sports team at a group discount rate of €65 per room.
- Eight rooms are set as double rooms, occupied by one person each at a single occupancy rate of €60 per room.

Occupancy:
Room occupancy $35 + 20 + 15 + 8$
                         = 78 rooms occupied out of 100 total
                         = 78 per cent room occupancy

Bed occupancy	35 rooms x 2 guests, 20 rooms x 2 guests, 15 rooms x 2 guests, 8 rooms x 1 guest = 148 guests
	148 guests out of maximum 200 guests =
	74 per cent bed occupancy

Revenue occupancy

35 rooms x €100	= €3,500
20 rooms x €75	= €1,500
15 rooms x €65	= €975
8 rooms x €60	= €480
Total revenue	= €6455

Theoretical maximum
100 rooms x €100   = €10,000
65 per cent (64.55 per cent) revenue occupancy

From these figures, the hotelier can easily see that on the night in question, the hotel had 78 per cent room occupancy, 74 per cent bed occupancy and 65 per cent revenue occupancy. We must always remember that any accommodation provider/hotelier would like to sell 100 per cent of the rooms (full occupancy) at rack rate.

GRADING

Grading is a very important yet often controversial feature of accommodation marketing. It was introduced to make it easier for guests and prospective guests to evaluate accommodation prior to purchase and is an inherent feature of hotel accommodation around the world.

The old Irish grading system caused much confusion to international guests, as it deviated from the world norm. An internationally recognisable classification system was required, and hence the star rating system was introduced to Ireland.

| ***** | 5 stars | Highest standard (Ireland and most countries) |
| * | 1 star | Low standard |

In the article 'Group Hotels' (*Travel and Tourism Analyst*, February 2003), Sangster notes that:

> *Star ratings symbolise the level of service, range of facilities and quality of guest care that you can expect. Hotels are required to meet progressively higher standards as they move up the scale from one to five star.*

He presents a definition of what constitutes each of the star ratings, as follows.

What hotel star ratings mean

One star
Practical accommodation with a limited range of facilities and services, but a high standard of cleanliness throughout. Restaurant/eating area. Three-quarters of bedrooms will have en-suite or private facilities.

Two star
Better equipped bedrooms, all with en-suite/private bathroom and a colour television. A lift is normally available.

Three star
Higher standard of services and facilities, including larger public areas and bedrooms, a receptionist, room service, laundry.

Four star
Accommodation offering superior comfort and quality; all bedrooms with en-suite bath, fitted overhead shower and WC. Spacious and well-appointed public areas. More emphasis on food and drink. Room service of all meals and twenty-four-hour drinks, refreshments and snacks. Dry cleaning service available. Excellent customer service.

Five star
A spacious, luxurious establishment offering you the highest international quality of accommodation, facilities, services and cuisine. There will be a range of extra facilities.

In some countries the star rating system extends to seven stars. Such hotels are extremely high quality. One such example of this is the United Arab Emirates, home to the seven-star Burj al Arab Hotel, which has become known as the world's most luxurious hotel, located in the new tourism hot spot of Dubai.

The grading system in Ireland is regulated by legislation. Fáilte Ireland has responsibility for grading Irish accommodation. There are also private grading systems in place around the world. Some of the best-known internationally are AA, RAC and Egon Ronay. These have become trusted names, and the quality systems they use (be it stars, ribbons, rosettes, etc.) have become trusted as a signifier of quality.

In conjunction with the star rating, a shamrock approved system denotes accommodation which is registered with and approved by Fáilte Ireland. This is often an important indicator for many tourists, given the amount of unapproved accommodation providers in Ireland, i.e. those offering accommodation without registering with Fáilte Ireland.

Fáilte Ireland outsources the grading of Irish accommodation, but still sets the standards, policies and framework for grading. It also monitors the effectiveness of the company to which it has outsourced these tasks. The RTAs and Shannon

Development approve the self-catering accommodation sector. For hotels and guesthouses, grading and approval is currently outsourced to a company called Tourist Accommodation Management Services Ltd (TAMS), while for B&Bs it is outsourced to Tourism Accommodation Approvals Limited (TAA). Their predecessor, Excellence in Tourism Ltd, caused outrage in the summer of 2004 by downgrading four prestigious Dublin hotels from five stars to four stars. These were:

- The Shelbourne Hotel, St Stephen's Green.
- The Radisson SAS, Stillorgan Road.
- Jurys Ballsbridge.
- The Conrad on Earlsfort Terrace.

Fáilte Ireland ordered their reinstatement as five-star pending their appeal on the downgrading. The Shelbourne Hotel decided to remain unclassified for the time being, and has since closed for refurbishment.

While grading is an important marketing tool, some accommodation providers remain unclassified for different reasons. Some are not long enough in business to be fully assessed, and so wait until they are established before seeking a star rating. Some are undergoing redevelopment and so wait for their star rating after the completion of the work. Finally, some are simply not happy with the grade they are awarded and so remain unclassified.

New Hotel and Guest House Regulations to come into operation on 1 May 2003

The Minister for Arts, Sport and Tourism, John O'Donoghue, TD, today welcomed the bringing forward of the commencement date for the new Bord Fáilte [now Fáilte Ireland] Hotel and Guest House Regulations, which set out the minimum requirements for such establishments. The new commencement date, agreed by all parties concerned, is 1 May next.

The main changes being introduced relate to the size of establishments, the size of rooms and arrangements for the provision of food and beverages. For example, the minimum number of rooms necessary for hotel status in urban areas will be reduced from twenty to fifteen, bringing it in line with the rest of the country; there will be significant increases in the minimum size requirements for guest bedrooms, and bathrooms must be en-suite; and while hotels will still be required to serve quality meals and refreshments at reasonable hours, they will no longer be required to maintain full restaurant-style service at all times.

'These new regulations are more reflective of modern best practice and changes in consumer tastes and practices,' said the Minister, who stressed the importance of offering our visitors the highest standards.

Source: Department of Arts, Sport and Tourism press release, 26 March 2003.

WHAT IS FIVE STAR?

Five-star hotels are the most luxurious hotel offerings in Ireland, as in many destinations. It is worth noting, however, that what makes a five-star hotel in Ireland may not be classed as a five-star hotel in other countries, and vice versa. Fáilte Ireland's *Classification System for Hotels in Ireland* is a twenty-seven-page document setting out the many criteria which a hotel wishing to be classified as a five-star hotel must satisfy. The document regulates standards in all aspects of the hotel, including reception, bedrooms, bathrooms, dining, bar and car park. The following are some of the requirements:

- A staff member must be present to park residents' cars and the hotel must have its own parking area.
- The hotel must have a lift if it is three or more stories high.
- There must be a porter's desk separate from the reception desk and it must be staffed by a uniformed concierge.
- Reception desk must be staffed twenty-four hours a day in city hotels.
- At least a quarter of all rooms must have a safety deposit box.
- They must have facilities to book theatre, car hire and travel.
- They must have fax, typing and photocopying facilities.
- Double rooms must be at least 18.5 metres square.
- TV and radio must be controllable from the bed.
- Twenty-four-hour valet service.
- Laundry facilities.
- Nightly bed linen turn-down service.
- Room service department, with full menus in each room.
- A manager, proprietor or senior deputy must be available twenty-four hours.
- At least one staff member on the day and evening shifts must be able to conduct business in French and German.

Dining in a five-star hotel is also regulated in the document. It includes the following key points:

- Dining facilities must include a *table d'hôte* menu (set menu) and an *à la carte* menu (various items prices individually).
- Napkins must be provided for all meals.
- Secure and staffed cloakroom facilities must be provided.

BUDGET HOTELS

On the opposite side of the scale from five-star hotels are budget hotels. A budget hotel is a limited-service lodging accommodation offering the benefit of good value for money in standardised, modern accommodation. The aim is to provide a good-quality, low-priced accommodation for leisure and business tourists who are looking for guaranteed standards at affordable prices. Budget hotels are similar to American motels (motor hotels), which are limited-service lodging accommodation located primarily along American highways and freeways. Before budget hotels, affordable prices were found in low star-rated hotels. Standards vary amongst budget hotel companies, but in general, the guest can expect a comfortable stay without the luxury of more expensively priced hotels. Therefore, the quality in budget hotels is usually as good as three- or four-star hotels without the frills. Budget hotels are sometimes referred to as the Ryanair of the hotel industry, as they perform their basic function at a reasonable price, but anything else the guest wishes for during the stay, e.g. breakfast, in-room movies, costs extra.

There have been major increases in the budget sector, reflecting visitor profile and domestic demands. They are popular with business and leisure travellers alike.

The French dominate the budget hotel market in Europe for many reasons. Generally, the French have long summer holidays and many take domestic holidays. Further, the French are committed to spending more on food and drink rather than accommodation. Finally, France as an inbound destination attracts many car-borne holidaymakers across its borders from other continental states, as well as via ferry and the channel tunnel from Ireland and Britain. Some examples of well-known French budget hotels include Urbis, Formule 1 and Ibis (part of Accor Group), the latter of which is a popular budget hotel brand in Ireland and Britain.

Budget hotels are attractive to tourists on a budget. They are also popular with those who wish to spend more on other aspects of their trip, such as entertainment, food and beverage, sightseeing, etc. They are also popular with groups who travel, such as conference delegates, clubs, societies and sports teams.

Budget hotels are challenging the traditional Irish guesthouse or B&B in many areas of the country. Often they are similarly priced, and guests may choose to forsake the inclusive cooked breakfast offered in the latter in favour of the standardised comfort of a budget hotel room. The emphasis in the marketing of budget hotels is on convenience, consistency and value for money, and in this regard, the budget hotels have excelled in Ireland. They have opened up hotel accommodation to price-sensitive sectors of the economy, and thus exerted a pressure on other lower-grade hotels as well as guesthouses and B&Bs. The customer is, of course, the biggest winner, as more competition leads to more favourable prices. The local tourism economy also benefits after the construction of a budget hotel, as any tourist destination needs a variety of quality and mixed-priced accommodation to satisfy the varying tourist needs.

Budget hotels are financially viable as they make savings on construction costs and in operating costs in comparison to other hotels. They are often built in suburbs or on sites which are out of town but still on the major transport routes to a city or town. An example of this is the Ibis Hotel at the Red Cow roundabout in south west Dublin. The land is cheaper than in a city centre site, yet the hotel is within a few minutes' walking distance to the LUAS tramline, on several bus routes and is located at the intersection of the N7 and M50, leading to any route within Dublin and throughout Ireland and directly to Dublin Airport by motorway.

During construction, a standardised approach is used, which reduces costs. The plans are often similar to or the same as the plans used for another budget hotel of the same chain in a different city. If several budget hotels are being constructed at the same time, economies of scale can be achieved if bulk materials are purchased together. This is also the case with regard to furniture and furnishings. It is usually the case that the beds, bedside lockers, television, lamps, carpets, bathroom fittings, wardrobes, bed linen and even framed pictures are identical in all rooms in any given budget hotel. Regular guests are also aware of this, and so often know to expect a standardised room, which appeals to many. The emphasis in budget hotels is on the bedrooms rather than lavish public areas like other hotels. The rationale behind this is that the bedrooms must be more comfortable, given that most guests spend more time there than in public areas such as the reception area.

In operating the budget hotel, there is extensive use of automation, as staff costs are kept to a minimum. Often, during less busy times such as the evening and overnight, a budget hotel can be a one-person operation. In many budget hotels, snacks and soft drinks are available through vending machines in the lobby or on each floor, as is ice. A tea and coffee maker is usually available in each room. Rooms also have extra pillows and blankets stored in them. This saves the guest taking up staff time by requesting these should they require them. Often, the guest can check out remotely via the television and the remote control and simply drop their key or key card into a drop box on their way out. Staff costs are generally an enormous expense for regular hotels. With a higher degree of automation and methods of reducing guest demands on hotel staff, budget hotels have successfully reduced staff costs and so can offer lower rates.

Buffet breakfasts and standardised menus are used in dining areas (if they are available). Like anything else extra, such as in-room movies, the guest pays for any food from a dining area, as nothing more than the hire of the room is included in the price.

Finally, another reason for the low price offered by budget hotels is the costs cut from their marketing and distribution approach. Many offer little or no commission to agents, but instead encourage prospective guests to book directly with the establishment or with their central reservations by telephone or via the internet. This cuts out the commission they would otherwise pay to agents.

Budget hotels should benefit from increasing popularity of short breaks in Europe. Their continuing expansion throughout Ireland means that existing and emerging European tourism-generating markets (such as Eastern Europe) have an opportunity to stay in affordable yet comfortable accommodation. Further, many budget hotel chains have opened up (or are opening up) their business model and brand names for franchise, which is one way of rapidly expanding.

FUTURE FOR THE ACCOMMODATION SECTOR

The accommodation sector in Ireland is vital to the continuing growth of the tourism sector as a whole. The government and the industry together must ensure that the sector never again experiences the capacity problems of the 1990s, where the visitors to Ireland grew at a phenomenal rate, but the accommodation available did not grow at the same rate, leaving a shortfall of bed stock. Looking further afield, we will most likely see the continued overseas expansion of Irish hotel chains such as the Jurys-Doyle group, as larger groups of hotels look for new markets to enter. A future target of such chains may be newly emerging economies such as Eastern Europe, India and China.

A consistent campaign of the Irish Hotels Federation is to reduce the VAT on Irish hotels from the higher rate to a lower rate. In their pre-budget submission to the Minister for Finance, they continually call for a reduction to the EU average of 10 per cent VAT on hotels, which they claim will reduce the cost of Irish hotels from amongst the costliest in Europe.

Many accommodation providers rely on conferences, functions and food and beverage income as part of their overall profitability. We will most likely see an improved ability to cater for conferences, seminars and business meetings in larger establishments.

The unapproved sector may also increase in importance. Already we see increased co-operation and marketing from organisations representing privately owned and run B&Bs and guesthouses which are not part of the Fáilte Ireland-approved accommodation listings. Indeed, we will most likely see increased marketing efforts by all accommodation providers and their representative organisations. Competition will increase for the domestic and out-of-state tourists as more and more establishments vie for the growing number of tourists. As the following articles highlight, no accommodation provider – but especially the smaller B&B – can stay still; they must continually adapt to the changing market demands.

Wake-up call for B&Bs
Traditional B&Bs are under pressure from hotels. Fáilte Ireland is running workshops to help them fight back. **Rosita Boland** *sits in on one.*

'Take a nice picture of your breakfast buffet for your website' is one of the suggestions Steve Dudley of Fáilte Ireland has for the assembled people from the B&B trade attending his one-day workshop in Ardee, Co. Louth about marketing themselves via the internet.

Broadcaster Derek Davis would possibly not agree with Dudley that putting a nice picture of your breakfast buffet on your B&B website will help to pull in the punters. At a recent food tourism seminar in Drumshanbo, Co. Leitrim, Davis said many tourists 'gag' when faced with the full Irish breakfast, with 'deep-fried sausages' and fried eggs 'which are started at 6 a.m. and kept alive in lukewarm fat'.

It's no secret that the Irish B&B trade is not in a healthy state. In 2000, there were 4,124 approved B&Bs in the state. There are currently 3,110; a drop of a quarter in less than a decade – a period when the number of tourists visiting the state was increasing. From May to October in 2005, B&Bs had a room occupancy of 47 per cent.

To help boost trade, Fáilte Ireland has been running one-day workshops around the country for the last six weeks, aimed at increasing bookings via the internet. By the time the workshops end this week, Fáilte Ireland estimates one in three of all B&B owners will have attended one of the workshops.

The twelve people gathered in the Leader office in Ardee run B&Bs in counties Meath, Monaghan, Louth and Sligo. Most of them have been in the trade for many years. While some have a minor web presence via links from other sites, only a few of them have their own designated website. Some, such as Maureen Treanor of Emyvale, Co. Monaghan and Roland Bond of Navan, Co. Meath, don't have any presence on the web at all. All of them want more guests, and they're hoping Dudley's workshop – which proves to be highly informative and interesting – can help.

At one point in the day, there's a heated debate about the advantages of staying in a B&B as opposed to a hotel.

'Americans want to talk to Irish people and they don't get that in hotels with all the foreign workers,' says Treanor. 'They get a taste of Ireland by staying with us.'

Paula Trappe, of Latlurcan, Co. Monaghan, says, 'We can give people a personal service; offer them information about tourist places to see locally, suggest where they eat.'

However, B&B owners find that they are no longer catering only for tourists.

Orla O'Grady of Blackrock, Co. Louth, for instance, has had her B&B full of builders for the last couple of months. But while people doing manual labour might well appreciate a robust breakfast, they're not on holidays and wouldn't necessarily be interested in either chatting at length to Irish people or finding out more about the scenic attractions of their surroundings. So what's the advantage to them of staying there, other than the simple fact that it's cheaper than the local hotel?

No one in the group likes getting into a conversation about pricing.

Maeve Walsh from Tubbercurry, Co. Sligo blames the increasing number of hotels offering low rates for the fall-off in B&B trade.

'It's the media's fault,' she says. 'And the government. They should be backing the B&Bs, and not the hotels.'

What about the reality of the free market, where, like it or not, hotel owners are just as entitled to try to get their own share of bed nights?

Walsh isn't having any of it. Her response is to say that she is convinced all the new hotels will fail, and to repeat her belief that the fault in loss of business lies elsewhere.

'The Irish themselves are running down B&Bs,' Eilish McConnell of Carrickmacross, Co. Monaghan remarks.

'I think it's disgusting the things they say. That we're old-fashioned. The media don't help either. Gerry Ryan is always making fun of us. But if you take the B&B away from Ireland, what do you have left? The B&B is unique; it's all about the home atmosphere, and staying with a family.'

Dudley has been all over the country in the last few weeks, running the internet workshops which he has been involved in since they started as a pilot scheme in 2000.

One of the things he has noticed is that the age profile of those turning up is consistently of an older generation.

Very few young people are either coming into the business now, or taking it over from family members.

Several times during the day I'm asked if I stay in B&Bs myself. I answer honestly that the only times I've used them in the last few years is when I've been attending funerals in rural areas – when I have found people in B&Bs to have been very kind and considerate at what is a distressing time – but that when I'm working, I prefer to stay in a hotel, where I can plug in my computer, talk to nobody and be anonymous. This does not go down well at all. Nobody is taking no for an answer.

'We could plug your computer in for you. We'd know you didn't want to talk to us if you told us you didn't want to talk to us,' explains Pauline Daly. 'We're as good as a hotel.'

But if Irish B&Bs are not always the first choice of Irish holidaymakers, it's also the case that Irish tourists are not top of the list for the B&B owners either.

'I much prefer the continentals,' says Pauline Daly of Mooretown, Co. Meath, who has run a B&B for twenty years with her husband, Brian.

'They get up early and are tidy. You can't get the Irish out of bed in the mornings.'

Source: Boland, R., 'Wake-up call for B&Bs', *The Irish Times*, 12 April 2006.

B&Bs face bleak future as tourists go bargain hunting

Change is afoot in the Irish tourism industry. Once upon a time, travel agents, hoteliers and B&Bs would have a fair idea by April of what to expect during the summer season. However, short-term planning and booking cycles by visitors now mean that tourist operators are lucky if they can realistically plan just a month ahead. Irish holidays are much more likely to be an impulse buy rather than a planned vacation. The tourism industry is adapting to this 'new paradigm', according to Fáilte Ireland, which they see as driven by the convenience of internet bookings and last-minute bargains.

'The pace of change is staggering,' Fáilte Ireland's chief executive Shaun Quinn told his members recently. 'Perhaps influenced by the strategies of low-cost airlines, the Irish consumer has become both acutely deal conscious and IT literate, and now expects to browse and book packaged offerings.'

As with every economic sector, when there is contraction the small fry at the bottom tends to get squeezed out by the big fish who can carry some losses over the medium term. In the case of the €4.1 billion Irish tourism industry, it is the traditional B&B and rural guesthouse that seem to be facing an uncertain future in the face of a massive expansion of hotel capacity and a ruthless pricing strategy. The backbone of Ireland's accommodation stock has always been the humble B&B. These days they are by no means humble. The sector has grown into a sizeable rural industry.

As competition increases from cheaper and more accessible holidays abroad and pressure mounts from Ireland's burgeoning budget hotel industry, the B&B industry is facing tough times.

'The prospects for us in Killarney look terrible this summer,' said Evelyn Murphy, who runs the Redwood Country House B&B in the Kerry town.

Murphy is not surprised that many B&Bs are considering closing down. 'We're doing okay ourselves because it's a big house we have, but if it continues like this in the future, then I'll have to pack it up too. Bord Fáilte [Fáilte Ireland] say the numbers are the same as last year, but it doesn't seem that way.'

Regional tourism offices are reporting an increasing amount of diversification among small B&B operators who are now offering other attractions including horse riding, murder-mystery weekends, angling, organic farm produce and massage or spa treatments to attract more visitors. According to official figures, the B&B industry peaked during the late 1990s, with 4,300 officially registered homes in 1998. By late 2003 a quarter of these had closed down.

However, the hotel industry is enjoying an upward trend. Unreleased government statistics show that twenty-two new hotels opened in 2003 and thirty-two in 2004. Another thirty-five hotels are planned for this year. This means that there has been an increase of 7,042 hotel rooms over three years. So what's happening?

The Family Homes of Ireland, the country's largest listing of accommodation, has seen its membership decline from nearly 1,000 premises to just 660 over the same three-year period. While there are some new premises coming on stream – more than 500 new rooms became available in 2002 and 2003 – a far larger number are closing or ceasing to trade. 'It's all to do with marketing,' according to Family Homes director Dóirin Hickey. 'Tourism Ireland don't market B&Bs as part of the attraction of coming to Ireland. If they are even marketed at all, it's as cheap accommodation when it should be as family accommodation, and an opportunity for foreigners to meet and talk to "real" Irish people.'

'Some B&Bs are going down the road of having a little check-in desk and bunches of keys hanging up. That mini-hotel ethos is not what a B&B is supposed to be,' he said. 'It's not worth opening the doors during the winter months because there's no real passing trade in an off-the-beaten track area like this,' said Hilda Sheridan, who runs the Castlerosse House B&B in Aughnacliffe, Co. Longford. 'It's a hard business to be in these days, and all those people who haven't invested or diversified over previous years will be in trouble now.'

Quinn, a senior lecturer of tourism in the Dublin Institute of Technology, said it was not just a question of attractive marketing for B&Bs and the simple issue of supply and demand. 'There's been a narrowing of prices between cheap hotels, guesthouses and B&Bs in recent times. Historically people would pay per person in Irish hotels, but now there are pay-per-room charges which are very attractive to holidaying families,' said Quinn. 'Irish people are much more travelled now and demand higher standards – they're not just looking for a bed, but an experience. B&Bs have a depressed image and are less attractive to domestic tourists because of the competition from low-cost hotels.

'For foreigners it's a little different, but many arrive with an image of a stout farmhouse serving a fresh Irish breakfast, whereas in reality they often find a big bungalow on the outskirts of a county town.'

Source: Kelly, M., 'B&Bs face bleak future as tourists go bargain hunting', *The Sunday Business Post*, 24 April 2005.

REVISION QUESTIONS

1. Define the various accommodation terms in use in Ireland.
2. What are the recent trends in accommodation in Ireland?
3. Illustrate your understanding of how hotels operate.
4. Discuss your understanding of budget hotels.
5. Why is hotel grading important and why are some hotels not graded?
6. What makes a five-star hotel?
7. What are the key financial indicators used in the hotel sector?
8. Why is it not always viable for a hotel to reduce prices to stimulate demand?
9. What competitive challenges are non-hotel accommodation providers facing?

ESSAY QUESTIONS

1. Compare and contrast Irish five-star hotels to budget hotels. In your answer, list some of the criteria necessary to become a five-star hotel and some of the reasons why budget hotels can sell rooms at such a reduced rate. Use examples.
2. What are the challenges facing the Irish accommodation sector nowadays? How has the sector changed in the last ten years?
3. 'The day of the traditional Irish B&B is well and truly over.' Critically assess this statement.
4. 'Quality is important in accommodation. A luxury hotel must satisfy many criteria.' Discuss this statement with reference to Irish five-star hotels and at least one quality foreign hotel.
5. The budget hotel phenomenon is growing in importance in Ireland and globally. Outline why this is happening. Discuss why budget hotels can offer competitive rates and still remain financially viable.
6. Evaluate the competitive strategies employed by international hotel companies with reference to case studies you have studied.
7. Outline the structure of the international hotel industry and explain the critical factors required for success in this industry.
8. Explain how you think hotels might position themselves in order to be successful in the long term.
9. The hotel industry in Ireland is changing rapidly at present. Explain how the sector is changing and assess the implications for the independent operator.
10. There are many features which characterise the accommodation product and some clear trends are emerging for the future. Discuss with reference to examples of your choice.

TASKS

Divide the class into two roughly equal groups. Each group should be given ten to fifteen minutes to develop opposing points on the following statements, followed by a forty to forty-five minute debate.

Statement: The future for the Irish and/or international hotel sector is positive.

Statement: Budget hotels are aimed at business travellers more than leisure travellers.

Statement: Most visitors to Ireland are happy to pay a premium for luxury accommodation.

Statement: B&Bs are outdated as a tourism accommodation offering.

ASSIGNMENTS

1. Write a report on the major changes in the Irish accommodation product in recent years and compare these changes to international changes in the sector. Present a synopsis of the report to an audience, e.g. your class.
2. Research some of the more luxurious hotels in (a) Ireland and (b) the world. Find out what makes them so luxurious. Compare what constitutes luxury offerings in Ireland with other countries.

Chapter 6

Transport

SUMMARY

Transport is vital for tourism. It is especially vital for Ireland; given that the destination is an island, access transport is a key issue. This chapter provides a comprehensive analysis of the forms of transport, focusing on access transport to Ireland as well as within Ireland. Comparisons are drawn where applicable between the transport options to and from (as well as within) Ireland, and various other European countries, from a tourism point of view.

Transport issues that are discussed include water-based transport such as ferries as a link to Britain and Continental Europe. The chapter also discusses land-based transport as a means of travelling around Ireland. Car hire and private coach transport is briefly outlined. Public bus and rail (including new and future proposed developments) are discussed in detail. Government initiatives and plans such as the National Development Plan and Transport 21 are illustrated in the chapter.

A substantial portion of the chapter deals with air transport and Ireland's reliance on it. The chapter outlines the Irish airline sector since the 1980s, characterised by the continuing battle between Ryanair and Aer Lingus for the passengers coming to and leaving Ireland. The chapter also presents Ryanair as an example of the low-cost airline (also known as low-cost carriers, LCC) model that is sweeping Europe and the world. Company profiles of Aer Lingus, Ryanair and Aer Arann exemplify Ireland's major airline players, and the major changes witnessed in the structure, operations and customer experience of these airlines are analysed. The changes and development of Irish airports are highlighted as they modernise and expand to serve the growing need of large numbers of travellers. Finally, the international airline alliance phenomenon is outlined.

For a chronology of the development of access transport to Ireland and internal transport within Ireland, please consult the timeline presented at the beginning of Chapter 2. The years highlighted in bold indicate that this entry is relevant to the chronology of the origins and development of Irish transport as relevant to the tourism industry.

LEARNING OUTCOMES

Having completed this chapter, the reader should be able to:
- Appreciate the importance of access transport to and from a destination, as well as internal transport within a destination.

- Contextualise access transport and internal transport in the case of Ireland.
- Appreciate Ireland's heavy reliance on air transport, not only for tourism.
- Understand the changes taking place in Irish aviation.
- Demonstrate a knowledge of how international transport marketing and distribution occurs.
- Understand the importance of other forms of transport for Ireland, including water-based and land-based transport.
- Demonstrate an understanding of the role of governments in the implementation of transport policy and future strategies, particularly in an Irish context.

INTRODUCTION

Transport is arguably the most important element of the tourism product. In order for tourism to take place, there must be movement away from the place of habitual residence. Many domestic tourists rely on their own privately owned transport, i.e. car, to get them to their destination. Indeed, many tourists from Northern Ireland visiting the Republic do the same, as do Southerners visiting the North. This has been made possible due to the vast improvements in the quality of roads and motorways between the major cities on the island of Ireland. Many visitors from Britain and Continental Europe also bring their cars via car ferries.

Similarly, Continental tourists engaging in domestic tourism and those visiting neighbouring countries, e.g. Germans visiting Austria or the Netherlands, French visiting Switzerland or Spain, often bring their own car or camper-van, relying on the vast network of motorways (some incurring a toll) to take them to their destination.

The Republic of Ireland has only one land border – Northern Ireland. For all other inbound tourists (and Irish outbound tourists), other forms of transport must be utilised. As an island, access to Ireland relies heavily on air and sea forms of transport, the latter losing their previously dominant positions due to the falling cost of the former. The routes between Ireland and Britain in particular are extremely congested all year round. The Dublin-London air route (between Dublin and the London region's five airports) is the busiest in Europe (according to the Dublin Airport Authority) and one of the busiest in the world. Similarly, the Irish Sea contains many busy shipping lanes. Britain is also often used as a hub for onward travel, e.g. land-bridge ferry connections to the Continent or onward flight connections via London Heathrow airport. However, more direct access routes to Ireland by air and sea have been opened in recent years, both by Irish and foreign transport operators. As indicated by Table 6.1, half (49 per cent) of all arrivals to and departures from Ireland are by air from Britain, while a quarter of all arrivals to and departures from Ireland are by air from mainland Europe. Only 1 per cent of all Irish arrivals and departures are directly by sea from mainland Europe. A small proportion of Ireland's visitors arrive and depart via Ireland's only land border, Northern Ireland. The majority of Ireland's arrivals from and departures to North America are direct access by air (59 per cent), while more than a quarter (27 per cent) of the traffic travels via Britain. Indeed, the vast majority of arrivals from and departures to the rest of the world (not Britain, mainland Europe and North America) are by air via Britain, due, no doubt, to the excellent international air hubs in Britain, including London Heathrow, which is just a one-hour flight from most parts of Ireland.

Table 6.1: How Tourists Arrived to/Departed from Ireland (2005, percentage)

		Total	Britain	Mainland Europe	North America	Rest of World
Air	From Britain	49	72	15	27	64
	From Mainland Europe	24	1	74	9	25
	Transatlantic	9	1	<0.5	59	2
Sea	From Britain	15	23	6	3	8
	From Mainland Europe	1	0	3	<0.5	<0.5
Via Northern Ireland		2	3	1	2	2

Source: Fáilte Ireland/Central Statistics Office.

Transport is important to tourism in three different ways:
1. **Access transport:** The means of travel to a destination.
2. **Internal transport:** The means of travelling around a destination.
3. **Main feature:** It can be the main feature of the trip, e.g. a cruise.

In this chapter, we are more concerned with the first two of the above three: access transport to Ireland and internal transport within Ireland. After the tourism downturn caused by the major international events in 2001 (foot and mouth disease, the 9/11 terrorist attacks on the US), access transport to Ireland was cut by many airlines (the dominant form of transport to and from Ireland). In particular, the vitally important transatlantic routes suffered. Capacity was cut by major airlines, including Aer Lingus and many American operators, as routes were axed or scaled back or airlines suffered bankruptcy. European routes suffered also, albeit not as severely.

Since then, however, there has been a rapid expansion in the number of routes served directly to and from Ireland. This dramatic expansion is not centred solely on Dublin, but also on other major airport hubs in the state (especially Shannon). The new routes have been opened by rapidly growing Irish airlines Aer Lingus, Aer Arann and of course, Ryanair. However, we see many foreign airlines expanding their routes to include Ireland, including large American carriers (such as Delta and Continental) and new European players (such as Transavia and German Wings).

There have also been major improvements in ferry transport to and from Ireland. Both Irish and foreign ferry operators have kept afloat amid fierce competition from low-cost airlines. It is often cheaper (and certainly quicker) to fly to your destination than to take a ferry. However, ferry travel is still appealing to car-borne tourists as well as being economical for larger groups. Improvements on the Irish Sea routes include faster crossings, e.g. Stena HSS, and larger ferries, e.g. Irish Ferries *Ulysses*.

The improvements in access transport to Ireland are proving successful, given the state's increasing visitor numbers and revenue. However, internal transport in Ireland is still a long way behind our European neighbours. Successive governments have launched plans (such as the National Development Plan, NDP) and many have turned into reality, such as the completion of many urban, suburban and intercity motorways or the upgrading of the railway network. However, the decades of under-investment in Irish infrastructure has not yet been readdressed. Without excellent internal transport to complement access to the Irish tourism market, government strategies to evenly spread the tourism spend to all regions of the state are pointless. Until this area is addressed effectively, inbound tourists will continue to focus their stay on the major urban areas of the state. The Transport 21 plan announced by the Irish government in November 2005 aims to address this problem (discussed later in this chapter).

MAIN FORMS OF TRANSPORT

The main forms of transport for tourism are listed below and discussed individually in the remainder of this chapter. It is worth noting that while specific examples refer to Ireland, the general forms of transport listed are relevant to most countries.

Air Transport

Scheduled flights:	Operate on a timetable, public can purchase easily through a travel agent, directly from an airline or online. Company examples: Aer Lingus, Ryanair, Air France.
Charter flights:	Predominantly organised by tour operators as part of a package holiday (perhaps including flight, accommodation and transfers). Sometime excess seats are sold to the public. Company examples: Budget Travel, First Choice.

Water Transport

Ferry services:	Ferry link from port to port. Different types of ferries include the large 'superferry' (like a floating village), the HSS (high-speed service operated by Stena) or a Seacat (smaller catamaran vessel, generally faster). Can be purchased through a travel agent, directly from a ferry operator or online. Company examples: Irish Ferries, Stena Line, P&O Irish Sea Ferries.
Cruise ships:	Classed as a luxury travel experience. Often involve expensive packages, including flight to connect you to port to meet vessel. Popular in the seniors market. Company example: P&O Cruises.

Canals and inland waterways:	Originally designed as a means of transport, they are particularly important as a tourist attraction in Ireland. Can include accommodation options, such as hiring a cruiser on a river or canal. Company example: Shannon River Boat Hire.
Viking Splash Tours:	An alternative way to sightsee in Dublin, using a World War II amphibious vehicle to take tourists on a trip around Dublin, both by land and by water. Concept originated in Boston, US.

Land Transport

Railways:	Under-utilised form of internal transport in Ireland. Suffered from decades of under-investment, far behind European neighbours. Some improvements recently. Company example: Iarnród Éireann – Irish Rail.
Private motor car:	Dominant form of internal transport. Road network greatly improved since economic prosperity, especially in cities and intercity links.
Car hire:	Dominated in Ireland by large international brands and smaller Irish operators. Located at major tourist points, such as air and ferry ports and railways stations. Company examples: Hertz, Budget, Europcar, Argus.
Coaches:	Slower, yet cheaper form of internal transport and access transport. Popular with price-sensitive Continental European visitors. Company examples: Bus Éireann, Eurolines.

As we can see from Tables 6.2 and 6.3, the different modes of transport used for tourist arrivals internationally depend on the region in question. For example, over half of all arrivals in the Americas arrive by air, with 41 per cent arriving by land (rail and road). The opposite is the case in Europe, where 55 per cent of tourists arrive by land and only 38 per cent by air. Perhaps this is testament to Europe's comprehensive interstate rail and motorway networks, developed as a main form of intrastate as well as interstate transport. Further expansion of such networks is a major strategy of EU transport policy. However, given the reduced cost and rapid expansion of air travel within Europe, we may see a trend towards the world average figures in the next decades. Globally, half of all tourists arrive in their destination by land, while 43 per cent arrive by air. Only 7.4 per cent arrive by water, which would have been a dominant form of travel a century ago.

Table 6.2: Arrivals by Mode of Transport in Millions of Arrivals (2004)

	Total	Air	Land	Water	Not Specified
World	763.2	327.9	376.1	56.7	2.6
Africa	33.2	16.0	14.6	2.6	0.1
Americas	125.8	66.8	51.9	7.0	0.1
Asia and Pacific	152.5	70.4	64.0	16.3	1.8
Europe	416.4	158.7	228.1	29.0	0.6
Middle East	35.4	16.0	17.5	1.9	0.0

Source: UNWTO 2004 (includes estimates for countries with missing data).

Table 6.3: Arrivals by Mode of Transport as Percentage of Arrivals (2004)

	Total	Air	Land	Water	Not Specified
World	100	43.0	49.3	7.4	0.3
Africa	100	48.0	43.9	7.8	0.3
Americas	100	53.1	41.3	5.5	0.1
Asia and Pacific	100	46.2	41.9	10.7	1.2
Europe	100	38.1	54.8	7.0	0.1
Middle East	100	45.3	49.5	5.3	0.0

Source: UNWTO 2004 (includes estimates for countries with missing data).

LAND-BASED TRANSPORT: CAR HIRE

Car hire involves renting a car from a company for a particular length of time at an agreed rate. It is very popular with business tourists and fly-drive tourists (those who fly to a destination and then hire a car to drive around a destination). There are 5,421 kilometres of roadway in Ireland, of which 192 kilometres (3.54 per cent) are motorway, while 285 kilometres (5.3 per cent) are dual carriageway. The remaining 4,944 kilometres (91.2 per cent) are single lane, according to the National Roads Authority (NRA) as of 31 December 2004. As Table 6.4 illustrates, not all of those who use a car on holidays to Ireland hire it – many bring their own with them. One-fifth of all visitors from Britain bring a car with them, thanks to the comprehensive ferry links between both islands. Almost half of North American visitors hire a car. However, more than half (59 per cent) of all visitors to Ireland neither hire a car nor bring one with them.

Table 6.4: Percentage of Visitors to Ireland Using a Car (2005)

	Total	Britain	Mainland Europe	North America	Rest of World
Car Brought	13	21	11	1	8
Car Hired	28	16	31	44	32
Car Not Used	59	63	58	55	60

Source: Fáilte Ireland.

The Irish road network is being consistently improved after decades of under-investment. Under the National Development Plan (2000–2006) and the Transport 21 plan (announced by the government in November 2005), the Irish government's commitment to internal transport infrastructure is being addressed. Like many of our Continental European neighbours, tolled motorways and tunnels seem to be a key feature of the government's strategy, making driving in Ireland costly.

The fly-drive concept (flying into an airport, picking up a hired car and dropping it back at that or another airport before departure) is extremely popular with tourists from the US. Many prefer the freedom of fly-drive tourism, perhaps landing in Shannon and departing from Dublin, taking their own hired car to visit and stay in towns and cities between their arrival and departure points. Often they complete a 'u' around the country – driving from Shannon to Dublin (or vice versa) via the southern regions, e.g. Limerick, Kerry, Cork, Waterford. Or perhaps they complete an 'n' around the country – driving via the northern regions, e.g. Galway, Mayo, Donegal, the border regions, parts of Northern Ireland and the north east. These routes are popular with fly-drive tourists.

Car hire companies can be divided into two categories:
- Large international companies or franchise operators.
- Small, locally based independent hire companies.

The international companies are the big brands, instantly recognisable to business and leisure travellers the world over. They charge similar prices, but offer a choice of cars, hiring locations and flexibility. Many also offer frequent-hirer schemes and loyalty bonuses such as upgrades. For these reasons, the big brands are particularly attractive to business travellers.

The 'big brand' international car hire companies are:
- Avis   www.avis.ie
- Budget   www.budget.ie
- Dollar Thrifty   www.thrifty.ie
- Enterprise   www.enterprise.com/ie
- Europcar   www.europcar.ie
- Hertz   www.hertz.ie
- National   www.nationalcar.com

Some Irish car hire companies:
- Argus   www.argusrentals.com
- Atlas   www.atlascarhire.com
- County   www.countycar.ie
- Dan Dooley   www.dan-dooley.ie
- Irishcarrentals.com   www.irishcarrentals.com

All of the above operate desks in Dublin Airport and many other airports, ferry ports, railway and bus stations throughout Ireland.

The expansion of outlets has been greatly aided by the introduction of franchising, where a local business trades under the hugely popular brand name with a franchise agreement. Other factors which have improved the distribution channels for international and Irish-owned car hire companies are as follows.

1. **Desk space:** Contracts are signed with port authorities (such as airport and ferry ports) to have desk space and/or exclusive rights at a location which is a major tourism hub. Often there is a bidding war at the end of a contract, as competitors try to gain access to such a lucrative market.

2. **Referral bookings from transport operators:** Transport operators such as airlines recommend one particular car hire company to their passengers. The passenger is usually offered a discount if they present proof of custom with the transport provider, e.g. boarding card. The transport provider usually gets a commission and the car hire company get an exclusive recommendation. For example, Ryanair gets commission from Hertz for every Ryanair passenger who presents their Ryanair boarding card at a Hertz desk.

3. **Other elements in the tourism product also provide referral bookings** for car hire companies. The hotel, guesthouse, restaurant or tourist information office gets a commission for every booking made with a car hire company. Frequently, individual staff members are offered monetary incentives for every guest that books with a particular car hire company as an incentive for loyalty to one particular company.

4. **Computer reservations systems** (such as Sabre and Galileo) allow travel agents to directly book car hire at a commission, along with other travel products, making the travel agent the one-stop shop for all travel needs.

5. The **internet** – which has revolutionised the world of travel and tourism – offers the car hire customer an easy, convenient and often cheaper source of information and place to reserve. It has made it easier for the customer to compare offerings and search for the best deals.

LAND-BASED TRANSPORT: COACHES AND BUSES

Coaches and buses are an important form of internal transport. They are important for commuters, both within Ireland's major urban centres and between them. They are also a lifeline for many smaller towns and villages dotted around the country.

Generally, coaches and buses are a quick-fix problem for many governments. It is cheaper to buy more coaches and buses and run them on already existing roads than it is to build new railway lines. They do not require major infrastructural planning, but can be put to service relatively quickly. The Irish government prioritises public transport in its transport strategies. Under the NDP and Transport 21, the focus remains on public transport. Major investment in city bus services are a feature of the plans. They also include dedicated lanes called quality bus corridors (QBCs), which have removed bottlenecks for many regular commuters and reduced travel times in cities.

Dublin has a relatively comprehensive public bus network. This is operated by Dublin Bus, a division of government-owned CIE (Córas Iompair Éireann – the Irish Transport Network). The company operates regular scheduled bus services, both day and night, and tours in the Greater Dublin area. In recent years, the market for bus services in Ireland has been deregulated, paving the way for several private operators to offer similar services, not just between cities but within cities. Many private bus companies challenge the dominance of Dublin Bus on their routes. Some also operate routes that Dublin Bus does not. Private operators also offer sightseeing tours in and around Dublin in a direct challenge to the Dublin Bus services.

Bus Éireann is a sister company of Dublin Bus in the CIE group. It operates scheduled city bus services in the major cities of the Republic apart from Dublin, i.e. Cork, Galway, Limerick and Waterford. Bus Éireann also operates provincial bus services, school bus services and an extensive **Expressway** coach service to most towns, cities and villages in Ireland.

Eurolines is 'Europe's Express Coach Network'. It is a collection of thirty-five different coach companies which operate services in twenty-five countries of Europe. Bus Éireann is a member of this network, providing linkage to the Irish market. Coach travel between the countries of Europe is a cheaper form of transport, although quite a slow form. In an Irish context, it involves taking a ferry to the western seaboard of Britain, and again from the eastern and southern seaboards of Britain onwards to Continental Europe. Land-based travel (especially in a bus) can be slow and ferry travel is slower. This sector is generally reserved for large parties (such as sports teams, school trips) and travellers on a budget. However, given the ever-falling price of air travel and its inherent convenience, we can see this mode of transport playing less of a role in access to Ireland. Yet with the influx of migrants to Ireland, predominantly from Eastern Europe since the accession of the ten new states to the EU on 1 May 2004, coach companies such as Eurolines have become appealing to a new form of price-conscious tourist: the economic migrant.

LAND-BASED TRANSPORT: RAILWAY

The 1,947 kilometres of the Irish rail network are run by Iarnród Éireann (Irish Rail), the third and final branch of the CIE group of companies. Iarnród Éireann operates regular scheduled services between many of Ireland's cities as well as commuter and regional services. Although many regional commuter lines have reopened in recent years or have been identified as a government transport priority to reopen, most of the commuter services operated by Iarnród Éireann are concentrated around the Greater Dublin area and surrounding towns, i.e. suburban commuter lines and DART services.

Figure 6.1: Ireland's InterCity Rail Network

Source: Iarnród Éireann.

Figure 6.2: Map of the Dublin Commuter and DART Network

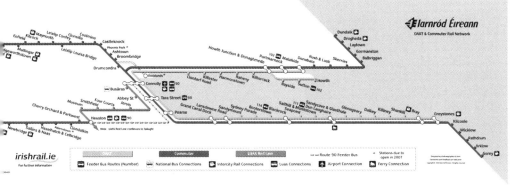

Source: Iarnród Éireann.

A map of the Cork-Cobh service is available at
www.iarnrodeireann.ie/your_journey/cork_cobh_map.asp.

LUAS is Dublin's newest light rail system. It is not part of Iarnród Éireann, but rather a private franchise operated by Connex, now called Veolia Transportation. At the moment, only two lines operate in Dublin, although there are future expansion plans linked into the Transport 21 plan. According to its website, the LUAS mission is as follows: 'LUAS connects you to Dublin city centre with a high-capacity, high-frequency, high-speed service. There are convenient stop locations and excellent levels of comfort and safety with easy access at all stops.'

The main InterCity routes operated by Iarnród Éireann are from two Dublin mainline stations: Dublin Connolly and Dublin Heuston.

- Dublin Connolly Station serves the north eastern and south eastern seaboard, as well as Sligo.
- Dublin Heuston Station serves the west, south west and Waterford routes.

After decades of under-investment, the Irish government is investing in the Irish rail network. It spent €1 billion as part of the NDP, largely in upgrading tracks, signals and carriages, and has major development plans for the railway infrastructure as part of Transport 21.

Figure 6.3: Map of the LUAS Network

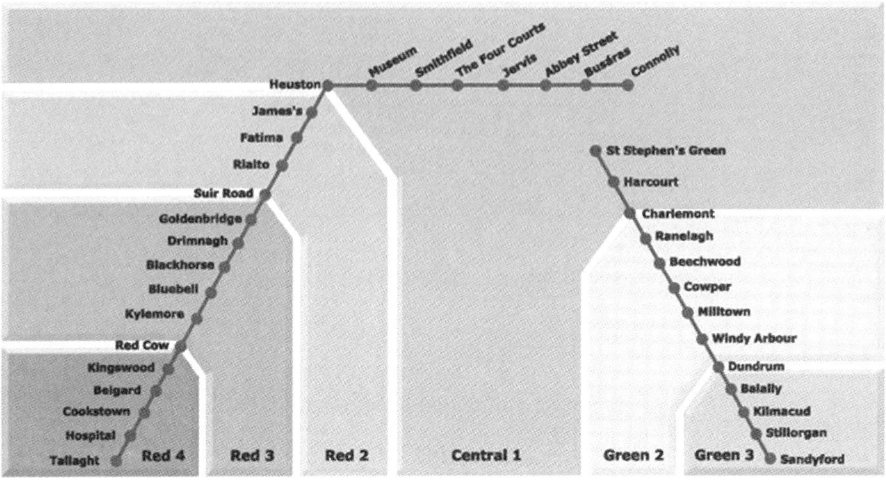

Source: www.luas.ie.

It is worth pointing out that there is a significant lack of railway service in the north west of the state. Tourists wishing to visit Donegal and surrounding regions must make do with a service connecting Dublin and Sligo. An onward commute by bus is necessary. This is at odds with government strategy, which plans to balance the tourism spread to the regions, especially the BMW region (Borders, Midlands and West), parts of which are underdeveloped in terms of tourism and have very poor visitor numbers compared to other regions. Such a strategy is only realistic with a complementary transport strategy to include public transport and efficient road access from the major tourist arrival points to this region. The government plans to address this problem under the Transport 21 plan (see below).

Ireland is well behind other EU states in terms of rail travel. In Continental states such as Germany and France, rail travel is a very important form of transport for commuting, leisure, business and freight. Given that states on the Continent are joined by land, as opposed to being totally surrounded by water (such as Ireland), it was inevitable that rail travel would develop to be a dominant force for state-to-state travel on the Continent. It is only quite recently that low-cost airlines have begun to challenge the dominance of rail transport internally on the Continent.

The governments of these states have invested heavily in rail travel in the past and continue to keep ahead of the rest in terms of new developments. Express services operate between many European cities. In Germany, the Deutsche Bundesbahn (German Federal Railways, www.bahn.de) operates the ICE service (the InterCity Express), a high-speed service popular amongst business travellers, boasting all the luxuries of first-class or regular travel for those who wish to pay for the privilege of time saving. The French counterpart is the TGV – train à grande vitesse – 'high-speed train' and is operated by SNCF (French Railways, www.sncf.com). These high-speed services are often more convenient than flying, given the reduced security and fewer check-in formalities, as well as train stations centrally located (as opposed to airports on the outskirts).

> The **TGV** (train à grande vitesse, French for 'high-speed train') is France's high-speed rail service, developed by GEC-Alsthom (now Alstom) and SNCF, the French national rail operator, and operated primarily by SNCF. Following the inaugural TGV service between Paris and Lyon in 1981, the TGV network, centred on Paris, has expanded to connect cities across France.
>
> The success of the first line led to a rapid expansion of the service, with new lines built to the south, west and north east of the country. Eager to share in the success of the French network, neighbouring countries such as Belgium, Italy and Switzerland built their own high-speed lines to connect with it. TGVs under other brand names also link to Germany and the Netherlands through the Thalys network, and to the United Kingdom through Eurostar. Several future lines are currently planned, including extensions within France and to surrounding countries. Towns such as Tours have become a part of this 'TGV commuter belt'.
>
> TGVs travel at up to 320 km/h (200 mph), which is made possible through the use of specially designed tracks, laid down without any sharp curves, and a range of features which make TGV trains suitable for high-speed travel. These features include high-powered electric motors, low axle weight, articulated carriages and in-cab signalling which removes the need for drivers to see lineside signals at high speed.
>
> TGVs are manufactured primarily by Alstom, now often with the involvement of Bombardier. Except for a small series of TGVs used for postal freight between Paris and Lyon, TGV is primarily a passenger service. Trains derived from TGV designs also operate in South Korea (KTX – Korea Train Express) and Spain (AVE – Alta Velocidad Española, or Spanish High Speed).
>
> Travel by TGV has largely replaced air travel between connected cities, due to shorter commuting times (especially for trips taking less than three hours), reduced check-in, security and boarding formalities and the convenient location of train stations in the heart of cities. Furthermore, the TGV is a very safe mode of transport, with no recorded fatalities due to accidents while running at high speed since operations began.
>
> Source: http://en.wikipedia.org/wiki/TGV.

WATER-BASED TRANSPORT: FERRIES

As an island, ferries are an important form of transport for Ireland. They form a vital link between Ireland and Britain as well as between Ireland and Continental Europe (either directly or via land-bridge through Britain). Up until and including the 1980s, flying was an unaffordable luxury for most Irish outbound tourists. The ferry was a slower yet cheaper alternative. In the days before the abolition of duty free shopping for intra-EU trips, countless shopper-tourists would enjoy a day trip from Dublin to Holyhead return in order to get their duty free entitlements.

Since the 1990s, ferry operators' business has changed dramatically. Duty free has been abolished for intra-EU trips and travelling with low-cost airlines has become cheaper. The price-sensitive traveller no longer has to suffer long, weather-dependent sea crossings. Indeed, flying to Britain from Ireland (or from Ireland to Britain) can be cheaper than travelling by ferry.

The ferry, however, does attract tourists wishing to bring their car (and caravan or even pets in some cases) with them on holiday. For sports teams and large groups, it can often be cheaper to travel by coach and ferry rather than flying. Increasingly, ferry companies have to employ novel approaches to make profits, including offering more on-board services and utilising the ferry for events like party cruises at off-peak times.

In Ireland, the main ports are on the eastern and southern seaboards, including:
• Dublin Port.
• Dún Laoghaire Port (South Dublin).
• Rosslare (Wexford).
• Cork.
• Belfast.
• Larne (Northern Ireland).

Most ferry companies serve the busy Irish Sea routes between Ireland (North and South) and the western seaboard of Britain.

For the ferry traveller wishing to travel between Ireland and Continental Europe, some ferry companies operate direct links to France, albeit mostly seasonally. Most ferry companies offer what is known as land-bridge options. This includes a ferry across the Irish Sea, as well as a ferry from Britain to Continental Europe, with a journey over land to connect the tourist from one British port to another. This is more economical to operate for the ferry companies than direct links from Ireland to Continental Europe.

Major ferry companies operating to/from Ireland include the following.

Irish Ferries
• Dublin/Dún Laoghaire to Holyhead (North Wales).
• Rosslare to Pembroke (South Wales).

Stena Line
• Dublin/Dún Laoghaire to Holyhead (North Wales).
• Rosslare to Fishguard (South Wales).
• Belfast to Stranraer (Scotland).
• Larne (NI) to Fleetwood (North England).

Brittany Ferries
* Cork to Roscoff (North France).

Swansea-Cork Ferries
* Cork to Swansea (South Wales).
* Cork to Pembroke (South Wales).

P&O Irish Sea Ferries
* Rosslare to Cherbourg (North France).
* Dublin to Liverpool.
* Larne to Troon (Scotland).
* Larne to Cairnryan (Scotland).

Isle of Man Steam Packet Company
* Belfast to Troon (Scotland).
* Belfast to Douglas (Isle of Mann).
* Dublin to Douglas (Isle of Mann).
* Dublin to Liverpool.

Economics of Ferry Operations

Ferry operations are highly seasonal, which is why there is often such a large variation in peak versus off-peak prices. Operating short sea ferry routes is expensive in terms of both capital investment and direct operating costs. We have seen many examples of cost-cutting measures in all forms of transport; ferry operations are no different. Such companies strive to achieve profits through a combination of maximum use of equipment plus on-board sales (much like low-cost airlines). Therefore, rapid turnaround in ports and round-the-clock sailings are the key to success for many operators. The Minister for Tourism noted in his end of year statement for 2005:

> For its part, sea access continues to deliver over 1 million visitors annually and remains a key strategic access route for tourism to the island. Tourism Ireland has been investing significant resources in the car touring segment of the British market and will be rolling out further enhanced programmes in 2006. A significant development in this area is the announcement of additional fast turnaround pier facilities...

Ideally the ferry companies would like an even volume of business all year round and a balanced flow of demand in both directions. However, as previously noted, ferry operations are extremely seasonal. Off-peak sailings on the shorter routes can be boosted by low fares with a wide range of discounted prices aimed at different market segments. Indeed, some ferry companies have come up with novel ways of supplementing profits during the off-peak period, including Christmas party cruises between Dublin and Holyhead return.

Irish Ferries cancels daily route

Irish Ferries yesterday scrapped one of its daily round trips from Dublin to Britain, citing weakness in the tourism market and rising fuel costs.

From next week, the company will operate four round trips a day instead of the usual five. The cancellation of one of the sailings will reduce capacity on the Dublin to Holyhead route by 7 per cent, according to Tony Kelly, marketing manager of Irish Ferries, which is owned by Irish Continental Group. Including the company's Rosslare to Pembroke route, overall capacity will be down by about 4 per cent, he said.

Irish Ferries currently runs two ships on the Dublin to Holyhead route, the *Jonathan Swift*, which is capable of carrying about 200 cars and focuses solely on the tourism market, and the *Ulysses*, which also caters for the freight market and has capacity for 1,300 cars.

Mr Kelly said the group had decided to cut one of the *Jonathan Swift's* daily sailings because, as a faster ship, it uses more fuel than the *Ulysses*.

NCB analyst John Sheehan described the decision as a good one for the company logistically, although said the reasons behind it – namely, declining passenger numbers – were negative. He said it shouldn't leave the company short of capacity in the long run as freight capacity would be unaffected and there remains ample car-carrying capacity on the other sailings to accommodate leisure travellers.

'Looking at the car market in the second half of last year, we figured we could manage quite well with four departures from Dublin,' said Mr Kelly.

'The *Swift*, being a faster craft, does consume considerably more fuel and therefore, with the state of the market, we considered this to be a prudent move.'

Irish Sea passenger volumes declined over the course of last year as increased competition from low-cost airlines cut into the industry's markets.

In the fourth quarter of last year, Ryanair announced increases in its capacity between Britain and Ireland, a move Mr Sheehan said may impact on Irish Ferries' passenger count in the future.

Source: Shoesmith, C., 'Irish Ferries cancels daily route', *The Irish Times*. 25 January 2006.

Challenges

The major problems with ferry travel are its low speed, and the problem of many ports located very far from major destinations. Luckily, Dublin Port and Dún Laoghaire Port are both quite central to Dublin as a tourism centre. However, the tourist-generating ports (such as Holyhead, Fishguard and Pembroke in Wales) are generally quite far from the main tourist-generating centres, i.e. the big British cities.

Ferry operators are suffering at the hands of low-cost airlines. It is proving more and more difficult to compete with low-cost airlines in terms of price and convenience. Ferry operators must continue to attract large touring parties. In this way, group travel may be cheaper than low-cost airlines. They must also launch more innovative products in a bid to attract different segments of the market that would not usually consider ferry travel. Changing strategies include mass marketing efforts to target passengers of low-cost air carriers and using internet reservations to reduce distribution costs and lower-paid non-Irish nationals as staff. An example of a unique marketing strategy is an Irish Ferries campaign stating 'with fares this low, flying is plane crazy'. The company is endeavouring to reposition itself as a low-cost operator. Its marketing logo even rebrands the company as 'IrishFerries.com – The Low Fares Ferry Company', and advises passengers 'to watch for the sting in the tail' with airlines – taxes and charges – as it claims all of its fares are inclusive of these. It further attacks the airlines by stating that Irish Ferries has 'no fuel charges' and 'no phantom taxes' and that it has a very strict baggage allowance – whatever fits in your car! This is a unique marketing strategy for a ferry operator, as it attacks the competition in areas where travellers are beginning to voice discontent with low-cost carriers, i.e. baggage charges, taxes, fuel surcharges and other charges.

AIR TRANSPORT: THE GATEWAY TO IRELAND

Air transport has become the dominant form of transport for access to Ireland and most tourist destinations. The cost of air travel has fallen dramatically in the last two decades, and if we are to believe industry leaders (such as Ryanair's charasmatic CEO, Michael O'Leary), they will continue to fall. The main reason for the reduction in cost can be summed up in one word: competition. In the early 1980s in Europe (like in the US in 1978), the process of deregulating the airline market began, opening Europe's skies to competition. And while it took some time for air travellers to feel the full economic effects of competition, Europeans now have the choice to travel on several airlines, and not just the previously state-owned airlines, or flag carrier, as they were known, e.g. Aer Lingus, British Airways, Air France.

In his end of year statement for 2005, the Minister for Tourism noted the following with regard to air access to Ireland:

> *Air access growth has been the big tourism story of 2005. Seat capacity from all our key markets has grown by double digits. Seats from Britain were up 16 per cent – most of which were directly to the regions. North America saw 4,000 additional seats come on stream – up 17 per cent on last year. Mainland Europe was up a phenomenal 31,000 seats, or 40 per cent on last year. Tourism Ireland has been working in strategic partnership with the carriers to maximise awareness of, and stimulate demand for, holidays in Ireland. In 2005, Tourism Ireland supported, through co-funded, co-operative marketing activities, the introduction of thirty-five new routes to the island of Ireland in 2005, twenty-four of which were to regional airports.*

There is no doubt that access to Ireland from all over the world has improved dramatically in recent times. Ireland is now extremely well serviced by air routes. Battling for position in the Irish market are Irish-owned airlines such as Aer Lingus and Ryanair, as well as smaller Aer Arann. However, given the increasing liberalisation of European airspace and the open skies and bilateral agreements with

North American countries, Irish operators are facing more competition nowadays than ever before. The ongoing battle for dominance in the lucrative Irish air market will inevitably result in one winner – the customer, as more competition brings better deals. Consider the cost of a return flight between Dublin and London twenty years ago compared to today. The increasingly affluent Irish traveller takes more trips abroad now than ever before. Many of these travellers are willing to pay a premium to avoid travelling through a major European hub, choosing rather to fly direct to their destination. Many airlines are answering this call and offering direct routes to a myriad of destinations, not just from Dublin, but from many regions of Ireland. Further, with the growing Irish population (especially the large immigrant communities), there is more of a demand for increased services to destinations not previously considered viable as a route, e.g. Eastern Europe, Asia, Africa.

O'Donoghue welcomes new direct air service to Belfast from New York as a major boost to tourism to the island of Ireland

Minister for Arts, Sport and Tourism, John O'Donoghue, TD, welcomed the announcement today of a new Continental Airlines route between Belfast International Airport and New York's Newark Airport as 'a major boost to tourism to the island of Ireland, particularly Northern Ireland and the North West. The daily service, due to become operational by June 2005, represents a significant milestone in opening up the enormous potential of the US market to Northern Ireland and the Border counties.'

Minister O'Donoghue said that improved air access is vital to the continued development of tourism throughout the island and a direct US service into Belfast will provide a huge impetus to the marketing efforts of Tourism Ireland.

Also commenting on the announcement, Paul O'Toole, chief executive of Tourism Ireland, said: 'The new direct transatlantic air service will provide a significant boost in US visitor numbers as well as substantial economic benefits. US visitors tend to stay longer and spend more than other overseas visitors – particularly on shopping, sightseeing, entertainment and internal transport.'

Source: Department of Arts, Sport and Tourism press release, 7 October 2004.

Ireland is the birthplace of Europe's largest low-cost operator, Ryanair. Nowadays, its major hub is located at London-Stansted airport, attracting the increasingly affluent population of England's south east and Greater London areas. The story of Irish aviation since the mid-1980s is a tale of fierce rivalry between Aer Lingus and Ryanair, a tale which has forced state-owned Aer Lingus to change into an organisation which is capable of competing effectively with Ryanair in the open marketplace that is its own backyard.

O'Donoghue welcomes new air routes for Shannon
John O'Donoghue, TD, Minister for Arts, Sport and Tourism, today [30 November 2004] welcomed the announcement by the Shannon Airport Authority and Ryanair of nine new routes – four from Britain and five from mainland Europe – that are expected to carry up to 1 million passengers in the first year of operation.

Minister O'Donoghue said, 'One of the objectives of national tourism policy is to facilitate a wider regional spread of business. I believe that the introduction of these new routes by Ryanair next year will be of major significance for tourism development, particularly in the Western regions. Tourism Ireland will be working with the airport and the airline to help support the development of inward traffic to Shannon from Britain and, in particular, key Continental European markets such as Germany, France and Spain.

'The Tourism Policy Review Group, in its *New Horizons for Irish Tourism: An Agenda for Action* report, identified access transport as one of the key strategic success drivers for Irish tourism. The development of regular and competitively priced routes from our key source markets is essential in helping to meet the ambitious growth targets for Irish tourism, which envisage an increase from 6 million to 10 million visitors by 2012.'

Source: Department of Arts, Sport and Tourism press release, 30 November 2004.

COMPANY PROFILE: AER LINGUS

www.aerlingus.com

Aer Lingus is Ireland's so-called 'flag carrier' airline. However, the concept of a specific airline carrying the flag (so to speak) of a nation is outdated in today's airline industry. Until September 2006, the airline was majority owned by the Irish government, with the remainder owned by staff, and is now a public limited company. It suffered terrible losses in the 1990s, which led to major restructuring between 2001 and 2004 under its previous CEO, Willie Walsh (now CEO of British Airways). Its current CEO is Dermot Mannion.

Aer Lingus services routes from Dublin, Cork and Shannon to Britain, Continental Europe, the US and Dubai (in the United Arab Emirates). Significant route expansion has been seen since 2002, and further routes are planned.

O'Donoghue welcomes new Aer Lingus service between Dubai and Dublin
John O'Donoghue, TD, Minister for Arts, Sport and Tourism, today [27 October 2005] welcomed the new Aer Lingus service between Dubai and Dublin. The new service, which will operate three times a week, is expected to carry 70,000 passengers in the first year and represents a major boost to inbound tourism from [Ireland's] new and developing long-haul markets.

Minister O'Donoghue said: 'I am delighted at Aer Lingus's announcement to launch a new service between Dubai and Dublin. As an island destination, it is vital that Ireland continues to grow and develop access routes into the country. In this regard the provision of this service is a welcome addition. This new service will allow direct travel to Ireland from Dubai and will also serve as a gateway into Ireland from new and developing tourism markets in the Middle East, Africa, the Far East and Australia.'

'This service is particularly important in terms of increasing the options available to long-haul travellers wishing to come to Ireland to enjoy a holiday or do business here. Ireland has much to offer the long-haul traveller – growth in visitor numbers of almost 30 per cent from markets such as Australia and New Zealand in 2004 is strong evidence of the potential from these markets. This service, along with the Gulf Air Bahrain service announced in July, will make Ireland significantly more accessible to these markets.'

Source: Department of Arts, Sport and Tourism press release, 27 October 2005.

British Airways (BA) is Aer Lingus's primary partner and rumours have been consistent about a possible BA takeover. A surprise Ryanair takeover bid was rejected by Aer Lingus in the winter of 2006. With the recent privatisation of the airline, the Irish government has insisted that any eventual takeover (by any airline) would come with a proviso that Irish passengers will not have to fly east before they fly west, i.e. routes from Irish airports will not be cut in favour of more economical routes from, for example, London. The airline was part of the OneWorld global airline alliance, but in 2006 announced plans to withdraw from it from 2007 (see article below).

There were major changes announced in August 2004 which ultimately changed the airline into a low-cost carrier (LCC) within Europe. These include:
- The abolition of short-haul business class (spring 2005).
- The abolition of short-haul cargo (however, 88 per cent of Aer Lingus cargo was destined for North America and Germany, and these two markets remain served).

Government will secure Heathrow slots
Aer Lingus's slots at Heathrow Airport in London will not be taken over by another airline in the event of a partial flotation of the company, according to the tourism minister, John O'Donoghue.

The minister said the government would retain the right to veto such a move. He supported the decision to sell part of Aer Lingus, as the airline required equity to expand its fleet and this would benefit Irish tourism. The government would retain sufficient shares in any sale to ensure that the strategic national interests would be protected, O'Donoghue said. Tender notices will be published this week seeking consultants to advise the government on the sale of Aer Lingus. A sale of at least a 51 per cent stake is considered necessary to generate equity for Aer Lingus's fleet expansion. It is envisaged that a consortium of six or seven investors could buy into the airline, leaving the state as the single biggest stakeholder, government sources said.

'Obviously, it is necessary for us to avoid a situation where Aer Lingus's valuable Heathrow slots were used by any new owners to provide additional transatlantic services into London, with Aer Lingus servicing the leg between London and Dublin or other airports only,' said O'Donoghue. 'This would only serve to increase the transit time to Ireland for tourists from the US and would only encourage them to spend part of their time in Britain, thereby reducing the value of their visit to the Irish economy. I'm quite satisfied that the sale of Aer Lingus would be conducted in such a way that we would be in a position to veto any such sale. All of these matters are safeguarded and tied down, and the dangers that exist to our national and strategic interests are protected.'

O'Donoghue said that a reduction of the state's shareholding in Aer Lingus would not lead to 'any weakening or abandonment of the brand abroad'.

The minister urged the early renegotiation of a bilateral agreement between Ireland and the US restricting Aer Lingus to flying out of six US airports. Rules forcing US airlines to match every flight into Dublin with one into Shannon would change, but the government would ensure that Shannon 'gets a soft landing', said O'Donoghue.

It was clear from the moves by Ryanair and American Airlines, which are flying into the West, that 'Shannon should not be looked upon as some kind of victim of European aviation policy', he said. 'It is necessary that there be further expansion of Aer Lingus services to Shannon. This is not a dog in the manger attitude.

'What I want to see in the future is that Aer Lingus would place significant emphasis on the inbound portion of any new routes and take account of the regions,' he said. O'Donoghue said business class should be retained by Aer Lingus on transatlantic flights, as the service played an important role in attracting high-spending visitors to Ireland. 'This type of business is very important, particularly for providers of high-end products in rural parts of Ireland where that business is not easily replaceable,' he said.

Source: Connolly, N., 'Government will secure Heathrow slots', *The Sunday Business Post*, 29 May 2005.

Aer Lingus plans to leave OneWorld

Aer Lingus has confirmed to its OneWorld partners that it intends to leave the alliance but retain bilateral links with a number of the grouping's key member airlines.

The timing and terms for its withdrawal will be considered at the next meeting of the alliance's governing board, but it is likely to be in early 2007, as the three new recruits lining up to join OneWorld board the alliance in its biggest expansion to date – Japan Airlines, the largest airline in the Asia-Pacific region; Malev Hungarian and Royal Jordanian.

Aer Lingus's strategy has changed fundamentally since it joined the alliance six years ago and is no longer convergent with OneWorld's. The alliance's key target market is the multi-sector, premium, frequent international traveller, while Aer Lingus has repositioned itself as a low-fares point-to-point carrier.

The departure of Aer Lingus – currently the smallest airline in OneWorld, with 13,765 million of the total 761,794 million available seat kilometres capacity offered in 2005 by its existing members – will come as the alliance's three recruits increase its capacity by more than 20 per cent. Talks are progressing between OneWorld and other airlines interested in joining.

Aer Lingus is in discussions with various OneWorld members with the aim of retaining strong bilateral links with them, and its intention is to conclude these agreements before its leaves OneWorld.

It has confirmed that it has no intention of joining another global alliance and that its key bilateral relationships will remain with OneWorld members.

Ireland will remain part of the OneWorld network through services operated by the alliance's other member airlines.

Source: OneWorld Alliance, 30 May 2006.

COMPANY PROFILE: RYANAIR

www.ryanair.com

Ryanair is Europe's leading low-cost, no-frills carrier and is an Irish-registered airline. It is a public limited company quoted on the Dublin, London and New York Stock Exchanges, whose shares have performed extremely well to date. It is famous for its no-frills approach and low prices, as well as its charasmatic CEO, Michael O'Leary. It operates almost 350 routes from sixteen bases around Europe, with London-Stansted being its primary hub. Indeed, English passengers make up the largest group of Ryanair passengers. The Ryanair concept is modelled (partly) on Southwest Airlines in the US. Ryanair was Europe's only major airline to post a profit in the turbulent climate of 2001. The airline operates routes mainly to and from secondary airports, mostly within Europe (although there are new routes open to North Africa).

Ryanair in their own words

Ryanair was Europe's original low-fares airline and is still Europe's largest low-fares carrier. In 2006 Ryanair will carry over 35 million passengers on 346 low-fare routes across twenty-two European countries. We have fifteen European bases and a fleet of over 100 brand new Boeing 737-800 aircraft, with firm orders for a further 138 new aircraft, which will be delivered over the next six years. These additional aircraft will allow Ryanair to double in size to over 70 million passengers p.a. by 2012. Ryanair currently employs a team of 3,500 people, comprising over twenty-five different nationalities.

We started in 1985 and had our IPO in 1997 when we floated Ryanair Holdings plc on Dublin and New York (NASDAQ) Stock Exchanges. We listed on the United Kingdom a year later. Ryanair joined the NASDAQ Top 100 in December 2002, reflecting the phenomenal increase of Ryanair's value and the commitment of its 1,800 staff [at the time].

Where we're going
Like Superman, we're going up, up, up and away. Ryanair will be Europe's largest airline in the next eight years.

How we're getting there
Low fares and friendly, efficient service – that's our way. And how do we do it? Superb cost management. Landing in airports that don't rip you off. Free seats when we're feeling generous. No frills on your flight – but we'll sell you food, drink and gifts. Punchy advertising that sometimes gets us in trouble. And we take on the high-fares guys when they try to block our routes and airport management when they want to charge us too much.

What we've done so far
Over the past ten years we've increased our annual traffic from under 700,000 to over 27 million passengers. Along the way we changed the face of air travel, broke higher-fare cartels, rocked airport monopolies and made it possible for millions to travel.

Milestones, millstones and monopolies
Milestones for us, millstones for our competitors and monopolies that needed to be broken. If only they taught history like this at school.
- **1985:** We started with a fifteen-seater turbo prop going from the south east of Ireland (Waterford) to London-Gatwick. Today, the plane wouldn't be big enough to carry the management team around.
- **1986:** Inspired by the story David and Goliath, we go after the big guys for a slice of the action and end up smashing the Aer Lingus/British Airways high-fare cartel on the Dublin-London route. With two routes under our belts we carry 82,000 passengers in the year. Of course, we had to buy two more turbo prop BA 768 planes to do it.
- **1990/91:** Well, we're pretty good at getting the passengers onto our planes but not so hot on managing our costs. We're losing money, so a new management team is brought in to sort it out. We relaunch as a 'low fares/no frills' airline, closely modelling the Southwest Airlines model in the US. The rest is pretty much history.
- **1995:** Happy 10th Birthday to us. And we've plenty to celebrate. By now, we're the biggest passenger carrier on the Dublin-London route, the largest Irish airline on every route we operate and we've carried 2.25 million passengers in the year.
- **1997:** This is the year the EU fully deregulated the air business, enabling us to open new routes to Continental Europe. We launched services to Stockholm, Oslo, Paris and Brussels. And we took time out to float Ryanair plc on Dublin and NASDAQ Stock Exchanges.
- **1998:** Forget your fifteen-seater turbo props. This year we put in a US$2 billion order for forty-five new Boeing 737-800 series aircraft. We're voted Airline of the Year by the Irish Transport Users Committee and voted Best Managed National Airline by *International Aviation Week*

magazine. Over the next few years we get used to these awards but we stick with our cost focus.

- **2000:** Well, if there was anyone going to make money out of a dot com business, who better than Ryanair? After much deliberation and watching others burn up money, we jump onto the internet with the launch of our new online booking site: ryanair.com. Within three months the site is taking over 50,000 bookings a week.

- **2001:** It's the first birthday for ryanair.com and again something to celebrate. Our new baby now accounts for 75 per cent of overall bookings. We also start operations at our European base in Brussels Charleroi.

- **2002:** We open Frankfurt-Hahn as our second Continental European base and announce a long-term partnership with Boeing which will see us acquiring up to 150 new Boeing 737-800 series aircraft over an eight-year period from 2002 to 2010. Today our web accounts for 94 per cent of our bookings – probably something to do with opening another twenty-six routes this year.

- **2003:** Is characterised by rapid expansion. We start the year by announcing we've ordered an additional 100 new Boeing 737-800 series aircraft to facilitate our rapid European growth plans. We acquired Buzz from KLM in April and relaunched thirteen Buzz routes in May. In February we open our first base in Italy at Milan-Bergamo, and in April we launch our Stockholm Skavsta base in Sweden, with six new European routes. In all, sixty new routes are added throughout 2003 to bring us a total of 127 routes.

- **2004:** Ryanair is named the most popular airline on the web for 2003 by Google, as www.ryanair.com continues to be the most searched travel website in Europe. We add twenty-four new B737-800 aircraft (sixty in total) and retire another five of the older 737-200s. We launch two new bases in Rome Ciampino and Barcelona Girona as well as adding further aircraft to the existing bases at Stockholm Skavsta, Frankfurt-Hahn and Milan-Bergamo. Ryanair.com now accounts for over 98 per cent of all Ryanair bookings.

- **2005:** We launch five new bases, at Liverpool John Lennon Airport, Shannon in the West of Ireland, Pisa, Nottingham East Midlands and Cork, giving us a total of fifteen bases throughout Europe in 2005. We retire the remaining 737-200 aircraft and replace them with brand new Boeing 737-800s. We now have the youngest fleet in the world with an average aircraft age of just two years. Our punctuality is also second to none, and we celebrate beating easyJet for punctuality every week for three years solid. We carry more passengers in August than British Airways on their entire worldwide network, making us 'The World's Favourite Airline'. We also reiterate our 'no fuel surcharge guarantee' as airlines such as British Airways, Air France and Lufthansa continue to supplement their already high fares with fuel surcharges. To celebrate our 20th birthday, we offer

100,000 seats at 99p, 100 times less than our 1985 fare! Year-end 2005: Passengers: 30,946,000, employees: people (y/e): 2,700.

- **2006:** We add more new aircraft to our fleet to enable us to carry 42 million passengers in the year, and in March we accept delivery of our 100th Boeing 737-800. By 2012, we will have 225 such aircraft, allowing the airline to grow to 70 million passengers per annum. In March we also commence our Check'n'Go service, giving passengers the opportunity to check in online across our entire route network, cutting queues at both check-in and boarding. May marks the launch of Ryanair's 16th and first French base in Marseille. We also announce our first routes outside of Europe, to Marrakesh, Fez and Oujda in Morocco, allowing North Africans to experience what Europeans have been enjoying twenty-one years: the lowest fares, the most on-time flights and the best customer service.

Source: www.ryanair.com.

New routes a major boost to tourism
John O'Donoghue, TD, Minister for Arts, Sport and Tourism, today [21 December 2005] welcomed the announcement by Ryanair and the Dublin Airport Authority of an additional eighteen routes between Dublin and Continental Europe, involving an estimated additional 1 million inbound passengers.

'These new routes represent a major boost to Irish tourism and will be greatly welcomed by the tourism industry,' Minister O'Donoghue said. 'Many of the new destinations are already being targeted by Tourism Ireland as part of their major marketing programme for 2006 which was announced earlier this month, with the support of the €40 million Tourism Marketing Fund available next year. The number of mainland European visitors to Ireland already tops 1.5 million and represents €1 billion in foreign revenue earnings. With five new aircraft based in Dublin from next spring, the targeted tourism growth of 7 per cent from Continental Europe for 2006 looks set to be readily achieved.

'It is important that the tourism trade capitalises on these new routes and puts together compelling and value for money holiday packages that will entice visitors here, with a particular emphasis on spreading business to all the regions,' the Minister concluded.

Source: Department of Arts, Sport and Tourism press release, 21 December 2005.

Aer Lingus soars 15 per cent after takeover bid
Aer Lingus was yet again the topic of the day in the Irish market yesterday as, less than a week after it officially floated on the ISEQ, rival low-cost carrier Ryanair made a bid for the group.

In Dublin, dealers said all eyes were on Aer Lingus, which jumped more than 15 per cent to end the day up 39 cent, at €2.90 – above the €2.80 a share offered by Ryanair. As many as 64 million units changed hands in Dublin, with a further 55 million trading in London as dealers reported significant hedge fund interest in the stock following the takeover bid.

Under stock exchange rules Ryanair is unable to buy any shares below the price of its offer and it's believed that some tactical players are seeking to push the share price up in order to force the company to raise its bid.

The news had a different effect on Ryanair's share price, sending it down as low as €8.33 early in the day, only to recover slightly to close down only 3 cent – less than half a per cent – at €8.67.

After the market closed, Ryanair said it had increased its holding in Aer Lingus to 19.2 per cent.

Source: Shoesmith, C., 'Aer Lingus soars 15 per cent after takeover bid', *The Irish Times*, 6 October 2006

O'Leary urges take up of Ryanair offer
Ryanair chief executive Michael O'Leary has again urged Aer Lingus shareholders to accept the €1.4 billion takeover offer for the former State airline, saying that on its own the company has little chance of increasing shareholder value.

In a letter to all Aer Lingus shareholders yesterday, Mr O'Leary said Ryanair 'remains convinced that its offer of €2.80 per Aer Lingus share is a generous price'. Shareholders have until 1pm on December 22nd to accept the offer. Mr O'Leary criticised Aer Lingus's response to its offer document, saying it 'completely' failed to address the significant issues that Ryanair has raised and about which it believes Aer Lingus shareholders should be gravely concerned.

These include the group's 'dismal' financial performance in the first half of this year, its declining load factors and failure to provide any details of how it intends to reduce costs.

The Takeover Panel last month ruled that Aer Lingus must reveal details of its cost-reduction plan after mentioning it in its response document. Aer Lingus proceeded to issue a circular, but it contained little detail and simply outlined 12 areas where the group would look to increase cost efficiency.

Ryanair has outlined specific things it would do to lower costs at Aer Lingus if the offer were to succeed, including compulsory redundancies.

In the letter, Mr O'Leary says that without Ryanair's offer he believes Aer Lingus will be unable to cut its costs as it will remain 'a small, regional airline with limited bargaining power and a minnow in comparison to the global mega carriers it competes with'. Earlier this week he said Aer Lingus's best future prospects were as part of an enlarged Irish airline group.

The letter also points out that Aer Lingus's share price has continued to trade below Ryanair's €2.80 offer price and describes this as evidence that the market has little confidence in Aer Lingus management delivering a better alternative to shareholders. Immediately following the October 5th bid Aer Lingus shares rose above the offer price, though recently the stock has been trading around the low €2.70 level. Yesterday the shares closed unchanged at €2.75.

At an extraordinary meeting earlier this week where Ryanair shareholders approved the takeover offer, Mr O'Leary admitted the bid was 'highly unlikely' to succeed. Shareholders representing about 40 per cent of Aer Lingus's total stock have already expressed opposition. Whatever the outcome, Ryanair has said it intends to stay on the Aer Lingus share register. The budget airline has spent €342 million becoming Aer Lingus's second-biggest shareholder with a 25.2 per cent stake, although Mr O'Leary earlier this week said the company hadn't yet decided whether it would raise its holding.

The European Commission is due to rule on the proposed takeover on Wednesday, a decision Mr O'Leary believes will determine the way several Aer Lingus shareholders decide to vote.

Source: Shoesmith, C., 'O'Leary urges take up of Ryanair offer', *The Irish Times*, 16 December 2006

O'Leary letter sparks racist row on Jordanians

The chief executive of Ryanair, Michael O'Leary, has triggered a major row by sending what has been described as a 'racist' letter to the Minister for Public Enterprise referring disparagingly to Jordan's national airline.

The letter from O'Leary was brought to the attention of Royal Jordanian Airlines and is understood to have caused such anger that the company is now considering referring the matter to the Jordanian government.

In the April 5 letter, O'Leary accused Mary O'Rourke of offering nothing to Irish tourism except '100,000 Jordanians stopping off for wee wees in Shannon'. He suggested her efforts might have done no more than create a couple of jobs for lavatory cleaners.

Royal Jordanian has increased its business into Ireland, with twenty-two flights a week using Shannon on stopovers between New York and the Jordanian capital, Amman. The airline picks up full catering services at Shannon and is regarded as an extremely valuable customer of Aer Rianta, the airports authority.

According to documentation released to *The Sunday Business Post* under the Freedom of Information Act, O'Leary's letter to the minister claimed that her tenure in Public Enterprise had been 'a disaster for Irish aviation and Irish tourism'.

'The fact that Royal Jordanian (airlines) will now be stopping off with 100,000 people for wee wees in Shannon will really guarantee the future of the airport and tourism in the Mid West region. Who knows, it might even create one or two jobs for lavatory cleaners in the area? It is a pity it won't do anything for car hire companies, restauranteurs, hotels or the wider tourism industry generally because it won't add one inbound visitor to Shannon or the Mid West region,' he wrote.

The correspondence is the latest in a series of vituperative personal letters to the minister and her department, criticising what O'Leary alleges is O'Rourke's protectionist attitude to Aer Rianta. His letter, marked 'strictly private and confidential', congratulates O'Rourke on her 'latest initiative in Shannon'.

Aer Rianta sources described O'Leary's references to Jordanians urinating in Shannon as 'racist' and said the correspondence was regarded as deeply insulting by the airline.

In his letter, which began 'Dear Mary', the Ryanair chief executive continued: 'Who cares, I hear you cry, if Irish people have to pay higher air fares? Who cares if traffic from our major market, the UK, is in decline? Who cares if there is no new route development between Ireland and Continental Europe?'

In a subsequent letter dated April 30, O'Leary referred to a formal complaint lodged by O'Rourke's department with the Advertising Standards Authority of Ireland concerning a Ryanair advertisement in two daily newspapers the previous week. The department complained to the chief executive of the Authority that the advertisement was 'not truthful, honest or decent' and that the picture of the minister was reproduced without her permission.

But O'Leary claimed the advertisement expressed Ryanair's view on a political issue and a matter of significant public interest, and was not in breach of the advertising code.

The Ryanair chief told O'Rourke that the letter was 'typical of the spurious waffle which always characterises your reaction to criticism'.

A spokesman for the department refused to comment on the O'Leary letters.

Source: Tynan, M.M., 'O'Leary letter sparks racist row on Jordanians', *The Sunday Business Post*, 27 May 2001.

Ryanair July numbers climb 23 per cent

Ryanair carried 3.94 million passengers in July, an increase of 23 per cent on the same month last year.

The load factor – a measure of how many seats the airline filled – was unchanged at 90 per cent.

Ryanair yesterday reported pre-tax profits of €128.6 million for its first financial quarter to the end of June, a jump of more than 75 per cent on the same period last year, despite a 52 per cent rise in fuel costs.

But chief executive Michael O'Leary warned that the airline was cautious on the outlook for the rest of its financial year. He said Ryanair expected more difficult trading conditions this winter, as it planned substantial route expansion.

Source: RTÉ, 'Ryanair July numbers climb 23 per cent', 3 August 2006.

Ryanair announces biggest ever expansion at Dublin – twelve new European routes start from December

Ryanair, Ireland's largest airline, today [9 August 2006] unveiled a significant expansion of its European operations at Dublin Airport. From December, Ryanair will base three new aircraft in Dublin Airport, create over 200 jobs and start services on twelve new routes from Dublin to points all over Europe. The new schedule of routes is as follows:

- Oslo (Norway) – daily.
- Madrid (Spain) – daily.
- Tampere (Finland) – four weekly.
- Vitoria (Spain) – four weekly.
- Billund (Denmark) – four weekly.
- Bologna (Italy) – four weekly.
- Grenoble (France) – three weekly.
- Friedrichshafen (Germany) – three weekly.
- Seville (Spain) – three weekly.
- Pula (Croatia) – three weekly.
- Almeria (Spain) – three weekly.
- Rzeszow (Poland) – three weekly.

These new destinations start in December 2006 and will be served by Ryanair on a year-round basis. They bring to sixty-three the number of UK and European routes served by Ryanair from Dublin and completes Ryanair's displacement of Aer Lingus as the national carrier of Ireland, as demonstrated by the following facts:

1. Ryanair carries 42 million pax [passengers] annually, five times more than Aer Lingus's 8 million.
2. Ryanair offers more routes from Dublin to the UK (eighteen) than Aer Lingus (seven).
3. Ryanair offers more routes from Dublin to Europe (forty-five) than Aer Lingus (twenty-eight).
4. Ryanair offers double the routes from Ireland to the UK and Europe (102) than Aer Lingus (fifty-one).
5. Ryanair carries 50 per cent more passengers to/from Ireland (12 million) than Aer Lingus (8 million).
6. Ryanair's average fare is €41. Aer Lingus's average euro fare is 60 per cent higher at €67.
7. Ryanair beats Aer Lingus on punctuality, fewer cancellations and fewer lost bags.
8. Ryanair brings more visitors to Dublin and Ireland than Aer Lingus.

Announcing these new routes in Dublin this morning, Ryanair's CEO Michael O'Leary said: 'Move over Aer Lingus! Ryanair is now Ireland's national airline and Aer Lingus is just a distant number 2. Passengers prefer Ryanair because we give them lower fares, many more destinations to the UK and Europe and a better passenger service in terms of newer aircraft, better punctuality, fewer cancellations and fewer lost bags.

'On every route where they have a choice, millions more passengers prefer Ryanair to Aer Lingus. Today's twelve new routes will end Aer Lingus's high-fare monopoly to destinations such as Madrid, Bologna, Almeria and Seville. Irish passengers who previously had no alternative to Aer Lingus's high fares and frequent delays on these routes will now have a low-fare, on-time option with Ryanair. Irish passengers will also enjoy Ryanair's low fares to new European destinations such as Norway (Oslo Torp), Denmark (Billund), Finland (Tampere) and Eastern Poland (Rzeszow), which are not currently served by Aer Lingus.

'This year Ryanair will carry 42 million passengers across its network. This is five times more than the annual 8 million traffic of Aer Lingus. Ryanair also carries 50 per cent more passengers than Aer Lingus to/from Ireland. The Irish people have voted with their feet and made Ryanair Ireland's number one airline. In the process Aer Lingus has been displaced as Ireland's national airline and now survives as just a distant number 2.

'In 2007, Ryanair will deliver 9 million passengers through Dublin Airport, sustaining 9,000 jobs in Dublin and generating a tourist spend of €2.5 billion. To celebrate these twelve new European destinations, Ryanair is launching a seat sale today with every seat on every one of these routes (except Grenoble and Friedrichshafen) being sold for just €12 one way (including taxes, fees and charges) for travel during the first month of operation. This offer will run for one week only and I urge everybody to book their seats as quickly as possible on www.ryanair.com because at such low prices, these seats will sell out fast.'

Source: Ryanair August 2006.

COMPANY PROFILE: AER ARANN

www.aerarann.com

Aer Arann is a small Irish airline, originally serving the link between the Aran Islands and the Irish mainland since the 1970s. It has expanded and now offers internal routes within Ireland, as well as routes to and from Britain and France. Its CEO is Padraig O'Ceidigh. Major technological and fleet investment in the past few years have led to its rapid growth. Aer Arann currently services the public service obligation (PSO) routes such as Dublin–Galway and Dublin–Cork, which are subsidised by the state. The airline was the first to offer a Cork–Belfast route. It is the largest airline operating from Cork Airport, and third largest from Dublin Airport. Aer Arann offer prices on domestic flights which are often not much more expensive than rail routes, e.g. €30, €40 each way on many domestic flights.

Aer Arann in their own words

In the 1970s Aer Arann began flying from Galway to the Aran Islands, providing an island-hopping air service from the mainland to each of the three islands.

In 1994 Padraig O'Ceidigh purchased Aer Arann and set about laying the groundwork for a feeder air service for Ireland and the UK.

Today, Aer Arann is one of the world's fastest-growing regional airlines, with a turnover in excess of €95 million per annum and passenger numbers of 1.15 million for 2005.

Aer Arann currently operates over 600 flights per week across thirty-five routes in Ireland, the UK and France. The airline has launched a total of twelve new routes for summer 2006, half of which are UK services including Cork to Cardiff and Newquay, Galway to Liverpool, Dublin to Inverness and the newly announced Cardiff to Dublin and Galway.

The Aer Arann fleet comprises eleven aircraft; five 50-seater ATR42s and six 66-seater ATR72s. The ATR turboprop aircraft has become renowned in the global air transport industry for reliability and efficiency. It is also a best seller in its class.

The aircraft provides passengers with a similar cabin environment to that of large jet airliners, combining wide aisles with generous headroom. These aircraft are specifically designed to provide efficient and comfortable transportation on short-haul routes, making them an ideal fleet for Aer Arann. The airline also has partnership links with SAS, Air France and British Airways.

Source: Aer Arann.

AIRPORTS IN IRELAND

Dublin Airport is the fourteenth busiest airport in Europe and is a vital gateway for Ireland. Increasingly, Irish airports are becoming hubs for international travel, although they still remain in the shadow of regional super-airports, such as London Heathrow and Paris Charles de Gaulle (see Chapter 2 for details on the development of Irish state-owned airports).

Table 6.5: Airports in Ireland

Belfast City	Galway
Belfast International	Kerry
City of Derry	Knock
Cork	Shannon
Donegal	Sligo
Dublin	Waterford

Table 6.6: Europe's Business Airports by Passenger Traffic (2005)

1. London Heathrow	UK	67 million
2. Paris Charles de Gaulle	France	51 million
3. Frankfurt International	Germany	51 million
4. Amsterdam Schiphol	Netherlands	42.5 million
5. Madrid Barajas	Spain	41.9 million
6. London Gatwick	UK	32 million
7. Munich Airport	Germany	29 million
8. Rome Leonardo da Vinci	Italy	29 million
9. Barcelona International	Spain	27.1 million
10. London Stansted	UK	22 million
11. Copenhagen Airport	Denmark	20 million
12. Malpensa Intl Milan	Italy	19.6 million
13. Manchester International	UK	19.2 million
14. Dublin International	Ireland	18.4 million
15. Zürich International	Switzerland	17.8 million
16. Stockholm Arlanda	Sweden	17.1 million
17. Düsseldorf International	Germany	16.7 million
18. Brussels Airport	Belgium	16.2 million
19. Oslo Airport	Norway	16 million
20. Vienna Airport	Austria	15.7 million
21. Atatürk Intl Airport	Turkey	15.6 million
22. Athens Intl Airport	Greece	14.3 million
23. Helsinki Vantaa Airport	Finland	13 million
24. Sheremetyevo Intl Moscow	Russia	12.2 million
25. Berlin Tegel Intl	Germany	11.1 million

Source: http://en.wikipedia.org/wiki/Airports_of_Europe.

Table 6.7: Scheduled Airlines Flying to/from Dublin Airport (2006)

Adria Airways	www.adria-airways.com
Aer Arann	www.aerarann.com
Aer Lingus	www.aerlingus.com
Air Baltic	www.airbaltic.com
Air Canada	www.aircanada.com
Air France	www.airfrance.com
Air Malta	www.airmalta.com
Air Southwest	www.airsouthwest.com
Air Transat	www.airtransat.com
American Airlines	www.aa.com

Table 6.7: Scheduled Airlines Flying to/from Dublin Airport (2006) (contd.)

Austrian Airlines	www.aua.com
British Airways	www.britishairways.com
British Midland	www.flybmi.com
CityJet	www.cityjet.com
Continental Airlines	www.continental.com
Czech Airlines	www.czechairlines.com
Delta	www.delta.com
Estonian Air	www.estonian-air.com
Euro Manx	www.euromanx.com
Finnair	www.finnair.com
Flybe	www.flybe.com
Flynordic	www.flynordic.com
German Wings	www.germanwings.com
Gulf Air	www.gulfairco.com
Hapag Lloyd Express	www.hlx.com/en
Helios Airways (now ajet)	www.ajet.com
Iberia	www.iberia.com
Lithuanian Airlines	www.lal.lt/en
Loganair	www.loganair.co.uk
Lot Polish Airlines	www.lot.com
Lufthansa	www.lufthansa.com
Luxair	www.luxair.lu
Malev	www.malev.com
Ryanair	www.ryanair.com
SAS Braathens	www.sasbraathens.no
SAS Scandinavian Airlines	www.scandinavian.net
Spanair	www.spanair.com
Swiss Airlines	www.swiss.com
Thomsonfly	www.thomsonfly.com
Transavia	www.transavia.com
US Airways	www.usairways.com

Source: Dublin Airport Authority.

Speech by John O'Donoghue, TD, Minister for Arts, Sport and Tourism, media launch of Gulf Air's new direct service between Bahrain and Dublin in Conrad Hotel, Dublin on Friday, 15 July 2005

I am delighted to be here today at the launch of Gulf Air's new direct service between Bahrain and Dublin.

Ireland is an island, and as such, our economic growth and our tourism growth, in particular, are closely bound up with access. 2005 will see significant increases in direct scheduled air capacity to the island of Ireland from key markets – peak season capacity from Britain will grow by 16 per cent, from mainland Europe by 40 per cent and from North America by 17 per cent. However, the focus of global economic development and tourism growth is moving east and we need to follow that in air access development. I see this as an issue of key strategic importance.

In this context, the service being announced today is most opportune and most welcome. This new service will allow direct travel to Ireland from the Kingdom of Bahrain and will also serve as a gateway into Ireland for more than forty cities in the Middle East, Africa, the Far East and Australia.

The service will increase the options available to long-haul travellers wishing to come to Ireland to enjoy a holiday or for business purposes.

Ireland has much to offer the long-haul traveller. Growth in visitor numbers of almost 30 per cent from markets such as Australia and New Zealand last year is strong evidence of the potential from these markets. From next December, Ireland will become more accessible to these markets than ever before.

As we are fully aware, the tourism and travel sectors have seen a lot of turbulence in recent years. Over-reliance on any one market is not prudent in the long term. We are particularly keen to increase visitor numbers and exploit the full potential of new and developing markets outside our traditional source markets of Britain, the US and Europe. Gulf Air's decision to open this route from December is a vote of confidence in that potential. I know Tourism Ireland, the agency responsible for marketing the island of Ireland overseas as a tourism destination, is keen to work with Gulf Air to maximise the tourism opportunities arising from the new service.

From a business perspective, this new service will facilitate the ever-growing commercial links between Ireland and the Middle East.

For all of these reasons, I believe Gulf Air's decision to initiate this Dublin–Bahrain service is well founded and one that will be well rewarded with both inbound and outbound business.

Source: Department of Arts, Sport and Tourism speeches archive, 15 July 2005.

AIRLINE REGULATIONS

Following deregulation of the US airline market in 1978, Europe began the process of deregulating its airline market in the early 1980s. National governments are no longer permitted to financially support the so-called 'state' or 'flag carrier' airlines.

Internationally, routes are assigned on the basis of agreements between governments of the countries involved. Fares are generally monitored by governments, but set by companies themselves. However, national governments approve and licence airlines.

O'Donoghue welcomes new air transport deal as a major boost for Irish tourism

John O'Donoghue, TD, Minister for Arts, Sport and Tourism, today [11 November 2005] welcomed the agreement negotiated by Martin Cullen, TD, Minister for Transport, with the US authorities in the context of the current EU–US Open Skies negotiations which resume in Washington next week.

The proposed new arrangements have major potential to open up a range of new air services between Ireland and the US. The US tourism market currently delivers close to 1 million visitors annually, representing a revenue spend of approximately €700 million. But the potential is truly enormous, in particular, when new gateways are opened beyond the current seven gateways.

'This is great news for the Irish tourism industry,' said Minister O'Donoghue. 'The US is our second largest tourism market. US visitors stay longer, spend more per capita and travel more widely in the country, which is critically important for improved regional spread of tourism.

'The objective in these negotiations was to ensure that prior to concluding an EU–US Open Skies Agreement we would move to protect our strategic interests in expanding air access to the US while at the same time ensuring an acceptable deal in so far as Shannon Airport is concerned.

'Market research carried out in the United States by the tourism agencies over the years has demonstrated a consistently high level of interest in Ireland as a holiday destination and a high level of unsatisfied demand. Unfortunately, we have suffered from a glass ceiling in the US market which has constrained our performance there due to the very limited number of direct access gateways and routes between Ireland and the US.'

Minister O'Donoghue said that he was delighted at the prospect of three further gateways being opened up for Irish carriers in addition to the existing gateways.

'I am particularly happy with the fact that the need for a transition phase for Shannon has been recognised. I believe that this breakthrough agreement represents a major opportunity for Ireland as a whole and it is imperative that the industry and public sector in the West, in particular, work together in a positive and integrated way to realise the great potential on offer. For my part, I will be asking the state agencies to take the necessary measures and work with the industry to capitalise on the very significant opportunities arising from today's most welcome announcement,' continued O'Donoghue.

'The Ireland US bilateral made sense at the time it was negotiated but we must now move on and grasp the opportunities for all regions arising from the experience of such a large potential tourism market that is well disposed to the Irish product offering.

'The signing of such an arrangement has long been an objective of Irish tourism policy and was a major recommendation in the report of the Tourism Policy Review Group, *New Horizons in Irish Tourism*, published in September 2003,' Minister O'Donoghue concluded.

Source: Department of Arts, Sport and Tourism press release, 11 November 2005.

THE ECONOMICS OF AIRLINE OPERATIONS

There is a large element of risk in introducing a new route. Success is not easy. Seat prices are traditionally high to compensate for a low load factor. However, some carriers (such as low-cost carriers) price seats lower at the launch of a new route to promote the route. As the route gains popularity, other carriers may enter, particularly on lucrative routes. Certain routes are very competitive, e.g. the Dublin to London route, which (according to the Dublin Airport Authority) is the busiest air route in Europe.

Many airlines suffered or disappeared in the 1990s and at the turn of the millennium. Indeed, the early years of the 2000s were not very promising, especially 2001. Nowadays, major restructuring is taking place.

Some of the leading European airlines are 'huddling together for warmth' as one newspaper article put it, referring to the fact that many airlines must work together to survive. International airline alliances and co-operative agreements are extremely important in such a climate.

Airline costs are generally divided between capital costs and operating costs. There are enormous investment costs in the airline business. Costs are usually a package of sale of aircraft plus subsequent provision of spares and/or maintenance. Many airline manufacturers offer attractive loan terms and trade-ins. This is especially true in the global competition between America's Boeing (www.boeing.com) and Europe's Airbus (www.airbus.com).

During turbulent times (such as between 2001 and 2004), airlines cut back on orders and leased instead to release capital. This causes major problems for airline manufacturers. One airline that took advantage of the downturn for Boeing was Ryanair. The airline negotiated a significant discount for 150 brand new Boeing 737s at a time when Boeing desperately needed orders.

Short-haul routes are more expensive to operate than long-haul in a mile-for-mile comparison because there is greater frequency of take-offs and landings and because short-haul aircraft spend more time on the ground.

Low-cost airlines such as Ryanair combat the second issue by ensuring their aircraft are back in the skies shortly after landing at a destination. The airline also only uses Boeing 737 jets, as they are fuel efficient. They also allow for easy and efficient embarking and disembarking of passengers, as they have front and rear passenger doors. Further, having one type of jet allows Ryanair to bulk buy parts and to hire and train a single type of maintenance crew.

Operating costs can be divided between direct and indirect:
- **Direct:** Salaries, fuel, in-flight catering, maintenance, depreciation, airport charges.
- **Indirect:** Marketing, reservations, ground-handling, etc.

Fuel cost is a key determinant of efficiency in the airline business. Fuel costs globally are priced in US dollars. This benefited European airlines between 2000 and 2004. As the euro was strong versus the US dollar, this provided a buffer against the rising cost of oil, which was offset by the rising value of the euro. However, in 2004 and 2005, the euro weakened against the US dollar and the cost of oil hit record highs in the summer of 2005. This resulted in higher direct operational costs. Many airlines passed this on to the customer in the form of an added fuel surcharge on flights. Some airlines actually distinguish themselves from the majority by promising not to impose a fuel surcharge at a later date, e.g. Ryanair. Airlines often engage in fuel hedging. This involves bulk purchase of aviation fuel (to be delivered as required) at a fixed agreed price. This can be advantageous to the airline. They can plan their fares based on a fixed price for the fuel they use. The airline will of course benefit if there is a subsequent rise in the cost of the fuel. However, fuel costs may fall, and the airline is obligated to pay the agreed prices, even if it is higher. The euro stabilised somewhat against the US dollar in 2006, and as a result so did the record high fuel prices.

PRESENT AND FUTURE CHALLENGES
Alliances and Co-operation

Many airlines are now part of international airline alliances, such as the OneWorld Alliance and the Star Alliance. These are marketing alliances, which allow the airlines to share services (customer service desks, business lounges in airports) as well as distribution methods in an effort to keep their costs down. These alliances are set to grow in importance as many airlines join up. However, Ireland's national airline, Aer Lingus, decided to leave OneWorld in 2006 (effective from 2007) as their business strategy of low-cost, point-to-point operator ceased to fit with the full-service model of the OneWorld airlines.

There are various other forms of partnership, of which these alliances and ultimately mergers are the more extreme. Basic alliances include code-sharing and interlining. The former denotes one aircraft operating under two flight codes by two carriers, and the single aircraft would usually be staffed by employees of both airlines. The benefit for the airlines in question includes filling one aircraft and sharing the route, rather than half-filling two aircraft and competing on the route. It also enhances both airlines' listings on reservations systems, as the flight appears under two codes for two distinct airlines. On the other hand, interlining is a looser form of partnership, where the airline that a customer checks in for on the first leg of their journey has the ability to interline (book ahead) their baggage and check-in for the entire journey. For example, if a customer is flying from Dublin to London with Aer Lingus, then onwards to Athens with British Airways from London, then the Aer Lingus check-in desk in Ireland would be able to provide the customer with their boarding cards for both legs of the flight and arrange for the customer's luggage to be transferred so they do not collect it until arrival at the final destination, i.e. Athens.

Security

The shock of commercial airliners being used as weapons of terror on 11 September 2001 changed the nature of air travel forever. As a result, many people are fearful of flying, and even those who do not fear flying may refuse to fly on airlines of certain nations that are perceived as terrorist targets. This presents huge challenges to the industry. Airlines which code-share with partner airlines may encounter passengers who believed they were travelling on an aircraft of Airline A, but in fact are travelling on an aircraft of Airline B (as is the nature of code-sharing). If Airline B is an airline of a country which is a perceived terrorist target, then some safety-conscious passengers may refuse to fly on such an airline.

Security at airports as well as on airlines must be continually improved and monitored if confidence in air travel security is to be maintained.

Technology

Technology continues to make it easier to distribute travel (see Chapter 9). Given the falling costs of access to broadband internet service, it will continue to become as much an everyday feature in homes as a television set. This allows the customer to shop around for travel. It also allows the transport operators to engage in disintermediation (cutting out the intermediary; see Chapters 8 and 9) in an effort to cut their distribution costs. Further technology such as enhanced mobile phones and palmtop devices will continue to provide opportunities and challenges for the transport provider.

Low-cost Airlines

Low-cost airlines seem here to stay, as their cost base and prices offered continue to fall. Indeed, it is hard to imagine how some can continue to cut costs. Even Ryanair's in-flight sick bags, once unused, double as a photo processing envelope by post. Aer Lingus seems to be succeeding in its goals to turn into a lower-cost operator in order to challenge Ryanair, primarily on the lucrative Ireland–Britain market. Further airlines may develop low-cost divisions in order to compete, although both KLM's Buzz and BA's Go low-cost brands were sold not long after their inception (Buzz to Ryanair). There can be only one clear winner in the continuing low-cost battle, and that is the air passengers.

Around 15 per cent of Ryanair's profits come from ancillary business – that is, not fares for air travel. This includes commissions from car hire operators, hotels, travel insurance, onward travel links (such as Stansted Express tickets), call cards and even their own MBNA credit card. It is no wonder that CEO Michael O'Leary claimed recently that all Ryanair flights should be free by 2014, with the passenger only having to pay airport charges and taxes, as Ryanair will by this stage, he ventured, be making all of its profits from ancillary business.

Yield Management and 'Bumping'

Most airlines oversell seats, the basic premise being that on any one flight, it is likely that some people will be delayed or not show up. As a service, airlines cannot store their excess capacity for resale tomorrow (like a shopkeeper can). Rather than a seat remaining empty, the airlines take a chance and oversell. This improves their overall revenue, and is known as yield management. Sophisticated software is sometimes used to work out what the likelihood of some customers missing the flight is. Even information such as road traffic accidents near airports which may delay passengers is taken into account.

'Bumping', or 'involuntary denied boarding', occurs when a passenger is denied boarding although they have a paid, confirmed ticket and have arrived at check-in at the designated time. The understandably irate passenger now has recourse to immediate compensation, according to new EU passenger rights (see Chapter 11), which were designed to discourage such airline behaviour.

IRISH TRANSPORT STRATEGY

On 1 November 2005, the Irish government announced a major €34.4 billion investment in Irish transport over ten years. The plan, aimed at delivering on-time, on-budget transport solutions for the whole country, was to be known as **Transport 21** (see www.transport.ie and www.transport21.ie). The press release from the Department of Transport summarises the key issues.

Connecting communities, promoting prosperity

Government launches 'twenty-first-century transport plan for twenty-first-century Ireland'

An integrated transport system for Dublin, to include seven new LUAS projects, two Metro lines, an underground station at St Stephen's Green integrating all services and the Western Rail Corridor are among the investments outlined today in Transport 21, the government's €34.4 billion transport investment plan.

Transport 21 also includes new commuter rail services for Cork City and Galway City, DART extensions in Dublin and a new road route connecting Donegal to Galway, Limerick, Cork and Waterford, known as the Atlantic Corridor.

An Taoiseach, Bertie Ahern, TD, launched Transport 21, a strategy which will see €9.4 million invested every day for the next ten years in Irish transport. The Taoiseach was joined by the Tánaiste, Mary Harney, TD, the Minister for Transport, Martin Cullen, TD, and the Minister for Finance, Brian Cowen, TD.

Minister Cullen outlined the details of Transport 21, nationally and in the Greater Dublin Area, saying Transport 21 had connecting communities and promoting prosperity at its core. Minister Cowen outlined the economic benefits of Transport 21 and detailed a series of value for money measures to ensure Transport 21 is delivered on time and on budget.

Speaking in Dublin Castle, the Taoiseach said Transport 21 signalled a new era for transport in Ireland. He said: 'We need and deserve a first-class transport system. We have all worked to generate the resources, now we must invest to continue to improve the lives of everybody. On transport, we have to move from far behind to the lead. Transport 21 is designed to achieve this objective and deliver benefits in every part of the country.'

The Tánaiste, Mary Harney, said: 'This programme will not merely meet the transport needs of our citizens, but also underpin our competitiveness into the future. Ireland is no longer a low-wage economy and we have no wish to return to being one. A comprehensive and efficient transport network is essential if we are to continue to improve our living standards while remaining competitive in the global marketplace.'

> Minister Cullen said: 'Transport 21 will deliver a twenty-first-century infrastructure for a twenty-first-century Ireland. It has connecting communities and promoting prosperity at its core. It is visionary, detailed, integrated and deliverable. Transport 21 seizes the historic opportunity to complete the transformation of our country.'
>
> Minister Cowen said: 'Transport 21 is a statement by government that transport investment merits top priority. Quality, integrated transport is critical for competitiveness, return on investment and regional development. Sound economics has enabled us to prepare Transport 21. Continued sound economics will sustain our stability and deliver Transport 21.'
>
> Source: Department of Transport, 1 November 2005.

The key points of the Transport 21 plan are:
- €9.4 million per day for transport for the next ten years.
- 175 million extra public transport users.
- 75 million extra suburban rail passengers.
- City centre to Dublin Airport in seventeen minutes by Metro.
- 80,000 more bus passengers per day.
- 80 million LUAS and Metro passengers per annum.
- Seven new LUAS projects.
- Dublin rail journeys – DART, LUAS, Metro, Suburban – in zero or one change of train.
- Doubling of park and ride sites in Dublin to seventy-four.
- 70 km of QBC in Cork.
- 187 new rail carriages.
- A train on the hour from Dublin to Cork.
- A train every hour at peak time from Dublin to Galway.
- A train every hour at peak time from Dublin to Limerick.
- A train every two hours off peak from Dublin to Galway.
- A train every hour off peak from Dublin to Limerick.
- A train every two hours from Dublin to Sligo.
- A train every two hours from Dublin to Tralee.
- A train every two hours from Dublin to Waterford.
- Four trains a day from Dublin to Westport, Ballina and Rosslare.
- Train service from Ennis to Claremorris.
- Galway: Commuter train service every day from Athenry to Galway City.
- Cork: Commuter train service every day from Midleton to Cork City.
- Cork: Commuter train service every day from Mallow, Blarney, Dunkettle and Kilbarry to Cork City.
- €9 million per annum for Rural Transport Initiative, serving more than 500,000 passengers.
- A saving of up to thirty-nine minutes by car from Dublin to Galway.
- A saving of up to forty-one minutes by car from Dublin to Cork.
- A saving of up to fifty-six minutes by car from Dublin to Waterford.
- A saving of up to seventeen minutes by car from Dublin to Limerick.

- 850 km of dual carriageway, 2+1 and single carriageway roads.
- Atlantic Corridor: Connecting the Gateways of Letterkenny, Sligo, Galway, Limerick, Cork and Waterford.

Table 6.8: Expected Completion Dates for Transport 21 Projects

2006	Introduction of hourly services on Dublin–Cork rail route
	Dublin Port Tunnel
2007	New Portlaoise train depot
	Delivery and introduction to service of 120 intercity railcars
	M1 Motorway
	M50 upgrade (Phase 1)
2008	Joining of the Tallaght and Sandyford LUAS lines in city centre
	LUAS extension from Connolly to Docklands
	LUAS extension Tallaght to Citywest (subject to developer contributions)
	Cork commuter rail service to Midleton
	Ennis–Athenry rail line (Western Rail Corridor)
2009	Dublin city centre rail resignalling project
	M3 Motorway
	Phase 1 of Navan Rail Link
	Opening of new Dublin city centre rail station
	Limerick Southern Ring Road
	Waterford City Bypass
	Galway–Athenry commuter rail services
2010	Metro West Phase 1 Tallaght to Clondalkin
	Kildare rail upgrade
	Sandyford LUAS line extension to Cherrywood
	Dublin–Cork Inter-Urban Motorway
	Dublin–Limerick Inter-Urban Motorway
	Dublin–Galway Inter-Urban Motorway
	Dublin–Waterford Inter-Urban Motorway
	M50 upgrade (Phase 2)
2011	Metro West Phase 2 Clondalkin to Lucan
	Athenry–Tuam rail line (Western Rail Corridor)
2012	Metro North
	LUAS extension from city centre to Liffey Junction
	Metro West Phase 3 Lucan to Blanchardstown
2013	Lucan to city centre LUAS
	Rail Safety Programme completed
2014	Metro West Phase 4 Blanchardstown to Ballymun
	Tuam–Claremorris rail line (Western Rail Corridor)
2015	Interconnector completed
	Extend electrification to Balbriggan, Maynooth, Navan, Hazelhatch
	Phase 2 of Navan rail link
	LUAS extension Cherrywood to Bray

Source: Department of Transport.

The 2011–2015 road programme will involve the development of approximately 150 km of dual carriageway, 400 km of 2+1 roads and 300 km of single carriageway. The sequencing of projects for implementation post-2010 will be decided by the National Roads Authority at a later date.

According to the Transport 21 plan, Dublin will be well served by public transport, both overground and underground, as shown in Figure 6.6.

Figure 6.6: Transport 21's Plan for Dublin

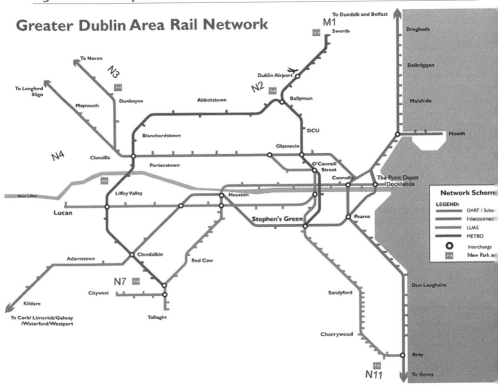

Source: Department of Transport.

The Transport 21 plan also envisages an impressive road network for the country, including upgrading and widening of existing motorways and national roads, as well as regional routes and the creation of an Atlantic Corridor.

Figure 6.7: Transport 21's Plan for Ireland

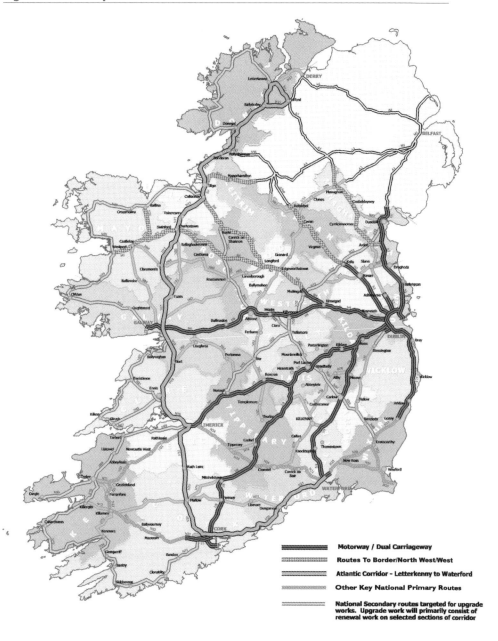

Source: Department of Transport.

The Transport 21 plan is an ambitious plan for Irish transport, which will serve Irish commuters as much as tourists. As mentioned earlier in this chapter, internal transport is vital for promoting a balanced regional spread of tourism, which is part of the government's tourism strategy. Innovative plans such as an Atlantic Corridor roadway connecting some of the regions with the least tourism numbers to various other access points of the country will address these issues. What remains to be seen, however, is if the commitment to the Transport 21 plan reaches fruition, and how long it will take before Ireland can boast a world-class network of roads, railways, public transport and access ports comparable to our European neighbours.

REVISION QUESTIONS

1. List Ireland's access transport options and give a brief background of some companies involved in each.
2. Comment on how each of the Irish transport operators has changed over the last ten years.
3. Highlight any deficiencies in access transport to Ireland.
4. What challenges do you foresee for the major Irish-owned access transport operators?
5. What are the key distinctions between full-service and low-cost airlines?
6. In your opinion, what does the future hold for both full-service and low-cost airlines in (a) a European and (b) a global context?

ESSAY QUESTIONS

1. What are the issues facing the (a) Irish and (b) global transport industry at present?
2. 'Traditional European airlines are locked in a battle with new market entrants and substitutes.' Discuss.
3. Southwest Airlines in the US and Ryanair in Europe have demonstrated how low-cost, no-frills service can be a formidable challenger to traditional so-called 'flag carrier' airlines. Is a low-cost strategy the only way forward for such 'old relics' of aviation?
4. 'Ryanair has done the impossible – taken on the large European airlines, and won.' Discuss.
5. 'People management is important in any industry, including the transport industries. However, not all airline management has harmonious relations with their staff.' Discuss this statement with relevance to at least one transport operator and compare/contrast it to at least one other one.
6. 'The continuing fierce battle between access transport operators in the Irish market results in one clear winner: the traveller to Ireland.' Discuss.
7. 'Ferry operators must develop innovative products if they are to survive in the current competitive climate.' Discuss.

8. Transport is one of the key components of the tourism product. Highlight the major recent trends in air transport in (a) Ireland and (b) Europe. Briefly discuss the challenges faced by the Irish airline industry.

9. 'Given the increasing trend towards shorter breaks, a modern and efficient transport system is essential for any destination wishing to grow its tourism industry.' Discuss.

10. You are employed as a consultant to the aviation sector. Detail your understanding of the critical strategies required for survival in the twenty-first century.

11. The low-cost airline model has been very successful to date, but only for a handful of airlines. Detail the causes for its success and outline what you perceive to be the future for such airlines.

12. On 1 November 2005, the Irish government announced a major €34.4 billion investment in Irish transport over ten years. The plan, aimed at delivering on-time, on-budget transport solutions for the whole country, is known as Transport 21. Given the critical importance of transport to the future success of Irish tourism, evaluate the contribution of Transport 21 to addressing Ireland's transport needs.

13. The provision of efficient and cost-effective transport is essential to the development of tourism for any country. Critically analyse the role of the state in facilitating both access transport to Ireland and internal transport within Ireland.

14. Ryanair was established in 1985. Twenty years later, it was the second largest airline in the world in terms of market capitalisation. Explain how Ryanair has managed to achieve this at a time when many 'traditional' airlines are struggling to survive.

15. You are employed as a consultant to Irish Rail with a brief to improve its product/service offering. Explain how you might approach this task in light of the developments of rail transport in Europe.

16. 'The airline business is extremely fragile and vulnerable. Consequently, many airlines are unable to compete in the long term and ultimately fail.' Discuss.

17. 'The Irish government is effectively managing the development of Irish transport infrastructure.' Critically assess this statement.

18. 'The emergence of no-frills airlines in Europe is an excellent example of a successful marketing strategy.' Discuss (with examples) whether you agree with this statement or not.

19. Rail transport in Europe is undergoing significant change at present. Outline (a) the nature of this change (b) the implications for the airline sector and (c) the challenges for the future.

TASKS

Divide the class into two roughly equal groups. Each group should be given ten to fifteen minutes to develop opposing points on the following statements, followed by a forty to forty-five minute debate.

Statement: The only survival option for airlines like Aer Lingus is to go low cost and offer no-frills services.

Statement: The sky is the limit for Ryanair.

Statement: Ryanair is to Europe what Southwest Airlines is to America.

Statement: Ferry operators cannot possibly win against low-cost airlines.

Statement: Although still behind its European neighbours, Ireland's internal transport has improved dramatically.

Statement: The Irish government does a good job developing transport infrastructure.

Statement: The Irish Rail network is inefficient and should be closed down in favour of more expressway bus routes.

ASSIGNMENTS

1. Write a report on the importance of the following in terms of tourism *to* Ireland and *within* Ireland:
   (a) Air transport.
   (b) Ferry transport.
   (c) Rail transport.
   (d) Car hire.
   (e) Coach/bus transport.
2. Research how ferry operators are marketed in Ireland and around the world and write a report on the comparisons and contrasts you find.
3. Research how airlines are marketed in Ireland and around the world and write a report on the comparisons and contrasts you find.
4. Write a report on the role of the EU in transport planning. In your report, pay particular attention to interstate rail projects and the European Open Skies policy. Present your findings to the class in the form of a twenty-minute multimedia presentation.

FURTHER INFORMATION SOURCES

See
http://ec.europa.eu/transport/air/rules/rights/index_en.htm for EU transport website.

See
http://ec.europa.eu/dgs/energy_transport/publication/videos_en.htm#tent for a thirteen-minute video on EU transport network plans.

See
http://ec.europa.eu/dgs/energy_transport/publication/videos_en.htm#motorways_of_the_sea for a ten-minute video on EU sea transport strategies.

See
http://ec.europa.eu/dgs/energy_transport/publication/videos_en.htm#single_european_s ky for a six-minute video on the Single European Sky.

See
http://ec.europa.eu/dgs/energy_transport/publication/videos_en.htm#europe_railways for a five-minute video on Europe of Railways.

Chapter 7

Visitor Attractions

SUMMARY

Chapter 7 presents the concept of visitor attractions and discusses its importance as part of the overall tourist experience. Some of the categories of visitor attractions are discussed with examples. In particular, international festivals, seaside resorts and sports as attraction are exemplified. The chapter moves on to analyse Irish visitor attraction categories and presents a list of top attractions on offer. It asks why Ireland does not have the type or style of visitor attractions of many destinations such as the Eiffel Tower or Disneyland. The chapter concludes by presenting some of the problems inherent with world and Irish visitor attractions and highlighting some possible future projections for the sector.

LEARNING OUTCOMES

Having completed this chapter, the reader should be able to:
- Define visitor attractions as well as categories and sub-categories of attractions.
- Demonstrate an understanding of the importance of various categories and sub-categories of visitor attractions.
- Identify the type of visitor attractions on offer in Ireland as well as the top attractions in the state.
- Understand some common problems affecting visitor attractions.
- Appreciate future projections for the sector.

INTRODUCTION

There has been much debate about what defines a visitor attraction. This is mainly due to the complex nature of the visitor attractions sector, as well as the different interpretations internationally of what a visitor attraction actually is. An acceptable definition for the purposes of this chapter comes from Walsh-Heron and Stevens (1990), as cited in Swarbrooke (2005):

> A visitor attraction is a feature in an area that is a place, venue or focus of activities and does the following things.
> 1. Sets out to attract visitors/day visitors from resident or tourist populations, and is managed accordingly.
> 2. Provides a fun and pleasurable experience and an enjoyable way for customers to spend their leisure time.

3. *Is developed to realise this potential.*
4. *Is managed as an attraction, providing satisfaction to its customers.*
5. *Provides an appropriate level of facilities and services to meet and cater to the demands, needs, and interests of its visitors.*
6. *May or may not charge an admission for entry.*

Another simple definition is that a visitor attraction is 'any site that appeals to people sufficiently to encourage them to travel there in order to visit it' (Holloway 1994).

In order to constitute a visitor attraction, the attraction itself must have the ability to attract tourists to visit it. A visitor attraction can be defined as encompassing both sights, i.e. things which the tourist believes are worth seeing, and sites (actual places, perhaps where an event takes place). The attraction can be broad or quite specific. An example of the former is a seaside resort, with all that goes with it. In an Irish or British sense, the traditional seaside resort may include the sea and beach itself, along with pubs, hotels, restaurants, pier, amusement arcades, etc. When considering large-scale sun beach resorts such as those of the Mediterranean, the previous are also prerequisites. However, many also promise regular sunshine and warm weather, as well as towns and villages which have been developed with the inbound beach and sun-worshipping tourist in mind, e.g. Costa Brava in Spain. An example of a specific attraction could be a single building, such as Amsterdam's Van Gogh museum.

Sightseeing and entertainment make up for an average estimated 4 per cent of the total tourist spend in Ireland, but it can be higher for tourists from some markets, e.g. North America; see Appendix D for further statistics on tourist spending patterns. These make up a vital component of the overall tourism product of any destination. Attractions must be managed properly, as dissatisfaction with any aspect of them can leave a negative impression of the entire holiday in Ireland.

CATEGORIES OF VISITOR ATTRACTIONS

Visitor attractions can be divided into several categories, depending on the nature of the attraction, as depicted in Figure 7.1. One way of categorising them is to divide them between either man-made or natural. Examples of the former include buildings such as a museum or great works of architecture such as the Eiffel Tower. Natural attractions are those which occur naturally without human input and include waterfalls, lakes and mountains. Swarbrooke (2005) makes a further division in the man-made category. The author believes that this can be further divided into 'human-made buildings, structures and sites that were designed for a purpose other than attracting visitors, such as religious worship' and those which are 'designed to attract visitors and are purpose-built to accommodate their needs, such as theme parks'.

A further category is events as attractions, which are usually one-off or annual events such as festivals, concerts and sporting competitions. It is further possible to sub-divide an event between man-made, e.g. concert, or natural, e.g. aurora australis or southern lights.

Figure 7.1: Categories of Visitor Attractions

Natural Attractions

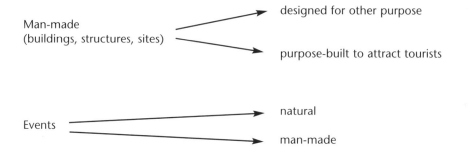

Some of the sub-divisions within each of the visitor attraction categories are listed below.

Natural attractions:
- Wildlife parks.
- Nature reserves.
- Flora (plants) and fauna (wildlife).
- Peatland.
- Forests (including Coillte forests in Ireland).

Man-made attractions (designed for other purposes):
- Historic properties.
- Castles.
- Churches and cathedrals, religious sites.
- Gardens (approximately forty in Ireland, e.g. Powerscourt).
- Parks.
- City parks, e.g. Phoenix Park.
- Workplaces.
- Birthplaces/living places of famous people, e.g. Irish literary greats.
- National monuments.

Man-made attractions (purpose-built to attract tourists):
- Museums and art galleries.
- Theme parks.
- Leisure attractions. (Eg. National Aquatic Centre)

Events (natural):

- Aurora borealis and aurora australis (northern and southern lights).
- Geysers (like Old Faithful in California).
- Winter solstice, e.g. at Newgrange.
- *Sports (International Scale))*

Events (man-made): *◁—————)*

- Festivals.   *Eg. Oxegen.*
- Concerts.

National Parks and Wildlife Service

Ireland's natural heritage is an integral part of our national inheritance and forms part of our sense of identity, providing resources of social, educational, recreational and aesthetic value.

The National Parks and Wildlife Service (NPWS), part of the Department of the Environment, Heritage and Local Government (DEHLG), manages the Irish state's nature conservation responsibilities under national and European law. NPWS is charged with the conservation of a range of ecosystems and populations of flora and fauna in Ireland. A particular responsibility of NPWS is the designation and protection of Special Areas of Conservation (SACs), Special Protection Areas (SPAs) and Natural Heritage Areas (NHAs). Consultation with interested parties is an integral element of the designation process. NPWS is also responsible for:

- The implementation of both domestic, e.g. Wildlife Acts 1976–2000, and international, e.g. EU Habitats and Birds Directives, legislation.
- The management and development of national parks and nature reserves.
- Overseeing licencing under the Convention on International Trade in Endangered Species (CITES) and the Wildlife Acts 1976–2000.

Source: National Parks and Wildlife Service.

FESTIVALS AS ATTRACTIONS

Countless festivals take place in Ireland and around the world. The dedicated festival website www.festivals.com claims that there are over 40,000 unique festivals which take place annually. Unfortunately, this website is primarily focused on the US and details very few festivals elsewhere. Many festivals have roots in ancient religious rites, while some constitute nothing more than an excuse to party. Ancient festivals have changed over the years to encompass many extra events and attractions which the participants have added on over the years.

Fáilte Ireland encourages and markets the many festivals taking place throughout Ireland. It lists 333 distinct festivals taking place all over Ireland annually, and groups the festivals into the following broad categories:

- Clan rallies.
- Drama/theatre festivals.
- Fairs.
- Film festivals.

- Gourmet festivals.
- Parades.
- Children's festivals.
- Arts festivals.
- Opera festivals.
- Comedy festivals.
- Celtic festivals.
- Traditional/jazz/bluegrass festivals.
- Craft and food fairs.
- Poetry and writing festivals.
- General festivals.
- Angling festivals.
- Walking festivals.
- Book festivals.
- Floral festivals.
- Heritage festivals.

O'Donoghue announces tourism grants of over €338,000

John O'Donoghue, TD, Minister for Arts, Sport and Tourism, announced grant assistance of €338,450 in respect of the Festivals and Cultural Events Initiative, 2006, which will be administered by Fáilte Ireland.

The amounts, set out hereunder, have been granted subject to the usual standard conditions:

- World Fleadh, Ballybunion, Kerry €100,000.
- Fleadh Cheoil na hÉireann, Letterkenny, Donegal €50,000.
- National and World Ploughing Championships, Tullow, Carlow €30,000.
- International Rose of Tralee Festival, Tralee, Kerry €36,500.
- Lord Mayor's New Years Day Parade, Dublin €24,825.
- Carrick Water Music Festival, Carrick on Shannon, Leitrim €17,000.
- Waterford Fringe Festival, Waterford €15,200.
- Johnny Keenan Banjo Festival, Longford €14,525.
- Cork International Folk Dance Festival, Cork €11,500.
- Yeats International Summer School and Festival, Sligo €10,250.
- Viking Boat Festival, Irish National Heritage Park, Wexford €8,550.
- Comórtas Peile na Gaeltachta, Spiddal, Connemara €7,750.
- The Brendan Kennelly Summer Festival, Ballylongford, Kerry €7,350.
- Gravity and Grace, Limerick €5,000.

Minister O'Donoghue said, 'I am delighted to announce these grants, which represent a further substantial injection of funds to enhance tourism countrywide. The provision of funding for such events permits the development and expansion of their role as an attraction for international tourists, allowing them to experience what we have to offer while at the same time affording an opportunity for local people to enjoy the benefits.'

Source: Department of Arts, Sport and Tourism press release, 10 May 2006.

Rather than presenting a definitive list of the world's biggest festivals, the following details some well-known as well as some more unusual world festivals. Some of the festivals in the annual calendar below are featured in the *Globe Trekker* travel series on television, produced by Pilot Film and TV Productions. The comprehensive website www.pilotguides.com provides a wealth of travel details, including the popular *Globe Trekker* series (as seen on the Travel Channel), which can be ordered on DVD or downloaded for around US$4.00 per episode. Further, travel writer Glen Kenner presents an entertaining if not somewhat rude portrayal of some of the world's more bizarre festivals on the website at www.2camels.com/destination4.php3.

January	**Ati Atihan, Philippines** Festival worshipping the Santo Niño (Sacred Child), including religious festivals, partying, parades and food. See www.ati-atihan.net for further information.
February	**Carnival, Port of Spain, Trinidad** Carnival festivals take place in many places around the world and the celebrations culminate on the last two days before Lent. One of the most colourful and exotic of these festivals takes place in the Caribbean island of Trinidad. For further information on Carnival in Trinidad, see www.seetobago.com/tandt/carnival/dates/cdcroots.htm.
March	**Las Fallas, Valencia, Spain** On 19 March each year, the burning of Las Fallas takes place in Valencia. Las Fallas are paper maché caricatures, constructed over an entire year. The aim is to present a satirical view of the woes of the world and eventually burn them on the final day of the sixteen-day festival. Its origins lie in the worship of the local saint. See www.fallas.com and choose the English language icon.
March	**St Patrick's Festival, Ireland and World** The patron saint of Ireland is celebrated by countless Irish worldwide. The largest festival takes place in New York, followed by Dublin and Birmingham in third place. The festival atmosphere engulfs the majority of the cities and towns taking part and culminates in a lively parade of floats and performers in the city and town centres. See www.stpatricksfestival.ie for the Irish festival.
March	**Battle of Oranges, Ivrea, Italy** 400 tons of oranges are thrown by townsfolk at each other, commemorating an ancient uprising against a local count. Over 100,000 people take part each year. See www.deliciousitaly.com/Piemontetour.htm and http://goitaly.about.com/b/a/248163.htm for further information.
March	**Mardi Gras, Sydney, Australia** Every March the streets, pubs, nightclubs and shops of Sydney are crowded as tens of thousands of locals and visitors attend Australia's largest gay and lesbian festival. More than 100 activities ranging from

parades to fashion shows, fairs to family events take place during the festival. See www.mardigras.org.au for further information.

April	**Moors and Christian Festival, Alcoy, Spain** This ancient three-day festival dates back to a 1276 battle between the native Spanish Christians and the Moors from North Africa and is commemorated at the site of the original castle where it took place in Alcoy, near Alicante in southern Spain, although similar festivals take place all over the region. It culminates in the Moors taking the castle in the morning of the final day, while the eventually victorious Christians retake it in the afternoon, just as it was in 1276. See http://en.wikipedia.org/wiki/Moros_y_Cristianos and www.sierracastril.com/Festivals.htm for further information.
May	**Cheese Rolling, Coopers Hill, Gloucestershire, England** On the last Monday in May, locals and visitors alike take part in the annual Cheese Rolling down a 300-yard steep hill in the English Cotswolds. Participants literally roll down the hill in pursuit of the cheese. Only fifty contestants take part, but thousands turn up to view the spectacle. See www.2camels.com/destination1.php3 for further information.
June	**Rath Yatra Festival, India** Religious festival honouring three Indian deities, when effigies of all three are taken in specially made chariots called Rathas, attracting enormous crowds. See www.2camels.com/destination46.php3 for further information.
July	**Gilroy Garlic Festival, Gilroy, California** A food festival that attracts people to sample and buy a wide variety of foods made from what the town is famous for – garlic. Examples of food include garlic popcorn and garlic ice cream. The festival always takes place in the last full weekend of July and has attracted over 3 million visitors over the years. See www.gilroygarlicfestival.com.
July	**Nadaam Festival, Ulaanbaatan, Mongolia** This is Mongolia's largest festival and is akin to its own version of the Olympic Games. It includes games such as wrestling, archery and horseracing. It takes place in Ulaanbaatan, the capital of Mongolia, as well as in every town, city and village. See www.csen.org/Mongol.Nadaam/Mongol.text.html and www.mongolia.co.uk/group_naadam.htm for further information.
July	**Love Parade, Berlin, Germany** This is one of the world's largest music festivals, attracting over 2 million visitors, the majority coming from other parts of Germany and Northern Europe. It is a celebration of techno music and it fills the streets and parks of Germany. The festival itself centres around dozens of large floats pumping techno tunes from world-renowned DJs, while the evenings involve partying in the Berlin nightclubs. Locals claim that the music is so loud that the birds in the Tiergarten (central park in Berlin) actually leave and it takes about a week after the festival for

them to return. Many locals do the same. See www.loveparade.net for further information.

| July | **Kirkpinar Oiled Wrestling, Kirkpinar, Turkey** |

This is an ancient festival dating back to 1357 attracting millions of visitors over a one-week period, and although the focus is on wrestling, several festival activities take place. See www.kirkpinar.com for further information.

| August | **La Tomatina, Bonul, Spain** |

This southern Spanish festival has unknown origins and involves hundreds of thousands of kilos of tomatoes being thrown by people at each other on the streets of the town. The tomatoes are leftovers from the regional tomato harvest. Legend has it that it was started by a disgruntled citizen throwing a tomato at the fascist dictator Franco in 1945. See www.latomatina.com for further information, as well as pictures and video clips.

| August | **Battle of Hastings, Hastings, England** |

A re-enactment of the 1066 battle which saw the Norman King William the Conqueror kill the English King Harold and claim the English throne. Saxon and Norman tent villages are reconstructed to attract visitors. See www.english-heritage.org.uk/1066 for further information.

| September to October | **Oktoberfest, Munich, Germany** |

This festival begins at the end of September in the Bavarian capital of Munich and is a twelve-day celebration of beer and fast food, originating from 1810, when Bavarian Crown Prince Ludwig celebrated his marriage with a massive party in the city. Although originally taking place in October (hence the name), the festival was moved to the end of September and beginning of October because of the better weather conditions. See www.oktoberfest.de/en for further information.

| November | **Tar Barrel Rolling, Ottery St Mary, England** |

This unusual festival takes place on Guy Fawkes Night (5 November). It commemorates the capture and execution of Catholic Guy Fawkes and his followers after their attempt to blow up Protestant King James I and his followers in the British Parliament. While most of Britain celebrates with bonfires and fireworks, the town of Ottery St Mary set alight barrels which have been tarred, and carry and roll them through the town full of people. See www.otterytourism.org.uk/events.htm for further information.

| November | **Day of the Dead, Mexico** |

This is a religious festival with pagan origins and is one of Mexico's biggest festivals, although one of the quietest and most personal. The family of deceased relatives set up shrines at burial sites and stay there overnight, praying and eating the prepared feast. See www.andespressagency.com/fea_02.html for further information.

December   **Klausjagen, Küssnacht, Switzerland**
On 5 December, the eve of St Nicholas' Day (now known internationally as Santa Claus), the Swiss town of Küssnacht is called Klausjagen (literally 'chasing Klaus', as in St Nicholas). This pagan festival has its origins in the Middle Ages, when townsfolk would make loud noises with bells and whips to chase away the winter darkness. St Nicholas was brought into it when the Christians turned the festival into a Christian one from its pagan roots. See www.pulseplanet.com/archive/Dec98/1767.html for further information.

State's biggest annual celebration is a crock of gold for business
The St Patrick's Festival is now worth €58.3 million to the economy and attracts 1.5 million people, about 40,000 of whom come from overseas.

Wherever you are in the world you would have to be pretty slow not to have noticed that today is St Patrick's Day. The festivities began last Sunday when the famous fountain in London's Trafalgar Square turned its waters green in honour of the patron saint of Ireland, and have continued throughout the week, with celebrations across the world from the US to New Zealand to Paris.

In Ireland, the festivities started on Wednesday and continue through to Sunday evening, with a range of activities, from the famous St Patrick's parade and funfair through to smaller events such as exhibitions and traditional markets.

Overall, the festival, which will attract about 1.5 million people, is worth €58.3 million to the economy, according to Fáilte Ireland. About 40,000 come from overseas, and of those, about half come especially for St Patrick's Day, says Mary Cosgrave, spokeswoman for Fáilte Ireland, which puts up some of the €2.5 million used to fund the festival.

The remainder of the money comes from corporate sponsorship and partnership agreements, according to a spokeswoman for the organisers.

'It is a very important day in the Irish tourism calendar,' says Cosgrave, adding that the fact that this year it falls on a Friday is even more beneficial to the industry. It encourages many people to make a weekend of it, and in some parts of the country marks a start to the tourism season.

This is not the case in Dublin, where tourism runs all year round and has already been boosted by Ireland's home rugby matches as part of the Six Nations tournament.

Unlike many other patron saint festivals, St Patrick's Day seems to be celebrated by everyone, whether they have Irish roots or not. This may have something to do with the long-standing history of Irish emigration, which means that there are many people with Irish roots scattered around the globe, or it may simply be because everybody likes a good excuse for a party and the Irish certainly know how to do that.

'We have had a huge amount of interest from overseas media,' says Cosgrave, adding that this is one of the busiest times for hotels and guesthouses in the Republic.

For those who cannot get to Ireland, there are plenty of events happening outside of St Patrick's home nation, generating further funds in those countries.

New York will today hold its 245th St Patrick's Day parade. Disneyland in Paris is hosting special events to mark the day, while Sydney will also hold its own parade. As mentioned, London hosted a parade last weekend which culminated in a street party in Trafalgar Square and an Irish food market in Covent Garden, while smaller parades were also held in Birmingham and Manchester.

It was because of the increasing overseas popularity of St Patrick's Day celebrations, and the fact that other countries' celebrations were starting to surpass those in Ireland, that the government in 1995 established the St Patrick's Day Festival.

The organisation was charged with developing an international festival over the holiday weekend. Its brief was to reflect the talents and achievements of Irish people and to showcase this around the world.

Since the creation of this body, most people will agree that Ireland has done itself proud in showing the rest of the world what it means to be Irish.

'For me, this is one of the best days of the year,' says Eimer Harris, who cannot wait to take her three children out to watch today's parade.

'It embodies all that is good about Irish society and shows what a great time can be had by everyone pulling together.'

According to Harris, the aim of the day is to make everyone want to be Irish. 'It certainly makes me glad I'm Irish,' she says, pointing out that in England, where her husband is from, St George's Day is not a national holiday.

The first St Patrick's Day festival was held over one day and one night on 17 March 1996. The attendance was estimated to be about 430,000.

In 1997, the word 'day' was dropped from the title and it became St Patrick's Festival, allowing for the elongation of the celebrations as it became a three-day event.

Since then, the festival has grown to become a five-day event. In the old days, preparations took only five months, but now the ever-expanding size of the festival means that it takes about eighteen months of planning to pull off what is Ireland's biggest annual celebration.

The main events of this year's 100-hour carnival, as it describes itself on the festival website, are an aerial music and acrobatic spectacle in Dublin's Smithfield, which hopefully you will have seen on Wednesday evening, an exhibition of arts and crafts at Farmleigh in Dublin entitled 40 Shades of Green, a treasure hunt for all ages which will test your knowledge of Dublin's streets as well as your ability to solve riddles and a funfair on Merrion Square. For more details, see www.stpatricksday.ie.

> Those of you living outside Dublin won't miss out, as there are events going on all over the country. Details can be found at www.st-patricks-day.com, or in your local papers.
>
> Source: Shoesmith, C., 'State's biggest annual celebration is a crock of gold for business', *The Irish Times*. 17 March 2006.

CRITICAL SUCCESS FACTORS

Swarbrooke (2005) notes that the success of visitor attractions is dependent on various factors, some under the control of the organisation owning and/or managing the attraction, and some out of their control. The author groups the factors under the following four headings, as presented below:

1. The organisation and its resources.
2. The product.
3. The market.
4. The management of the attraction.

Success is greatly improved, according to Swarbrooke, if **the organisation** developing and managing the attraction has previous experience in such a venture, as previous experience should reduce problems occurring. However, as certain large-scale attractions prove, e.g. Disneyland Paris, even the largest and most experienced organisation can make mistakes. Further, if the organisation has their own financial resources, this reduces the necessity for external capital from loans and investors.

In a highly competitive market with sophisticated and informed customers, a unique **product** is essential for success. However, a new or unique idea is not an automatic success factor. There must be an interest created in the new concept. Further, competition can replicate similar products very quickly and easily, and so unique products need to constantly adapt and update.

Swarbrooke (2005) notes that visitor attraction products should include:

- A variety of on-site attractions.
- Special events to promote variety.
- A high-quality environment.
- Good visitor facilities.
- Good customer service.
- A fair price.

The **market** targeted by the attraction must be a growth market. This includes seniors markets, given the rising average age in many countries (including most European countries). This market typically has higher levels of disposable income. Other market segments which must be catered for include those who wish to visit an attraction to learn something, as well as those who wish to become actively involved in the attraction. Interactive visitor centres and recreations of events (such as medieval banquets at Bunratty Castle) afford the visitor the opportunity of feeling part of the attraction. Attractions offering family products with a variety of activities for multiple age groups are also essential. Finally, the market for green and health attractions is also growing strongly. The successful attraction will be one which can offer and adapt to the changing demands of their market segments.

Attractions must also be **managed** effectively for success. This includes ensuring properly trained employees deal with all aspects of managing the attraction, including customer service, sales and marketing, financial controllers and human resources. Managers (or management teams) must also understand the changing nature of the business environment in which they operate, including competitive pressures and the threat from substitutes. The successful attractions manager will also monitor their performance and engage in short-, medium- and long-term planning for the future. Swarbrooke (2005:139) notes that a systematic, professional approach to marketing is vital for success in attractions. The author continues by listing the marketing factors which must be taken into account:

- Giving adequate attention to market research so that they know their market and its tastes and preferences.
- Recognising that marketing is not just about producing brochures and placing advertisements.
- Taking a longer-term strategic view rather than just a short-term tactical approach.
- Appreciating that there is not one big 'public' but many different market segments with different needs and desires.
- Spending a significant proportion of turnover on marketing year in, year out rather than just spending money on an ad hoc basis in response to crises.
- Accepting the importance of word-of-mouth recommendations and acknowledging the value of giving the existing visitor a first-rate experience to encourage positive recommendations.
- Employing specialist sales and marketing staff while training all staff to realise that they are also part of the marketing effort, because to the customer they are all part of the core product.

IRISH VISITOR ATTRACTIONS

Many visitor attractions are members of marketing organisations such as Fáilte Ireland, RTAs, Heritage Island, Heritage Towns, Houses, Castles and Gardens of Ireland, or county and local tourism organisations.

Speech by John O'Donoghue, TD, Minister for Arts, Sport and Tourism, on the occasion of the 'sod turning' for the new visitor experience at the Cliffs of Moher on Tuesday, 21 June 2005 at 4.15 p.m.

Deputy Mayor of Clare, Chairman of Shannon Development, ladies and gentlemen.

It is with great pleasure that I find myself here with you today to formally acknowledge the start of work that will produce a state-of-the-art visitor experience for those coming from all over the world to see one of Ireland's greatest natural attractions, the Cliffs of Moher. Over the years the cliffs have been made popular by our musicians, our artists, our writers and now apparently even by our advertisers.

Anyone who has ventured up the path, and I am told that there are approximately 750,000 visitors annually, has been greeted by one of the most phenomenal sights to be found in Europe.

From the best vantage point at O'Brien's Tower, a visitor can see the Aran Islands as well as the Twelve Pins and the Maum Turk Mountains to the north in Connemara and Loop Head to the south.

What they see beneath them are sheer walls of rock measuring 8 kilometres long by 214 metres high, boldly thrusting their face out towards the unforgiving Atlantic which pounds these cliffs with all its fury and might. Yet paradoxically, the cliffs serve as home and safe haven to many. Vast colonies of birds nestle along the cliff ledges, including fulmars, puffins, guillemots, kittiwakes, razorbills and many varieties of gull. Designated as a Special Protection Area for Birds by the EU Birds Directive in 1989, the cliffs and their surrounding grassland and heath play host to up to 30,000 breeding pairs of seabirds every year.

As wonderful as all this is, a great deal is lost to the visitor who is not imaginatively informed about the birds and other local flora and fauna, who knows nothing of the local history of the area and the origins of its unique geography, and is served by inadequate facilities. Thus it became necessary to give serious consideration to an improved visitors' centre that would meet these needs and all the other expectations of tourists and visitors.

The setting and design of such a centre is obviously of concern to all who wish to preserve this wonderful vista and resource. And so it is that the two agencies, Clare County Council and Shannon Development, who for the past twenty years have co-operated in the development and joint management of the original visitor facilities, have made a supreme effort to be sensitive and accommodating to everyone's perspective on how the new visitor centre should progress. Today, therefore, we are finally formally recognising the commencement of construction of a visitors' centre for the largest tourist attraction on the western seaboard.

The design of the new centre is both imaginative yet fully integrated with the natural and rugged beauty around it. From the winning design of Reddy O'Riordan Staehli Architects, selected from an architectural competition over a decade ago, the building is to be partly cut into the side of the hill and the hillside is to be regraded to completely envelop the structure. The landscaping and remounding of the hill will reflect the existing topography of the landform.

The visitors' centre will overcome the limitations of the previous centre and, with its two storeys, will feature a circular exhibition area, a shop, a restaurant, a tourist information area, toilet facilities and an auditorium/ audio visual area. Included in the work are substantial cliff edge improvement works and the introduction of cliff rangers as visitors' guides.

This project is being put in place by Clare County Council and will cost approximately €29 million. In May 2004 I was very pleased to announce that the Tourism Product Management Board, which is serviced by Fáilte Ireland, approved an EU grant of almost €10 million, and in the same month the government gave sanction to Clare County Council to borrow a sum of up to €15 million from the European Investment Bank to develop the project.

It is expected that the centre will be open for the 2007 tourism season. Shannon Development, through its subsidiary, Shannon Castle Banquets and Heritage Ltd, will assist with the management of the centre by running the retail unit and tourist information desk within the centre as well as operating these temporary visitor facilities during the construction phase. Shannon Development will also join Clare County Council in marketing the attraction.

When completed, it is expected that this development will deliver a world-class visitors' experience. So convinced are Clare County Council of this, they are actively campaigning to have the Cliffs of Moher designated a World Heritage Site, a development I applaud and support.

Source: Department of Arts, Sport and Tourism speeches archive, 21 June 2004.

Government will not intervene in Vega City

The government has refused a request to intervene in the debate on the proposed theme park for north Dublin.

The Minister for the Environment has been asked by a local councillor to appoint an independent adjudicator to examine the proposals for Vega City, a €7 billion theme park planned for a site near Lusk, Co. Dublin.

The €7 billion proposals were rejected on Monday evening by Fingal county councillors after planning officials advised that the proposals were unrealistic. The consortium behind the proposals had also refused to reveal the financial backers who were willing to invest the €7 billion in the park.

An overwhelming majority of councillors – nineteen to one – accepted advice from planning officials that the plans were unacceptable.

The county manager, Mr Willie Soffe, said the plans lacked detail and credibility – they were unsustainable for the area and violated existing planning guidelines.

Source: Reid, L., 'Government will not intervene in Vega City', *The Irish Times*, 27 November 2003.

Nature Reserves

There are seventy-seven nature reserves spread across sixteen counties in the Republic of Ireland. They are defined as an area of importance to wildlife, which is protected by the government. Not all of the nature reserves are state owned, but all come under the responsibility of the National Parks and Wildlife Service (NPWS, www.npws.ie). For a full list and description of all seventy-seven reserves, see www.npws.ie/NatureReserves/.

National Parks

There is an international agreement on what defines the term 'national park'. Ireland subscribes to this agreement, established in 1969 by the International Union for the Conservation of Nature (IUCN). The three criteria needed under this agreement to be classed as a 'national park' are as follows, according to the NPWS:

1. *Where one or several ecosystems are not materially altered by human exploitation and occupation; where plant and animal species, geomorphological sites and habitats are of special scientific, educational and recreational interest or which contain a natural landscape of great beauty;*
2. *Where the highest competent authority of the country has taken steps to prevent or eliminate as soon as possible exploitation or occupation in the whole area and to enforce effectively the respect of ecological, geomorphological or aesthetic features which have led to its establishment;*
3. *Where visitors are allowed to enter, under special conditions, for inspirational, educational, cultural and recreational purposes.*

There are six national parks in the Republic of Ireland, run by the National Parks and Wildlife Service:

* Killarney National Park, Co. Kerry   (10,289 hectares)
* The Burren National Park, Co. Clare   (1,673 hectares)
* Connemara National Park, Co. Galway   (2,957 hectares)
* Glenveagh National Park, Co. Donegal   (16,958 hectares)
* Wicklow Mountains National Park, Co. Wicklow   (15,925 hectares)
* Ballycroy National Park, Co. Mayo   (11,779 hectares)

For full details on each of Ireland's national parks, see www.npws.ie/NationalParks/.

Miscellaneous Natural Landscape

Ireland is famous for its natural landscape. Many tales have been told of its beautiful scenery. Travel journalists and state tourism marketing agencies alike have moulded and shaped Ireland's natural landscape to their advantage in their descriptions of Ireland. Guiney (2002) is just one of many authors who lists some of Ireland's natural landscapes of importance to tourism, and the following is a sample of some.

* Giant's Causeway, Co. Antrim.
* The Burren, Co. Clare.
* Aillwee Caves, Co. Clare.
* Killarney, Co. Kerry (mountains and lakes).
* Glendalough, Co. Wicklow.
* Clew Bay, Co. Mayo.
* Bantry Bay, Co. Cork.
* Cliffs of Moher, Co. Clare.
* Dunmore Caves, Co. Kilkenny.
* The River Shannon.
* Errigal, Co. Donegal's highest mountain.
* Skellig Islands, Co. Kerry (nine miles south west off the Kerry coast).
* Connemara, Co. Galway.

IRELAND'S TOP FEE-PAYING ATTRACTIONS

Many of Ireland's most visited attractions are fee paying. Fees for Irish attractions are consistent with international rates, although some attractions can be much more expensive in Ireland. Similarly, some attractions are actually cheaper or free in comparison to many other cities. Many of Ireland's state-owned museums and galleries are free to enter, and all the visitor is asked for is a contribution when exiting. However, this is not obligatory. We can contrast this to Berlin, for example, where state museums and galleries are generally only free on the first Sunday of each month.

The price paid at visitor attractions depends on several factors, including the time of year, cost of running the attraction, size and composition of the visiting party (students, children and OAPs usually get discounts) and current economic climate. Ireland's attractions do not discriminate based on the nationality of the visitor. For example, an American tourist pays the same as an Irish one or a German one. The fees apply to all nationalities. This is not the case all around the world. In Rome, visitors to the Colosseum pay a different price based on nationality. There is one rate for all EU citizens (a passport must be shown) and a significantly higher rate for all other nationalities. In India, several attractions have a rate for Indian nationals and all other nationalities. The non-Indian rate can be as much as twenty times the rate paid by Indian nationals.

Ireland's fee-paying visitor attractions are situated all over the country. However, there is a disproportionate spread of visitors to fee-paying visitor attractions across Ireland's tourism regions, as shown below from Fáilte Ireland figures. Almost one-third of the spend made by visitors at Ireland's fee-paying attractions is concentrated in the capital.

- Dublin: 29 per cent
- South East: 14 per cent
- Midlands East: 15 per cent
- South West: 15 per cent
- Shannon: 13 per cent
- West: 11 per cent
- North West: 4 per cent

The types of attractions chosen by visitors to Ireland's fee-paying visitor attractions are as follows:

- Historic houses and castles: 20 per cent
- Interpretative centres/museums: 32 per cent
- Parks and gardens: 7 per cent
- Monuments: 17 per cent
- Other attractions: 24 per cent

The top three visitor attractions are all in Dublin. Ireland's most visited attraction is Dublin Zoo, followed closely by the popular Guinness Storehouse, whose Gravity Bar allows visitors to sample the finest pint of Guinness as well as unique food with a Guinness theme or flavour, all enjoyed from high above the city, affording the visitor a 360-degree panoramic view of Dublin. Trinity College, with the world-famous Book of Kells on display, takes the number three spot. Other attractions in the top ten include castles, a cathedral, a wildlife park, the Waterford Crystal factory and the Brú na Bóinne Visitor Centre for the megalithic passage tombs at Newgrange and Knowth in Co. Meath.

Table 7.1: Top Ten Irish Fee-Paying Visitor Attractions (2003)

2003 Ranking	Attraction	Number of Visitors	2001 Ranking
1	Dublin Zoo	772,322	2
2	Guinness Storehouse	738,000	1
3	Trinity College/Book of Kells	467,513	3
4	Bunratty Castle and Folk Park	307,145	5
5	Waterford Crystal	303,000	4
6	Fota Wildlife Park	301,313	8
7	Blarney Castle	300,000	6
8	St Patrick's Cathedral	275,922	7
9	Rock of Cashel	245,316	9
10	Brú na Bóinne	216,957	13
	Total for Top Ten Irish Fee-Paying Visitor Attractions	3,927,488	

Source: Fáilte Ireland.

IRELAND'S TOP NON-FEE-PAYING ATTRACTIONS

As mentioned above, many of Ireland's most visited attractions have no fees. This includes many state-owned museums and galleries housing priceless works of art from internationally famous artists. The most visited non-fee-paying attraction is the National Gallery of Ireland in Dublin. The Cliffs of Moher in Co. Clare ranks second.

Table 7.2: Top Ten Irish Non-Fee-Paying Visitor Attractions (2003)

2003 Ranking	Attraction	Number of Visitors
1	National Gallery of Ireland	706,000
2	Cliffs of Moher	650,000
3	Irish Museum of Modern Art	309,000
4	National Museum of Archaeology and History	260,000
5	National Museum of Decorative Arts and History	136,868
6	Chester Beatty Library	134,161
7	Natural History Museum	118,705
8	National Museum of Country Life	112,270
9	Cashel Heritage Centre	75,000
10	Triona Design	65,000
	Total for Top Ten Irish Non-Fee-Paying Visitor Attractions	2,567,004

Source: Fáilte Ireland.

Fáilte Ireland's Visitor Attractions Survey
Fee-charging attractions generated an estimated 11.3 million visits in 2003. This is broadly in line with the number of visits recorded in the fee-charging sector in 2001 (11.2 million).

Dublin attracted an estimated 3.3 million visits to its charging attractions in 2003. This represents a 29 per cent share of total visits to fee-charging attractions and is a significantly larger share than that achieved by other regions. Attractions in the capital have gradually increased their share of total visits over the last decade.

Interpretative centres/museums, including industrial heritage sites, are the most popular types of fee-charging attractions. In 2003, this category generated an estimated 3.6 million visits (32 per cent of total visits). Since 2001, however, historic houses/castles and monuments have increased their overall share of visits at the expense of interpretative centres/museums and other attractions.

Dublin Zoo (with 772,322 visits), Guinness Storehouse (738,000) and Trinity College/Book of Kells (467,513) are the leading fee-charging attractions in terms of visits (as they were in 2001). Of the top three, Guinness Storehouse and Trinity College/Book of Kells have played a key role in attracting and catering for international visitors to Dublin. The top ten fee-charging attractions recorded a 6 per cent growth in combined visits between 2001 and 2003. These 'flagship' attractions currently account for a 35 per cent share of all visits to fee-charging attractions.

There has been a reduction of eight minutes in the average 'dwell time' at fee-charging attractions to an average of one hour twenty-three minutes. This factor is likely to have had some bearing on visitor expenditure patterns.

Income generated by fee-charging attractions
Admissions income at fee-charging attractions in 2003 is estimated to have been of the order of €54 million. This represents a marginal increase on estimated admission income in 2001. Although attractions generate a further estimated €46 million from other sources of income, i.e. catering, retail, etc., the evidence suggests that the proportion of income from these other sources relative to admission income has declined in recent years.

The ratio of admissions income to other income types varies significantly according to different types of attraction. Interpretative centres/museums, wildlife attractions, historic sites/monuments and historic houses/castles are heavily reliant on admissions. For parks/gardens and industrial heritage attractions, on the other hand, a greater share of total income is generated from retail and other sources.

Marketing activity
Fee-charging attractions spent an estimated €4 million on marketing in 2003. Advertising and brochure production/distribution accounts for almost three-quarters of marketing expenditure.

Just over one-third of fee-charging attractions currently claim membership of a marketing organisation and a number of these retain membership of more than one organisation.

Human resources

In 2003, there were an estimated 2,527 individuals employed in fee-charging attractions in Ireland. This represents a significant reduction from the estimated numbers employed in the sector in 2001. Consistent with the findings from the 2001 Visitor Attractions Survey, the overwhelming majority of employees in the fee-charging sector are retained on a part-time and/or seasonal basis, including unpaid volunteers and those on social employment schemes.

Approximately half of the fee-charging attractions interviewed conducted formal in-house training programmes in 2003. Consistent with findings from the 2001 Visitor Attractions Survey, participation in training programmes was highest where wildlife attractions are concerned.

Non-charging attractions

Estimates of attendances at non-charging attractions should be treated with caution. Unlike fee-charging attractions where most sites maintain a record of visitor throughput, the opposite is often the case in the non-charging attractions sector.

The audit carried out by Tourism Development International at the outset of the Visitor Attractions Survey identified 105 non-charging attractions. Sixty-three non-charging visitor attractions supplied information in relation to attendances. Collectively, these attractions generated an estimated 3.3 million visits in 2003. No upward adjustment has been made to take account of non-responding attractions.

The National Gallery (706,000 visits) and the Cliffs of Moher (650,000) are Ireland's leading non-charging attractions. The latter is of strategic importance where international tourism is concerned.

Non-charging attractions achieve a more even distribution of visits throughout the year than do fee-charging attractions. However, at fifty-five minutes, average 'dwell time' at non-charging attractions is significantly shorter than the average dwell time at fee-charging attractions (one hour twenty-three minutes).

Income generated by non-charging attractions in 2003 is estimated to be of the order of €14 million. A very significant proportion of income is accounted for by grants, donations and other fundraising.

An estimated 1,500 individuals are employed in the non-charging sector. Unlike the fee-charging sector, most jobs in the non-charging sector are of a full-time nature.

(See www.webtourism.ie/vas/results/ for charts depicting the above.)

Source: Visitor Attraction Survey, Fáilte Ireland.

SEASIDE RESORTS AS VISITOR ATTRACTIONS

Seaside resorts in Ireland and Britain originally developed as an attraction for wealthy city-dwellers, and eventually for all. Large seaside towns such as Brighton and Torquay in England were designed with the London visitor in mind. Similarly, Irish seaside towns such as Bray, Courtown and Tramore developed as seaside resorts aimed at Dubliners.

There has been a major decline in recent decades in the numbers in Ireland and the UK visiting home seaside resorts. This has been due to many reasons:

- Pollution of seaside resorts in recent years, especially those near large cities.
- Irish and British weather is not always favourable for enjoying the seaside.
- The relatively good value of travelling to foreign seaside resorts such as Spain, coupled with the increase in wealth and levels of disposable income of Irish and British workers.
- Legislation providing for statutory paid holidays.

Many Irish and British seaside hotels and resorts, as well as other tourism products associated with them, are either losing money or closing down. Some have refocused on attracting foreign tourists rather than domestic, including a focus on English language learners from abroad. Domestic tourism agencies such as Ireland's Fáilte Ireland have launched several marketing campaigns to encourage Irish holidaymakers to take their break at home rather than abroad. However, as the Irish economy grows, more exotic foreign holidays lure the Irish-earned euros from Irish holidaymakers' pockets.

Ireland and Britain are not alone with regard to this problem. The Spanish coastline, which is traditionally Europe's playground, has suffered a decline as newer resorts open, e.g. Cyprus, Greece, Turkey, Eastern Europe, and other long-haul destinations, e.g. Australia, America, Asia, Africa, become affordable. Concerns about skin cancer are also damaging the sun-sea-sand package holiday market worldwide.

SPORTS AS VISITOR ATTRACTIONS

Sports are increasingly becoming more and more important in Irish and world tourism. Millions of tourists travel every year to support their favourite team, players or participants in international fixtures, be it soccer, rugby, basketball, athletics, tennis or any one of the myriad of sports played throughout the world. Sports tourists are often dedicated fans who pay above-average prices to follow their team to an international fixture. Specialist travel agents and tour operators have developed to serve this lucrative market. However, sports tourism is important for both inbound and outbound tourism. Many international games are played in Ireland on a regular basis, including qualification matches for large-scale events like the FIFA World Cup and the annual Six Nations Rugby Championship.

O'Donoghue welcomes GAA decision to facilitate international fixtures of other sports in Croke Park

John O'Donoghue, TD, Minister for Arts, Sport and Tourism, today [17 January 2006] welcomed the agreement between the GAA, FAI and the IRFU

on Croke Park being used to accommodate international soccer and rugby
fixtures during 2007.

Minister O'Donoghue said: 'The GAA, FAI and the IRFU are to be
congratulated on reaching this agreement. The GAA decision to facilitate
important international fixtures in other sports is very welcome and reflects
great credit on the association.

'The people of Ireland have a passion for sport and will applaud this
initiative during the period when Lansdowne Road is not available. It
removes the spectre of Ireland playing "home" internationals outside of the
state, a prospect which would do little for our standing overseas. Instead, we
now have the reality of access to one of Europe's finest stadia, which the
GAA has developed at its own initiative, supported by the government, and
which is a splendid showcase for our national games.

'The FAI and the IRFU are to be congratulated on reaching this
agreement with the GAA, which reflects credit on their respective sports,
ensures that their athletes will have renewed momentum in playing home
games and retains a major commercial spin-off for Ireland,' the Minister
concluded.

Source: Department of Arts, Sport and Tourism press release, 17 January 2006.

In Ireland, sports and tourism are uniquely connected. Since 1997, the minister
responsible for tourism has also had the responsibility for sport. This was Jim
McDaid between 1997 and 2002, followed by John O'Donoghue between 2002 and
2007. This dual role means that sports initiatives were encouraged which often
benefited tourism. Examples of these include Ireland's hosting of the 2003 Special
Olympics World Summer Games, the biggest sporting event in the world in 2003,
and the first time the Special Olympics were held outside of the US. Similarly, the
2006 Ryder Cup held at the K Club in Co. Kildare showcased Irish golf and Ireland
to the world. The Minister noted:

*Sports tourism is of growing importance in the tourism mix and Fáilte Ireland,
through the International Sports Tourism Initiative, has played an important role
in attracting more than 100 international events to this country, spanning a wide
diversity of sports from equestrian events to sailing and from motor sport to
hockey. Golf is a perfect example of sports tourism, attracting as it does high-
spending visitors, who stay in high-quality accommodation, travel throughout
the regions and, according to Fáilte Ireland research, show a high level of interest
in Irish cuisine, culture and heritage.*

The unsuccessful joint bid with Scotland to host the 2008 European Football
Championship (lost to another joint bid from Switzerland and Austria) would have
furthered this world representation of Ireland as a sporting nation.

Success of Irish athletes and teams in international events has also helped
Ireland's image as a sporting nation. Gold medals at Olympic Games and world
championships and the European and international success of Ireland's soccer and

rugby teams (as well as Ireland's excellent provincial rugby performances) are all examples of the many Irish achievements in the field of sport.

The following articles (press releases and speeches from the Department of Arts, Sport and Tourism) highlight how some of the more publicised events in and near Ireland have benefited Irish tourism and Ireland as a whole.

Sports ministers discuss Olympic opportunities in Dublin

John O'Donoghue, TD, Minister for Arts, Sport and Tourism in the Republic of Ireland, and David Hanson, MP, Northern Ireland's Minister for Culture, Arts and Leisure, met today in Dublin for discussions on a number of sports issues.

Minister O'Donoghue said: 'London hosting the 2012 Olympics and Paralympics offers tremendous potential and that the attraction of Ireland to overseas teams participating in the Games for acclimatisation and preparation purposes is an area on which our sports councils could co-operate.' David Hanson said, 'John O'Donoghue and I both agreed that there were tremendous opportunities for both Northern Ireland and the Republic to benefit from the London 2012 Olympic Games. The existing close working relationships which exist both at departmental and sports council levels will provide a solid basis from which to go forward.'

Source: Department of Arts, Sport and Tourism press release, 12 October 2005.

O'Donoghue announces special funding for Ryder Cup programmes

John O'Donoghue, TD, Minister for Arts, Sport and Tourism, today [23 February 2006] has announced the provision of an additional €4.5 million for Fáilte Ireland to support an enhanced programme of marketing and promotion activities around the Ryder Cup. The money is included in the Revised Estimates Volume 2006 published today [23 February 2006] by Brian Cowen, TD, Minister for Finance.

The Minister said that the overall aim of the programme, which will be mounted by Fáilte Ireland with the participation of Tourism Ireland, is to expand the impact on the economy, and the legacy in tourism and economic terms, of the Ryder Cup in Ireland. The programme includes a national branding programme and a number of golf marketing initiatives.

Minister O'Donoghue said: 'As one of the world's top corporate entertainment events, the Ryder Cup provides a unique opportunity to showcase Ireland far beyond tourism or golf. It provides the vehicle through which Ireland can be projected to an estimated 1 billion viewers around the world, in addition to the estimated 2,000 journalists and media personnel attending. The proposed programme is intended to create a tangible legacy for Ireland in terms of enhanced international reputation, awareness of our economic, social and cultural successes, and appeal as a destination for both general and special interest tourism. By bolstering the tourism agencies' golf and tourism marketing efforts both at home and overseas, it will help to optimise the very significant investment made in attracting the Ryder Cup over previous years.'

The Minister said that it had also been agreed that Fáilte Ireland engage with the European Tour for delivery of an appropriate complementary programme of events around the Ryder Cup, including the official opening and closing ceremonies and other initiatives intended to raise the profile of the occasion within Ireland. 'Ryder Cup opening and closing ceremonies are very high-profile and professionally managed events in which host nations in the recent past have invested heavily so as to enhance their international standing in attracting and staging events of this calibre,' said the Minister. 'Ireland should not be an exception and funding will be available for Fáilte Ireland to support the European Tour in delivering an appropriate programme staged to the highest possible standards.'

The benefits of the Ryder Cup, which will take place in the K Club, Co. Kildare, from 22–24 September 2006, are enormous and include:

- Television coverage to over 550 million homes worldwide, with a potential audience of up to 1 billion viewers.
- Over 2,000 international media personnel will report from Ireland before and during the event.
- 40,000 people will attend the event each day at the K Club.
- 5,000 people will work on site at the course for each of the six days – including personnel from high-profile international corporations who will take retail and corporate hospitality space in the tented village.

'It is unlikely that Ireland will ever again host a sporting event which attracts as much worldwide interest as the Ryder Cup. The event, together with the Olympics and the soccer World Cup, ranks in the top three sporting events in terms of international interest and publicity. I am delighted that the funding which is being announced today will ensure that Ireland maximises the enormous potential that exists to capitalise on the event,' the Minister concluded.

Source: Department of Arts, Sport and Tourism press release, 23 February 2006.

Speech by John O'Donoghue, TD, Minister for Arts, Sport and Tourism, at a media briefing for the Ryder Cup at the K Club, Straffan, Co. Kildare

Ladies and gentlemen of the press: I am delighted to be here today at the K Club as Minister for Arts, Sport and Tourism to address you as we begin the official countdown to the 2006 Ryder Cup.

To those of you whom I know, it is good to see you again. To those of you with whom I am not yet acquainted, may I extend a warm welcome to Ireland.

It is a truly significant day when we consider that a mere ten weeks from today we will all once again be gathered at this magnificent venue for the much-anticipated start of the 2006 Ryder Cup. The countdown, of course, has been underway from as far back as 1998, when Ireland signed the agreement with the PGA European Tour to host the Ryder Cup, but the start of the European Open is the official reminder that Ireland is but one golf event away from the honour of hosting the most revered of international golfing events and the third biggest sporting event in the world after the Olympic Games and the FIFA World Cup.

Ireland, as you know, has made an enormous contribution to golf and the Ryder Cup since the event first took place in 1927. Golfers from Fred Daly in 1949 to Padraig Harrington, Paul McGinley and Darren Clarke in 2004 have all played pivotal roles in epic Ryder Cup encounters. We remember with pride the heroics of Christy O'Connor, Senior, who played in ten successive Ryder Cups, winning eleven matches between 1955 and 1973, and the never to be forgotten two iron approach shot by Christy O'Connor, Junior to the eighteenth green at the Belfry in 1989, which clinched a win over Fred Couples of the US and was vital to Europe retaining the trophy.

Hosting the 2006 Ryder Cup is an enormous honour for Ireland not just because of its prestige as one of the world's leading sports events, but because it allows us to present a New Ireland to a worldwide audience already familiar with our proud culture, heritage and rich traditions.

The Ireland of today is a far remove from the land of our ancestors and our success in hosting the 2006 Ryder Cup has also presented us with a unique opportunity to showcase what it is that has led to our economic prosperity and what it is that makes Ireland one of the world's leading tourist destinations.

It is for these reasons that the government was fully supportive of the bid to bring the 2006 Ryder Cup to Ireland and I am delighted that an allocation of €4.9 million was made through Fáilte Ireland towards the €9.5 million that will be paid to the Tour. I am equally delighted that the balance is being funded by our three partners, Bord Bia (the Irish food board), Waterford Crystal and Allied Irish Bank (AIB).

I would also like to recognise the very substantial investment that has been made in the Ryder Cup by Dr Michael Smurfit and the K Club, which won the bid to stage the event. This investment has included the design and construction of a new golf course and clubhouse, the expansion of the hotel and the provision of a host of ancillary services for the event.

It is fitting, therefore, that the Ryder Cup 2006 matches should be played here by the banks of the Liffey in Co. Kildare on the challenging K Club course that is such a fine example of the magnificent facilities which are available to golfers in Ireland.

The eyes of the golfing world are already training their sights on Ireland in growing numbers that are expected to reach 1 billion television viewers in 150 countries during the Ryder Cup matches.

During this unique window of opportunity we have much to tell the world about Ireland. We will showcase our traditional values of a spectacular landscape, a welcoming people, a rich cultural heritage and a modern tourism infrastructure. We will highlight Ireland as a mature golfing destination with more than 400 courses including 40 per cent of all the genuine links courses in the world, with hundreds of welcoming clubs, some of which have been established for more than a century. We will focus attention on the many parkland courses and golf resorts and a golf environment that offers exceptional value for money at every level of the market – a combination of factors which led to Ireland being declared 'International Destination of the Year 2004' by the International Association of Golf Tour Operators.

The world has an estimated 60 million golfers, a growing number of whom are taking golfing holidays. Research conducted by Fáilte Ireland indicates that many of these golfers already hold Ireland in high regard as a golfing destination. UK golfers rank Ireland second in the world for quality of golf courses and half of American golfers are considering Ireland for their next golf trip. On the other hand, only 6 per cent of US golfers have visited Ireland, so we have a perfect opportunity, through Ryder Cup 2006, to convert this positive level of awareness into a decision to visit this country.

The Ryder Cup will also provide an opportunity to address an international corporate audience which tends to have a keen interest in golf, and in the process to promote business tourism into Ireland. More than 250,000 visitors came to Ireland to participate in corporate meetings, international conferences and incentive trips in 2005, representing an increase of 23 per cent on the previous year. Overall, business tourism in Ireland grew by 5 per cent to 857,000 visits and was worth €457 million, with the Dublin market recording a 26 per cent increase in the number of incentive conferences choosing the Irish capital. The new National Conference Centre, which is now at an advanced planning stage, will further boost this valuable sector of the tourism industry.

My department and Fáilte Ireland plan to grasp with both hands the opportunity to leverage the Ryder Cup to promote Irish tourism through a series of initiatives which will enable us to engage a worldwide audience not only in the golf, but also in a rich visual and aural tapestry that will reflect the destination that is Ireland.

In a creative and innovative initiative, we have reached agreement to introduce a spectacular opening ceremony to Ryder Cup 2006, which international television networks around the world have undertaken to broadcast in its entirety. The traditional introduction of the teams and players on Thursday, 21 September will be incorporated into a ceremony that will be in the tradition of the opening of the World Cup or the Olympic Games. It will incorporate a pageant featuring Macnas, Cos Ceim and the Spanish theatre group Els Comediants and will be followed by the playing of a specially commissioned Ryder Cup anthem, composed by Donal Lunny. More than 300 actors, dancers and musicians will participate in the pageant, which will follow the official opening of the Ryder Cup 2006 by the President of Ireland. The ceremony will also include the raising of the flags of the nations and the playing of the anthems.

That event will be preceded by the Ryder Cup Gala Dinner, where leading Irish artistes and theatre groups will also perform while the presentation of the Ryder Cup by An Taoiseach at the conclusion of the matches will also be framed by a visual celebration of the event.

A truly exciting week in Co. Kildare will also include Ryder Cup Race Day, which takes place at the Curragh on Tuesday, 19 September. This very special day will feature the inaugural running of the Shelbourne Hotel Goffs Million, which carries a prize of €1 million for the winner. Two races being staged on that day will feature, exclusively, graduates of the 2005 Goffs Million Sale, thereby attracting owners from more than twelve countries around the globe who were purchasers at that sale. The card carries a total prize fund of €2.4 million, making this Ryder Cup Race Day one of the great racing events of the season.

These and many other events related to Ryder Cup 2006 are elements in a multi-faceted national endeavour to achieve sustained growth in the Irish tourism industry, which experienced its fourth consecutive year of growth in 2005 when visitor numbers reached a record 6.8 million and foreign exchange earnings grew by 5 per cent to almost €4.3 billion. The industry employs more than 240,000 people and is again on a growth pattern in this current year, which will of course be stimulated by the Ryder Cup.

This historic island is blessed with a treasury of culture and heritage which is deeply appreciated by a growing number of visitors and which can provide a compelling reason to visit Ireland. From the pre-historic monuments of Newgrange dating back to 3200 BC to the early Christian monasteries, the Celtic and Norman castles and the architectural heritage of Victorian and Georgian buildings, we can offer visitors a rich array of places to see and enjoy. The targeted marketing of our cultural heritage is being stepped up by Fáilte Ireland and Tourism Ireland with recent initiatives, including a new joint publication from Fáilte Ireland and the Northern Ireland Tourist Board highlighting many of the monasteries, churches, round towers and high crosses to be found throughout this island. The publication will be of interest and value to the 61 per cent of holiday visitors travelling to Ireland who regard interesting culture and heritage as very important when choosing their holiday.

We therefore have much to offer our sporting visitors, be they golfers, sailors, hill walkers or anglers or participants in the myriad of sports that are enjoyed in this country. We can offer them a spectacular and unique landscape, a rich cultural heritage, hundreds of festivals and musical events, fine food, friendly pubs and most of all the *cead mile fáilte* of the Irish people.

Significantly, too, we can attract visitors to an environment which, despite the economic development of recent times, remains green and clear. Much work has been undertaken to improve the quality of our fishing lakes and rivers, to conserve stocks of fish and game, to increase natural energy production, to encourage environmentally friendly farming and to guarantee that this Emerald Isle retains the unique quality of life which it can offer its citizens and visitors.

These are just some of the images of Ireland which will be shown to the world as we grasp the opportunity to showcase our country during the Ryder

Cup. The benefits of staging the event will not, of course, end with the final putt on the eighteenth green. We will, through Tourism Ireland, continue to leverage the positive images created by Ryder Cup in ongoing campaigns in key overseas markets which we confidently expect will pay handsome dividends in terms of golfing, business and leisure visitors.

Source: Department of Arts, Sport and Tourism press release, 6 July 2006.

PROBLEMS WITH VISITOR ATTRACTIONS

All around the world, visitor attractions are facing competition from competing attractions locally and internationally. Word of mouth is an important marketing tool in tourism. If a visitor to a particular destination recommends it to a friend or relative, this improves the chances of the friend or relative considering visiting the attraction. If, on the other hand, they hear negative reports on the attraction, they may discourage the prospective visitor. Some problems with visitor attractions are discussed below. It is worth noting that this list is not exhaustive, nor is it limited to Ireland.

Overcrowding, Delays and Queues

Tourism is a seasonal business in many destinations. This results in an increase in demand at peak times, such as summer in Ireland. Such an increase in demand puts pressure on attractions. Visitors may be forced to wait in a queue to enter the attraction. An example of this is the queues for rides and attractions at a Disneyland resort at major holidays or during school breaks, some of which can be over an hour long in blistering heat. Large-scale attractions such as these deal with queues and delays by making it more comfortable for visitors to stand in a queue. This includes mist sprays in queues to keep the visitors cool in soaring temperatures, as well as video displays relating to the ride or show to keep them entertained and interested. The actual layout of the winding queue also gives the visitor the impression that the queue is a lot shorter than it actually is. This is also achieved by locating the front part of the queue indoors, where the person joining the queue at the end cannot see.

Lack of Parking

A lack of parking at many attractions is a discouraging factor. Many large attractions have multi-storey car parks, as well as space for coaches and dedicated public transport links, e.g. Disneyland Resort Paris. Parking facilities and transport links are essential for the success of a tourist attraction.

Lack of Cleanliness

Given the problems of overcrowding, it is inevitable that many attractions will suffer from litter problems. Litter is a major problem for many Irish cities and has been commented on by tourists. Large music and horseracing festival attractions advertise in advance for litter pickers, who are employed for the duration of the festival to collect and dispose of litter. Litter must be controlled at attractions, as an untidy attraction will yield a negative impression of the attraction in the mind of many visitors.

Poorly Trained/Rude Staff

The tourism sector in Ireland is largely non-unionised and pay is traditionally low. As a result, there is a large labour turnover and high level of short-term employees and seasonal workers. Training is seen as an investment by many managers and proprietors of tourism enterprises, and many are unwilling or unable to invest in training for staff who subsequently leave their position. This often causes a negative customer service experience, which frustrates and annoys many visitors. Further, many staff working in tourism enterprises such as visitor attractions do not have English as a first language, which can also frustrate many visitors, considering almost three-quarters of Ireland's tourism arrivals come from the UK and North America.

High Admission Fees

While many attractions are free, a large number of attractions have an admission fee. Some admission fees are modest and cover the management and maintenance of the attraction and any visitor centre which may accompany it. However, some visitor attractions are profit-making enterprises and the entrance fees can be expensive. Sometimes, fees are increased to discourage demand so that overcrowding can be avoided. These fee increases usually take place at peak periods when there is the highest demand, often causing disappointment to visitors on a budget. Further, gift shops or cafés at attractions are often over-priced, according to many visitors.

Maturity

Many visitor attractions around the world have reached or are reaching the maturity stage in their life cycle. This is characterised by the majority of those wishing to visit an attraction having done so. There are other opportunities for such visitor attractions in emerging markets, and marketing efforts may be redirected to such markets.

FUTURE OF VISITOR ATTRACTIONS

Ireland's population, like that of Europe's, is ageing. In the past, the Irish economy necessitated young Irish people to emigrate in the search for work, and so Irish people grew older abroad. This is no longer the case. An ageing population with higher levels of disposable income than ever witnessed in Ireland will inevitably result in a demand for different kinds of products, including different kinds of domestic tourism products. Older generations are more interested in visitor attractions such as heritage sites, natural attractions and museums rather than the party-style beach resorts such as Ibiza or concerts, pubs or nightclubs. This should create a long-term boost to Irish and international visitor attractions that fall into the categories they desire.

Another growth opportunity for visitor attractions is the domestic and international tourist seeking active leisure holidays, where they participate in activities and events linked to specific attractions. Niche holidays with an emphasis on physical activities and mental stimulation are set to increase.

Inevitably, newer technologies will improve the visitor experience at many attractions. Interactive visitor centres (such as the GAA Museum at Dublin's Croke Park) offer a better visitor experience. The internet is just one technological revolution that has made it easier than ever for interested tourists to find information on attractions, both before and after a visit. It is also a powerful marketing and distribution tool for any attraction. Other technology, such as translator headsets in museums, allows multilingual exploration of artwork and artefacts.

Apart from all of the positive aspects that the future may hold, there are some concerns regarding the conservation of sites, including how sustainable they will remain in the future. Many sites must discourage visitors if age-old attractions (such as at Newgrange) are to survive as visitor attractions. Careful and responsible planning is needed from all governments who control the world's visitor attractions to conserve and preserve them for future generations of tourists to enjoy.

The Motivation for Change

The following are the main types of circumstances that can cause managers to feel they must make changes to their attractions (Swarbrooke 2005: 334):

1. Changes in consumer behaviour, such as the growing interest in green issues, animal welfare and healthy eating, and the desire to learn something new on a visit to an attraction.
2. New legislation and regulations which affect the attraction's operations.
3. A deterioration in the state of the economy which may result in less attraction visits being made and visitors looking for more attractions which are perceived to offer value for money.
4. Demographic changes which threaten to reduce the size of the market which the attraction currently targets.
5. Reductions in visitor numbers and/or income.
6. Complaints about the attraction from existing customers.
7. Poor performance by marketing intermediaries or suppliers.
8. The actions of competitors.
9. The opinions of key stakeholders, such as major investors in the case of private attractions, or councillors in relation to local authority museums.

REVISION QUESTIONS

1. Define what is meant by a 'visitor attraction'.
2. List and explain the categories of visitor attractions.
3. What are the problems facing Irish visitor attractions?
4. What are Ireland's top visitor attractions and why?
5. How do the attractions on offer in Ireland compare to international attractions?
6. How large of a role do festivals play in attracting visitors to a destination?

7. Is the risk of environmental damage too high a price to pay for making a natural attraction available to the public?
8. Is the success of an attraction dependent on how close any information/interpretative centre is located to it?
9. Do visitor attractions serve the locals as well as the visitors? If so, how?
10. Are the arts important as a tourist attraction?

ESSAY QUESTIONS

1. Ireland does not market itself as a tourist destination like sun destinations of the Mediterranean. Instead, it relies on alternative approaches. Outline your understanding of such approaches and highlight their importance to Ireland.
2. Discuss the development and decline of Irish and British seaside resorts.
3. Why hasn't a Disneyland-style theme park emerged in Ireland? If such a theme park was to emerge, in your opinion:
    (a) What would it be like?
    (b) Who would it target?
    (c) Would it be successful?
    (d) Where could it be located?
    (e) Would it be Irish or internationally owned?
    (f) Would it have specifically Irish attractions or would they be generic?
4. 'Ireland cannot rely on world-renowned tourist attractions, such as the Pyramids or the Eiffel Tower, to attract large numbers of tourists, nor are we likely to ever develop single attractions such as Disneyland that can claim to bring extra tourists to Ireland in their own right. Instead we must mould our heritage in its broadest sense and promote and present it to visitors so that the result is a transformation in the quality of the entire holiday experience.' (Source: *Developing Sustainable Tourism*, Fáilte Ireland.) Critically analyse this statement, using examples to illustrate your answers.
5. 'Heritage tourism is as important to Irish tourism as sunshine and beaches are to the Mediterranean.' Discuss.

TASKS

Divide the class into two roughly equal groups. Each group should be given ten to fifteen minutes to develop opposing points on the following statements, followed by a forty to forty-five minute debate.

Statement: Ireland may not have the sunshine weather of many of our competing tourism destinations, but the visitor attractions are world class.

Statement: Disneyland size and style theme parks would not be successful in Ireland.

Statement: Man-made visitor attractions are more popular internationally than natural visitor attractions.

ASSIGNMENTS

1. Write a brief report (for a fictional client) on the Irish visitor attractions you would recommend such a client to visit on their next trip to Ireland. Ensure that your report encompasses a variety of visitor attractions from various regions of Ireland. You should use a short brochure style and then expand briefly on each attraction. Your aim is to promote the particular set of attractions.

2. You are a tourism management consultant. The owner of a German theme park company has approached you and asked you to inform her about the Irish visitor attractions product, as she hopes to set up a large-scale theme park on the outskirts of north Co. Dublin. Advise your client of the current state of the visitor attraction market in Ireland (including the different categories of attractions and some examples of the most popular attractions). Further, advise her of what you believe the restrictions to such a venture might be. Finally, raise any other issues that you think may be relevant to her decision.

Chapter 8

The Travel Industry (Travel Retailing and Tour Operations)

SUMMARY

Chapter 8 outlines the past, present and predicted future of travel agents (retailer) and tour operators (wholesaler) and discusses their diluted role as distributors for the large players in the industry throughout the world. It begins with an overall introduction to the industry, followed by the first half dedicated to tour operations and the second half to travel retailing (travel agents). The chapter presents the Irish regulations required to become a travel agent and tour operator and discusses why these regulations are so strict. It looks at the operations of the traditional travel agent and tour operator and presents the key success drivers for the industry. The stages in organising a package tour are also presented in detail. In addition, the chapter highlights the recent trends and challenges faced by the traditional small travel agents and tour operators, most notably from the internet and larger, internationally owned organisations, and will lead the reader into the next chapter on the travel industry's biggest threat: e-commerce. The chapter concludes by outlining the organisations that both travel agents and tour operators are affiliated to.

LEARNING OUTCOMES

Having completed this chapter, the reader should be able to:
- Understand the nature of the travel industry.
- Identify the difference between the traditional travel retailer and tour operator.
- Appreciate the regulations imposed on the industry.
- Understand the organisation and structure of travel retailers and tour operators.
- Identify key success drivers.
- Appreciate the competitive forces in the industry.
- Illustrate the stages in the organisation of a package tour.
- Understand the role of e-commerce.
- Identify the organisations representing the interests of the Irish travel industry, both at home and abroad.

INTRODUCTION

Tour operators, along with travel agents and ground handling agents, make up the travel industry, which are traditionally the main channels of distribution for the tourism industry. The tour operator's traditional role is one of a wholesaler, who organises a package tour and sells it on to a travel agent (the retailer). The travel agent would then sell it on, at a commission, to the customer.

The roles of tour operators and travel agents are continually becoming blurred. The distinction between the two no longer exists in many cases. Many tour operators are forsaking travel agents as a method of distribution, choosing instead to sell direct to the customer. At the same time, many travel agents no longer seem content with buying package holidays wholesale and selling them on to customers at a profit; instead, they organise the package themselves and sell it to their customers, cutting out the middleman. This process has become known as 'disintermediation'.

Travel agents and tour operators taking on each others' roles is only part of the competitive situation at present. Many smaller Irish operations are being challenged by larger foreign firms that can offer customers better deals due to their large bargaining power.

The biggest competitive threat of all comes from relatively new technology. The internet and its mass proliferation have made it possible for online tour operators and travel agents to flourish. Offering travel products online direct to the customer drastically reduces distribution costs. Further problems for the traditional travel retailers come from principals (product providers such as Aer Lingus or Irish Ferries) who have become e-tailers in their own right, as they encourage their customers to book direct on their website at a reduced fare and cut out any and all intermediaries. (The role of e-commerce is discussed in detail in Chapter 9.)

In Ireland, tour operators and travel agents are represented by the Irish Travel Agents' Association (ITAA, www.itaa.ie) and the Irish Tour Operators' Association (ITOA, www.itoa-ireland.com), discussed in more detail below.

TOUR OPERATIONS

Irish tour operators organise inclusive tours for outgoing tourists. Traditionally, they have organised package holidays which they sell wholesale to travel agents to destinations outside Ireland. The traditional package holiday includes a combination of any of the following:

- Travel to/from destination.
- Travel from airport to accommodation and return to airport.
- Accommodation.
- Catering (full board, half board, breakfast).

Most of the sun holidays to seaside resort destinations such as Costa del Sol (Spain), the Algarve (Portugal) or Agia Napa (Cyprus) include at least the first three listed above, with the option of the tourist paying a supplement for the fourth. Sometimes all inclusive packages will include activities such as water sports, golf, excursions and children's entertainment. In addition, tour operators usually have a courier or representative agent at the destination to care for customers and organise things from the destination.

Regulations

In Ireland, package holidays are regulated by many Irish and European laws and regulations, ranging from advertising standards to consumer law and contract law. Further, the Transport Act 1982 and the Package Holidays Act 1995 are particularly relevant to tour operators (the latter is discussed in Chapter 11).

A tour operators license is required under the Transport Act 1982 before organising package holidays. In order to be issued with a license, a tour operator must apply to the Department of Transport. The following are required in order to apply:

- An application form two months in advance of trading as a tour operator.
- Company audited accounts.
- Financial projections of future tour business.
- Copies of the brochures and booking terms and conditions that will be used.
- Arrangements for a bond – with cash, insurance or a bank (around 10 per cent of projected turnover). This was initiated after numerous companies went bankrupt in 1984 and left thousands of tourists stranded abroad.
- Proof of competent and experienced staff.
- An annual fee, based on company turnover.

The Department of Transport will issue a one-year licence if it is satisfied that these conditions have been met in full.

Different Types of Packages

New and innovative packages are consistently being developed by tour operators in order to meet changing consumer demands. A sample of some of the traditionally popular types of packages is listed below:

- Summer sun holidays.
- Winter sun holidays.
- Winter ski holidays.
- Short break holidays.
- Long-haul holidays.
- Round-the-world trips.
- Cruises.
- Group escorted tours.
- Fly-drive packages.
- Special interest packages, e.g. religious holidays, golf holidays.
- Conferences and incentive tours.

MAJOR IRISH TOUR OPERATORS

Appendix C   provides a detailed database of contact details for more than sixty tour operators in Ireland to enable the reader to research in further detail. These include telephone and fax numbers as well as e-mail and web addresses and postal addresses.

Tours to Ireland

There are many tour operators around the world that offer tours to Ireland. Most tours to Ireland can be categorised as follows.

Group escorted holidays

This is a package which involves a tour operator's representative accompanying the travelling tour party as a guide. This form of package is popular with American tourists. It is also known as 'blue rinse' tourism, given that so many people on such tours are senior citizens (blue rinse referring to a hair colouring used by many older American women).

Short break holidays

Given Ireland's relatively cheap, efficient and regular air access from Britain and Continental Europe, short break holidays such as weekend breaks to Ireland's cities and towns have become increasingly popular with British and other European tourists. Often such tourists can purchase packages inclusive of flights and accommodation at the last minute, from either travel retail outlets, direct from tour operators or (more and more) online.

Special interest holidays

Ireland has a lot to offer in terms of special interest holidays. It offers many world-class golf resorts which are the envy of golfing destinations the world over. Similarly, Ireland is famous for its equestrian heritage and horse-racing and horse-breeding enthusiasts alike recognise and choose Ireland as their destination of choice. Traditionally, Ireland was chosen as a cheaper alternative for foreign students wishing to learn the English language. It is now often just as expensive as other destinations, if not more. However, there is still a large language learning market. Finally, the perception of Ireland as a green destination leads to many tourists choosing Ireland as a destination for nature holidays, perhaps including a stay and participation on a working farm.

Biggest Irish tourism fair gets underway

Over €800 million worth of business is expected to be generated at Ireland's largest tourism trade fair.

Meitheal 2006, which was opened by the Minister of Arts, Sport and Tourism earlier today, takes place over the next two days in Killarney, Co. Kerry.

The fair presents Irish firms in the tourism sector with an opportunity to win business with over 300 tour operators from around the world.

Around thirty overseas markets are represented at this year's event, with a strong representation from new and developing tourism markets such as China, Russia, Ukraine and India.

The fair has been jointly organised by Fáilte Ireland, the national tourism development authority, and Tourism Ireland.

Shaun Quinn, chief executive of Fáilte Ireland, said: 'Irish tourism has managed to transform itself to the changing needs of visitors while also maintaining and building on its traditional success factors.

'This is an ongoing process and Meitheal plays an important role as Irish tourism businesses meet key and potential customers face to face. It is a highly efficient manner of both doing business and building market intelligence.'

Source: 'Biggest Irish tourism fair gets underway', *The Irish Times*, 8 May 2006.

ORGANISING THE TOUR

Organising a package holiday of any type is an extremely complex procedure given the regulations which must be followed and factors such as the myriad independent organisations that the package organiser must contract, e.g. transport providers to the destination, then within the destination, accommodation, retailers, marketers, etc. There are also external environmental variables out of the organiser's control, such as international events (natural and man-made), changing regulations and economic climate. Thus organising a package tour can take place up to two years in advance of the actual tour taking place.

The procedure for organising a package tour is generally as follows (Guiney 2002):

1. Choose destination.
2. Decide transport to destination.
3. Decide on accommodation.
4. Organise transport from airport to accommodation and return to airport.
5. Work out retail price.
6. Prepare brochure.
7. Payment in advance.
8. How does the customer book?

1. Choose destination

The destination is chosen on the basis of popularity with the target market, the climate in the destination as well as the customs and the general cost. Like most products and services, destinations go through a product life cycle. Many traditional package holiday destinations have reached maturity or saturation stage in their life cycle, as the majority of the target market who wish to travel there have already done so. Such destinations stay alive by attracting newer generations as well as tourists from newly developing markets. Further, like a fashion product, a destination may be the 'in' place to travel to in one particular season and not the next.

Cost is also a factor to consider. At times of economic success in an outbound market, higher-priced luxury packages will sell better than in times of an economic downturn. The cost of food, drink, entertainment, gifts and other items in the destination is also a key factor when deciding on a destination.

The climate and customs of the destination must be similar or tolerable to the prospective outbound tourist. Tourists may wish to escape from a cold climate to a warmer one for their holiday, but they do not wish to feel uncomfortably warm. Similarly, the local custom in the destination must permit the outbound tourist to enjoy what they expect to enjoy on their holiday. It is for this reason that many outbound tourists will not visit many Islamic countries, as the sale of alcohol is not permitted in many.

2. Decide transport to destination

The method of travel to the destination is a key cost factor. Most package tours charter an entire aircraft, or block book seats on one. Indeed, many tour operators own their own fleet of aircraft specifically devoted to the tour operator's business. Traditionally, an airline registered in either the tourism-generating or destination country is used.

The package organiser must decide key details such as the date and time of flights, as this will have an impact on other variables, such as availability of landing slots at airports, availability of transfer links to accommodation and availability of accommodation.

The organiser must also decide to pay for all the seats on the aircraft or all of the seats block-booked, or else agree a sale or return basis with the airline. In the case of the former, the organiser runs a risk of not filling the aircraft and thus making a loss on the unused seats. However, economies of scale can be reached by booking larger amounts. The latter is the more expensive option, but will release the organiser from its obligation to absorb the loss of any unsold seats. In either scenario, any unsold seats may be sold to the general public as seat-only fares by either the organiser or the airline itself. Anyone purchasing such a flight flies to the destination, but that is all they receive. They are not entitled to accommodation or transfers to resorts. Although not permitted, it is often the case that those who take this option make their own way to a resort and sleep on the floor or couch in the apartment of friends who have paid for the full package holiday.

3. Decide on accommodation

The type of accommodation chosen has a great deal of influence on the price of the package. There are various options of accommodation, as discussed in Chapter 5. In the standard sun package holiday (such as the Spanish coastline or islands), the most common form of accommodation is purpose-built package holiday apartments. The apartments come in various qualities and forms and the room combinations also vary. Most have at least one bedroom, bathroom, kitchen and lounge area. Many also have a balcony. The couch usually also converts to a bed to increase the occupancy. Apartments also range in terms of facilities and services. Many have swimming pools, bars, restaurants and children's activity centres. Any meal options which are included (such as breakfast buffet) will inevitably impact on the price.

The location of the accommodation is also a key consideration and is highly dependent on the target market. Younger party-goers will be keen to ensure they are accommodated close to the nightlife in a resort, while young family groups may be more concerned with proximity to the beach and activity centres.

The organiser must enter negotiations with an accommodation provider or management company in the destination to get the best price for the time required.

4. Organise transfers from airport to accommodation and return to airport

Most packages will include transfers from the arriving airport to the accommodation upon arrival, and again from the accommodation back to the airport when departing. This is usually organised with a local coach company. In the case of many sun holidays, the airport may be located a significant distance from the accommodation, so coach journeys of two or three hours are not uncommon.

5. Work out retail price

The next stage is a costing exercise. The cost price and the eventual retail price must be derived. The organiser must ensure that all costs are covered, including distribution costs and commissions (if any), and that a profit can still be achieved. At this stage, any free child places and discounts, e.g. for early booking or payment, must be factored in, as must provisions for unknown variables such as fuel surcharges incurred by airlines.

An important factor which must be considered is the issue of demand and supply. At peak holiday periods (such as August for sun travel, or school holidays), the price charged by tour operators is generally maximum, as the demand at this time often exceeds supply. At off-peak periods, the price is usually at the opposite end of the scale in order to stimulate demand.

6. Prepare brochure

The brochure describes all aspects of the tour. It is a very important marketing tool for a package organiser. Pictures of destinations and the models used are picked carefully to convey an effective and targeted message. The brochure must adhere to Irish and EU regulations, e.g. Misleading Terms in Advertisements, Package Holidays and Travel Trade Act 1995. The latter of these Acts mandates that certain information be placed in brochures, including:

- Price.
- Provision for price revision.
- Payment timetable.
- Security of deposit.
- What happens if the customer or organiser is forced to cancel.
- Contact information of the organiser.
- All times and dates.
- Passport and visa requirements (if any).
- Vaccination requirements (if any).
- Insurance options.
- Means and categories of transport.
- Type and grade of accommodation.
- If any meals are included.

- Any other terms and conditions deemed necessary.

Due to the complexity of the requirements, brochures are generally prepared at least a year in advance of the holiday taking place.

7. Payment in advance

Tour operators generally have to pre-pay accommodation and transport providers, or at least partly pay them. Therefore they need to get a deposit at the time of reservation. To do this, they often offer discounts and deals such as free child places to encourage early booking and early payment.

8. How does the customer book?

Traditionally, the two options for the customer were to book direct with the tour operator or to book through a distributor such as a travel agent. This still occurs. However, the situation has become more complicated. Many tour operators have decided to cut out the intermediary, i.e. travel agent, so that they do not have to pay a commission to them. Similarly, many travel agents have commenced organising their own package holidays rather than purchasing them wholesale from the tour operator. This has created a blur in the definition of an organisation as either a tour operator or a travel agent. As we shall see in Chapter 9, both tour operators and travel agents are facing the growing threat of the internet as a distribution channel, not just for package holidays, but for all forms of travel.

Tourists rejecting 'rip-off' Ireland

Tour operators anticipate a bumper week of bookings for foreign package holidays and say that 'rip-off Ireland' is driving Irish and foreign holidaymakers to alternative destinations. Positive predictions for the domestic market over the next twelve months mask a worrying slump in profits and a lack of essential reinvestment.

The Irish Tour Operators' Federation (ITOF) predicts that this year will see further increases in the numbers of people jetting off to the sun, despite predictions that the domestic tourist industry is set for growth.

The federation reports that just under 1 million Irish people took cheap package holidays last year and believes that this January will be the busiest ever for the booking of cheap getaways. The main locations for Irish holidaymakers remain Majorca, the Canary Islands, the Spanish mainland and Portugal.

ITOF president Niall McDonnell believes the problems bedevilling tourism in Ireland will benefit his end of the industry.

'All the indications suggest that a lot of people who stayed at home last summer are going to book abroad in 2004,' he said. 'According to our research, people have had enough of "rip-off Ireland". A lot of the anecdotal evidence would suggest that people are fed up staying at home and paying over-the-top prices for eating out and accommodation.

'The introduction of the euro has introduced a huge amount of transparency into going abroad. Irish people are now comparing the price of a meal in their local restaurant to that in the south of Spain or Portugal. The days when a package holiday was regarded as a luxury option are long gone. Prices have been coming down for the last ten years.'

Source: Colgan, P.T., 'Tourists rejecting "rip-off" Ireland', *The Sunday Business Post*, 4 January 2004.

TRAVEL AGENTS

While tour operators are traditionally the wholesalers of the travel industry, travel agents are traditionally the retailers, the point of contact for the customer wishing to purchase travel products. They are the distributors for the travel product. They do not own the product they are selling, but are the sales agents for the tour operator (wholesaler) or for the producer (known as the principal, e.g. airlines, ferry companies, cruise liners, hotels). Their role is to provide a convenient location for customers who are considering a trip to find travel information and complete a reservation, at a cost which is at least comparable with competing forms of reservation.

There are in excess of 460 travel agents in Ireland, of which 370 are affiliated to the ITAA. Most of them employ fewer than ten people. There is a trend towards the formation of larger chains, especially in cities, e.g. Budget Travel and Sunway Travel.

Travel agents sell travel products at a commission. That is, they purchase travel products from wholesalers, i.e. tour operators, as well as principals, e.g. Aer Lingus, Bus Éireann, hotels, car hire companies, at a reduced rate, mark up the price and sell to the customer. Products sold by travel agents include:

* Flights.
* Ferry tickets.
* Cruises.
* Car hire.
* Hotels.
* Rail tickets.
* Coach tickets.
* Packages.
* Insurance.

Travel agents also provide information on visa, passport and health requirements for destinations as well as often having employees who have visited a selection of the destinations on offer. A large amount of travel agents' staff time is spent dealing with information requests such as prices and availability of single products such as flights, or package products such as two-week sun holidays. The key to profitability for travel agents is to turn as many such requests as possible into actual reservations. Travel agents do not get commission on providing free information!

Irish travel agents are represented by and affiliated to the Irish Travel Agents' Association (ITAA) and International Air Transport Association (IATA). Through the ITAA, they are affiliated to the European Confederation of Travel Agents' Associations (ECTAA) and the Universal Federation of Travel Agents' Associations (UFTAA). See below for further details.

TRAVEL AGENCY REGULATIONS

Travel retailing is another area of the travel industry with strict regulations. In order to sell travel products, a travel agency license is necessary. The requirements are similar to those of a tour operator's license. The following must be included with any application:

- A copy of audited accounts and/or a financial projection must be provided with all applications.
- Must prove employees hold IATA and ITAA qualifications to sell travel products.
- Must prove that they have paid a bond (usually 4 per cent of projected income – less than the amount paid by tour operators) in order to protect customers in case the agency goes out of business.

If the Department of Transport is satisfied that all of the requirements have been met, it issues a license to sell travel.

KEY SUCCESS DRIVERS

The success of any travel agency depends on many factors. Two key drivers for success in the traditional travel retailer are the quality of customer experience delivered by competent, informed and customer-orientated staff (discussed below) and the location of the outlet. Usually, it must be situated in a prime retail location (main street or shopping mall) with enough business to sustain its operations.

A travel agent does not need much room for stock, as most of the stock is in the form of brochures. Therefore, agency costs can be held down by sacrificing office space. This can be offset, however, by consumer demand for travel agents to be situated in a convenient location, e.g. Grafton Street, which usually have higher retail rental costs.

STAFFING AND OPERATIONS

In order to sell travel products, staff must be highly trained and proficient in several key skills. Inevitably, customer service and interpersonal skills are vital, as the traditional travel agent interacts with the customer face to face or on the telephone. A warm, friendly, professional approach is a prerequisite for maintaining customer satisfaction and retention.

Staff in travel agents also require a knowledge of sales theory and the skills necessary to convert an information request into a reservation. Further, skills on up-selling are beneficial to profitability. Computer skills are vital for agency staff. The use of computer reservation systems (CRS) such as Galileo (used by the majority of Irish agencies), Sabre, Worldspan and Amadeus is essential to the efficient operation and success of travel agents (see Chapter 9 for a detailed discussion of CRS).

As in any organisation, there are several different roles that must be fulfilled in a travel agency. Apart from the actual person selling the travel (travel agent or travel consultant), there are a host of other individuals without whom a travel agency would not be able to operate effectively. The titles, roles and number of these individuals are dependent on the size and scope of the travel agency operations. They include administrators, receptionists, sales managers, accounts officers, marketing/promotions managers, etc.

It is easy to provide customers with information about simple travel products such as flights. It becomes more complex and time consuming when organising multiple products, such as tailor-made packages. In general, experienced staff will become very familiar with the reservations system in use and will be able to search more quickly using short cuts learned along the way. An example of this is using airport or airline codes, e.g. DUB for Dublin, LHR for London Heathrow, EI for Aer Lingus, LH for Lufthansa, etc. The consultant will then present the customer with the best options to match their needs while also ensuring high commission-paying principals are presented, i.e. travel providers that pay the agency the highest commission. The consultant's task is to disseminate the information to the customer and aid them in their decision-making process. The ultimate goal is to encourage the customer to make a reservation. Often, the consultant will offer to place the travel products on hold in the customer's name for twenty-four to seventy-two hours in order to give the customer time to consider the offer.

Regarding complex packages, more detailed knowledge of the resort and its constituent components is required. Often, larger travel agencies such as Trailfinders will welcome you at reception and ask you what type of product and geographical area you are considering. Depending on your answer, you will be directed to a specific consultant with specific knowledge in your desired product or region, most likely from familiarisation trips as well as their own experience living or travelling there. This results in a more informative approach to the customer experience. Such consultants may know important criteria which they can use to aid the customer's information-gathering and decision-making process. It is not possible that a travel consultant can know so much information about every resort that they sell. The ideal situation is that each consultant would be a specialist in a specific area from first-hand knowledge. However, even in such a desirable scenario, not all travel consultants would be on duty at all times that the establishment is open. Often, competent travel consultants do their best to be informative on destinations they have not visited, gaining insight instead from travel literature.

Important decision-making criteria for choosing a package include:
- Typical weather at a particular location at any given time of year.
- Entertainment options.
- Whether it is family friendly.
- Cost of general items, food, drink, entertainment, shopping.
- Transport at the location, including transfers.
- Types and standards of accommodation.
- Local culture and customs and similarity of these to the customer's.
- General amenities and services.

RECENT TRENDS AND CHALLENGES: TRAVEL AGENTS AND TOUR OPERATORS

Small travel agents are losing business to larger Irish and foreign-owned chains of agencies. These have more bargaining power with principals and so demand higher commission. They can also afford more advanced administration and reservation systems and rental of the best retail premises in prime retail locations. They can afford expensive television marketing campaigns and usually negotiate favourable credit agreements with principals. They may become a trusted household name. Some have become so trusted that they issue money in the form of travellers' cheques, e.g. Thomas Cook.

However, there is also a continuing trend of a blurring of roles between travel agents and tour operators. Vertical and horizontal integration is taking place in this sector on a grand scale. Travel agents are no longer content to buy the package from the tour operator and sell it on to the customer. Instead, they organise the package themselves and receive all the profits. Similarly, tour operators often no longer see travel agents as a viable form of distribution, opting instead for the direct sell approach. Some tour operators do not even wish to be reliant on the transport providers, and so either charter or lease their own aircraft, e.g. www.mytravellite.com. Similar examples exist with accommodation.

Traditional travel agents and tour operators are losing business to these mega-companies who can attract customers with lower prices through economies of scale. However, even these larger travel companies operating in the retail environment are not immune from the immense pressures presented by recent technological advancements. Distribution of travel products has been revolutionised by the internet. There has been a continuing shift away from the traditional form of travel retailing to web-based travel e-tailing, offering the customer better value and more options from countless online intermediaries and travel companies. The growing dominance of e-commerce (conducting business online) is discussed in Chapter 9.

Although the onslaught of the web is one of the largest upheavals in the travel industry's history, it is not the only one. Recent years have presented several major challenges to the industry.

Book Direct

Because of aggressive promotions to customers to make direct bookings with principals such as airlines, and even with tour operators by telephone and internet, travel agents have been facing falling demand. Despite this increasing competition, profits must be achieved to stay in business.

Commission

Commission has been steadily reduced to agencies, especially from airlines, e.g. Ryanair, Aer Lingus. Such airlines and other principals see reduced commission (or no commission) and encouraging customers to book direct as cost-cutting measures in the distribution of their products, which enables them to provide a low-cost service, e.g. Ryanair. Some agencies still sell products for principals that do not offer them commission. In such cases, a service charge is added to the product purchased.

Customer Care

In such a tough business climate, travel agents must ensure a fast turnaround of customers in their premises in order to gain profits. However, this must be achieved without jeopardising customer care. Customers are more demanding nowadays than ever before, and if they do not receive the level of service they expect, they can easily take their business elsewhere.

Economic Climate

Although Ireland's economy is performing exceptionally well, the tourism industry is highly impacted by events in the global economy rather than just one economy. The recent global economic downturn since 2001 has caused many financial challenges for the tourism industry as a whole.

Terrorism and War

People are more afraid to travel as a result of terrorist events such as those in the US on 11 September 2001 and in the UK on 7 July 2005, as well as in popular resorts such as Bali and traditionally popular city destinations such as Madrid. Immediately after such events there is a notable decrease in tourism to the destination in question as well as international traffic. This decrease has tended to level off over time. A similar demand decrease occurs at time of war, such as the American-led invasions of Afghanistan in 2001 and Iraq in 2003.

Natural Disasters

Similar to terrorist attacks, natural disasters such as the Asian tsunami of 26 December 2004, earthquakes, hurricanes and volcanic eruptions (to name just a few) cause an immediate short-term decline in demand for a particular destination as well as a decline in international tourism traffic. A similar result occurs at times of agricultural and disease crises, such as the threat of foot and mouth disease in Ireland in 2001, SARS in 2003 and the bird flu threat in 2006.

Inflation

Inflation leads to higher costs of conducting business. In recent years in Ireland there have been large increases in staff and administration costs, including the cost of energy, insurance and rent. Increasing world oil prices also pose their own challenges, as it increases the cost of travel. Often, travel agents and tour operators are forced to pass on a surcharge for fuel which has been imposed by transport providers.

Currency Fluctuations

Since the introduction of the euro single currency, fluctuations within participating countries have been removed. However, fluctuations still exist between the value of the euro versus other world currencies. Of particular concern is the value of the euro versus the US dollar. Fluctuations in the euro-dollar relationship impact on the price of travel, due to the fact that oil is priced in US dollars. In the period 2002 to 2005, the massive increases in the price of oil were offset by the strengthening of the euro versus the US dollar. However, the euro weakened against the US dollar in 2005, causing the full impact of fuel price increases to be felt in Europe. The euro stabilised somewhat against the US dollar in the first half of 2006.

REPRESENTATIVE ORGANISATIONS

The ITAA

The Irish Travel Agents' Association (ITAA, www.itaa.ie) was founded in 1970 from the merger of the Alliance of Irish Travel Agents and Irish Provincial Travel Agents. It acts as a representative voice for 370 retail travel agents and twenty-two tour operators in Ireland. All ITAA members are licensed and bonded with the Government Commission for Aviation Regulation, according to the Transport (Tour Operators and Travel Agents) Act 1982 and the Package Holidays and Travel Trade Act 1995. It is a condition that all members must employ only fully qualified staff and must display a membership sticker in their premises window. Affiliation to the ITAA implies security and professionalism to the customer, as membership implies that they have complied with statutory regulations in relation to licensing and a bond. Further, it implies that the customer will receive professional, independent advice, up-to-date information as well as value and excellent customer service. According to their website:

> Members of the ITAA are governed by a set of rules and regulations in their Memorandum [see www.itaa.ie/memorandum.pdf] and Articles of Association [see www.itaa.ie/articlesofassociation.pdf] and by-laws which comprehensively deal with all aspects of standards relating to the consumer. Therefore, consumers can be assured that where they deal with members of the ITAA, that providing excellence in standards of services is the norm rather than the exception.

Irish holidaymakers joining the world's most adventurous – ITAA president

Travel agents point to increase in direct air destinations as key to changing consumer patterns.

James Malone, president of the Irish Travel Agents' Association (ITAA), said Irish holidaymakers are increasingly curious about destinations that only a few years ago would not even have been contemplated.

Speaking at the announcement of Holiday World Show 2006, Mr Malone, the principal of Rathgar Travel, said, 'Agents across the country are reporting increased interest in destinations in the Middle and Far East, in cities in the US and Canada that were rarely discussed before and in both adventure and cruise holidays and in complex "round the world" itineraries.'

'The market here in Ireland is changing so fast that Irish travellers are beginning to resemble the Dutch and the Scandinavians in their thirst for

---

new destinations and holiday experiences.

'A key feature has been the opening up of new long-haul destinations from Irish airports – with flights to the Gulf, South Africa and an ever increasing number of North American cities rewriting the rules of long-haul travel for those who want to avoid transiting through London.'

Mr Malone urged consumers who are planning now for their 2006 holidays to take advantage of the Holiday World Show at the RDS from 27 to 29 January to get a real sense of the destinations and holidays that are on the market.

'No amount of web-based research can compare with a real face-to-face discussion with even one of the 800 exhibitors that will be in the RDS. Agents, tour operators and destination specialists will be on hand to help you spot the best deals, the right locations and the traps to be avoided.'

ITAA chief executive Simon Nugent stressed the benefit to consumers of working with a travel agent when planning their holidays, both during and after the Holiday World Show: 'Only an ITAA member will take you through the wide range of options in terms of airlines, package holiday operators, accommodation providers and help you find value in terms of car hire, etc. The cost of travel has come down but a holiday is still a major investment for any family. You need to be sure that you are getting value for money and that your money is protected. That peace of mind is what your travel agent's bond is all about.'

Source: ITAA press release.

ITOA

The Irish Tour Operators' Associations (ITOA, www.itoa-ireland.com) represents thirty-four Irish members as well as overseas member companies who 'package and promote the various elements of the Irish tourism product for marketing overseas'. The organisation promotes Ireland as a destination among its 4,000 overseas partners, which include tour operators, large retail travel groups as well as operators in the conference, incentive and events sub-sectors.

The organisation divides tour operators into three categories, as follows:

1. **Professional conference organisers:** Managing all aspects of conferences and congresses.
2. **Destination management companies:** Managing corporate meetings and incentive programmes in a destination.
3. **Ground handling agents:** Organises destinations arrangements on land for group tours as well as individuals; acts as local representative.

The Irish tour operator provides a comprehensive packaging, booking and reservations service for the overseas travel trade. On occasion the operator also acts as an Irish representative of overseas tour operators, wholesalers and traffic generators. The Irish tour operator, by virtue of expert knowledge of the availability of home products, as well as bulk purchasing and allocation rates and facilities, can provide a comprehensive and flexible service on an individual, group or specialised basis for preordained and planned programmes or for specifically requested and designed requirements. As a service to the travel trade, the chief benefits are product knowledge, on-the-spot operational and negotiating ability, plus bulk purchasing and servicing facilities.

In 2002 alone, ITOA handled over 450,000 visitors, who contributed over €400 million in tourism revenue to the Irish economy. This represents approximately 20 per cent of all overseas holidaymakers to Ireland.

ITOA is responsible for 75 per cent approx. of the packaged market, that is, people having two or more elements of their holiday prepaid. Members have been instrumental in developing the conference, incentive and events markets to Ireland. Almost 28 per cent of ITOA business comes from these niche segments.

ITOA generates over €110 million in exchequer revenue on an annual basis. And because, uniquely in the commercial sector, it promotes every aspect of the tourism product, ITOA contributes to the achievement of the National Development Plan and the Tourism Development Strategy (2000–2006) objectives of:
- More balanced regional growth/development.
- Promoting a better spread of the economic benefits of tourism.
- Extending the tourism season.

ITOA has been pioneering in developing new markets, such as those in Eastern Europe.

In terms of jobs, ITOA is directly responsible for 7,000 in the Irish economy with an additional 3,500 indirectly. It generates an annual turnover of €200 million.

Source: ITOA website, July 2006.

IATA

'We represent, lead and serve the airline industry' is the motto for the International Air Transport Association (IATA, www.iata.org). Founded in Havana, Cuba in 1945 as a successor to the International Air Traffic Association established in 1919 and based in The Hague, it has built its reputation for more than sixty years and now represents 270 airlines across more than 140 nations, representing 94 per cent of international scheduled air traffic. (See www.iata.org/membership/airline_members.htm for a current list of full membership.)

The organisation is 'the prime vehicle for inter-airline co-operation in promoting safe, reliable, secure and economical air services – for the benefit of the world's consumers' (IATA 2006). Its website takes the three key drivers of 'representing', 'leading' and 'serving' from its motto and explains how it achieves these.

Representing...

IATA seeks to improve understanding of the industry among decision makers and increase awareness of the benefits that aviation brings to national and global economies. It fights for the interests of airlines across the globe, challenging unreasonable rules and charges, holding regulators and governments to account, and striving for sensible regulation.

Leading...

IATA's aim is to help airlines help themselves by simplifying processes and increasing passenger convenience while reducing costs and improving efficiency. The groundbreaking Simplifying the Business initiative [see www.iata.org/whatwedo/simplibiz/] is crucial in this area. Moreover, safety is IATA's number one priority, and IATA's goal is to continually improve safety standards, notably through IATA's Operational Safety Audit (IOSA) [see www.iata.org/ps/services/iosa/index.htm]. Another main concern is to minimise the impact of air transport on the environment [see www.iata.org/whatwedo/environment/index.htm].

Serving...

IATA ensures that people and goods can move around the global airline network as easily as if they were on a single airline in a single country. In addition, it provides essential professional support to all industry stakeholders with a wide range of products and expert services, such as publications, training and consulting. IATA's financial systems also help carriers and the travel industry maximise revenues.

...For the benefit of all parties involved:

For consumers, IATA simplifies the travel and shipping processes while keeping costs down. Passengers can make one telephone call to reserve a ticket, pay in one currency and then use the ticket on several airlines in several countries.

IATA allows **airlines** to operate safely, securely, efficiently and economically under clearly defined rules.

IATA serves as an intermediary between airlines and **passenger** as well as **cargo agents** via neutrally applied agency service standards and centralised financial systems.

A large network of **industry suppliers** and **service providers** gathered by IATA provides solid expertise to airlines in a variety of industry solutions.

For **governments**, IATA seeks to ensure they are well informed about the complexities of the aviation industry to ensure better, long-term decisions.

Source: IATA.

For a full history of the IATA, see www.iata.org/about/history.htm.

ECTAA

Through the ITAA, Irish travel agents are affiliated to the European Confederation of Travel Agents' Associations (ECTAA, www.ectaa.org). Its mission is to represent and promote the European travel industry, with particular focus on travel agents and tour operators. Its tasks include:

- Monitoring the European Commission, European Parliament, European Council and other institutions for issues relating to tourism.
- Informing members of activities relating to European institutions which may affect them.
- Consulting with national organisations and trades as to matters affecting them to achieve an umbrella European perspective.
- Bringing the concerns of members to the European Union institutions and decision makers.

Founded in 1961 in Germany, its headquarters are now located in Brussels. As of 2006, it represents twenty-four of the twenty-six national associations of travel agents and tour operators of the EU (excluding Lithuania and Slovenia, with two associations from Spain), as well as four affiliate members from Bulgaria, Croatia, Romania and Turkey and two observers from Norway and Switzerland. In total, more than 120,000 travel agencies and tour operators across Europe are represented, with an estimated combined annual turnover of circa €60 billion.

> 'ECTAA is now recognised by industry and decision makers in Brussels alike as the representation of the travel agents and tour operators and is an esteemed consultation partner on any policy issue, legislation or action having an impact on the travel agents' and tour operators' activities.'
>
> Source: ECTAA, 2006.

REVISION QUESTIONS

1. Define a 'tour operator' and a 'travel agent/retailer'.
2. What is the definition of a package tour according to the relevant regulations?
3. List and briefly discuss the process involved in organising a package tour.
4. Define the term 'organiser' of a package tour.
5. Briefly outline the regulations that a tour operator must follow.
6. List some of the types of packages.
7. Outline some of the types of information a travel agent should know.
8. How are travel retailers regulated?
9. List the types of product sold by travel retailers.
10. Identify the key success drivers in travel retailing.
11. Comment on what you think the future may hold for Irish tour operators and travel retailers.

ESSAY QUESTIONS

1. Discuss the competitive position facing tour operators in Ireland (use examples to illustrate your answer).

2. The role of travel retailers and tour operators has become blurred in recent years. Outline the traditional role of each and briefly discuss the current situation. List and briefly discuss the competitive forces impacting on both.
3. 'Given the growing dominance of e-commerce in the travel and tourism industry, there is no longer a need for the traditional travel agent.' Critically assess this statement.
4. 'There is a constant battle in travel retailing between small travel agents and larger high street chains. Further, e-commerce is competing (and winning) against both small and larger travel agents.' Discuss this statement.
5. Define the term 'disintermediation' and explain why it is such a threat to the traditional travel industry.
6 Identify and analyse the recent trends and challenges faced by (a) the Irish and (b) the international travel industry. Comment on how these challenges may be addressed.

TASKS

Task 1
In your opinion, what does the success of a travel agency depend on? Use the macro and task business environment to structure your answer.

The macro environment:
- Political.
- Economic.
- Socio-cultural.
- Technological.
- International.

The task environment:
- Threat from competitors.
- Threat from suppliers.
- Threat from customers.
- Threat from substitutes.
- Threat from new entrants.

Task 2
Divide the class into two roughly equal groups. Each group should be given ten to fifteen minutes to develop opposing points on the following statements, followed by a forty to forty-five minute debate.

Statement: Tour operators should keep to organising tours, while travel retailers should keep to selling them. There should be no blurring of these roles.

Statement: There is no longer a need for a travel retailer.

Statement: The Irish travel industry is not adapting quickly enough to new business models and customer demands.

ASSIGNMENTS

1. You have been contracted by a foreign business consortium who wishes to set up a travel retail chain in Ireland. They are unsure of the regulations they must follow and of the competitive situation. Write a report for the client outlining the regulations and what you believe the current competitive situation is. Offer suggestions and advice to the client on how to compete effectively in the Irish travel retail market. Prepare a ten-minute presentation summarising the report for the clients.

2. Research the various organisations Irish travel agents and tour operators are affiliated to. Write a report on their functions. In the report, analyse how relevant they are to the successful operation of (a) the Irish industry and (b) an individual tour operator or travel retailer.

Chapter 9

E-commerce in the Travel Industry

SUMMARY

From a business-to-business (B2B) point of view, technology has vastly improved the flow of communication and information and has revolutionised the business models employed by small and large travel organisations. The use of central reservations systems (CRS) and global distribution systems (which were developed to improve such communication and distribution) is outlined and discussed. A profile of the major operators is presented.

From a business-to-customer (B2C) point of view, e-commerce, primarily in the form of the internet, has dealt a major blow to the traditional travel retailer (the travel agent) and the travel wholesaler (the tour operator). Although we have seen in the previous chapter that a 'blur' has emerged between the roles of both travel retailers and tour operators in recent years, causing competition between them, they both have a common competitor: the mass-proliferation of the internet. This has led to a generation of tourists and travellers who have in effect cut out the intermediary in favour of no-frills, low-cost travel at the expense of the traditional travel agents and tour operators.

Travel e-tailing is gaining momentum, and travel e-tailers operating in the so-called 'marketspace' (rather than in the traditional 'marketplace') are succeeding in attracting more and more travellers to their websites in an effort to bypass traditional distribution channels and thus save costs. This chapter looks at how and why, and asks the question: can travel e-tailers be beaten, or should travel retailers simply join them?

LEARNING OUTCOMES

Having completed this chapter, the reader should be able to:
- Appreciate the importance of technology in B2B and B2C relationships in the tourism sector.
- Understand the importance of e-commerce in the marketing and distribution of travel products.
- Appreciate the growth and dominance of e-commerce in various facets of life, including tourism.
- Define the concepts of e-tailing in the marketspace in the sector.
- Understand the competitive pressures exerted by e-commerce on smaller and traditional organisations in the industry.

INTRODUCTION

The entire tourism industry has been affected by the rapid advancements in technology, primarily since the 1990s. Twenty years ago, no one could have predicted that a six-digit reference number taken from a computer screen and picture ID would replace a travel ticket, that a flight could be sold for one cent (plus taxes and charges) on a website or that a customer would feel secure entering their credit card details online. Yet all of these things have happened. Technological revolution, primarily in the form of the mass proliferation of the World Wide Web, has made it easier and cheaper than ever for travellers to find information and make travel reservations to any destination they choose, especially suitable for the independent traveller. Table 9.1 illustrates how holidaymakers to Ireland (visitors who stated that their primary purpose for visiting Ireland was a holiday) arranged their holiday. As we can see, the vast majority of holidaymakers to Ireland organised their holiday independently.

Table 9.1: How Holidaymakers to Ireland Arranged Their Holiday (2005) (per cent)

	Total	Britain	Mainland Europe	North America	Rest of World
Package	21	15	22	32	18
Independent	79	85	78	68	82

Source: Fáilte Ireland.

It has also allowed travel distributors, both intermediaries and principals, to market their products and services to a wider audience than ever before, and more efficiently. It is inevitable that technology will continue to improve and present new opportunities as well as challenges for the travel industry. In this chapter, we will begin by looking at some of the technology that travellers do not often encounter – the systems used by the principals and their agents. We will then proceed to look at some of the recent advancements as well as some likely future trends in direct contact between the principals and agents and their customers. This latter point is heavily influenced by the process we previously identified as disintermediation, i.e. cutting out the intermediary, primarily with the aid of technology.

TECHNOLOGY IN THE TRAVEL INDUSTRY

Even as far back as the early 1980s, technological advancement was beginning to play an enormous role in the management, marketing and distribution of travel-related products and services. Apart from the internet, which the majority of this chapter will be devoted to, the most important technology used in the travel industry are central reservation systems (CRS) and global distribution systems (GDS). These systems are designed for the use of the travel industry itself, rather than the travelling public, although they help travel retailers and e-tailers (online retailers) to better serve the travelling public with timely, accurate and wide-ranging information with which to make their final travel decisions.

The CRS were developed before GDS by the airline companies as a system to control seat reservations, flight and crew schedules. Later, travel agents linked into the CRS to take allocation of airline seats, sell them and issue tickets. The CRS also has the ability to allow airlines to link to each other. Apart from airline seats, CRS can also provide information on and sell other travel products, such as accommodation and car hire. Although most discussion of CRS centres around the airline industry and traditionally the distribution of such travel products via travel agents, hotels also use internal CRS, known as property management systems, e.g. MS Protel, to manage their operations.

GDS 'link several CRS to a mainframe computer that has a large database. GDS sell a range of travel products, including airline seats, car hire, and hotel rooms' (Guiney 2002: 360). GDS are mostly owned by airlines (see below). The four major GDSs are Galileo, Amadeus, Sabre and Worldspan.

Galileo (www.galileo.com)	
Slogan:	'Together we can achieve more'
Owned by:	Aer Lingus, Air Canada, Alitalia, Austrian Airlines, British Airways, Olympic, Swiss Air, TAP, United Airlines, US Airways
Set up:	In 1991 with the merger of United Airlines' Apollo system and Swiss-based Galileo International (BA, KLM, Swiss Air)
Based in:	Denver, Colorado in the US
Located in:	66 countries, with 33,000 outlets
Airlines:	500
Hotels:	208 hotel chains (37,000 premises)
Car hire:	47 firms
Enquiries:	66 million per day
In Ireland:	Galileo is used by over three-quarters of Ireland's travel retail outlets

Galileo's corporate mission is outlined below.

Galileo mission statement
Our mission is to be the leading provider of travel information and transaction processing worldwide by deploying solutions that drive measurable results for our customers.

Listen
We believe in the power of partnership. We listen to our customers to identify and develop opportunities for success.

Learn
We listen to customer needs and industry concerns at global conferences, one-on-one sales visits and in our training classes. Our industry expertise

and unique relationships allow us to promote dialog to better understand the needs of those we serve.

Deliver

Finally, it is not enough to simply meet the challenges of building world-class technology solutions. We must guarantee client satisfaction by always delivering the right solutions in the right place, at the right time.

Source: Galileo, July 2006.

For a complete history of Galileo, see www.galileo.com/galileo/en-ie/about/History/.

According to Guiney (2002: 361), the following are the core functions of Galileo:

1. *Flight availability on over 400 airlines can be checked, both for direct and indirect flights.*
2. *There are over 2 billion fares available on Galileo's database, updated three times a day. The fares are displayed with the cheapest fares first.*
3. *The flight is then booked. Information is collected about the flight, the passenger and the travel agency booking the flight. This is then sent to the Galileo database, and from there to the airline's CRS.*
4. *The next stage is to produce airline tickets based on the information from three databases, i.e. fares, availability and booking file.*
5. *Seating allocation on the aircraft can be chosen in advance.*
6. *Clients' files are also kept on the database, and they can be useful when a client returns to book a new flight.*
7. *A queuing system controls the workflow of the business and increases its efficiency. Queues operate within the travel agency, between the travel agency and Galileo, and between Galileo and the suppliers. Any changes in flights, times, etc. are put onto the queue, which the travel agency accesses.*
8. *RoomMaster is the hotel booking service that Galileo provides. The 37,000 hotels are linked either directly or indirectly to the Galileo system.*
9. *CarMaster allows travel agents using Galileo to reserve cars all over the world.*
10. *Galileo's Information System provides general information about consulates, visa and health requirements.*
11. *Galileo productivity helps travel agents to improve their operations, giving access to old records to be used for marketing purposes.*

Worldspan (www.worldspan.com)

Slogan:	'Travel technology so advanced, it's simple'
Owned by:	Delta, Northwest, TWA
Set up:	1990
Based in:	Atlanta, Georgia in the US

Located in:	60 countries, with 15,000 outlets
Airlines:	414
Hotels:	29,000
Other:	38 other travel service providers, e.g. cruise and tour operators. Also linked to ferry operators, railway operators, Eurostar
Enquiries:	250 million per day
In Ireland:	Growing in importance

Worldspan company profile
Worldspan is a leader in travel technology services for travel suppliers, travel agencies, e-commerce sites and corporations worldwide.

Utilising some of the fastest, most flexible and efficient networks and computing technologies, Worldspan provides comprehensive electronic data services linking approximately 700 travel suppliers around the world to a global customer base.

Worldspan offers industry-leading fares and pricing technology such as Worldspan e-Pricing, hosting solutions and customised travel products. Worldspan enables travel suppliers, distributors and corporations to reduce costs and increase productivity with technologies like Worldspan Go! and Worldspan Trip Manager XE...

Globally, Worldspan is the largest transaction processor for online travel agencies, having processed 59 per cent of all GDS online air transactions during the twelve months ended March 31, 2006.

Source: Worldspan, July 2006.

For a complete history of Worldspan, see
www.worldspan.com/home.asp?fPageID=7&fBUCatID=.

According to Guiney (2002: 362), the following are the core functions of Worldspan:

1. *Profiles of passengers.*
2. *Checking of airline schedules and availability.*
3. *Airline fares.*
4. *Airline reservations.*
5. *Worldspan Hotels Select allows the travel agent to make hotel reservations.*
6. *Worldspan Car Select allows the travel agent to organise car hire bookings.*
7. *Queues for information on passengers, changes in flight details and messages between the airline and travel agent.*
8. *Production of tickets and other travel documents.*
9. *Other information systems including Worldspan Traveller Supplies, Travel Guides.*

Amadeus (www.amadeus.com)

Slogan:	'Your technology partner'
Owned by:	Air France, Iberian and Lufthansa
Set up:	1987
Based in:	France, Germany and Spain
Located in:	215 countries, with 86,000 outlets
Airlines:	440
Hotels:	35,000
Car hire:	55 firms
Enquiries:	30 million per day

Amadeus company profile

The leading provider of IT solutions to the travel and tourism industry

Within a very short timeframe, Amadeus has become a world leader in providing the travel industry with superior solutions to manage the distribution and selling of travel services.

We regularly enhance our products and services with the benefit of input from our various customer groups who actively participate in forums. This way we ensure that the solutions we offer fulfil the required expectations.

Our products and services are used by our distinct customer groups in differing ways. Nearly 75,000 travel agencies and more than 11,000 airline sales offices use the Amadeus system to run their business. Many of the industry's leading travel service providers use our modular technology to optimise their distribution and internal operational requirements.

Our tagline, **'Your technology partner'**, reflects the approach we take towards our clients. We focus on building and maintaining mutually beneficial long-term relationships. Through this stability we develop a deep understanding of where we can maximise our clients' success. And all this is provided via the outstanding customer service that forms the backbone of the Amadeus experience.

Amadeus, a truly global company

Amadeus has established a global presence for the world-class service it delivers:

- Seventy-five local Amadeus commercial organisations present in over 215 markets worldwide.
- Five regional centres.
- Three research and development centres.
- Over 6,500 employees.
- Over 100 nationalities in our central sites alone.

Source: Amadeus, July 2006.

For a complete history of Amadeus, see www.amadeus.com/amadeus/x5126.html.

Sabre (Semi Automated Business Research Environment)
(www.sabre-holdings.com)

Slogan:	'Connecting people with the world's greatest travel possibilities'
Owned by:	American Airlines
Set up:	1976, although separate from American Airlines since 1995 (still a major shareholder)
Based in:	South Lake, Texas in the US
Located in:	45 countries, with 59,000 outlets
Airlines:	4,540
Hotels:	53,000
Car hire:	54 firms
Other:	Cruise operators, ferry operators, railways operators, Eurostar, tour operators

Sabre company profile

Our mission is clear – to connect people with the world's greatest travel possibilities. As a world leader in the travel marketplace, Sabre Holdings merchandises and retails travel products and provides distribution and technology solutions for the travel industry. Sabre Holdings supports travellers, travel agents, corporations and travel suppliers around the world through its three companies:

- **Travelocity**, the most popular online travel service.
- **Sabre Travel Network**, which includes the world's largest global distribution system (GDS), connecting travel agents and travel suppliers with travellers.
- **Sabre Airline Solutions**, the leading provider of decision-support tools, reservations systems and consulting services for airlines.

From building the first computer reservations system in the 1960s, to blazing the trail for online travel in the 1990s, to delivering the sophisticated, cutting-edge travel solutions of today, Sabre Holdings has made innovation its business.

Source: Sabre, July 2006.

For a complete history of Sabre, see www.sabre-holdings.com/aboutUs/history.html.

GullNet

GullNet is an extranet service for Gulliver members. Initially available to both serviced and self-catering premises which operate on an allocation basis with Gulliver, the service is to be the electronic link of choice connecting Gulliver and its members.

An extranet service makes use of standard internet technology to provide a specific service to a closed group of users. The GullNet service is a site on the public internet, but with access restricted to members of Gulliver through the use of user names and passwords. Users are permitted only to access information records on their own premises or organisation. Under no circumstances would a user from one premises be able to view booking details or modify information for another premises.

The added benefits to our members are:

- Immediate retrieval of booking and cancellation notifications.
- Ability to query past bookings and cancellations on the database by guest name, arrival date, booking date or booking reference.
- Members can update selling prices for the various products offered, allowing flexibility for different situations.
- Room/unit availability maintenance.
- Premises data maintenance.
- Notice boards which allow organisations such as Bord Fáilte [now Fáilte Ireland], the Northern Ireland Tourist Board, Gulliver InfoRes and the various Regional Tourism Authorities to disseminate notices or messages to the relevant users.
- A fast, efficient and reliable system which will be maintained by our own IT staff. This means immediate service if any assistance is required. Also, the staff on the helpdesk are always at hand for any queries if needed.
- An easy-to-use, user-friendly system.
- From mid-1999 online bookings will be available through the Bord Fáilte [now Fáilte Ireland] website.

The equipment needed to access the system is a PC, modem and a subscription to an internet service provider.

Source: Gulliver.

E-TAILING VERSUS RETAILING

E-tailing is the internet form of retailing (e = electronic, as in e-mail, e-commerce, e-banking, etc). There has been phenomenal growth in recent years in technology in so many areas of commerce. For example, bank customers can conduct the majority of their transactions online rather than queuing in branch queues. This allows banks to close more branches in order to keep costs down.

There has also been a revolution in online shopping. New online e-tailers, e.g. www.cd-wow.com, www.play.com, www.amazon.com, www gifts.ie, as well as traditional retailers selling their products online, e.g. www.tesco.ie, www.next.co.uk, www.buy4now.ie, have made it possible for customers to shop from the comfort of their own home at any time. Online shopping has damaged sales of many retailers in many sectors, such as bookstores and music stores. However, many co-exist, satisfying different sectors of a market.

Some of the advantages of e-tailing are discussed below.

Lower Cost

Generally, the purchase power of larger online stores, coupled with a global market, allows large online e-tailers to demand more favourable purchase prices for the products and services, which they then mark up and sell online. E-tailing also leads to lower distribution costs, and expensive retail premises are often forsaken in favour of a well-designed website. Marketing costs and direct targeted marketing are also more affordable online. Some of these cost savings can be passed on to the customer, while the rest can be turned into higher profits than available through traditional retailing.

Ease of Comparison

It is much easier to shop around among several online e-tailers from the one location, i.e. sitting at an internet-enabled PC or laptop, than physically visiting or telephoning multiple competing retailers. There are also websites which act as hubs, collecting prices from several other e-tailers and presenting them to the online customer for comparison. Global price comparison has been made easier with the introduction of the euro single currency as well as the online display of prices in multiple currencies and online currency converters which provide real-time accurate conversions.

Round-the-Clock Shopping

Websites offer the ability for the customer to visit online e-tailers anytime they feel like it, twenty-four hours a day, seven days a week, 365 days a year. Physical retailers cannot match this ability, as the costs would be extremely high.

Convenience

When a customer shops from the convenience of their own home or at their office PC, they can avoid traffic problems, searching and paying for parking, getting caught in the rain, standing in queues and a myriad of other inconveniences that customers were forced to endure before the advent of online e-tailing and online services. No longer does a customer of most services have to queue at their lunch break (having spent half of it in their car getting to and from the premises) in order to conduct their business.

These are just some of the many advantages of conducting business online using e-commerce tools such as the internet. There are no doubt countless other examples which could take up many pages.

Ireland.ie

The www.ireland.ie website was set up by Fáilte Ireland as a comprehensive tourist website, with a goal of making it easier for tourists and potential tourists to find information about Ireland and to book online. It features constantly changing themes and specials, as well as a special regional focus, which changes regularly. The late availability link allows the last-minute tourist to reserve easily at literally the last minute to avail of the best deals. The website targets busy individuals who have little time, do not want to read reams of text and want a source they can trust. The aim is to challenge consumers, to excite them with the product range and to satisfy convenience needs. Ireland.ie drives convenience at all levels. It simplifies the

> information and booking route, shortcuts the decision-making process and offers bundled price offers. Its booking engine allows the viewer to reserve online easily and securely.

There are of course two sides to every story. There are several disadvantages to the technology revolution that has made so many people's lives easier by offering e-tailing. Some of these are discussed below.

Not Everyone Has Access to the internet

Many people do not have regular access to a PC or laptop in their home or work lives, and may have to use an internet café to avail of e-tailing. No matter how they eventually get access to the internet, the cost of access in Ireland is a prohibitive factor. The cost of broadband access for home users in Ireland is amongst the very highest in Europe, and the bandwidth (speed and amount of information that can be downloaded and uploaded) is smaller, resulting in slower speeds and more time waiting for pages to open. Online e-tailers such as Ryanair rely on access to the internet for their customers to reserve seats on their flights, but many simply do not have access. This results in some travel agents offering to reserve seats on a Ryanair flight via their own internet connection, but charging the customer a reservation fee for the service.

Not Everyone Can Use the Internet

Even those who do have access to the internet may not be able to use the technology. This is particularly true of older generations, who may find the new technology confusing and complicated.

Lack of Trust in Technology and Lack of Human Contact

Many people who buy products online call the customer service telephone number advertised to ensure that their order online was successful. Many do not trust the technology and need absolute confirmation that their purchase was handled correctly. Further, for many, human contact is imperative in business transactions, as many do not wish to conduct business with a machine. Finally, many customers are fearful that their details will be passed on to third parties who will use their e-mail or physical addresses for junk mail marketing purposes. The laws protecting such information in the customer's home country (Data Protection Act in Ireland) may not be adhered to by a company operating from another legal jurisdiction.

Credit/Debit Card Issues

This is perhaps the most important factor contributing to some customers choosing not to purchase products and services online. Many people simply do not possess a credit card, and while more and more websites will accept a debit card (such as Laser and Maestro in Ireland and Switch and Solo in the UK), many will not. Security in regard to all types of card transactions is paramount, and customers often fear the prospects of computer hackers obtaining their card details and using them for fraudulent purposes. This is a valid concern, so most e-tailers now offer secure payment technologies which encrypt card details upon sending and can only be deciphered by the company's host computer. Security fears still exist, however. Further, many e-tailers add a handling fee for using credit cards instead of debit cards, e.g. www.ryanair.com and www.aerlingus.com, which may not be applicable if they were to use their credit cards in physical retail outlets.

Despite these disadvantages, once customers take the plunge and try an online booking and it is successful, they tend to move to that form of e-tailing rather than the traditional retailing. Further, many become an advocate of this type of transaction and inform their family, friends and work colleagues of its simplicity and efficiency.

Jurys-Doyle bids to join online booking group

Jurys-Doyle is in talks with hotel groups Hilton, Forte and Accor to join its pan-European internet offering. The Irish hotel group is trying to boost its internet sales; currently they account for only 3 per cent of total bookings.

Jurys-Doyle, which posted a 70 per cent increase in pre-tax profits to €50 million at year end, aims to sell 15 per cent of its room stock over the internet by 2005, according to chief executive Pat McCann.

The company announced a 106 per cent increase in turnover to €219 million and earnings per share of 68.3 cent, up 25.7 per cent. The shares closed at €7.60 last Friday.

'Over the next period of time, we'll come together with businesses like airlines to co-operate to offer complementary internet offerings. We are in discussions as we speak,' McCann said.

NCB Stockbrokers expect the group will link into Aer Lingus's future website as an extension of its current airline loyalty tie-up. This also holds out the potential of further link-ups with airlines in the OneWorld alliance, which includes American Airlines and British Airways.

The Jurys-Doyle website is managed by the US internet company Pegasus, which offers the hotel site on major search engines including Microsoft Expedia travel site, Lastminute.com and Priceline.com.

The market is likely to view the formation of business alliances as a positive step for the hotel group, and preferable to a stand-alone policy.

There is still a relatively low level of internet penetration in the hotel sector and Jurys-Doyle's 3 per cent figure is in line with figures for the US, according to NCB analyst Shane Matthews. The internet is seen as a way of both keeping costs low and expanding into new markets.

'It's still early days for the hotel industry and I have not heard of any hotel that is particularly strong in the area. The business is not as internet friendly as the airline business, because there are multi-point procedures, different rates, corporate rates and a very substantial level of discounting. The internet is not totally geared up for this type of business,' he said.

Jury's-Doyle did not join the alliance last year when Hilton, Forte and Accor struck a deal on an internet offering. Last year it launched its own central reservations operations to maximise room occupancy. This is seen as key to its internet strategy, as it receives 2,500 calls per day. This number is converted into a 30 per cent bookings rate.

'We would see this system as acting as a backbone for their internet offering which currently accounts for 2 to 3 per cent of bookings over the longer term,' according to NCB.

Source: Connolly, N., 'Jurys-Doyle bids to join online booking group', *The Sunday Business Post*, 16 July 2000.

FIGHTING BACK

Traditional travel retailers, i.e. those operating in the *marketplace*, can counter-attack against travel e-tailers, i.e. those operating in the *marketspace*, by offering specific and exclusive products that cannot be reserved anywhere else. This involves developing exclusive distribution contracts with certain principals. This is not always practical, however, as many principals wish to ensure the widest possible distribution strategy and refuse to limit themselves to narrowly defined distribution channels.

A further method of ensuring retail survival is to organise a co-operative marketing approach to jointly promote and sell the offerings of constituent members. An example of an organisation engaged in such practices is the ITAA (see Chapter 8).

However, the major advantage a travel retail outlet has over a travel e-tailer is the personal touch. As efficient as it is, the internet cannot provide the human contact that so many customers demand before they will part with their hard-earned money. Customers have become more sophisticated and demand better customer service. The situation was changing even before the mass proliferation of the internet, according to Holloway and Plant (1994):

> In the past, travel agencies have been seen largely as 'order takers' – a convenient point for the purchase of travel arrangements – but competition has now forced a reappraisal of the role, and agents are placing greater emphasis on the ability of their staff to sell, to establish rapport with their clients, and to offer a superior level of **product knowledge**, so that clients actively seek them out to receive advice, particularly for the independent, tailor-made travel arrangements that provide greater earning potential than the standard package holidays.

Travel retailers that have highly skilled, customer-orientated staff that meet and exceed customer expectations by providing informed recommendations have a unique proposition that no machine can offer. Such professional service should occur before the reservation takes place at the time of the information request, at the time of reservation and even after the fee has been received. Travel retailers often contact customers after their return from their trip to ensure their satisfaction. By doing this, the customer feels valued, and this improves customer loyalty and retention.

John O'Donoghue, TD, Minister for Arts, Sport and Tourism, speaking at the launch of the Tourism Ireland website, www.discoverireland.com, Innovation Centre, Northern Ireland Science Park, Belfast

Tá an áthas orm bheith anseo I mBéal Feirste inniu, le Angela Smith, chun an suíomh nua idirlíon de chuid Tourism Ireland a sheoladh.

I'm delighted to be here today, along with Minister Angela Smith, to launch Tourism Ireland's global suite of websites.

In a fiercely competitive global economy, no industry can afford to sit back and reflect on its achievements, no matter what level of success it has enjoyed in the past.

These 'next generation' websites have been designed as a central tool to entice over 8 million overseas visitors to our shores annually. They are a welcome and necessary development in presenting Ireland to its best advantage overseas.

The tourism and travel business is undergoing rapid and widespread change. So much of that change is driven by the internet. An ever-growing number of holidaymakers use the internet to plan and book holidays and this is borne out by Tourism Ireland's research.

I find it striking, for example, that 70 per cent of our target audience in the US market use the internet for tourism and travel bookings.

Fáilte Ireland's Visitor Attitude Survey shows that almost 50 per cent of holidaymakers to Ireland view the internet as the most important source of information for planning holidays in Ireland – up from 8 per cent in 1997.

We have come a long way from the days when a John Hinde postcard was the main international visual marketing tool for Irish tourism.

The internet has developed into a tool of critical importance to Irish tourism in the battle to stay competitive. It is being used across the full range of the industry throughout the island – from top hotel chains to B&Bs – to present their product to an ever-growing audience.

Our recent tourism policy review, *New Horizons*, clearly identified new technologies and the internet as immensely important in driving growth in the tourism sector.

This launch of Tourism Ireland's new sites is therefore a significant milestone in advancing the objectives set out in our national tourism strategy. It also demonstrates that Tourism Ireland is committed not just to moving with the times, but to staying ahead of consumer trends and providing its customers and its industry partners with the best possible service.

These new websites will provide the user with world-class levels of choice and customisation. They will also allow Tourism Ireland to provide a more compelling and comprehensive picture of holidays in Ireland, which can be tailored to the needs of consumers in each market.

An impressive twenty-seven separate market sites, in fourteen different languages, will be launched between now and the end of July. This level of specification will allow potential visitors to view the huge range of holidays and activities which are waiting to be discovered throughout the island of Ireland. Such a large range of individual market sites will also help underpin efforts to further broaden our customer base.

The website development will also tie in with Tourism Ireland's new three-year global advertising campaign. This €50 million campaign is targeting an audience of 200 million people worldwide. Research has shown that a major part of that audience needed more information about what a holiday in Ireland might involve and the new sites seek to address that need.

From a North-South perspective, today's launch is also very significant for a number of reasons. Firstly, it represents the culmination of many months' work by the key tourism players on this island – Tourism Ireland in close collaboration with the industry on the island, the Northern Ireland Tourist Board, and Fáilte Ireland. All of them have played a vital part in developing this website – not only through their participation in the E-Marketing Partnership Group, but in working towards a comprehensive e-marketing strategy for the island of Ireland.

As many will know, trying to keep apace with developments in the e-world can be an expensive business. By working closely together on this suite of websites but also on a wider e-marketing strategy for the island, there are very clear and tangible benefits to be gained by the three agencies and the industry.

Pooling the high level of expertise which exists within the agencies and the industry is also hugely important in ensuring this strategy is soundly based and positioned to benefit all stakeholders.

Source: Department of Arts, Sport and Tourism speeches archive, 30 March 2006.

Ireland.ie founder has tourist market in his sights

Fáilte Ireland's consumer website, www.ireland.ie, was recognised as one of the best in Ireland when its project manager, Alan Kelly, won the e-government award at the Irish Internet Association Net Visionary Awards last year.

The website was launched in 2004 to help people find inexpensive short activity holidays in Ireland. Since it was launched, the number of visitors to the website has increased by 150 per cent, and it is expected the site will have generated more than €500,000 in sales leads.

'I first registered the domain name www.ireland.ie in 2000, and had to get permission from the Department of the Taoiseach to actually use it,' said Kelly.

'Ireland.ie is the primary site for people wishing to take a break in Ireland. It has about 20,000 pages of tourist information, from attractions and activities, to events and accommodation. Last year, we had more than 1 million hits.'

A native of Portroe on the banks of Lough Derg, Kelly studied history and English at UCC. He later attended Boston College and obtained a degree in e-commerce from the Smurfit Business School.

'After college, I worked in the history department in UCC, and went on to become a freelance journalist. In 1998, I joined Bord Fáilte [now Fáilte Ireland] to develop their online content, which was a challenging but rewarding role,' said Kelly.

'My job entails managing Fáilte Ireland's e-business strategies and developing Ireland.ie into Ireland's premier domestic online channel, as well as creating marketing synergies online between multiple tourism propositions.'

Kelly enjoys the diversity of the job most of all, working in design and dealing with people involved in the tourism industry. 'There is so much passion out there to promote one's own bailiwick. It's great to work with these people and see them meet their goals.' Kelly's main aim is to create a single destination database for Ireland that will service all channels, provide a database for the Irish holiday home market and help sell Ireland abroad.

'Irish sites need to differentiate themselves much more in the future. Online space is becoming increasingly cluttered and competitive. Irish tourism agencies will need to use their "official" status to stand out and act as honest brokers,' said Kelly.

'That said, content is king, and no matter what facilities a tourism site has, if the content is not up to date and in the local language, the site will not be a success.'

Source: Hayes, C., 'Ireland.ie founder has tourist market in his sights', *The Sunday Business Post*, 29 January 2006.

POSSIBLE FUTURE TRENDS FOR E-COMMERCE AND TRAVEL

It is inevitable that technology will continue to advance. No one can tell what future advancements are likely, but if we were to predict based on the current trends, we may see an increasing trend towards using the internet for planning, organising, reserving and paying for countless travel and related products and services, not to mention thousands of other product categories. New devices may be developed to make the process even easier. Even today, internet-enabled palm-top devices and mobile communication technology allow the owner to use a wide variety of internet functions on the move.

Many travel organisations may exit their traditional distribution channels in favour of e-commerce, following in the footsteps of companies like Ryanair. Many may throw in the towel in the long fight against e-tailing and decide to maintain a dual approach of e-tailing and retailing, e.g. Club Travel.

Payment methods are also likely to continue to change. Perhaps one day soon, all of the credit, debit and ATM cards will be replaced by one all-encompassing smart card, acting as all of the above as well as a passport, driving license and medical information card all combined into one small credit card-sized card.

Society is becoming more technology focused, and only organisations that develop truly customer-focused e-commerce strategies will survive, especially as the internet generation grows older and demands products to satisfy various specific stages in the individual's life. Public and private tourism marketing and development organisations must realise this. As the following speeches and article show, e-tourism is becoming more and more of a key strategic focus for the success of tourism organisations, both on the island of Ireland and beyond.

Speech by John O' Donoghue, TD, Minister for Arts, Sport and Tourism, at the e-Marketing Tourism in the 21st Century Conference in the Abbey Gate Hotel, Tralee, Co. Kerry on Friday, 23 April 2004 at 1.00 p.m.

Chairman, ladies and gentlemen: Today's seminar on e-marketing is yet another example of why Kerry remains at the cutting edge of tourism in Ireland. I must congratulate James Clifford and his team for their initiative in organising this event and for bringing such an impressive line-up of speakers here to share their views on the importance of e-marketing and e-business technologies generally for tourism development, both in the region and on the island as a whole.

As a key player in bringing tourism business to the regions, Michael Cawley from Ryanair will, I'm sure, have highlighted the pivotal role a strong website can play as a cost-efficient tool for generating business. With his many years' experience in the policy field at regional level, John Leonard from Shannon Development touched on how local initiatives in this field can tap into national and regional tourism strategies. As a successful entrepreneur in the e-business, Dr Stewart Stevens is ideally placed to share valuable experiences on Fexco's operations in the tourism sector.

The Gleneagle Hotel uses e-technologies and the web to great effect and, in that regard, Patrick O'Donoghue is a great exponent of the virtures of e-marketing. This afternoon I understand Michael Rosney, representing the Kerry branch of the Irish Hotels Federation, will explain some of the important things one needs to know when marketing on the web. And finally, Maura Moynihan from Cork-Kerry Tourism will share her views on how Kerry and Cork regions can make the most of the e-way.

As many of you will be aware, the Tourism Policy Review completed last year identifies information and communication technologies as one of the key strategic success drivers of the tourism sector for the next ten years. Nowhere is this more evident than in the promotion and marketing of Ireland and its myriad of tourism products.

The rapid advances in technology and communications, and in particular the dramatic increase in internet usage, have changed business practices and communication methods forever. In 2002, consumers worldwide spent €5.8 billion through the internet, of which €1.1 billion was spent on the tourism product. Research shows that the second highest usage of the web is the purchase of the tourism product in terms of booking flights, hotel rooms, car hire and package holidays. Data produced by Tourism Ireland shows that the organisation's eighteen market sites attracted 1.3 million unique visits in 2002. In 2003, the number of unique visits jumped to 5.2 million, a massive 300 per cent increase in traffic. This year, Tourism Ireland forecasts up to 8 million visits.

As everyone in the industry knows only too well, the internet has impacted on the travel and tourism industry more than on any other. Not only does it influence the consumer's choice of holiday destination or package but, crucially for the industry, it also influences the consumer's booking pattern. By facilitating price comparisons, the internet also focuses the consumer on the comparative value of the offering and consumers are becoming increasingly value focused. Increased processing speeds and keyword searches of mammoth databases can be carried out for highly specific offers. Perfect matching of a customised demand with supply is technically possible. Such technology plays to the strengths of Ireland's SMEs and their ability to offer a personalised service.

Over the past few years, consumers have become increasingly aware that late booking can often yield better value, particularly if they are flexible in their destination or package preference. Convincing a customer of the value of visiting a particular destination and converting that interest into a holiday purchase is therefore becoming increasingly competitive. Our own airlines have been at the forefront of a revolution in low-cost air travel and their model supports the early bird who is prepared to book well in advance.

The challenge for the industry – both the tourism agencies and individual tourism enterprises – is to ensure that we have customer-friendly e-marketing applications that play to our strengths.

Enterprises that have the capability to use ICTs effectively in areas such as customer relations management, marketing, payment, cost control, yield management, training and human resource management will have a competitive advantage.

The internet also allows comprehensive data capture about potential customers, their preferences and behaviour and facilitates better-directed marketing activity, in turn increasing the potential for winning repeat business. In developing its all-island contact centre, Tourism Ireland has invested significantly in order to tap into huge potential for adding value when providing information to people interested in taking a holiday in Ireland. In dealing with the initial query from the caller, the contact centre uses a brand new customer enquiry and information system to build up an efficient and valuable customer database.

Tourism Ireland will continue to monitor the changing patterns and preferences regarding how customers choose to communicate with us and will be ready to implement such channels in line with consumer demand. The objective is to communicate with the customer through his or her preferred channel.

For its part, Fáilte Ireland is making great strides currently in the area of e-business. The organisation now has a number of websites. Its corporate site, launched late last year, provides the industry with all the necessary research, planning and business information that they require. This year Fáilte Ireland's consumer site – Ireland.ie – is the main point of sale for the home market. This indeed marks a change from the time when one could only ring up a phone number or browse a brochure to look at these offers.

Also, the organisation is promoting the various products and regions of Ireland more directly through the electronic medium with great success as more and more people find out about the diversity of the Irish tourism product.

Of course, key to the success of any new initiatives by Tourism Ireland and Fáilte Ireland is maximum industry participation. In this highly competitive global marketplace, we need to set out our stall and convey the many attributes and uniqueness of the Irish product. Every customer search should be rewarded with an attractive offer. This is what we mean by putting the customer first. This is relevant for all tourism enterprises, big and small, and I would urge everyone involved to come on board.

To facilitate the tourism industry, Tourism Ireland together with Fáilte Ireland are implementing an Information and Communication Technologies Development Programme this year. This programme has been developed to help accelerate the exploitation of the potential of information and communication technologies and e-commerce for the tourism industry. Working together, we can successfully manage the evolving trends in customer communication and be at the leading edge to ensure we capture the consumer's initial interest in holidaying in Ireland and turn it into actual business.

Source: Department of Arts, Sport and Tourism speeches archive, 23 April 2004.

Speech by John O'Donoghue, TD, Minister for Arts, Sport and Tourism, opening the EU conference on Digitisation of Heritage and Culture (LUND Principles) in St Patrick's Hall, Dublin Castle on Tuesday, 29 June 2004 at 9 a.m.

It is a pleasure to welcome you all here today. I wish to welcome the National Representative Group members of the member states of the European Union and, in particular, the representatives from our new member states. Welcome also to the European Commission, our guests from Norway, Russia, Canada and Israel, as well as the local and national managers of the cultural heritage areas of museums, libraries and archives.

This conference is the final element of a successful and varied six-month programme of my Department of Arts, Sport and Tourism for the Irish Presidency. It is fitting that the title of the conference is 'Access All Areas: Serving the User', as it presents a very important topic for today. It focuses on making culture accessible to everyone. This conference will provide further signposts on the cultural roadmap of Europe. Many European cultural bodies and institutions are involved in digitisation initiatives, some of which will be presented here. Considerable effort and financial resources are being invested in these projects across Europe. In order to get the full benefit at local and European levels from this investment, digitisation initiatives across the member states need to be more visible.

Cultural content has been identified by the Information Society Commission of Ireland as a driver for internet take-up. Local content, which is of interest to all, but particularly to the population of a particular area, acts as an important incentive to attract new users online. The digitisation of large amounts of local content across the country as a result of initiatives like the Cultural Heritage Project therefore has a national significance, which goes beyond adding value to museums, public libraries and archives.

The creation of cultural portals like Ask About Ireland provide shop windows for users to access the rich cultural history of Ireland. The Ask About Ireland website focuses on the digitisation and provision of new modes of access to cultural heritage material in museums, libraries and archives. Its purpose is the provision of access online for citizens to their cultural holdings. Users can look at true-to-life three-dimension images of artefacts from the National Museum of Ireland. They can browse through the flora of the Burren, a unique limestone landscape in County Clare, the pages of the *Dublin Evening Telegraph* of 1904 or follow the spectacular walking route of the North Kerry Way, all samples of the material from the local studies collections in public libraries. The work of the national institutions such as the National Museum, the National Library, the National Archives as well as public libraries, local museums and archives in digitising and uploading the material is an investment in the future of the culture and heritage of Ireland.

Later today, following the conference, you will have the opportunity to visit the National Museum of Ireland, which includes amongst its varied collections this country's unique collection of portable antiquities. The Museum of Archaeology and History is the national repository for all archaeological objects found in Ireland. It houses over 2 million artefacts, which range in date from 7000 BC to the late medieval period. Among its holdings is one of the finest collections of prehistoric gold artefacts in Europe as well as an unrivalled collection of early medieval decorated metalwork.

I hope our overseas guests are enjoying their visit to Ireland and are availing of the opportunity to experience some of the unique aspects of Irish heritage. I hope also that all the guests here today greatly benefit from this conference. I am sure that this event will be of great advantage in advancing the accessibility of European culture online. It is more than appropriate, then, that the papers of the conference will be available to read or to download from the MINERVA website. Moreover, through the developments of the last few years, which you are discussing here today, you will be able to access the rich culture of Ireland from your homes on your return. Likewise, we will all be able to access your remarkable European culture online.

Source: Department of Arts, Sport and Tourism speeches archive, 29 June 2004.

UNWTO and Microsoft to boost e-tourism for development: Africa to be primary target

Cape Town, South Africa, 11 July 2006 – The UN World Tourism Organization and Microsoft Corporation today announced a long-term partnership to expand information communications technology in the tourism sector. It will provide ICT systems and tools for emerging tourism economies to improve their export competitiveness, product quality and support skills. Its primary focus will be on Africa.

In his keynote speech at the Global Leaders Forum for Africa, Microsoft Chairman and Chief Software Architect Bill Gates cited the public/private partnership with United Nations World Tourism Organization (UNWTO) as the kind of implementing programme that will help over 40 million people in Africa drive toward future economic growth. Gates said, 'Microsoft wants to play a hands-on role to help countries and entire regions develop their knowledge-based economy, create jobs, spur growth and enable innovation. We can do this by providing easy and affordable access to technology and helping our partners build robust local software economies.'

The collaboration with Microsoft has two immediate projects, which were announced today:

- The creation of a new portal called 'Windows on Africa' developed through co-operation between UNWTO and NEPAD. The portal will showcase Africa in a globally competitive way: it will be able to be replicated at the national and local levels. It will be capable of linking to visitor centres, museums and libraries. Ultimately, it will even provide real-time advice via PDAs and mobile devices with destination-specific data.

- Support for the UNWTO Emergency Response System by creation of a portal to aggregate information on catastrophes affecting tourism to provide a new framework for improved industry response. The portal will bring together public and sector-specific data, incorporating tools for information sharing and improved messaging. It will assist tourism destinations and stakeholders to respond more rapidly and effectively in emergencies and help recovery programmes. The portal will be used initially to strengthen industry preparedness for a potential avian flu pandemic.

'This agreement is a huge leap forward for tourism-driven job creation, export income and capacity building for the world's poorest countries – especially in Africa, where it will be integrated into our programmes to alleviate poverty through sustainable tourism (ST-EP). It links Microsoft's outstanding technology and solutions with UNWTO's central role of advancing the sector as an instrument of development,' said Francesco Frangialli, Secretary General of UNWTO.

He added, 'Equally importantly over the next five years, we will collaborate closely to build a leading-edge ICT dimension into all of our key programmes, ranging from improved access for tourists through electronic border clearance, to better-quality service through distance training and sustainability management at destinations.'

Source: UNWTO.

REVISION QUESTIONS

1. Define:
   - (a) B2B.
   - (b) B2C.
   - (c) GDS.
   - (d) CRS.
   - (e) E-tailing.
   - (f) Marketspace.
2. How has technology benefited (a) B2B and (b) B2C relationships?
3. How did CRS and GDS develop, and why did they develop?
4. Outline the advantages and disadvantages of e-tailing.
5. What is e-ticketing, and how might it benefit (a) travellers and (b) transport providers?
6. List some (a) Irish and (b) international online intermediaries and e-tailers.
7. How are traditional retailers fighting back?
8. What do you predict for the future in terms of travel and e-commerce?
9. List the ways that e-commerce has made your life easier in the last year.
10. Are there any general drawbacks to e-commerce in modern everyday transactions?

ESSAY QUESTIONS

1. 'New technology has revolutionised the distribution of travel products.' Discuss this statement with reference to *either* the transport sector *or* the accommodation sector.
2. 'The process of disintermediation is as relevant to success in the accommodation sector as it is in the transport sector.' Discuss.
3. 'Ultimately, the critical success factors for survival [of travel retailers] will be the ability to offer customers a fee-based and value-added service. Travel agencies will need to reinvent their operations, and in the process think of new ways in which to reach, satisfy and keep their customers. Alliances must be forged, the service must be improved and the product range must be expanded in order for travel agents to gain a competitive edge in the future.' (Source: 'Future of Travel Agents', *Travel and Tourism Analyst*, November 2001.)

   Discuss this statement, using examples. In your answer, you should list and briefly discuss the strategies that travel retailers can employ for success in the current market.
4. 'The world of travel is continuing to undergo major transformations in the way it communicates with its consumers, in the scale and geographical extent of markets to which it caters, and in the business models it uses.' (Source: 'E-Travel in Europe', *Travel and Tourism Analyst*, May 2004.)

   Discuss this statement, drawing examples from articles/reports you have read.
5. The process of disintermediation has led to a complete revolution in the travel retail and tour operations market, and e-commerce has a large part to play in this process, as do many other factors. Analyse and discuss the current situation.

6. Critically analyse this statement: 'So far, it has been proved that "clicks need bricks", and while companies without clicks are at a clear disadvantage unless they develop an internet strategy, companies relying entirely on the internet are even more disadvantaged without either market or alliances with so-called "old economy" companies.' (Source: Andrew Sangster, 'The Importance of Technology in the Hotel Industry', *Travel and Tourism Intelligence*, No. 3 (2001): 48.)

TASKS

Divide the class into two roughly equal groups. Each group should be given ten to fifteen minutes to develop opposing points on the following statements, followed by a forty to forty-five minute debate.

Statement: Traditional travel outlets on high streets are obsolete.

Statement: Clicks need bricks – online agencies cannot survive without a physical presence.

Statement: E-commerce alienates a large proportion of the population.

Statement: Security fears are a major drawback to shopping online.

ASSIGNMENTS

1. Research the various online intermediaries and principals offering their products and service online direct to the customers. Write a report on the world's largest providers and compare and contrast what they offer.
2. List the Irish travel agents and tour operators that offer their products and services online with a full booking facility. Survey the students in your class as to whether a full booking facility would encourage more students to use that website rather than a physical travel agent/tour operator with an information website without a full online booking facility.
3. Survey fifty people with the following questions (yes or no answers) and compile the results into a short report and presentation analysing and discussing the results:
   (a) Have you bought any (travel) goods online in the last six months?
   (b) If yes, was it from an Irish website?
   (c) Were you worried about giving your personal or payment details online?
   (d) Does a website with a secure payment facility provide reassurance?
   (e) Do you find shopping (for travel) online easier?
   (f) Do you find it better value?
   (g) Would you recommend shopping online to a friend/relative?

Chapter 10

Business Tourism

SUMMARY

Chapter 10 outlines the importance of business tourism as a lucrative section of the tourism industry. The chapter begins with an introduction to the concept of business tourism and highlights the key criteria needed for a destination to attract business tourism. The bulk of the chapter presents the varying forms of business tourism, including business meetings (meetings, conferences and congresses), incentive travel as well as exhibitions and trade fairs. The chapter concludes by outlining how Ireland fares against other European countries in this market and highlights some of the strategies under discussion to improve Ireland's share of world business tourism.

LEARNING OUTCOMES

Having completed this chapter, the reader should be able to:
- Define business tourism as distinct from leisure tourism.
- Understand the different types of business tourism.
- Understand the economic benefits of promoting business tourism.
- Appreciate the key criteria needed to attract business tourism to a destination.
- Understand the competitive position of Ireland relative to other countries in this sector.

INTRODUCTION

Business tourism is distinct from leisure tourism in that its participants are usually visiting a destination on behalf of their company or organisation (which pays their costs) for business purposes rather than solely for enjoyment, relaxation, entertainment and all of the other things we have come to associate with leisure tourism. Business tourism is the highest-spending form of tourism since business tourists are usually spending the company's money on their trip, in comparison with leisure tourists, who spend their own money. Naturally, tourists spending their own money are more careful than tourists spending someone else's!

The principal characteristics of business tourism can be summarised as follows (according to the NITB):
- It is at the high-quality, high-spend end of the tourism spectrum.
- It is year round, peaking in spring and autumn, but generally balanced year round, sustaining full-time employment.

- It competes with leisure tourism and relies on much the same physical infrastructure (and so facilities built for either business or leisure tourists can be enjoyed by both).
- Investment in business tourism facilities has a proven track record of regenerating urban and inner city areas, e.g. Belfast, Manchester, Birmingham.
- Business tourism stimulates future inward investment, as businesspeople see the attractions of a destination while travelling on business or to attend a conference, exhibition or incentive and then return to establish business operations there. They can also become unpaid 'ambassadors' for a destination by communicating to colleagues and others their positive impressions and favourable experiences.
- The higher quality of personal service demanded by business tourists requires more labour-intensive service suppliers, which in turn translates into higher levels of job creation.
- Approximately 40 per cent of business travellers will return with their families as leisure visitors to destinations they have enjoyed visiting on business.

Business tourism to Dublin up 26 per cent in 2005

Business tourism in Dublin increased by 26 per cent in 2005, according to Fáilte Ireland.

The national tourism development authority, in conjunction with Tourism Ireland and Dublin Tourism, was outlining its business and marketing plans for 2006 to tourism operators in the Dublin region at a meeting this morning.

Fáilte Ireland chief executive Shaun Quinn said the tourism industry was 'reasonably optimistic' about its prospects for the coming year.

He welcomed the increase in business tourism last year and said progress on the National Conference Centre [NCC] project boded well for Dublin's development as a leading conference venue.

It is estimated that around 20 per cent of visitors to the country are here on business. Ireland's slice of the €40 billion global business tourism industry is currently valued at €400 million.

'The continued development of this sector is very important, as a business tourist spends on average 70 per cent more than leisure travellers, and many stay on for longer visits around the country,' said Mr Quinn.

Looking to the year ahead, he said that the hosting of the Ryder Cup offered an enormous opportunity to the capital, but he urged businesses to take a longer-term perspective of the event and avoid opportunistic pricing.

Mr Quinn also warned that Ireland's VAT rate of over 10 per cent was a major competitive disadvantage in attracting business meetings and conferences to the country.

Tourism Ireland, the overseas tourism marketing agency, has set a revenue target of €4.2 billion for 2006, driven by a projected 8.5 million overseas visitors to the island of Ireland this year.

Chief executive Paul O'Toole said: 'While we expect conditions to be largely favourable again for Dublin this year, there can be no complacency. It will be important, for example, that the proposed developments in Dublin Airport are brought to fruition.'

Tourism Ireland has a budget of €50 million to carry out overseas campaigns this year, the highest ever level of funding for frontline tourism marketing.

Source: Carr, A., 'Business tourism to Dublin up 26 per cent in 2005', *The Irish Times*, 16 January 2006.

More than 250,000 visitors took part in what is sometimes called **MICE tourism** (meetings, incentive, conferences and exhibitions) in Ireland in 2005, accounting for a total 857,000 business-related visits, or around one in every eight visitors. This 5 per cent increase on the previous year was worth €457 million to the Irish economy. The Ryder Cup provided Ireland with an opportunity to address an international corporate audience (which research shows tends to have a keen interest in golf), and in the process promote business tourism into Ireland.

Table 10.1: Percentage of Visitors Citing 'Business' as Main Reason for Visiting Ireland (2005)

	Total	Britain	Mainland Europe	North America	Rest of World
Business	13	12	17	7	12

Source: Fáilte Ireland.

Business tourism can be divided into the following key areas:
* Business meetings.
* Incentive travel.
* Exhibitions and trade fairs.

Business tourism to approach €500 million in annual earnings by 2007
The value of business visitors to Ireland, whether attending meetings, conferences or on incentive trips, is targeted by Fáilte Ireland, the national development authority for tourism, to rise 17.5 per cent to €470 million by 2007 – or almost half a billion euro. Approximately 150 people attended Fáilte Ireland's first Business Tourism Forum conference in Dublin today.

Minister for Arts, Sport and Tourism, Mr John O'Donoghue, TD, opened the conference and reiterated that the National Conference Centre is one of his main priorities. He said, 'There has been enormous investment in Ireland's tourism infrastructure, both private and public, and this was a necessary precursor to expanding our business tourism sector. There are areas that still need to be addressed. I am committed to ensuring that the contract for the National Conference Centre is awarded by summer 2005. Nobody should be in any doubt that this project will be delivered. There are real challenges, but they will be addressed and overcome as a priority.'

The Business Tourism Forum was set up by Fáilte Ireland in July of this year to drive growth in the business travel sector, which is already worth €250 million a year to Ireland. This rises to €400 million when incentive travel is included and Fáilte Ireland is targeting a 17.5 per cent increase in value to €470 million by 2007 – almost half a billion euro. A business visitor spends on average 70 per cent more than holiday makers during their stay in Ireland. Business tourism meets many national objectives in terms of the high yield per visitor and the fact that it is most active during the autumn and winter months but has a number of distinguishing characteristics, including long lead-in times for association conferences and a generally more demanding customer.

Ms Gillian Bowler, chairwoman of Fáilte Ireland, said, 'I am very pleased to see the level of commitment and interest in business tourism. Despite all the predictions and technological developments, it remains the case that people are travelling to meet and do business in greater numbers than ever before.

'Ireland's proposition to business visitors can build on that for holidaymakers, but it is very different in some important respects. It relies less on our traditional warmth of welcome, and more on a focus on the modern Ireland. Air access is crucially important, and this has greatly improved for Ireland in recent years, although there is more to be done. Business visitors are very demanding, and Ireland's improved infrastructure of four- and five-star hotels throughout the country means that we can now go about servicing their requirements in a serious way. For large conferences, novelty in the destination is an important selling point, and this is something Ireland can provide once the conference centre is up and running,' she concluded.

Peter Malone, chairman of the Business Tourism Forum, said, 'This autumn we held a number of consultative sessions with groups across the sector – from transport to accommodation to event managers. A number of issues came through very strongly at those sessions, and here again today at the first Business Tourism Forum conference.

'Ireland is the only European country with a VAT rate of over 10 per cent that does not reimburse businesses for hotel and restaurant expenses and this is a major competitive disadvantage in attracting business meetings and conferences to the country, according to the delegates at Fáilte Ireland's first Business Tourism Forum conference in Dublin today. Our main competitor for international meetings, the UK, makes a point of promoting its deduction allowances. At a time when the Irish tourism industry is already trying hard to manage a rising cost base in order to provide a competitive product, this policy is surely due for revision. It is also an impediment for businesses located in Ireland,' Mr Malone said.

'Another issue very much on people's minds is for Ireland to preserve business-class air access, and in particular interlining of luggage between airlines. Because we are an island destination, many international businesspeople fly to Ireland from larger hub airports. They have no desire to collect and carry luggage through connecting terminals.

'Finally, in a positive sense, the industry recognises that we must take a partnership and co-operative approach to developing business tourism in Ireland – "Team Ireland". There are some very practical things that can happen quickly, such as creating a single, shared database of meeting planners, improving the information we have on business tourism in Ireland and revitalising the very effective Conference Ambassador programme, particularly with the medical, pharmaceutical and financial sectors and academics. I am very confident that the focus and momentum now behind business tourism will yield dividends over the next two to three years,' Mr Malone concluded.

Speakers at the conference included incentive travel expert David Hackett, economist Jim Deegan, Dan Flinter and Paul Keeley of Fáilte Ireland. Kevin O'Malley, consultant surgeon at the Mater Hospital, shared his experience of and insights from the Conference Ambassador role. In 2003, he was involved in bringing 1,800 vascular surgeons to Ireland for their European conference.

In 2005, Fáilte Ireland will implement a concerted programme to promote business tourism, both among Irish tourism businesses and through Tourism Ireland, in overseas markets. Key initiatives include:

1. Branding Ireland as a 'perfect place to meet'.
2. A suite of appropriate marketing materials, including websites and DVDs.
3. Revitalising the Conference Ambassador programme.
4. Developing an international database of meeting planners and incentive buyers.

Source: Fáilte Ireland, 23 November 2004.

Any destination wishing to benefit from business tourism of any kind must be able to answer 'Yes' to the following checklist:

1. Does the city have excellent conference facilities?
2. Are they easily reachable from the airport?
3. Does the city have a comprehensive transport network?
4. Are there resources for cultural activities and entertainment in the delegates' spare time?
5. Is the cost favourable?
6. Is the culture (a) similar to the organisation's or (b) accepting of the organisation's culture?
7. Is the organisation's language understood by at least some in the destination?

Transport is a key consideration. Ireland's transport network is far behind some of its European neighbours, such as Germany and France. Cities in Germany have underground train stations serving the conference centres. In fact, in some cities there are multiple underground lines for the conference centre, e.g. Berlin. In some German cities, there are dedicated underground lines that only operate at times of conferences or trade fairs, e.g. Stuttgart. A comprehensive and reliable transport network is a prerequisite for any city seeking to be classed as a business tourism destination.

Fáilte Ireland appoints consultants

Fáilte Ireland, the national tourism body, is to appoint a team of external consultants in an effort to boost the corporate tourism market in Ireland... The consultants will be appointed later this month and will draft a wide-ranging business plan to help Ireland attract more international conferences and business meetings. The move is part of a broader effort by Fáilte Ireland to market Ireland as a business destination more comprehensively. Last year, it established a Business Tourism Forum under the chairmanship of Peter Malone, the former chief executive of the Jurys Hotel Group. A request for tenders for the development of a Business Tourism Development Plan was issued last week, and the deadline for submissions is this Wednesday. The contract is initially for one year, but the deal can be extended for a further twelve months by Fáilte Ireland. According to the tender document, the plan 'will encompass a wide range of initiatives' ranging from attracting international conferences to helping the Irish tourism industry to improve its standards. The consultants will also develop 'a detailed marketing plan with sales initiatives that drive customer acquisition retention and development strategies'. The document states that the core target markets are Britain, France, Germany and the US.

A 'framework for co-operation' will also be developed with Irish stakeholders to agree on new initiatives, while the consultants will also evaluate the effectiveness of how Irish business tourism is currently promoted overseas.

Business tourism is a lucrative market, with visitors attending conferences or corporate meetings spending on average 70 per cent more money than regular holidaymakers. Many also stay on for longer visits around the country.

This summer, 1,200 harpists came to Dublin for the World Harp Conference, while 6,000 beekeepers attended the World Apiculture Conference last month.

Source: Kehoe, I., 'Fáilte Ireland appoints consultants', *The Sunday Business Post*, 11 September 2005.

Call for business tourism tax breaks

Annual revenues from business tourism in the Republic could double to €1 billion by 2010 if measures are taken now to encourage the sector, according to Fáilte Ireland.

The tourism development authority yesterday called on the government to remove VAT for business travellers to create a regime similar to that of the UK.

Fáilte Ireland, which has created a new business tourism brand, wants Aer Lingus to make it easier to make group bookings and for construction to start on the National Conference Centre.

Peter Malone, chairman of the Fáilte Ireland Business Tourism Forum, pointed out that people visiting the Republic for business tended to produce a...higher yield than holidaymakers.

Visitors coming for conferences, incentive trips or business meetings are also less dependent on seasons, he said.

Mr Malone said the removal of VAT for costs such as accommodation and meals would significantly boost the tourism sector. He is hopeful that it might be addressed in December's Budget, having been reassured by the Minister for Finance, Brian Cowen, it is 'very high on the agenda'.

Fáilte Ireland estimates that the measure would result in an annual tax loss of €25 million for the exchequer, but argues that this would be more than outstripped by the additional tourism spending that would result. 'It's very important – it sends a great message,' said Mr Malone. 'I would be disappointed if by 2010 we weren't at €1 billion in revenues,' he added.

Source: McCaffrey, U., 'Call for business tourism tax breaks', *The Irish Times*, 23 May 2006.

BUSINESS MEETINGS

Every day around the world thousands of meetings take place where businesspeople from different parts of a country – or indeed the world – come together to do business. Often, these meetings last for more than one day, or there is a significant distance to travel, and so an overnight stay is required away from the businessperson's place of habitual residence. Business meetings are vital for the tourism industry, not least in Ireland. During off-peak leisure travel periods, business tourism can keep a hotel in profit.

In general, we can divide business meetings between corporate meetings and associate meetings. In the former, the aim of attending is to do business with someone else. In the latter, people with a common interest or who belong to a common organisation meet to exchange ideas and information.

Business meetings are sometimes known as conferences or conventions. The term 'congress' is also often used. This refers to an international conference, i.e. a conference whose delegates come from different parts of the world to converge on one location for their meeting.

The Union of International Associations (UIA) based in Brussels estimates that between 7,000 and 10,000 congresses take place annually.

The world's top congress destinations are the US, France, the UK, Germany and the Netherlands. Paris is the world's top destination for business tourism, followed by London, Brussels, Vienna, Geneva and Berlin. Notably, all of these cities are in Europe. These cities are so prominent because of their facilities and excellent transport links.

In the 1950s, the vast majority (80 per cent) of congresses were held in Europe. However, by the 1990s, this figure had fallen to 60 per cent. In the future, we may see a further drop in Europe's share of the market, as newly emerging destinations such as Thailand, India and China compete to host conferences and congresses. Although these destinations are located quite far from many of the world's key business centres in Europe and North America, the cost of travel to the destination can be offset by the relatively cheaper cost of accommodation, food and beverage, entertainment as well as conference facilities. Further, more exotic places may appeal to delegates and encourage a delegate who was not considering attending to in fact travel.

The most popular time of the year for congresses is September, followed by May. In Ireland, spring and autumn are also busy for domestic conferences, e.g. political parties, trade unions, other national organisations. The winter months (December, January and February) are the least popular.

Around one-third of conferences have fewer than 100 participants, while just less than one-third have between 100 and 250 participants. Around a quarter of conferences have between 250 and 1,000 participants and only less than 10 per cent have more than 1,000 participants. Two-thirds of delegates bring their spouse.

The organisation of conferences and especially congresses can take place years in advance, given the amount of organisation necessary.

INCENTIVE TRAVEL

There are many ways to motivate and reward staff, especially sales staff that reach and exceed sales targets. As management theory suggests, money ceases to be a motivating factor for many once sales staff earn a high income. Travel is one form of motivation and reward for staff which is growing in popularity. It can serve as a welcome acknowledgement of work done or an incentive to sales staff to reach and exceed their sales targets, hence the term 'incentive travel'.

The type of travel organised and the various elements of the package are usually chosen to match the lifestyles and aspirations of the staff who are participating. Therefore, an incentive travel trip for a group of twenty to twenty-five-year-old telesales agents will take a very different form to one for a group of forty to fifty-year-old senior financial services agents, for example.

The area of incentive travel is continually growing and is predicted to be a major growth market. The traditionally popular city break destinations of Europe, such as London, Paris, Amsterdam, Dublin and Prague (to name just a few), are important destinations for incentive travel. Most incentive travel comes in the form of short break trips, such as weekend breaks; longer breaks where a section of a company's staff are away for extended periods would interrupt the running of a company.

However, destinations further afield are becoming more popular. Eastern Europe is projected to be a major future incentive destination. The main barriers to Eastern Europe as an incentive destination (poor infrastructure, poor ground handling) are being addressed, primarily with EU funding since the accession of the Central and Eastern European states to the EU. This region has a great deal to offer, such as cities full of culture and heritage, attractive scenery, national cuisine, local customs as well as some well-known wines and beers. With infrastructural improvements, Eastern Europe will be set to compete effectively with the traditional short break destinations of Europe, and not just in terms of incentive travel, but all forms of travel.

It is interesting to note that there is a marked difference in incentive travel between the US and Europe. In the latter, only around one-third of incentive travellers take their spouses along, compared to almost three-quarters in the US.

EXHIBITIONS AND TRADE FAIRS

Exhibitions and trade fairs are large events offering various products and services for display, and most for sale. They may be open to the general public, e.g. Ideal Homes Exhibitions or the Opportunities Careers Fair in the RDS Dublin, or invited specialists (members of a specific organisation). Some of the larger exhibitions and trade fairs have become synonymous with the products and services which they display. For example, the Paris Air Show is the world's most prestigious showcase for the latest aircraft, both civilian and military. The ITB Travel Trade Fair in Berlin is the world's largest travel trade fair, with estimates of over 30,000 visitors from the trade and circa 100,000 from the general public.

Exhibitions and trade fairs cause immediate and direct boosts for transport, accommodation and other services in the host city. They also cause an indirect boost to retailing, communications, entertainment, food and beverage, etc. One can see, therefore, that there is major potential for direct and indirect tourism revenue from this lucrative form of business tourism. It is for these reasons that national and regional governments get involved in encouraging exhibitions and trade fairs to their region as well as lending marketing assistance. There is fierce competition between governments to host these events. Britain, France and Germany earn billions of euro from exhibitions and trade fairs alone (estimated to be worth €40 billion worldwide), compared to Ireland's circa €4 billion from all forms of foreign tourism.

Exhibitions and trade fairs are often combined with conferences, as there is a captive audience attending a conference or congress and they are potential buyers for related products. Therefore, adding an exhibition to a conference can be a useful way of offsetting the cost of the conference, as the organisers charge the vendors for the privilege of selling at the conference. An example of this is school and college book publishers attending the annual meetings of the teachers' unions.

> **Speech by John O'Donoghue, TD, Minister for Arts, Sport and Tourism, at 'Business Tourism – Exploiting the Potential' – Fáilte Ireland Business Tourism Forum, in the Four Seasons Hotel, Ballsbridge, Dublin 4, Tuesday, 23 November 2004 at 8.30 a.m.**
>
> I am delighted to be here today and to see such an excellent representation from the tourism and hospitality sector. Many of you are already successful in targeting business tourism, others have more recently recognised the potential it offers both to your own businesses and to Irish tourism nationally.
>
> The Tourism Policy Review Group has set challenging targets to double overseas visitor spend to €6 billion by 2012 and to increase visitor numbers from 6 to 10 million. Within this, a specific objective is to increase the share of promotable segments, which includes holiday, language and incentive and conference travel, to half of all visitors to Ireland. The report also identifies conference and incentive travel as a key opportunity market for growth.
>
> There are issues that must be addressed through a partnership approach between industry, the tourism agencies and government if we are to achieve

these objectives. Specifically related to the business tourism sector, I know that the absence of a dedicated National Conference Centre is a major impediment to optimising growth, a fact that is reflected in the report of the Tourism Policy Review Group.

Most of you here know that I secured agreement from government in June 2003 for the provision of a National Conference Centre through an open competitive procurement process. Following this, I established a High Level Steering Group comprising representatives of my department, the Office of Public Works, Fáilte Ireland and the Department of Finance to agree the parameters of a procurement process. In November 2003, a Notice inviting Expressions of Interest in the provision of a National Conference Centre in the Dublin area was issued. Four submissions were received in response to the Notice and following evaluation, three candidates were short-listed to proceed to the next stage of the competition.

The procurement process being undertaken is necessarily complex. As part of the procedural requirements of the public-private partnership arrangement under which the provision of the National Conference Centre is being pursued, a public sector benchmark exercise and a benefit assessment must be undertaken before the next detailed proposals stage can be initiated. These exercises are being carried out and I am glad to say are close to finalisation. In addition, every effort is being made to complete as soon as possible the detailed project contract documentation required. The objective is to issue Invitations to Tender to the three pre-qualified candidates before Christmas. Allowing some months for necessary engagement with the selected tenders, current indications are that a preferred bidder could be selected by late summer 2005. My personal priority and that of the government is to have this project brought to a conclusion at the earliest possible date while ensuring that the relevant procedures and guidelines relating to the process are closely observed and that nothing is done that might jeopardise its successful conclusion.

In more general terms, clearly a great deal of progress is also being made through the Business Tourism Forum initiative, which has revitalised and refocused the sector. The consultative approach being taken by Fáilte Ireland is proof of the success of the partnership model in this industry. I understand that the sessions held to date have been remarkably useful, open and frank. Everyone realises that they have a part to play. Today's conference will continue and formalise the discussion and agenda setting for the development of the sector going forward, resulting in a very clear action plan.

The investment, both public and private, in our tourism infrastructure in recent years was a necessary precursor to expanding our market share of the global business tourism sector.

Ireland can offer the quality product demanded by discerning business visitors combined with a unique tourism experience. That is the essence of value – offering the customer a product that exceeds their expectations for a competitive price, not necessarily the cheapest.

Every high-yielding business visitor offers more than just a single opportunity. Not only is their individual trip to Ireland of significant economic benefit, often during the winter months, but there is also the opportunity for Ireland to provide them with such an excellent experience that they return, perhaps for another business meeting, or perhaps with family for a holiday, or with friends to explore some of Ireland's exceptional golf courses or other attractions.

Ireland has already proved itself as a world-class location for business. Now we must do the same for business tourism to prove ourselves as a world-class location for doing business. I am confident that with the energy and commitment of the people here today, that will happen.

Source: Department of Arts, Sport and Tourism speeches archive, 23 November 2004.

FUTURE OF BUSINESS TOURISM

Ireland's tourism officials and the government have made it clear that encouraging business tourism is a key strategic priority. The provision of a National Conference Centre in Dublin is a key driver of the strategy. Plans are in place for such a conference centre but have been delayed several times. Improvements in Ireland's transport network have continued. Public transport initiatives such as the LUAS and the Transport 21 plan (see Chapter 6) will all improve the infrastructure. The roads network is continually improving, and recent extensions of motorways around Dublin and the rest of the country have greatly improved the road transport network. Dublin's Port Tunnel aims to continue this infrastructural improvement.

Marketing efforts by public and private tourism agencies will inevitably focus more on attracting business tourism, given that it is such a high-spending sector of the tourism industry. However, lack of conference facilities, the perceived high cost of Ireland as a tourism destination and the lack of transport facilities in comparison to other European countries will need to be addressed in much more detail if Ireland is to compete effectively in the area of business tourism. Transport in particular is a major barrier for Ireland, given that it is an island. International delegates with time constraints only have air travel as a viable option if considering business travel to Ireland. Routes into and out of Ireland are relatively competitively priced by many airlines, including Ryanair and Aer Lingus. However, the lack of a business-class service on intra-European routes by the national carrier Aer Lingus since 2005 has led to claims that Ireland is actively discouraging business tourism. Most other European destinations have business-class services on the flights servicing them. Even trains travelling between the major business hubs of Europe have dedicated business carriages, where there is wireless broadband internet available as well as secretarial services and basic business supports such as photocopying and fax. Such intercity services (such as the ones provided by Deutsche Bundesbahn – German Federal Railways) are often a more viable option for the business traveller who wants to travel from city to city (not to out-of-town airports) and who wants to be able to wander around a business traveller-orientated train with their mobile phone in use, rather than being restricted on board a plane without the use of certain communication devices that are not permitted on board. Even on longer journeys, overnight cabins on trains are relatively inexpensive, and the traveller can sleep most of the way to their destination and arrive fresh to conduct their business. Ireland is taking steps in the right direction, but is certainly decades behind its continental neighbours in this regard.

Fáilte Ireland's **Business Tourism Forum** has developed a business tourism brand and website, www.irelandinspires.com, in an effort to further develop business tourism. It is aimed at meeting, conference and incentive trip planners and includes presentation tools to assist planners when making presentations on Ireland to the decision-makers in the organisation.

The following articles outline the press releases by the Department of Arts, Sport and Tourism of the proposed National Conference Centre (NCC), from the announcement of the plan through to the awarding of the tender, between June 2003 and November 2005. They are presented to illustrate the procedures that the government follows in planning and organising a development on this scale.

JUNE 2003: National Conference Centre

The Minister for Arts, Sport and Tourism, Mr John O'Donoghue, TD, announced today [25 June 2003] that the government has taken a major step towards the realisation of one of the key tourism commitments in the Agreed Programme for Government – to ensure the construction of a state-of-the-art National Conference Centre (NCC) in Dublin.

Following a consultative process with promotional, tourism industry and other bodies and consideration of various financing options, the government has agreed in principle to the provision of an NCC by way of a leasing arrangement through an open competitive procurement process.

The government has authorised Minister O'Donoghue to set up a steering group, including senior representatives of his department, the Office of Public Works, the Department of Finance and Fáilte Ireland. This group will advise on an up-to-date specification for the NCC and its operational requirements with a view to agreeing the parameters for an open and competitive procurement process, which it is envisaged will be carried out under the auspices of the OPW.

'On the basis of consultations undertaken by my department and the recent research reviewed, I am totally convinced of the need for a dedicated National Conference Centre if Ireland is to realise its full potential in the international conference market. Independent estimates put the level of additional annual foreign revenue that could be earned from such a facility at between €25 million to €50 million, which would represent a very welcome boost for Irish tourism,' Mr O'Donoghue concluded.

According to Fáilte Ireland, the current level of overseas conference and meetings visitors to Ireland each year is in the region of 120,000, with Dublin being by far the most popular region. Conference visitors are high spenders who, if the experience is right, will extend their stay or return later for private holidays. It has been estimated that an additional 30,000 annual visitors could be generated through the availability of a dedicated centre.

The National Conference Centre has the support of the key elements of the tourism industry and business interest groups and was specifically endorsed in the recent interim report of the Tourism Review Group.

Source: Department of Arts, Sport and Tourism, 25 June 2003.

* * *

NOVEMBER 2003: O'Donoghue announces initiation of National Conference Centre procurement process

John O'Donoghue, TD, Minister for Arts, Sport and Tourism, has announced that a Notice Inviting Expressions of Interest in the provision of a National Conference Centre in the Dublin area, with an expected minimum delegate capacity of the order of 2,000, has been issued for publication in the Official Journal of the European Union. The time limit set for the receipt of requests to participate is 21 January 2004.

'The publication of this Notice represents another important milestone on the road to achieving a National Conference Centre for Ireland,' said the Minister, adding that 'if acceptable proposals are received, the National Conference Centre could, as envisaged by the Notice, be constructed before end 2007.'

In relation to the location of the centre, Minister O'Donoghue said that those expressing interest are required to propose a site in the Dublin area but that, in addition, the state has reserved the right to identify an appropriate site within its ownership or control.

Minister O'Donoghue said that the establishment of a National Conference Centre in Dublin in partnership with private sector investors is one of the key actions to support tourism product development and innovation identified in the recent Report of the Tourism Policy Review Group.

Source: Department of Arts, Sport and Tourism, 13 November 2003.

* * *

JANUARY 2004: Four candidates for the provision of a National Conference Centre in Dublin

John O'Donoghue, TD, Minister for Arts, Sport and Tourism, announced today [22 January 2004] that four submissions have been received in response to the Office of Public Works' advertisement for Expressions of Interest in the provision of a National Conference Centre in the Dublin area. The closing date for receipt of submissions was 5.00 p.m. on Wednesday, 21 January 2004.

The Minister said that he was pleased with the level of interest in participating in the competition. 'The fact that there are as many as four candidates will enhance the competitive nature of the process.

'All the submissions will now undergo detailed evaluation by an assessment panel representative of my department, the Office of Public Works and its advisors, the Department of Finance, Fáilte Ireland and the National Development Finance Agency. A separate panel will subsequently evaluate the site proposals, which candidates were also required to put forward.'

Minister O'Donoghue said that he expects the next stage of the process, whereby qualified candidates with acceptable sites will be invited to submit a 'response to site proposal', to be initiated next month. 'Subject to the acceptability of proposals, the National Conference Centre could, as envisaged under the process, be constructed before end 2007.'

Source: Department of Arts, Sport and Tourism, 22 January 2004.

* * *

DECEMBER 2004: O'Donoghue announces next stage of National Conference Centre competition
John O'Donoghue, TD, Minister for Arts, Sport and Tourism, today [10 December 2004] announced that tenders are being invited from the three short-listed consortia interested in providing a National Conference Centre in the Dublin area. The three consortia are:

• Anna Livia Consortium
• Michael McNamara & the Leopardstown Club Consortium
• Spencer Dock International Conference Centre Consortium.

Minister O'Donoghue said, 'Each of the consortia is now being provided with the relevant tender documentation by the Office of Public Works. The preparation of this documentation has been demanding and time consuming, with details requiring careful scrutiny and consideration, and I am very pleased that it has been completed in time to issue before the holiday period and that the next stage of the procurement process is now underway.' The closing date for receipt of Tenders is 18 March 2005.

Source: Department of Arts, Sport and Tourism, 10 December 2004.

* * *

MAY 2005: O'Donoghue welcomes submission of tenders by two consortia for the provision of a National Conference Centre in Dublin.
The Minister for Arts, Sport and Tourism, Mr John O'Donoghue, TD, today [20 May 2005] welcomed the submission of tenders for the provision of a National Conference Centre in Dublin. Today was the deadline for the receipt of tenders by the Office of Public Works. Tenders were received from the Anna Livia Consortium and the Spencer Dock InterNational Conference Centre Consortium and will be evaluated in accordance with the provisions of the competition.

The selection of a Provisional Preferred Tenderer is scheduled for later in the summer, with the award of the contract, subject to government approval, expected before the end of the year.

Source: Department of Arts, Sport and Tourism, 20 May 2005.

* * *

NOVEMBER 2005: O'Donoghue announces designation of Spencer Dock InterNational Conference Centre Consortium as Provisional Preferred Tenderer for the provision of a National Conference Centre in Dublin
Following approval by the government, the Minister for Arts, Sport and Tourism, John O'Donoghue, TD, today [16 November 2005] announced that Spencer Dock InterNational Conference Centre Consortium is being invited to become the Provisional Preferred Tenderer (PPT) for the provision of a National Conference Centre in Dublin. The decision was taken by the National Conference Centre Steering Group following a detailed assessment and evaluation of tenders received against award criteria set out in the Invitation to Negotiate document.

In accordance with the competition process, the next step will be for the contracting authority, the Office of Public Works, to negotiate, settle and agree any required amendments to the project agreement with the PPT and for the PPT to resolve all outstanding due diligence issues. Assuming that these negotiations prove successful, the next step is the appointment of the PPT as Preferred Tenderer (PT). During the Preferred Tenderer phase, the PT will develop and provide the full range of project documents which will require review and approval by the contracting authority.

'I am delighted that a further critical stage in the process of delivering a world-class National Conference Centre for Dublin has been completed. I look forward to the early completion of the next stages and to a final decision by government next year,' the Minister said. He added that he was particularly pleased that the commitment in the Programme for Government to the provision of a National Conference Centre has taken this further major step to final implementation.

'On the basis of consultations undertaken earlier by my department and research reviewed, I am totally convinced of the need for a modern, dedicated National Conference Centre if Ireland is to realise its full potential in the hugely valuable international conference market,' Minister O'Donoghue concluded.

Source: Department of Arts, Sport and Tourism, 16 November 2005.

REVISION QUESTIONS

1. Why is the business tourism market such a lucrative one?
2. What is the difference between a congress and a conference?
3. Write a brief paragraph on the importance of each of the following:
   (a) Business meetings.
   (b) Incentive travel.
   (c) Exhibitions and trade fairs.
4. How does business tourism differ from leisure tourism?
5. What does the future hold for this sector, in your opinion?
6. What facilities and services are needed for business tourism?
7. How is business tourism promoted?

8. Why do so many Europeans not take their spouse on incentive trips in comparison to Americans, in your opinion?
9. Why is Dublin/Ireland not a popular conference destination?

ESSAY QUESTIONS

1. Discuss the potential for business tourism for Ireland.
2. List the different forms of business tourism and briefly discuss each of them.
3. Outline the situation in Ireland regarding business tourism.
4. Compose a list of deficiencies that must be addressed if Ireland is to compete effectively for business tourists.
5. 'Although current government strategy is to encourage business tourism, reduction in business-class travel to and from Ireland is hindering efforts.' Discuss.
6. 'The provision of a National Conference Centre will do little to boost business tourism considering the current high taxation of business tourism.' Discuss.

TASKS

Task 1

ABC Ltd is a London-based insurance firm. As an incentive trip for their top twenty sales executives, they have commissioned your executive travel agency to organise a weekend trip to Ireland for these executives and their spouses (forty people in total). You are required to plan the entire trip, from the moment they land at the airport in the region they are visiting in Ireland (18:00 on Friday evening) to the moment they depart (18:00 on Sunday evening), including transport, food, drink, entertainment, excursions etc., for the full forty-eight-hour period. Allow eight hours for sleep per night and a total of no more than six hours for private time during the whole weekend.

You have a total budget of €120,000 for the entire group for the entire weekend. You do not have to include the price of flights from London to Ireland. Your task is to obtain quotes, to prepare a full brochure for the weekend and to deliver a presentation to an audience presumed to be the board of directors of ABC Ltd. You must spend within 10 per cent of your budget, and your commission is to be no more than a maximum 15 per cent of the total (to be included in the €120,000).

Task 2

Divide the class into two roughly equal groups. Each group should be given ten to fifteen minutes to develop opposing points on the following statements, followed by a forty to forty-five minute debate.

Statement: Ireland should forsake business tourism in favour of leisure tourism.

Statement: Business tourists should not stay in luxury hotels and travel on first/business class.

Statement: The Irish government does little to support business tourism.

ASSIGNMENTS

1. You are a tourism consultant. You have been commissioned by a South African client to write a report on business tourism in Ireland. Illustrate the main points of such a (fictional) report in your answer. You should comment on incentive travel, exhibitions and trade fairs as well as business meetings.

2. You are a civil servant and are asked by the Minister for Tourism to compile a report on how Ireland can develop its business tourism potential. Compile the report, paying particular attention to the facilities and infrastructural developments that are needed.

Chapter 11

Tourism Law

Important note: The information given in these pages is for assistance only and no responsibility is accepted for any error or inaccuracy. Full legal advice should be obtained.

SUMMARY

This final chapter presents an important area for the study of tourism. Rather than providing a legal interpretation of various laws and regulations relevant to tourism, this chapter outlines some of these and gives a brief synopsis of their major points, highlighting how they affect Irish tourism. Some of the laws and regulations discussed are specifically related to the area of tourism and hospitality, e.g. the Package Holidays Act 1995, the Hotel Proprietors, Act 1963, EU air passengers' rights, the Intoxicating Liquors Act 2003 and 2005, while others are included because of their importance to the area, e.g. the Employment Equality Act 1998, the Equal Status Act 2000, the Equality Act 2004 and finally the Public Health (Tobacco) Act 2002 (smoking ban legislation).

LEARNING OUTCOMES

Having completed this chapter, the reader should be able to:
* Demonstrate a basic understanding of some key tourism legislation.
* Understand how other relevant legislation may impact on the tourism sector.
* Appreciate the customer protection enshrined in Irish and European legislation.

INTRODUCTION

Like any other sector, tourism is regulated by Irish and European law. As well as the many statutes, regulations and directives that govern all forms of business, e.g. contract law, consumer law, credit law, there are certain pieces of legislation which are specifically aimed at the tourism and hospitality industry in Ireland. Examples of these include the Package Holidays and Travel Trade Act 1995 and the Hotel Proprietors' Act 1963. These are discussed in detail in this chapter. The intoxicating liquor legislation is also important for the tourism and hospitality industry and so it is presented and discussed in this chapter as well. Finally, the relevance of equality legislation, the impact of the smoking ban and the changes in EU passengers' rights are also discussed.

These pieces of legislation are simply a sample of some of the more commonly discussed areas in tourism law. Further regulations referring to specific branches in the tourism sector, e.g. travel agency licenses, are discussed as they arise in any particular chapter in the book. It is important to note at this stage that the discussion in this chapter is not proposed to be a legal interpretation of the respective pieces of legislation, but rather a rough interpretation of them and their implications for the Irish tourism and hospitality industry.

THE PACKAGE HOLIDAYS AND TRAVEL TRADE ACT 1995

The Package Holidays and Travel Trade Act 1995 originated as an EU Directive, which must be incorporated into the national law of each of the EU member states. The main provisions of a Directive cannot be altered by a national parliament. The EC Package Travel Directive came into operation on 1 January 1993 and the Irish Act implementing the Directive came into operation in 1995.

Before the Act was implemented, the main areas of legislation dealing with package holidays in Ireland included:
- The Sale of Goods and Supply of Services Act 1980.
- The Consumer Information Act 1978.
- The Transport Act 1980.

Definition

According to the Act, a package is a holiday that is sold or offered for sale, is prearranged by an organiser and is a combination of at least two out of the following three:
- Transport.
- Accommodation.
- Other services not ancillary to transport or accommodation.

In order to constitute a package, at least one overnight stay must be included. Once there is a combination of any two of the above for sale, the organiser is obliged to follow the regulations governing a package holiday and cannot price components separately.

The Organiser

The organiser is a 'person who other than occasionally' organises packages for sale, and he or she is legally liable for the whole package, even the subcontractors. This includes all package holidays of any kind, once they are prearranged. The term 'other than occasionally' is placed in the Act to ensure that someone who organises an annual school trip, for example, would not be in breach of the Act. However, organising a monthly school trip and selling it to students could be construed as breaching the Act, as this is 'other than occasionally'. Similarly, outings for clubs and societies may be governed by the Act if they are a regular occurrence. Even conferences may be included if they satisfy the 'two out of three' rule above. However, in order to be governed by the Act, at least one overnight stay on the conference, school trip or club outing must be included. Therefore, day packages are not governed by the Act. A tourist booking service offering products which satisfy the definition of a package must comply with the Act.

Transfers from the port of travel, e.g. airport, ferry port, to the accommodation is not considered to be an individual element, but rather it is ancillary to the transport element, and so does not count as one of the criteria in the 'two out of three' rule. In general, anything offered along with, for example, transport or accommodation must account for a significant element of the package. In considering whether such an element accounts for a significant element, we can ask 'would people have purchased the package if X was not available?' where X is the significant element.

The Brochure

A brochure for the package must contain the majority of the following information under the Act. However, in practice all of the information below is included.
* All elements of the package.
* Full itinerary.
* Must contain actual details and must not mislead.
* Must be legible, accurate and comprehensible.
* For foreign trips, customers must be informed in writing or verbally about passport and visa requirements.
* Destination information.
* Means and category of transport.
* Type and grade of accommodation.
* Details of full price.
* Payment timetable.
* Security of deposits.
* Insurance options.
* Minimum number of people required.
* Cancellation deadline.
* Meal options.
* Outward/inward delay arrangements.
* Vaccination requirements.

The Contract

Under the terms of the Act, a contract must be provided to the customer when booking. For all contracts, the following must be included (for last-minute contracts, the customer should be advised of the following information verbally and receive a written copy later).
* Destination.
* Dates.
* Transport (dates, times, points).
* Meals.
* Minimum number of people.
* Itinerary.
* Visits.
* Organiser's name and address.
* Price, provision for price revision, tax, extra fees.

- Any special requirements.
- Complaints procedure.

Price Revision

Once the package has been booked and a contract is entered into, a price revision cannot occur unless specifically stated in the contract. Price revisions sometimes take place due to an increase in fuel charges. In the event of a price revision, the organiser must provide details on how the revision is calculated. They must also detail the duties, taxes, landing charges or any other related fees. If the price revision is due to large exchange rate fluctuations, an explanation of how the rate is used must be presented. At the time of booking, the contract and/or brochure should state the last date at which a price revision can take place, and the Act states that no revision may take place within the last thirty days prior to departure. Any price increase of less than 2 per cent may not be passed on to the customer, but instead must be absorbed by the organiser. Finally, the customer has the right to a full refund if they are not satisfied with the price revisions for whatever reasons.

Before Departure

Before departure, the organiser is legally obliged to ensure that the customer is furnished with details on all transport, connections and the accommodation as well as contact details for representative(s) in the destination. For minor travellers (those under sixteen years old), such contact details are particularly important. Further, the organiser should provide the customer with details of insurance options for their package.

Change and Cancellation

The customer must be informed immediately if the package is changed or cancelled. At that stage, they have the right to withdraw with a full refund. Alternatively, they can opt to take an equivalent or superior package (often by paying a premium on the latter), or a reduced-value one with the difference refunded. The organiser is also liable for cancellations and changes out of their control, such as those made by subcontractors.

Protection against Insolvency

The Act mandates that anyone selling package holidays must protect their customers against their business becoming insolvent, and to do this, they must:
- Have a bond; or
- Be a member of an authorised institution with a reserve fund; or
- Be a member of an approved body (with or without bond); or
- Be a member of an authorised institution; or
- Have their own insurance.
   This provision is enforced by criminal law as well as civil law.
   The Package Holidays Act provides that an Authorised Officer may be appointed by the government or by the Director of Consumer Affairs to investigate any alleged breaches. The Authorised Officer has a large amount of power for investigative

purposes, and the penalties for not co-operating with an Authorised Officer include a fine and/or imprisonment.

Case Law: *Jarvis v. Swan Tours*

This case law from the UK is an extremely important precedent which influences how many courts in Ireland deal with the Act. The case centres on a barrister named Mr Jarvis who booked a two-week ski holiday. The first week did not live up to his expectations, but the second week was a disaster, according to Mr Jarvis, as the resort was almost empty and the promised entertainment was almost non-existent. Upon return, Mr Jarvis took a case against Swan Tours. Originally, Mr Jarvis was awarded half of his costs, as he enjoyed benefits of half the holiday, i.e. the first week. However, the Court of Appeal awarded him double the cost of the package for the emotional damage caused. This precedent can be applied in many Irish cases.

Benefits of the Act

The benefits of the Act include enhanced consumer protection in a European framework. This is especially important as many European package organisers operate outside the confines of their own state by offering their packages to multiple markets in Europe. The benefits clearly lie with the consumer, as the package organiser's liability is better defined. However, it is not solely the individual consumer that benefits – the tourism industry as a whole stands to gain from such legislation, as anything that increases consumer protection and in turn enhances confidence has the power to fuel growth in the industry.

Problems with the Act

There are several problems inherent in the Act, including the lack of a definition of what a tourist is. There is also ambiguity regarding services and facilities that are implied to be included, e.g. a leisure centre at a hotel resort. There is no reference to compensation in the EU Directive, but the Act makes reference to compensation of up to double the cost for an adult. There is also confusion regarding hotels offering special breaks (such as two nights' bed and breakfast and one evening meal). Is the evening meal ancillary to the hotel (and so not part of the 'two out of three' rule constituting a package) or is it separate? Finally, the Act leaves organisers open to claims for compensation for many areas out of their control. This includes not only subcontractors, but also uncontrollable variables such as the weather or an act of God.

THE HOTEL PROPRIETORS' ACT 1963

Like all sectors of the tourism industry, accommodation providers must adhere to their responsibilities and obligations under many pieces of Irish and EU legislation. Examples of such include legislation to protect employees, such as the vast plethora of Irish employment legislation and the Safety, Health and Welfare at Work Act 2005, as well as legislation designed to protect guests and consumers, such as laws governing food and hygiene, law of torts (in relation to guests injuring themselves) and fire regulations, to name but a few. The most relevant statute to the hotel sector is the Hotel Proprietors' Act 1963. This Act places certain duties upon hoteliers; the main duties are set out below. A major criticism of the Act is that it is very dated and does not fully reflect the changing needs and expectations of hotel guests. For example, in a hotel/spa resort, do the duties of the Act apply to the spa as well as the hotel if they are advertised as the one entity?

The Hotel Proprietors' Act covers all hotels registered with Fáilte Ireland but excludes all other forms of accommodation, such as guesthouses, B&Bs and similar types of accommodation. Different forms of legislation also apply to these other types of accommodation. For example, a guesthouse must have a minimum of seven and maximum of thirty bedrooms and must by law register in Fáilte Ireland's Register of Guesthouses.

A hotel is described as premises that are used primarily for lodging and sleeping of travellers who present themselves with or without prior arrangement, and the premises should serve meals and refreshments within reasonable hours. A register of residents must be kept.

Duty to Receive Guests and Guest's Property

The Act provides that a hotelier has a duty to receive all comers unless there is reasonable grounds for refusal, including drunkenness or the safety of the staff and guests.

The hotelier also has a duty to receive property of the guests and is liable for a guest's property. This is in place even if the guest does not arrive, once they have engaged the accommodation. What this means is that if a guest sends on his or her luggage, but the guest himself or herself misses their flight and does not arrive, the hotelier is still responsible for the safety of the guest's luggage. This provision is in place once the guest has engaged, i.e. booked, accommodation, even if they do not arrive.

Liability

The Act places the responsibility for the safety of the guest with the hotelier, as well as their property. The hotelier's liability for damage is limited if the damage is caused by an act of God, by the guest him/herself or if the damage occurs outside the hotel premises. Similarly, the hotelier is not liable if the damage occurs outside the time that accommodation is engaged, e.g. after check-out.

However, liability for damage is not limited if it was due to an act or default of the proprietor or his/her servant. Further, there is no limit on liability for the guest's property where the proprietor accepts goods for specific safe-keeping, or in the case where the goods were offered to the proprietor or a servant for safe-keeping and they refused to accept it. Even a guest's car which is parked on the street outside the hotel (and not in a dedicated hotel car park) is the responsibility of the hotelier. Signs claiming 'cars parked at owner's risk' are invalid and the hotelier is responsible for damage or theft. There is a condition that the owner of the car must inform the hotelier or his/her servant that the car is parked there.

Notice

The Act contains a notice which must be clearly placed at reception or at the front door. The notice explains to guests their rights under the Act. The text of the notice is as follows.

Damage to, or Loss or Destruction of, Guests' Property

Under the Hotel Proprietors' Act, 1963, the proprietor of a hotel, as defined by the Act, may in certain circumstances be liable to make good damage to, or loss or destruction of, a guest's property, even though it was not due to any fault of the proprietor or staff of the hotel.

This liability, however,
(a) extends only to the property of persons who have engaged sleeping accommodation in the hotel;
(b) is limited to £100 in the case of any one person, except in the case of motor vehicles and of property which has been deposited, or offered for deposit, for safe custody.

A hotel, as defined by the Hotel Proprietors' Act, 1963, is an establishment which provides or holds itself out as providing sleeping accommodation, food and drink for reward for all comers without special contract, and includes every establishment registered as a hotel with Bord Fáilte Éireann.

Lien on Guest's Property

The Act provides for a lien on and right to sell any and all property of a guest if money is owed to proprietor. Controversially, the goods need not be owned by the guest as long as the proprietor is not aware of this. Further, the guest need not be an overnight guest, and the lien extends to motor vehicles. If the debt is not paid after six weeks, the goods may be sold at auction. The surplus after the debt and the cost of auction must be returned to the guest. This applies to goods even if they are stolen, once the hotelier is not aware of this.

INTOXICATING LIQUOR LEGISLATION

The Intoxicating Liquor Act 2003 was introduced to amend the Licensing Acts 1833 to 2003 and is focused on addressing concerns about the level and pattern of Irish alcohol consumption. The Act does, however, have an impact on tourists, given that Irish pubs are world famous and most visitors to Ireland will experience an element of Irish pub culture.

The Department of Justice outlines the Act under the following headings (source: www.justice.ie).

Combating Drunkenness and Disorderly Conduct

The Act contains revised provisions, including stronger penalties, in relation to the sale and supply of intoxicating liquor to drunken persons and drunkenness in licensed premises, as well as stronger provisions relating to the maintenance of order and the prohibition on disorderly conduct on licensed premises.

Enforcement and Sanctions

Wider use of temporary closure orders where licensed premises are found to be in breach of the licensing laws, for example in relation to permitting drunkenness or disorderly conduct, or supplying alcohol to drunken persons. Further, the Act provides for the extension of enforcement powers under the licensing laws to non-uniformed gardaí.

Trading Hours

Closing time on Thursday nights was brought back to 11.30 p.m. from the original 12.30 p.m. (partly to combat absenteeism from employment on Fridays). There is also a new provision which will allow local authorities to adopt resolutions in relation to the duration of special exemption orders in their areas. The courts shall have regard to such resolutions when granting special exemption orders. Finally, there is now a prohibition on the provision of entertainment during the thirty minutes' drinking-up time.

Admission and Service

In this regard, amendments of the Intoxicating Liquor Act 1988 were made to include a prohibition on supply of intoxicating liquor to under 18s, and consumption by under 18s only with the explicit consent of a parent or guardian. Licensees are to have discretion to exclude under 18s from bars of licensed premises at any time but will be required to exclude them after 9.00 p.m. Moreover, a child (under fifteen) may be excluded from a bar if it appears to the licensee that the duration of the child's presence in the bar could reasonably be regarded as injurious to the health, safety or welfare of the child. These requirements are particularly sensitive for tourism, given that many tourists considering Ireland may decide not to visit, as they cannot bring their child under fifteen years of age to a bar with them on holidays, as they can in many destinations. There is also a new requirement whereby persons under twenty-one, other than those accompanied by a parent or guardian, must carry an age document in the bar of the licensed premises. This may also cause problems for tourists under the age of twenty-one.

---

9 p.m. bar limit for children silly, say hoteliers

Hoteliers have urged the government to ease the 'silly and unsociable' restriction on the hours people aged under eighteen can legally be present in hotel bars.

Irish Hotels Federation chief executive John Power said the current provisions of the 2003 Intoxicating Liquor Act were anti-family and were damaging Ireland's attractiveness as a tourist destination.

He said a relaxation of the hours during which children were permitted to be in bars, introduced by Minister for Justice Michael McDowell last October, did not go far enough.

Mr McDowell extended until 10 p.m. in the summer months the time which those aged under eighteen must vacate a licensed premises. For the remainder of the year, a 9 p.m. time limit applies.

Mr Power, in Cork yesterday on the eve of the hotels federation's annual conference, said it was 'ridiculous' that families staying in a hotel could not have a meal in the bar area after 9 p.m., where they might also enjoy musical entertainment.

He said the law should be amended to allow children in the company of a parent or guardian to participate in food and entertainment in the bar until at least 10.30 p.m. all year round.

'At the moment we have to ask families to leave the bar area after 9 p.m. It is unsociable and silly, given that these children are under parental supervision,' he added.

'Families go away to spend time together. This law runs entirely contrary to that.'

Mr Power said it was estimated that more than 2 million family holidaymakers visited Ireland each year and these were negatively affected by the legislation.

He also claimed it was 'incredulous' that government departments did not seem to work in uniformity on national policy, with the Department of Tourism promoting Ireland to family holidaymakers and the Department of Justice creating laws 'to discourage family holidays'.

Source: Dooley, C., '9 p.m. bar limit for children silly, say hoteliers', *The Irish Times*, 7 March 2005.

Equality Structures and Amendments to Equal Status Act 2000

The Act provides for a transfer of jurisdiction in certain cases of alleged discrimination in licensed premises from the Equality Tribunal to the District Court. There is also an amendment of the Equal Status Act 2000, where the discretion of licensees to exclude children and persons under eighteen years from the bar of licensed premises is safeguarded by law. Further, licensees are to be permitted to set a minimum age for the sale and consumption of intoxicating liquor at a level above the statutory minimum of eighteen provided the policy is publicly displayed and operated in good faith.

Other Provisions

The Act prohibits consumption of intoxicating liquor (sold for consumption off the premises) in the vicinity of a licensed premises or in an off-license. The Act specifies particulars to be affixed to any container in which intoxicating liquor is sold for consumption off the premises which enable the identity of the licensee and the licensed premises concerned to be identified, in order to enforce this section of the Act.

The concept of a 'happy hour' (lower-price sales of alcohol during a limited period on any day) will be prohibited. This is in contrast with many of Ireland's competing tourism destinations. The reasoning behind this last provision is to prohibit or restrict licensees from engaging in promotional practices that are intended or likely to encourage persons to consume alcohol to an excessive extent.

The 2003 legislation has been further enhanced and updated by the Intoxicating Liquor (Codification) Bill 2005 (this Bill was passed and is now the Intoxicating Liquor Act 2005), and the major points of this are presented in the Minister for Justice's speech when launching the Bill.

Minister's statement at launch of Intoxicating Liquor (Codification) Bill, 15 April 2005

I am glad to have this opportunity to announce that the government has approved my proposals for a comprehensive codification of our liquor licensing laws. These proposals are set out in the General Scheme of the Intoxicating Liquor Bill 2005 which I am publishing today and on which I am seeking the views of the public and interested parties.

The main purpose of the proposed Bill is to streamline and modernise our liquor licensing laws. This will involve repealing the Licensing Acts 1833 to 2004 and replacing them with updated provisions more suited to modern conditions. **The existing stock of over 600 licensing provisions that are currently spread across about 100 statutes will be repealed and replaced by this Act.** That in itself will represent a significant contribution to the process of regulatory reform to which this government has committed itself.

As regards the reforms contained in the Bill, I want to state that they are underpinned by the following policy considerations:

- Encouraging the consumption of food with intoxicating liquor. I want to repeat what I have said many times on this subject: we need a cultural shift in this country in our approach to alcohol consumption, a shift towards moderate social consumption and away from the excessive consumption patterns and binge drinking that so often results in alcohol-related harm.
- Countering the trend towards 'super pubs' by encouraging a more rational spatial strategy involving the development of smaller café-bar outlets serving local areas and their communities.
- Promoting coherence between the planning and licensing codes and strengthening the role of local authorities in licensing matters.

The Bill contains a broad range of reform proposals and the details are set out in an information note that I have already circulated. I want to draw attention to the following reforms in particular:

- Proposed creation of a new café-bar licence.
- A new streamlined District Court procedure for all retail liquor licences.
- A new requirement that proof of planning permission and compliance with both planning conditions and fire safety standards be presented to the District Court with all applications.
- A new provision whereby the applicant's knowledge of the licensing laws may also be taken into account by the court in deciding whether or not to grant a certificate.
- A new nightclub permit for nightclub operators that would replace

special exemption orders to be granted by the District Court.
- New theatre licence provisions which will require application to the District Court for a certificate and which also contain new arrangements for opening hours.
- Replacement of five types of manufacturer's licence with a single producer licence.
- Replacement of four types of wholesaler's licence with a single wholesale licence.

As regards the creation of a café-bar licence, this was a key recommendation in the Final Report of the Commission on Liquor Licensing. That Commission was a broadly representative body which included representatives of the licensed trade and hospitality sector and which was ably chaired by Mr Gordon Holmes. It concluded that the historically restrictive nature of the licensing laws had resulted in the development of 'super pubs' which, while generally well managed and catering for an important segment of the market, tended to create noise and nuisance for local residents and made compliance with and enforcement of the licensing laws more difficult for licensees and the gardaí alike. The Commission also considered that large numbers of people emerging from such premises at closing time increased the risk of public disorder.

The Commission considered that Continental-style café-bars – which would be required, as a condition of the licence, to provide food as well as alcoholic and non-alcoholic beverages – could provide an atmosphere and ambience that encouraged moderate social consumption of alcohol. The government has agreed with my proposal to launch a public consultation process and I would value the responses of interested parties and, in particular, the views of the general public in relation to the Commission's proposal.

With a view to ensuring that café-bar licences would not lead to abuses or contribute to alcohol-related harm, the following safeguards would apply:
- The licence would be available only for premises of less than 130 square metres.
- It would not be available for premises engaged in 'take away' sales of food.
- Hot meals and non-alcoholic beverages would be provided for consumption on the premises during opening hours.
- The sale of alcohol for consumption off the premises would not be permitted.
- Exemption orders for extended opening hours would not be allowed.

Moreover, in order to ensure responsiveness to local circumstances and enhance local government, it is envisaged that local authorities could, by adopting a resolution, determine that café-bar licences would not be granted in the whole or a specified part of their areas.

In bringing forward proposals to reform the licensing laws, I am conscious of public concerns in relation to alcohol-related harm in our society. For this reason, the proposed Bill contains safeguards that are intended to combat such harm. These include:

- Extending the jurisdiction of the courts to all retail licences and nightclub permits and giving specified notice parties and the public the right to object to the grant of a licence or permit.
- Streamlining the system for renewing licences and clarifying the right of members of the public to object to such renewal on stated grounds.
- Strengthening provisions designed to combat sales to under-age persons by, for example, requiring all off-licences to have written policies and control procedures.
- Creating a new offence of being in possession of a forged garda age card.
- Increasing the levels of penalties and sanctions, including a proposal that all temporary closure orders should involve closure for a minimum of two days.

The Bill does not propose any significant changes to existing opening hours. Certain changes which were recommended by the Commission on Liquor Licensing were introduced in the Intoxicating Liquor Act 2003, e.g. earlier closing on Thursday night, and no significant changes are proposed in this Bill. A number of relatively minor adjustments are included, relating mainly to the longer opening hours permitted under general exemption orders and exemptions for special events. In all cases the reforms are intended to clarify the law with a view to improving compliance and facilitating enforcement by the gardaí.

The proposed Bill prohibits drunkenness and disorderly conduct in licensed premises as well as the supply of intoxicating liquor to, and consumption by, under 18s in licensed premises. The new licensing arrangements set out in the Bill will allow the gardaí to object to applications for retail licences, nightclub permits, special exemption orders and club registrations on the grounds of an undue risk of public nuisance or a threat to public order or safety. In addition, the gardaí will be able to apply to the District Court to have a nightclub permit revoked on those grounds.

The licensing provisions will continue to be complemented and supported by public order legislation. The gardaí already have extensive powers under the Public Order Acts of 1994 and 2003 to deal with incidents of intoxication or disorderly conduct in public places. The 2003 Act makes provision for both exclusion and closure orders arising from such incidents.

It goes without saying that reform of licensing law is a complex process. This arises from the need to take account of a broad range of public policy objectives while at the same time seeking to accommodate the demands of a range of interested parties and the general public.

Liquor licensing law has, for example, a role to play in contributing towards the attainment of the following public policy objectives:

- Combating alcohol-related harm and promoting public health.
- Protecting vulnerable groups, especially young people.
- Maintaining public order.

- Ensuring coherence with spatial planning and development objectives.
- Taking account of the needs of local residents and others likely to be adversely affected by decisions concerning the siting of licensed premises.
- Accommodating the legitimate needs of the tourism and leisure sectors.
- Improving market access to the licensed trade in order to ensure fair competition.
- Protecting consumers against anti-competitive practices and behaviour.

In the proposed Bill, I am seeking to establish an appropriate balance between these at times competing policy objectives. My primary purpose is to modernise and streamline licensing law in order to make it more accessible and user friendly for the licensed trade, the courts and members of the public alike; to reduce alcohol-related harm, especially among young people; and to improve compliance with licensing law by licensees and its enforcement by the gardaí.

This is obviously a policy area where views differ and where sincerely held beliefs diverge greatly. I believe there is a need for rational debate and for constructive dialogue on how best to address the problems of alcohol-related harm in this society. I believe that we can forge a broad measure of consensus on how the liquor licensing laws can contribute to that process and that is why I have decided to invite submissions from interested parties and the general public on the Bill.

AIR PASSENGERS' RIGHTS

The EU has introduced strict rules for its airlines to combat several practices which result in travel frustrations to many passengers. These came into force on 17 February 2005 throughout the EU. The main provisions are presented below.

Denied Boarding and Cancellation

If a passenger turns up on time for a flight and is denied boarding or the flight is cancelled, the airline must offer the passenger financial compensation and assistance. This applies to any flight including charters from any EU airport, as well as flights from any airport outside the EU to any EU airport (if operated by an EU airline).

When there are too many passengers for the number of seats available, the airline must first ask for volunteers to give up their seats in return for agreed benefits. These must include the choice of either refund of the ticket (with a free flight back to the initial point of departure, when relevant) or alternative transport to the final destination.

Those who do not volunteer but are still denied boarding must be paid compensation of varying amounts, depending on the distance of the flight:

- €250 compensation for flights of less than 1,500 kilometres.
- €400 compensation for flights within the EU, and for other flights between 1,500 kilometres and 3,500 kilometres.
- €600 for flights over 3,500 kilometres outside the EU.

The above compensation rates may be halved if the delays are less than two, three or four hours, respectively, for each of the three categories. Further, the airline is obliged to give passengers a full refund and to repatriate them to their initial point of departure when relevant, or provide alternative travel to the final destination. Meals, refreshments, communication facilities and accommodation (as well as transfer to accommodation) must also be provided when necessary.

The same rights and levels of compensation apply if a flight is cancelled and the passengers are not informed at least two weeks prior to the date, unless a similar routing is offered with little disruption in terms of time. Cancellations which delay a passenger for more than five hours entitle the passenger to a full reimbursement.

Any refunds offered must be in the form of cash, bank transfer or cheque and must be paid within seven days. Airlines are permitted to offer travel vouchers, but the passenger is not obliged to accept these.

Long Delays

Similar to the rules for denied boarding and cancellations, if a passenger turns up on time for a flight and the flight is delayed, the airline must offer the passenger certain assistance. Again, this applies to any flight including charters from any EU airport, as well as flights from any airport outside the EU to any EU airport (if operated by an EU airline). Passengers are entitled to meals, refreshments and communication facilities, and accommodation (as well as transfer to accommodation) must also be provided when necessary. This is an entitlement when the delay is as follows:

- Two hours' delay or more for flights up to 1,500 kilometres.
- Three hours' delay or more for flights within the EU and for other flights between 1,500 kilometres and 3,500 kilometres.
- Four hours' delay or more for flights over 3,500 kilometres outside the EU.

For any delays over five hours, the passenger is entitled to a full refund with a free ticket back to the passenger's initial point of departure when relevant.

Further rights are enshrined in the legislation for delays caused by EU airlines in non-EU airports, as well as for baggage damage or loss, and even death and injury. In the past, charter flights were exempt from such passenger rights. However, this legislation applies to both scheduled and charter flights.

Given the amount of code sharing and co-operation between airline alliances around the world, it is often the case that a passenger books with one airline but the route is operated by another. In such a case, a passenger has the right to claim any of these rights from the airline with which they have a contract, or from the airline actually operating the flight if they are different.

New rights for air passengers in the whole EU
Loyola de Palacio, European Commission vice-president in charge of transport and energy, welcomed the definitive adoption by the Council and the European Parliament of the proposal of regulation to protect the rights of air passengers when facing denied boarding, cancellation of their flight or a long delay. 'The passengers' rights action is one of the major initiatives of this Commission in order to put the citizens at the heart of EU policies,' she

said. 'Too many times, air passengers are victims of practices which deserve that they receive a fair treatment and proper compensation: henceforth, they will all benefit from new strengthened rights,' she added. The regulation should enter into force in the coming weeks and new rights will apply by 2005. Loyola de Palacio concluded: 'As we did in the past, the European Commission will ensure that the passengers are informed of their new rights and proper information will be given in all airports.'

Roughly a quarter of a million air passengers each year get a bad surprise at EU airports when checking in for their flight. They have bought a ticket and reserved a place. They are then told by the operator that their flight has been overbooked and they have to take a later one. Denied boarding causes passengers great inconvenience and loss of time. Equally bad surprises are cancellations without warning and delays that leave passengers stranded for hours at an airport.

The new regulation will replace the existing one dating from 1991. This has severe limitations as it does not effectively deter airlines from denying boarding or cover cancellations for commercial reasons or long delays. Nor does it apply to non-scheduled flights, chartered by tour operators.

This will change radically with the new regulation, which will give passengers effective, all-round protection once it comes into effect in around one year's time.

Source: EU press release, Brussels, 26 January 2004.

Air passenger rights in the European Union
Under EU and Irish law, all travellers have certain rights when travelling by air with European airlines. All European airlines, travel agents, tour operators and all other businesses involved in providing air transport services must observe your rights. These rights relate to issues such as your right to receive accurate information about flights and reservations, obligations of travel agents, liability in the event of loss of baggage or accidents, compensation for overbooked flights, etc.

Information about flights and reserving your ticket
You have the right to neutral and accurate information when enquiring about or booking a flight through a travel agent. In other words, your travel agent must supply you with objective information, i.e. information that does not favour one airline over another or selective information about availability, when you enquire about flights and bookings from its computerised reservation system until you suggest a preference or give the travel agent an option. This means your travel agent is obliged to supply information to you about all the options available for a journey in the following order:
- Non-stop flights, i.e. flights that operate directly from one point to your destination.
- Flights with intermediate stops (flights that operate with a stopover and then proceed to destination).

- Connecting flights, i.e. a flight between two points where you must get on another flight to continue your journey.
- All the fares available from various airlines.

Your travel agent must give you access to the information that is shown up by the computer system if you request this, either by allowing you to see the screen or by printing out this information for you. In turn, airlines are obliged to provide all information to the computerised system so that this information is available to your travel agent and to you. If you book your ticket with the airline, your travel agent must pass on all information available in the computer system about:

- The airline that will provide the service (if this is different from the airline mentioned on your ticket).
- Changes of aircraft that may occur during your journey.
- Stops en route during your journey.
- Transfers between airports that may occur during your journey.

Check-in and boarding
If you have a valid ticket and have confirmed your reservation and presented yourself at check-in at the airport within the time specified by the airline but you are not allowed to board the aircraft because the flight is overbooked, you are entitled to compensation under EU law.

Air travel as part of a package holiday
If you are travelling by air as part of a package tour or holiday purchased in Europe, you must receive clear, accurate and precise information from the organiser about your trip.

Data protection
Passengers reserving air tickets in Europe have the right to know about any personal details held or stored about them on computer reservation systems, what this information is to be used for and who is in control of this information. When your travel agent is making a reservation on your behalf using a computer system, he or she must tell you why the information is necessary, how long this information is being stored for and the name of the computer operator and how to contact this organisation. Anyone who requests this information must be given free access to information that is being stored about him or her on the computer reservation system. The Data Protection Commission in Ireland is in place to uphold your rights to information held about you on computer.

Liability in the event of an accident
In the event of an air accident, there is no financial limit on the liability of an EU airline for damages sustained by you in the event of death, wounding or any other bodily injury. Passengers that are travelling with an EU airline will receive full compensation in the case of an accident, regardless of where

it happens, i.e. within or outside the EU, and will receive up-front payments if necessary to help with any immediate economic hardship.

The EU airline will without delay and in any event, not later than fifteen days after the person entitled to compensation has been identified, make an advance payment to meet immediate economic needs in line with the hardship suffered as a result of the accident. If someone dies, the advance payment shall not be less than 15,000 SDR (approx. €21,600) per passenger. It is important to note that an advance payment **shall not constitute recognition of liability** and may be offset against any subsequent sums that are paid on the basis of EU air carrier liability. Generally, these payments are not returnable. To help resolve smaller claims, when responding to damages claims by passengers up to a level of 100,000 SDR (approx. €144,000), EU airlines can only be exonerated from their liability if the damage was caused by, or contributed to by, the negligence of the injured or deceased passenger.

Enforcing your air passenger rights
The above rights have been set down either directly in EU law or in Irish law that has been introduced to bring EU legislation into effect. Airlines, travel agents, tour operators and all other businesses involved in providing air transport services must observe them. You should be aware of your rights and be prepared to defend them.

If you feel your rights have not been respected and you have not received the level of treatment or compensation to which you are entitled, you should contact the Aviation Regulation Division at the Department of Transport or the Office of the Director of Consumer Affairs and inform them about it. You can also contact the Directorate-General for Transport and Energy of the European Commission.

Where to apply
All travel agents and tour operators in Ireland are required to be state bonded, which means that if your travel agent or tour operator collapses or goes out of business, your money and your holiday bookings are protected. If your holiday commences in the United Kingdom (including Northern Ireland) and is sold by an operator there through an Irish retailer, you should check with the retailer that there is security in place in the event of insolvency. Where booking is made directly with a tour operator or agent in the United Kingdom (including Northern Ireland), the consumer should check that its security covers them.

Source: www.oasis.gov.ie.

THE PUBLIC HEALTH (TOBACCO) ACT 2002

It is illegal to smoke tobacco in any enclosed workplace in the Republic of Ireland since 29 March 2004, according to the Public Health (Tobacco) Act 2002. The law was introduced to protect all workers from the harmful effect of tobacco smoke. This law has a major impact for choosing Ireland as a tourist destination. Given the climate of Ireland, a tourist who smokes may not wish to stand outside in the winter cold and rain to enjoy their habit when they can do so from the comfort of a bar or restaurant in many other destinations. However, we do see a move towards smoking bans in public places in other countries (California and New York in the US and Northern Ireland and Britain to some degree as well). There are certain exceptions to the smoking ban rule, including prisons and detention centres, nursing homes, hospices, psychiatric institutions, religious order homes, maternity homes, third-level education residential facilities and bedrooms in hotels, guesthouses and B&Bs. Although these workplaces are excluded from the legislation, the management must have due consideration to the health and well-being of their staff. Further, although they are not obliged to forbid smoking, they have the right to do so if they so wish under the legislation.

A fine of up to €3,000 may be imposed upon anyone who is found to be in breach of the ban, and the legislation is part of a wider strategy (including the abolition of ten packs of cigarettes) to discourage the 25 per cent of all Irish people who smoke from doing so.

EQUALITY LEGISLATION

The Employment Equality Act 1998 and the Equal Status Act 2000 (both amended by the Equality Act 2004) rule out any and all discrimination on the following nine grounds:

* Gender.
* Marital status.
* Age.
* Disability.
* Race, colour, nationality, ethnic or national origins.
* Religion.
* Sexual orientation.
* Family status.
* Membership of the Travelling community.

A person may not discriminate under any of the nine grounds in the provision of goods and services, accommodation, disposal of premises or education. The legislation also rules out discrimination in all aspects of employment, including dismissal, equal pay, harassment, sexual harassment, working conditions, promotion and access to employment. Harassment on the basis of any of the nine grounds is also forbidden by law. Entertainment establishments such as pubs and nightclubs that discriminate face the very real possibility of losing their license, while employers found guilty of breaching the legislation are open to severe punishment.

Under the Equal Status Act, discrimination occurs when a person is treated less favourably, was in the past, or is likely to be, on the basis of one of the nine grounds. The law also covers discrimination by association. For example, if you are not a Traveller but are discriminated against because you are with a Traveller, the law covers you.

There are certain exemptions in the Act when discrimination is allowed. An example which is particularly relevant to the accommodation sector is refusing service if the proprietor of a business believes there to be reasonable grounds of substantial risk of damage to property or criminal or disorderly conduct. Another example of permitted discrimination is when special rates for goods and services are offered for couples, people with children, people of a certain age, e.g. youth discount, OAP discounts, as well as people with disabilities, often referred to as positive discrimination.

REVISION QUESTIONS

1. What are the key provisions of the following?
   (a) Hotel Proprietors' Act.
   (b) Package Holidays Act.
   (c) Intoxicating Liquors Act.
   (d) EU air passenger rights.
   (e) Smoking ban.
   (f) Equality legislation.
2. How does each of the above provisions impact on (a) domestic tourism and (b) international tourism to Ireland?
3. How does each of the above provisions impact on foreign tourists' impression of Ireland?
4. Why is an understanding of equality legislation important in tourism?
5. How does the smoking ban impact on Ireland's competitive position?

ESSAY QUESTIONS

1. 'In order to operate effectively in a tourism enterprise, an understanding of the legal framework within which an organisation must operate is essential.' Discuss.
2. The EU protects its consumers from practices by large organisations that it deems unfavourable. Give an example of EU legislation protecting consumers in terms of travel and highlight how it impacts on the operation of the organisations in question.
3. The Hotel Proprietors' Act 1963 confers a duty on the proprietor of a hotel to receive all comers unless he has 'reasonable grounds for refusal'. What might constitute 'reasonable grounds' and what effect does the Equal Status Act 2000 have on the conferred duty above?
4. Outline in which situations one would be regarded as an 'organiser' under the Package Holidays Act 1995.

TASKS

Divide the class into two roughly equal groups. Each group should be given ten to fifteen minutes to develop opposing points on the following statements, followed by a forty to forty-five minute debate.

Statement: The Irish government does not do as much as the EU to protect travellers and tourists as consumers.

Statement: The smoking ban is a good thing for Irish tourism.

Statement: Travellers and tourists do not know their rights.

ASSIGNMENTS

1. You are a legal advisor to firms in the travel business. A tour operator has approached you seeking advice in terms of its obligations under the Package Holidays Act 1995. Write a report to advise your client.
2. You are required to research cases of how Irish businesses have been impacted by equality legislation and have lost cases. Pay particular attention to the outcomes of such cases and give recommendations of how negative situations can be avoided in future.

FURTHER INFORMATION SOURCES: EU INFORMATION AND VIDEO CLIPS ONLINE

See
http://ec.europa.eu/transport/air/rules/rights/doc/2005_01_19_apr_poster_en.pdf
for the poster of passenger rights which must be displayed at ports.

See EU video explaining air passenger rights (10 minutes 38 seconds) at
http://ec.europa.eu/dgs/energy_transport/publication/videos_en.htm#passengers_rights.

See
http://ec.europa.eu/transport/air/rules/rights/doc/commitment_airlines_en.pdf
for Airline Passenger Service Commitment on Air Passenger Service, developed by the EU in consultation with the airlines.

See
http://ec.europa.eu/transport/air/rules/rights/doc/commitment_airports_en.pdf
for Airport Voluntary Commitment on Air Passenger Service, developed by the EU in consultation with airports.

Appendix A

Glossary of Terms and Abbreviations

INTRODUCTION

Appendix A presents a glossary of tourism terms and abbreviations as used throughout the book.

à la carte **menu**: Various items prices individually.

Act: A piece of legislation which has been approved by Parliament.

ADS: Approved Destination Status.

ARI: Aer Rianta International.

arrivals: Tourists coming to a destination.

associate meeting: People with a common interest or who belong to a common organisation meeting to exchange ideas and information.

AVE: Alta Velocidad Española, or Spanish High Speed, although '*ave*' also means 'bird' in Spanish.

B&B: Bed and breakfast.

B2B: Business to business.

B2C: Business to customer.

BA: British Airways.

bandwidth: Speed and amount of information that can be downloaded and uploaded.

basic occupancy rate: Percentage of rooms used on any given night.

bed nights: Number of rooms available in a particular timeframe, e.g. 100 rooms x 365 nights in a year = 36,500 bed nights in a year for a 100-room hotel.

bed occupancy rate: Number of guests physically accommodated as a percentage of maximum capacity.

bed stock: Number of rooms available in a hotel/city.

BF: Bord Fáilte.

Bill: A proposed piece of legislation which has yet to be approved by Parliament.

BMW region: Borders, Midlands and West region of Ireland.

BOAC: British Overseas Airways Corporation, formed by the merger of Imperial Airways and British Airways Ltd. It became known as British Airways in 1974 following a merger with British European Airways.

budget hotel: Limited service but usually comfortable lodging accommodation.

bumping: Also known as **involuntary denied boarding** – occurs when a passenger has a paid and confirmed flight ticket, but is not permitted to travel due to the flight being oversold.

business meeting: Businesspeople coming together to do business (nationally or internationally). Sometimes known as conferences or conventions. Can be further divided between corporate meetings and associate meetings.

Business Tourism Forum: Fáilte Ireland's forum for discussion and development of business tourism in Ireland.

CAA: Cork Airport Authority.

CarMaster: Galileo's car hire reservation service.

carrier receipts: Payments to a transport carrier of a particular country.

carrier: A form of transport, e.g. airline.

categorisation: Refers to separation of accommodation by type.

CERT: The Council for Education, Recruitment and Training.

CIE: Córas Iompair Éireann – the Irish Transport Network.

classification: Physical features of accommodation, e.g. Georgian townhouse.

code-sharing: One aircraft operating under two flight codes, jointly run by two individual carriers working together.

conference: A business meeting with several delegates.

congress: An international conference; a conference whose delegates come from different parts of the world to converge on one location for their meeting.

convention: A business meeting with several delegates.

corporate meeting: The aim of attending is to do business with someone else.

CRS: Central reservations systems.

CRS: Country of Residence Survey.

CSO: Central Statistics Office.

DAA: Dublin Airport Authority.

Dáil: For the purposes of this book, a Dáil is defined as a session of Irish government between two general elections, lasting a maximum of five years.

DAST: Department of Arts, Sport and Tourism.

DEHLG: Department of the Environment, Heritage and Local Government.

destination management companies: Manage corporate meetings.

Deutsche Bundesbahn: German Federal Railways.

Directive: A piece of EU legislation which must be incorporated into the national law of each of the member states of the EU.

disintermediation: Cutting out the intermediary from the distribution channel.

domestic tourism: Residents of a given country travelling within that country.

e-commerce: Conducting business on the internet.

ECTAA: European Confederation of Travel Agents' Associations.

e-tailer: An online retailer.

exhibition: Large events offering various products and services for display, and most for sale.

extranet: Using standard internet technology to provide a specific service to a closed group of users, i.e. not public like the internet.

F&B: Food and beverage.
FI: Fáilte Ireland.
fly-drive concept: Flying into an airport, picking up a hired car and dropping it back at that or another airport before departure.
full board: Room and breakfast as well as lunch and dinner.

GDP: Gross domestic product.
GDS: Global distribution systems.
GNP: Gross national product.
grading: Quality rating assigned by reputable agency.
ground handling agents: Organise destination arrangements on land for group tours as well as individuals; act as a local representative.

half board: Room and breakfast with either lunch or dinner.
holidaymakers: Visitors who state that their primary purpose for visiting a destination was a holiday.
hotel chain/consortia: Group of hotels that co-operate in key functional areas, e.g. marketing and distribution.
hotel: A lodging accommodation offering rooms for hire for leisure or business; of varying quality depending on grading.
hotelier: Hotel manager or management company running a hotel.

IATA: International Air Transport Association.
ICE: InterCity Express rail service.
ICT: Information and communication technology.
IHF: Irish Hotels Federation.
inbound tourism: Non-residents received by a destination country from the point of view of that destination.
incentive travel: Travel as a reward for staff, usually sales staff upon reaching sales targets. An alternative to financial rewards.
interlining: The airline has the ability to book a customer's baggage ahead onto another flight and/or another airline and (in most cases) provide the customer with an onward connection boarding card and confirmed seat number.
invisible export: Foreign tourist coming to a destination, e.g. Ireland, buying local products and services.
invisible import: Local tourist, e.g. Irish person, spending home-earned currency, e.g. euro, on foreign goods and services in a destination abroad.
IOSA: IATA's Operational Safety Audit.
ITA: Irish Tourism Association (1893–39).
ITAA: Irish Travel Agents' Association.
ITAS: Irish Tourist Assistance Service.
ITB: Irish Tourist Board (1939–52).
ITIC: Irish Tourist Industry Confederation.

ITOA: Irish Tour Operators' Association.
IUCN: International Union for the Conservation of Nature.

KTX: Korea Train Express.

LCC: Low-cost carriers.
load factor: A measure of how many seats are filled by an airline as a percentage of total seats available.
LVA: Licenced Vintners Association.

marketspace: The online marketplace.
MICE: Meetings, incentive, conferences, exhibitions.
motel: Motor hotel, an American budget hotel offering.

NCC: National Conference Centre.
NHA: Natural Heritage Areas.
NITB: Northern Ireland Tourist Board.
NPWS: The National Parks and Wildlife Service.
NRA: National Roads Authority.
NTDA: National Tourism Development Authority.
NTO: National Tourism Organisation.

OPW: Office of Public Works.
outbound tourism: Residents travelling to another country from the point of view of the country of origin.

package tour/holiday: A travel offering including any two of transport, accommodation and any third element not ancillary to transport or accommodation.
Pan Am: Pan American World Airways, the main airline of the US from the 1930s until its collapse in 1991.
pax: Passengers.
principals: Travel product providers/producers, e.g. airlines, car hire companies, hotels.
professional conference organisers: Manage all aspects of conferences and congresses.

QBC: Quality bus corridor.

rack rate: Full published rate, not discounted.
revenue occupancy: Total revenue on one particular night in comparison to maximum revenue (full occupancy at rack rate).
RoomMaster: Galileo's hotel reservation service.
RTA/RTO: Regional Tourism Association/Organisation.

SAA: Shannon Airport Authority.
SABRE: Semi Automated Business Research Environment.
SAC: Special Areas of Conservation.
SIPTU: Services, Industrial, Professional and Technical Union.
SNCF: French Railways.
SOT: Survey of Overseas Travellers.
SPA: Special Protection Areas.
ST-EP: Sustainable Tourism – Eliminating Poverty.

table d'hôte menu: Set menu.
TBI: Tourism Brand Ireland.
TGV: Train à grande vitesse, French for 'high-speed train'.
TIL: Tourism Ireland Ltd.
TIO: Tourist information office.
tour operator: Traditionally the wholesaler of the travel industry.
tourism destination: Country or region where a tourist travels to.
tourism-generating country/region: Country or region where the tourist comes from.
trade fair: Large events offering various products and services for display, and most for sale.
travel agent: (As an organisation) traditionally the retailer of the travel industry; (as an individual) a person working in a travel retail outlet advising and reserving travel products for their customers.
travel consultant: An individual working in a travel retail outlet advising and reserving travel products for their customers; usually possesses superior product knowledge, perhaps on specific regions or destinations.
Travelocity: Online travel e-tailer, owned by SABRE.
TVSS: Tourist Victim Support Service, now the ITAS – Irish Tourist Assistance Service.
TWA: Trans World Airlines, now part of American Airlines (the world's largest airline in terms of passenger numbers and second only to KLM-Air France in terms of total operating revenue).

UFTA: Universal Federation of Travel Agents Associations.
UIA: Union of International Associations.
UNWTO: United National World Tourism Organization.

VAS: Visitor Attractions Survey.
VFR: Visiting friends and relatives.

Worldspan Car Select: Worldspan's car reservation service.
Worldspan Hotels Select: Worldspan's hotel reservation service.
WTO: See UNWTO.

Appendix B
Tourism Web Resources

INTRODUCTION

Appendix B provides a detailed list of internet resources referenced in the book and more websites for further research and reading in the areas covered in the book, as well as other relevant areas. These resources are a vital companion to the reader, as they serve to keep the material in the book topical. The resources provide up-to-date information, provided by the relevant organisations and web hosts.

In order to avoid duplication, organisations that appear in Appendix C (the list of contact details of several organisations for further research) will not appear in this appendix. The web addresses of these organisations appear in the contact details directory of Appendix C, along with e-mail and postal addresses and telephone and fax numbers.

THE IRISH GOVERNMENT

The Irish government, all departments and agencies www.irlgov.ie
Department of Arts, Sport and Tourism www.arts-sport-tourism.gov.ie/
Department of Transport www.transport.ie
Department of the Environment, Heritage and Local Government www.environ.ie

WEBSITES OF IRISH TOURISM AGENCIES

Fáilte Ireland corporate information www.failteireland.ie
Fáilte Ireland tourist information www.ireland.ie
Tourism Ireland corporate informationn www.tourismireland.com/corporate
Tourism Ireland tourist information www.discoverireland.com

PRESS RELEASES AND SPEECHES ON TOURISM

For a full and up-to-date list of all of the Minister's speeches
and press releases, see www.arts-sport-tourism.gov.ie/

DEPARTMENT OF ARTS, SPORT AND TOURISM PUBICATIONS ARCHIVE

www.dast.gov.ie/publications/list_publications.html

DÁIL DEBATES AND PARLIAMENTARY QUESTIONS ON TOURISM

The following links contain the text of parliamentary questions and debates in the area of tourism. Sometimes these take place in the middle of discussion of other topics dealt with during Dáil business. If the tourism-specific discussion is not immediately apparent on the following links, it is recommended that the reader perform a search for the keyword 'tourism' to find the relevant discussion on the topic.

22 October 2002	www.gov.ie/debates-02/22Oct/Sect2.htm
20 November 2002	www.gov.ie/debates-02/20Nov/Sect2.htm
30 January 2003	www.gov.ie/debates-03/30Jan/Sect3.htm
26 February 2003	www.gov.ie/debates-03/26Feb/Sect3.htm
16 April 2003	www.gov.ie/debates-03/16Apr/Sect3.htm
12 June 2003	www.gov.ie/debates-03/12Jun/Sect3.htm
8 October 2003	www.gov.ie/debates-03/8Oct/sect2.htm#11
18 November 2003	www.gov.ie/debates-03/18nov/sect1.htm#4
18 December 2003	www.gov.ie/debates-03/18dec/sect3.htm#14

25 February 2004
       http://debates.oireachtas.ie/ddebate.aspx?f=dal20040225.xml&ex=997#n997
6 April 2004
   http://debates.oireachtas.ie/DDebate.aspx?F=DAL20040406.xml&Ex=148#N148
25 May 2004
       http://debates.oireachtas.ie/ddebate.aspx?f=dal20040525.xml&ex=123#n123
1 July 2004
       http://debates.oireachtas.ie/ddebate.aspx?f=dal20040701.xml&ex=1093#n1093
20 October 2004
               http://debates.oireachtas.ie/ddebate.aspx?f=dal20041020.xml&page=
               1&ex=h12-1#h12-1
1 December 2004
http://debates.oireachtas.ie/DDebate.aspx?F=DAL20041201.xml&Node=H10#H10
17 February 2005
http://debates.oireachtas.ie/ddebate.aspx?f=dal20050217.xml&page=1&ex=h9#h9
22 March 2005
   http://debates.oireachtas.ie/DDebate.aspx?F=DAL20050322.xml&Node=H3#H3
10 May 2005
           http://debates.oireachtas.ie/DDebate.aspx?F=DAL20050510.xml&Dail=
           29&Ex=All&Page=1
16 June 2005
http://debates.oireachtas.ie/ddebate.aspx?f=dal20050616.xml&node=h10-1#h10-1
26 January 2006
http://debates.oireachtas.ie/DDebate.aspx?F=DAL20060126.xml&Node=H11#H11
1 March 2006
http://debates.oireachtas.ie/DDebate.aspx?F=DAL20060301.xml&Node=H10#H10
25 April 2006
   http://debates.oireachtas.ie/DDebate.aspx?F=DAL20060425.xml&Node=H4#H4

TOURISM POLICY REVIEW

www.tourismreview.ie

NORTHERN IRELAND REGIONAL TOURISM

www.coastofdown.com
www.causewaycoastandglens.com
www.derryvisitor.com
www.discovernorthernireland.com
www.ni-tourism.com
www.kingdomsofdown.com
www.fermanaghlakelands.com
www.gotobelfast.com

WEBSITE OF THE UN WORLD TOURISM ORGANIZATION

www.unwto.org

NEWSPAPER WEBSITES AND GENERAL RESEARCH

	www.sbpost.ie
	www.ireland.com
	www.examiner.ie
	www.unison.ie
	www.economist.com
	www.mintel.com
Central Statistics Office	www.cso.ie
Free online encylopaedia	www.wikipedia.org

TRAVEL INDUSTRY REPRESENTATIVE BODIES

ITOA	www.itoa-ireland.com
ECTAA	www.ectaa.org
ITAA	www.itaa.ie
ITAA Memorandum of Association	www.itaa.ie/memorandum.pdf
ITAA Articles of Association	www.itaa.ie/articlesofassociation.pdf
IATA	www.iata.org
Full history of the IATA	www.iata.org/about/history.htm
IATA current airline membership	www.iata.org/membership/airline_members.htm
IATA Simplifying the Business Initiative	www.iata.org/whatwedo/simplibiz/
IATA's Operational Safety Audit (IOSA)	www.iata.org/ps/services/iosa/index.htm
IATA's environmental strategies	www.iata.org/whatwedo/environment/index.htm

SAMPLE ONLINE INTERMEDIARIES

www.expedia.com
www.lastminute.com

www.laterooms.com
www.e-bookers.com
www.travelocity.com
www.gulliver.ie

IRISH HOTELS FEDERATION (IHF)

IHF corporate website	www.ihf.ie
IHF reports	www.ihf.ie/reports/
IHF *InnSight Magazine*	www.ihf.ie/news/innsight/
IHF tourist website	www.irelandhotels.ie

CAR HIRE

Argus	www.argusrentals.com
Atlas	www.atlascarhire.com
Avis	www.avis.ie
Budget	www.budget.ie
County	www.countycar.ie
Dan Dooley	www.dan-dooley.ie
Dollar Thrifty	www.thrifty.ie
Enterprise	www.enterprise.com/ie
Europcar	www.europcar.ie
Hertz	www.hertz.ie
Irishcarrentals.com	www.irishcarrentals.com
National	www.nationalcar.com

GLOBAL DISTRIBUTION SYSTEMS (GDS)

Galileo	www.galileo.com
History of Galileo	www.galileo.com/galileo/en-ie/about/History/
Worldspan	www.worldspan.com
History of Worldspan	www.worldspan.com/home.asp?fPageID=7&fBUCatID=
Amadeus	www.amadeus.com
History of Amadeus	www.amadeus.com/amadeus/x5126.html
SABRE	www.sabre-holdings.com
History of SABRE	www.sabre-holdings.com/aboutUs/history.html

MISCELLANEOUS WEBSITES

Aer Lingus	www.aerlingus.com
Airbus Aircraft Manufacturers	www.airbus.com
An Óige (Irish Youth Hostel Association)	www.anoige.ie
Deutsche Bundesbahn (German Railways)	www.bahn.de
IHF Accommodation Listings (now www.irelandhotels.com)	www.beourguest.ie
Border, Midlands and West Region	www.bmwassembly.ie

Boeing Aircraft Manufacturers	www.boeing.com
Tour operator	www.cietours.ie
Connex (now Veolia), operator of LUAS	www.connex.net/en/
German tour operator	www.dertour.de
EU Energy and Transport Division	http://ec.europa.eu/dgs/energy_transport
World (but primarily US) festival listings	www.festivals.com
Hotel group	www.fitzpatrickhotels.com
Irish business tourism website	www.irelandinspires.com
Coach company	www.irishcoaches.ie
Farmhouse Marketing Organisation	www.irishfarmholidays.com
Ferry company	www.irishferries.com
Industry representative organisations	www.itic.ie
The Licenced Vintners Association (LVA)	www.lva.ie
Tour operators	www.mytravellite.com
National Development Plan	www.ndp.ie
Details of Ireland's six national parks	www.npws.ie/NationalParks/
List and details of Ireland's seventy-seven nature reserves	www.npws.ie/NatureReserves
National Roads Authority	www.nra.ie
Travel details and site to purchase well-known television travel programmes such as *Globe Trekker*	www.pilotguides.com
Cruise operator	www.pocruises.com
Ryanair	www.ryanair.com
Shannon River Boat Hire	www.shannon-river.com/
SNCF French Railways	www.sncf.com
Ferry operator	www.stenaline.ie
Festival information	www.stpatricksday.ie
Festival information	www.stpatricksfestival.ie
Festival information	www.st-patricks-day.com
Irish information resource	www.totalireland.com/index/tourism/airports/
B&B/guesthouse marketing organisation	www.townandcountry.ie
Visitor Attractions Survey charts	www.webtourism.ie/vas/results/

Appendix C

Contact Details for Tourism Organisations

INTRODUCTION

Appendix C provides a comprehensive list of contact details for tourism organisations in Ireland in order to assist the reader with further research for assignments, for revision or for examinations. These details include public tourism organisations on the island of Ireland as well as several private organisations in the area. Listings for the travel industry are also provided. The list is not intended as an exhaustive list, but rather a sample of some of the more commonly discussed organisations relevant to Irish tourism. Where appropriate, the contact details for the consumer, i.e. tourist, are presented separate to the contact details for the industry, i.e. corporate.

GOVERNMENT

Department of Arts, Sport and Tourism (IRL)
Kildare Street, Dublin 2
Tel (from Republic): 01 631 3800
E-mail: webmaster@dast.gov.ie
Web: www.arts-sport-tourism.gov.ie
Fax (from Republic): 01 661 1201

Department of Transport
Transport House, 44 Kildare Street, Dublin 2
Tel (from Republic): 01 670 7444
E-mail: info@transport.ie
Web: www.transport.ie

Department of Enterprise, Trade and Investment (NI)
Netherleigh, Massey Avenue, Belfast, BT4 2JP
Tel (from Republic): 048 9052 9900
E-mail: information@detini.gov.uk
Web: www.detini.gov.uk

Department of the Environment, Heritage and Local Government
Custom House, Dublin 1
Tel (from Republic): 01 888 2000
E-mail: press-office@environ.ie
Web: www.environ.ie
Fax (from Republic): 01 888 3272

Fáilte Ireland (Corporate)
Baggot Street Bridge, Dublin 2
Tel (from Republic): 01 602 4000
E-mail: info@failteireland.ie
Web: www.failteireland.ie
Fax (from Republic): 01 855 6821

Fáilte Ireland (Tourist Info)
Baggot Street Bridge, Dublin 2
Tel (from Republic): 1850 230 330
E-mail: online form
Web: www.ireland.ie

Tourism Ireland Limited (Corporate)
5th Floor, Bishop's Square, Redmond's Hill, Dublin 2
Tel (from Republic): 01 476 3400
E-mail: corporate.admin@tourismireland.com
Web: www.tourismireland.com/corporate
also
Tel (from Republic): 01 476 3435
E-mail: research@tourismireland.com

Tourism Ireland Limited (Tourist Info)
5th Floor, Bishop's Square, Redmond's Hill, Dublin 2
Tel: market dependent
E-mail: online form
Web: www.discoverireland.com

NITB (Corporate)
St. Anne's Court, 59 North Street, Belfast, BT1 1NB
Tel (from Republic): 048 9023 1221
E-mail: online form
Web: www.nitb.com
Fax (from Republic): 048 9024 0960

NITB (Tourist Info)
St. Anne's Court, 59 North Street, Belfast, BT1 1NB
Tel (from Republic): 048 9023 1221
E-mail: online form
Web: www.discovernorthernireland.com
Fax (from Republic): 048 9021 0960

NITB (Dublin)
16 Nassau Street, Dublin 2
Tel (from Republic): 01 679 1977
E-mail: infodublin@nitb.com
Web: www.discovernorthernireland.com
Fax (from Republic): 01 679 1863

Office of Public Works (OPW)
51, St Stephen's Green, Dublin 2
Tel (from Republic): 01 647 6000
E-mail: info@opw.ie
Web: www.opw.ie
Fax (from Republic): 01 661 0747

Heritage Data for Ireland
6 Ely Place Upper and 7 Ely Place, Dublin 2
Tel (from Republic): 01 888 2000
E-mail: gis@duchas.ie
Web: www.heritagedata.ie
Fax (from Republic): 01 888 3272

National Parks and Wildlife Service
7 Ely Place, Dublin 2
Tel (from Republic): 01 888 2000
E-mail: natureconservation@environ.ie
Web: www.npws.ie
Fax (from Republic): 01 888 3272

RTAs: REPUBLIC OF IRELAND

Dublin Tourism
Dublin Tourism Centre, Suffolk Street, Dublin 2
Tel (from Republic): 01 605 7700
E-mail: marketing@dublintourism.ie
Web: www.visitdublin.com
Fax (from Republic): 01 605 7757

South West Tourism
Áras Fáilte, Grand Parad, Cork
Tel (from Republic): 021 425 5100
E-mail: corkkerryinfo@failteireland.ie
Web: www.corkkerry.ie
Fax (from Republic): 021 425 5199

Ireland West Tourism
Áras Fáilte, Forster Street, Galway
Tel (from Republic): 091 537 700
E-mail: info@irelandwest.ie
Web: www.irelandwest.ie
Fax (from Republic): 091 537 733

East Coast and Midlands Tourism
Dublin Road, Mullingar, Co. Westmeath
Tel (from Republic): 044 934 8761
E-mail: eastandmidlandsinfo@failteireland.ie
Web: www.eastcoastmidlands.ie
Fax (from Republic): 044 934 0413

North West Tourism
Aran Reddan, Temple Street, Sligo
Tel (from Republic): 071 916 1201
E-mail: northwestinfo@irelandnorthwest.ie
Web: www.irelandnorthwest.ie
Fax (from Republic): 071 916 0360

South East Tourism
41 The Quay, Waterford City
Tel (from Republic): 051 875 823
E-mail: southeastinfo@failteireland.ie
Web: www.southeastireland.com
Fax (from Republic): 051 876 720

Shannon Development
Shannon Town Centre, Co. Clare
Tel (from Republic): 061 361 555
E-mail: tourisminfo@shannon-dev.ie
Web: www.shannonregiontourism.ie
Fax (from Republic): 061 363 180

RTAs: NORTHERN IRELAND

Belfast Visitor and Convention Bureau
47 Donegall Place, Belfast, BT1 5AD
Tel (from Republic): 048 9024 6609
E-mail: info@belfastvisitor.com
Web: www.gotobelfast.com
Fax (from Republic): 048 9031 2424

Derry Visitor and Convention Bureau
44 Foyle Street, Derry, BT48 6TE
Tel (from Republic): 048 7126 7284
E-mail: info@derryvisitor.com
Web: www.derryvisitor.com
Fax (from Republic): 048 7137 7992

Fermanagh Lakeland and South Tyrone Tourism
Wellington Road, Enniskillen, BT74 7EF
Tel (from Republic): 048 6632 3110
E-mail: info@fermanaghlakelands.com
Web: www.fermanaghlakelands.com
Fax (from Republic): 048 6632 5511

The Causeway, Coast and Glens
11 Lodge Road, Coleraine, BT52 1LU
Tel (from Republic): 048 7032 7720
E-mail: mail@causewaycoastandglens.com
Web: www.causewaycoastandglens.com
Fax (from Republic): 048 7032 7719

Sperrins Tourism
The Manor House, 30 High Street, Moneymore, BT45 7PD
Tel (from Republic): 048 8674 7700
E-mail: info@sperrinstourism.com
Web: www.sperrinstourism.com
Fax (from Republic): 048 8674 7754

Armagh Marketing
40 English Street, Armagh, BT61 4BA
Tel (from Republic): 048 3752 1800
E-mail: info@visitarmagh.com
Web: www.visitarmagh.com
Fax (from Republic): 048 3752 8329

Kingdoms of Down
40 West Street, Newtownards, BT23 4EN
Tel (from Republic): 048 9182 2881
E-mail: info@armaghanddown.com
Web: www.kingdomsofdown.com
Fax (from Republic): 048 9182 2202

AIRPORTS

Dublin Airport Authority
Dublin Airport, County Dublin
Tel (from Republic): 01 814 1111
E-mail: information.queries@dublinairport.com
Web: www.dublinairport.com

Shannon Airport Authority
Shannon Airport, County Clare
Tel (from Republic): 061 712 000
E-mail: customercomments@shannonairport.com
Web: www.shannonairport.com

Cork Airport Authority
Cork, Ireland
Tel (from Republic): 021 431 3131
E-mail: marketing@corkairport.com
Web: www.corkairport.com

AIRLINES

Adria Airways
Web: www.adria-airways.com

Aer Arann
Level 5, The Atrium, Dublin Airport, County Dublin
Tel (from Republic): 01 844 7700
E-mail: info@aerarann.com
Web: www.aerarann.com
Fax (from Republic): 01 844 7701

Aer Lingus
Dublin Airport, County Dublin
Tel (from Republic): 0818 365 000
E-mail: online form
Web: www.aerlingus.com
Fax (from Republic): 01 886 3832

Air Baltic
Web: www.airbaltic.com

Air Canada
Web: www.aircanada.com

Air France
Web: www.airfrance.com

Air Malta
Web: www.airmalta.com

Air SouthWest
Web: www.airsouthwest.com

Air Transat
Web: www.airtransat.com

American Airlines
Web: www.aa.com

Austrian Airlines
Web: www.aua.com

British Airways
Web: www.britishairways.com

British Midland
Web: www.flybmi.com

CityJet
Web: www.cityjet.com

Continental Airlines
Web: www.continental.com

Czech Airlines
Web: www.czechairlines.com

Delta
Web: www.delta.com

Estonian Air
Web: www.estonian-air.com

Euro Manx
Web: www.euromanx.com

Finnair
Web: www.finnair.com

Flybe
Web: www.flybe.com

Flynordic
Web: www.flynordic.com

German Wings
Web: www.germanwings.com

Hapag Lloyd Express
Web: www.hlx.com/en

Helios Airways – now ajet
Web: www.ajet.com

Iberia
Web: www.iberia.com

Lithuanian Airlines
Web: www.lal.lt/en

Loganair
Web: www.loganair.co.uk

Lot Polish Airlines
Web: www.lot.com

Lufthansa
Web: www.lufthansa.com

Luxair
Web: www.luxair.lu

Malev
Web: www.malev.com

Ryanair
Dublin Airport, County Dublin
Tel (from Republic): 0818 30 30 30
E-mail: online form
Web: www.ryanair.com
Fax (from Republic): 01 812 1213

SAS Braathens
Web: www.sasbraathens.no

SAS Scandinavian Airlines
Web: www.scandinavian.net

Spanair
Web: www.spanair.com

Swiss Airlines
Web: www.swiss.com

Thomsonfly
Web: www.thomsonfly.com

Transavia
Web: www.transavia.com

US Airways
Web: www.usairways.com

FERRIES

Irish Ferries (Corporate)
PO Box 19, Alexandra Road, Dublin 1
Tel (from Republic): 01 855 2222
E-mail: info@irishferries.com
Web: www.irishferries.com
Fax (from Republic): 01 855 2272

Irish Ferries (Tourist)
PO Box 19, Alexandra Road, Dublin 1
Tel (from Republic): 0818 300 400
E-mail: info@irishferries.com
Web: www.irishferries.com
Fax (from Republic): 01 855 2272

Stena Line
Ferry Terminal, Dún Laoghaire, Co. Dublin
Tel (from Republic): 01 204 7777
E-mail: info.ie@stenaline.com
Web: www.stenaline.ie

Brittany Ferries
Tel (from Republic): 021 427 7801
Web: www.brittanyferries.ie

Swansea-Cork Ferries
14 Union Quay, Cork
Tel (from Republic): 021 437 9820
E-mail: sales@swanseacorkferries.com
Web: www.swanseacorkferries.com
Fax (from Republic): 021 421 5814

P&O Irish Sea Ferries
Tel (from Republic): 01 407 3434
E-mail: online form
Web: www.poirishsea.com

Isle of Man Steam Packet Company
E-mail: online form
Web: www.steam-packet.com

LAND-BASED TRANSPORT

Coras Iompair Éireann (CIÉ)
Heuston Station, Dublin 8
Tel (from Republic): 01 703 4701
E-mail: online form
Web: www.cie.ie

CIE Tours International
35 Lower Abbey Street, Dublin 1
Tel (from Republic): 01 677 1871
E-mail: online form
Web: www.cie.ie

Iarnród Éireann (General)
Connolly Station, Dublin 1
Tel (from Republic): 01 836 6222
E-mail: online form
Web: www.irishrail.ie

Iarnród Éireann (Corporate)
Connolly Station, Dublin 1
Tel (from Republic): 01 836 3333
E-mail: online form
Web: www.irishrail.ie

Bus Éireann (General)
Busáras, Store Street, Dublin 1
Tel (from Republic): 01 836 6111
E-mail: online form
Web: www.buseireann.ie

Bus Éireann (Corporate)
Head Office, Broadstone, Dublin 7
Tel (from Republic): 01 830 2222
E-mail: online form
Web: www.buseireann.ie

Dublin Bus
59 Upper O'Connell Street, Dublin 1
Tel (from Republic): 01 872 0000
E-mail: online form
Web: www.dublinbus.ie

Eurolines
c/o Bus Éireann
E-mail: online form
Web: www.eurolines.ie

Irish Coaches
Ulster Bank Chambers, 2–4 Lower O'Connell Street, Dublin 1
Tel (from Republic): 01 878 8898
E-mail: info@irishcoaches.ie
Web: www.irishcoaches.ie
Fax (from Republic): 01 878 8916

ACCOMMODATION AND RESTAURANTS

Irish Hotels Federation (Tourist)
13 Northbrook Street, Dublin 6
Tel (from Republic): 01 497 6459
E-mail: info@ihf.ie
Web: www.irelandhotels.com
Fax (from Republic): 01 497 4613

Irish Hotels Federation (Corporate)
13 Northbrook Street, Dublin 6
Tel (from Republic): 01 497 6459
E-mail: info@ihf.ie
Web: www.ihf.ie
Fax (from Republic): 01 497 4613

NI Hotel Federation
Midland Building, Whitla Street, Belfast BT1 1JP
Tel (from Republic): 048 9035 1110
E-mail: office@nihf.co.uk
Web: www.nihf.co.uk
Fax (from Republic): 048 9035 1509

Restaurants Association of Ireland
11 Bridge Street, City Gate, St Augustine Street, Dublin 8
Tel (from Republic): 01 677 9901
E-mail: info@rai.ie
Web: www.rai.ie
Fax (from Republic): 01 671 8414

Gulliver Ireland
Tel (from Republic): 00800 668 668 66
Web: www.gulliver.ie

Irish Country Holidays
Old Church, Mill Strett, Borrisokane, Co. Tipperary
Tel (from Republic): 067 27790
E-mail: info@country-holidays.ie
Web: www.country-holidays.ie
Fax (from Republic): 067 27791

Irish Farmhouse Holidays
2 Michael Street, Limerick
Tel (from Republic): 061 400 700
E-mail: info@irishfarmholidays.com
Web: www.irishfarmholidays.com
Fax (from Republic): 061 400 771

Town & Country Homes Association
Belleek Road, Ballyshannon, Co. Donegal
Tel (from Republic): 071 982 2222
E-mail: admin@townandcountry.ie
Web: www.townandcountry.ie
Fax (from Republic): 071 982 2207

Ireland Farmhouse Holidays
2 Michael Street, Limerick
Tel (from Republic): 061 400 700
E-mail: farmhols@iol.ie
Web: www.irishfarmholidays.com
Fax (from Republic): 061 400 771

MISCELLANEOUS ORGANISATIONS

Heritage Island
Marina House, 11/13 Clarence Street, Dún Laoghaire
Tel (from Republic): 01 236 6890
E-mail: info@heritageisland.com
Web: www.heritageisland.com
Fax (from Republic): 01 236 6895

Irish Genealogy
E-mail: info@irishgenealogy.ie
Web: www.irishgenealogy.ie

An Taisce
Tailor's Hall, Back Lane, Dublin 8
Tel (from Republic): 01 454 1786
E-mail: info@antaisce.org
Web: www.antaisce.org
Fax (from Republic): 01 453 3255

ITIC (Irish Travel Industry Confederation)
17 Londford Terrace, Monkstown, Co. Dublin
Tel (from Republic): 01 284 4222
E-mail: itic@eircom.net
Web: www.itic.ie
Fax (from Republic): 01 280 4218

Houses, Castles and Gardens of Ireland
16A Woodlands Park, Blackrock, Co. Dublin
Tel (from Republic): 01 288 9114
E-mail: info@castlesgardensireland.com
Web: www.castleireland.com
Fax (from Republic): 01 288 9114

ITAA (Irish Travel Agents Association)
Heaton House, 32 South William Street, Dublin 2
Tel (from Republic): 01 679 4179
E-mail: info@itaa.ie
Web: www.itaa.ie
Fax (from Republic): 01 671 9897

UNWTO
World Tourism Organization, C/Capitán Haya, 42 28020 Madrid, Spain
Tel (from Republic): 00 34 91 567 8193
E-mail: tourcom@unwto.org
Web: www.unwto.org
Fax (from Republic): 00 34 91 567 8218

TOUR OPERATORS

ITOA (Irish Tour Operators Association)
PO Box 65, Bray, Co. Wicklow
Tel (from Republic): 01 286 1107
E-mail: info@itoa-ireland.com
Web: www.itoaireland.com
Fax (from Republic): 01 286 1107

Airtours
Tel (from Republic): 0818 202020
E-mail: info@mytravel.ie

American Holidays
18/19 Duke Street, Dublin 2
Tel (from Republic): 01 673 3800
E-mail: info@americanholidays.ie
Web: www.americanholidays.ie

Arrow Tours
40 West Street, Drogheda, Co. Louth
Tel (from Republic): 041 983 1177
E-mail: res@arrowtours.ie
Web: www.arrowtours.ie

Balkan Tours
5/6 South Great Georges Street, Dublin 2
Tel (from Republic): 01 679 4333
E-mail: mail@balkan.co.uk

Belleair
12 Pembroke Road, Dublin 4
Tel (from Republic): 01 660 4333
E-mail: info@dltmail.co.uk

Breakaway Tours
12 South Leinster Street, Dublin 2
Tel (from Republic): 01 607 9999
E-mail: break@neenantrav.ie

Brittany Ferries
Tourist House, 42 Grand Parade, Cork
Tel (from Republic): 021 427 7801
Web: www.brittanyferries.com

Budget Travel
134/5 Lower Baggot Street, Dublin 2
Tel (from Republic): 01 661 1403
Web: www.budgettravel.ie

Canamerica
67 Middle Abbey Street, Dublin 2
Tel (from Republic): 01 872 0444
Web: www.canamerica.ie

Carribean Collection
Drury's Avenue, Midleton, Co. Cork
Tel (from Republic): 021 463 4921

Celebration Travel
CFBA Business Park, Dunhill, Co. Waterford
Tel (from Republic): 051 396 448

Celtic Horizon Tours
Tel (from Republic): 01 628 8801
E-mail: info@celtichorizonstours.com
Web: www.celtichorizontours.com

CIE Tours International
35 Lower Abbey Street, Dublin 2
Tel (from Republic): 01 703 4014
E-mail: reservations@cietours.ie
Web: www.cietours.ie

Citiscapes
The Chimney Stack, 1A, Crowe Street, Dublin 2
Tel (from Republic): 01 677 5533
E-mail: book@citiscapes.ie
Web: www.citiscapes.ie

Classic Connection
Carrowkeeran, Murrisk, Westport, Co. Mayo
Tel (from Republic): 098 64006

Classic Resorts
24/25 Lower Liffey Street, Dublin 1
Tel (from Republic): 01 874 5000
Web: www.classicresorts.ie

Concorde Travel
47 Capel Street, Dublin 1
Tel (from Republic): 01 872 7066
E-mail: info@concordetravel.ie

Croatia Tours
19 Eden Quay, Dublin 1
Tel (from Republic): 01 878 0800
E-mail: info@croatiatours.ie
Web: www.croatiatours.ie

Crystal Holidays
18/19 Duke Street, Dublin 2
Tel (from Republic): 01 433 1080
E-mail: info@crystalholidays.ie
Web: www.crystalholidays.ie

Cyplon Holidays
561–563 Green Lanes, London, N8 0RL, UK
Tel (from Republic): 01 478 1500
E-mail: sales@cyplon.co.uk
Web: www.cyplon.co.uk

Delta Travel/Globespan
Sackville House, 5 Sackville Place, Dublin 1
Tel (from Republic): 01 874 7666
E-mail: deltatravel@eircom.net

Destinations
29 Lower Dorset Street, Dublin 1
Tel (from Republic): 01 855 6677
E-mail: sales@destinations.ie
Web: www.destinations.ie

Direct Holidays
17 Talbot Street, Dublin 1
Tel (from Republic): 01 886 0400
Web: www.direct-holidays.ie

Directski.com
Tel (from Republic): 01 433 6202
E-mail: sales@directski.com
Web: www.directski.com

East Cork Travel Worldchoice
Church Lane, Midleton, Co. Cork
Tel (from Republic): 021 463 3233
E-mail: info@eastcorktravel.ie
Web: www.eastcorktravel.ie

EU Tours
Ballinagar, Ballylinan, Co. Laois
Tel (from Republic): 059 914 5176
E-mail: euawarenesstours@oceanfree.net

Falcon Holidays
Tel (from Republic): 01 605 6500 / 5655
Web: www.falconholidays.ie

French Holidays Centre
3 Marlboro Street, Cork
Tel (from Republic): 021 427 2527

GLA Pilgrimages Abroad
64 Middle Abbey Street, Dublin 1
Tel (from Republic): 01 873 1444
E-mail: pilgrimages@eircom.net

Go Holidays
28 North Great George Street, Dublin 1
Tel (from Republic): 01 874 4126
E-mail: info@goholidays.ie
Web: www.goholidays.ie

Harry Cahill Tours
Tel (from Republic): 01 670 5123
Web: www.harry-cahill-travel.ie

Heffernans Travel
Pembroke House, Pembroke Street, Cork
Tel (from Republic): 021 427 1081
Web: www.heffernans.ie

Inghams
29 Herbert Lane, Dublin 2
Tel (from Republic): 01 661 1377
E-mail: info@inghams.co.uk
Web: www.inghams.ie

Irish Ferries
Ferryport, Alexandra Road, Dublin 1
Tel (from Republic): 01 855 2222
E-mail: info@irishferries.com
Web: www.irishferries.com

Italiatour
4/5 Dawson Street, Dublin 2
Tel (from Republic): 01 671 7821
E-mail: italyforlovers@italiatour.ie

Just Portugal
9B Lower Abbey Street, Dublin 1
Tel (from Republic): 01 878 7675
E-mail: justportugal.info@justportugal.ie
Web: www.justportugal.ie

Keith Prowse Travel
Irish Life Mall, Dublin 1
Tel (from Republic): 01 878 3500
E-mail: dublin@keithprowse.com
Web: www.keithprowsedublin.com

Keller Campotel
6 Merrion Row, Dublin 2
Tel (from Republic): 01 661 8833

Keller Travel
Main Street, Ballinaslow, Co. Galway
Tel (from Republic): 0909 642 131
E-mail: info@kellertravel.ie

Keycamp Holidays
78–80 South Mall, Cork
Tel (from Republic): 021 425 2300

Landround Travel Ltd.
College House,71–73 Rock Road, Blackrock, Co.Dublin

LSA Travel
19 Lower Main Street, Portlaoise, Co. Laois
Tel (from Republic): 0502 21510

Magic Holidays
18/19 Duke Street, Dublin 2
Tel (from Republic): 01 433 1057
E-mail: mail@magicholidays.ie

Norvista/Nortours
1st Floor, 11 Parliament Street, Dublin 2
Tel (from Republic): 01 677 9944
E-mail: reservations@norvista.ie

Norwegian Coastal Village
12 Pembroke Road, Dublin 4
Tel (from Republic): 01 667 7778
E-mail: info@dltmail.com

PAB Travel
53 Middle Abbey Street, Dublin 1
Tel (from Republic): 01 873 3411
E-mail: info@pabtours.com

Panorama
Tel (from Republic): 0818 202020
E-mail: info@mytravel.ie
Web: www.panoramaholidays.ie

747 Sunflight Holidays
82 Aungier Street, Dublin 2
Tel (from Republic): 01 478 7070

SHG (Specialist Holiday Group Ireland Ltd)
18/19 Duke Street, Dublin 2
Tel (from Republic): 01 433 1073
Web: www.americanholidays.ie

Slattery's Sun
1 Russell Street, Tralee, Co. Kerry
Tel (from Republic): 1850 673 673
E-mail: info@slatterys.com
Web: www.slatterys.com

Stein Travel
77 Lower Camden Street, Dublin 2
Tel (from Republic): 1890 408 408
E-mail: info@steintravel.ie
Web: www.steintravel.ie

Sunscapes
6 Castle Street, Bray, Co. Wicklow
Tel (from Republic): 01 274 4040
E-mail: book@sunscapes.ie
Web: www.sunscapes.ie

Sunway
Tel (from Republic): 01 288 6828
Web: www.sunway.ie

Sunworld
Tel (from Republic): 01 881 4300
E-mail: res@sunworld.ie
Web: www.sunworld.ie

The Travel Department
83 Main Street, Ranelagh, Dublin 6
Tel (from Republic): 01 406 2222
E-mail: traveldpt@iol.ie
Web: www.thetraveldepartment.ie

Tony Heverin Travel
11 North Frederick Street, Dublin 1
Tel (from Republic): 01 874 6443

Topflight
Jervis House, Jervis Street, Dublin 1
Tel (from Republic): 01 240 1700
E-mail: info@topflight.ie
Web: www.topflight.ie

TQ3 J Barter Travel Solutions
92 Patrick Street, Cork
Tel (from Republic): 021 427 4261
E-mail: info@barters.com
Web: www.barters.com

Travel Focus
5 Marlboro Street, Cork
Tel (from Republic): 021 425 1025
E-mail: travelfocus.info@travelfocus.ie
Web: www.travelfocus.ie

Tropical Places
18/19 Duke Street, Dublin 2
Tel (from Republic): 01 433 1020
E-mail: holidays@tropicalplaces.ie
Web: www.tropicalplaces.ie

Tour America
62 Middle Abbey Street, Dublin 1
Tel (from Republic): 01 878 3500
E-mail: info@touramerica.ie
Web: www.touramerica.ie

Tullys Travel Ltd
137 Tullow Street, Carlow, Co. Carlow
Tel (from Republic): 059 913 6100
E-mail: info@tullys.ie
Web: www.tullystravel.net

Twohig Travel
31 Dawson Street, Dublin 2
Tel (from Republic): 01 648 0800
E-mail: info@twohigs.net
Web: www.twohigs.com

Unique Destinations
47B Patrick Street, Dún Laoghaire, Co. Dublin
Tel (from Republic): 01 663 8792
E-mail: info@uniquedestinations.ie

United Travel
2 Old Dublin Road, Stillorgan, Co. Dublin
Tel (from Republic): 01 215 9300
E-mail: info@unitedtravel.ie
Web: www.unitedtravel.ie

Villa & Golf Vacations
3 Sandyford Village, Sandyford, Dublin 18
Tel (from Republic): 01 207 5300
E-mail: info@villa-golf.ie

Appendix D

Tourism Statistics

INTRODUCTION

Appendix D presents the most recent tourism statistics available at the time of publication. This enables the reader to contextualise the facts and figures presented throughout the various chapters in the book. Regularly updated tourism statistics for Ireland are available online at www.failteireland.ie/research.

Table D.1: Ireland's Top Ten Tourism-Generating Countries (Arrivals, 2005)

Country	Arrivals	% Global Share
Britain	3,640,000	49.6%
US	854,000	11.7%
Germany	402,000	5.5%
France	310,000	4.2%
Italy	190,000	2.6%
Spain	171,000	2.3%
Netherlands	157,000	2.1%
Australia/New Zealand	137,000	1.9%
Poland	125,000	1.7%
Denmark/Sweden	98,000	1.3%
Total from Top Ten	6,084,000	82.9%
Total Overseas	6,763,000	92.2%
Northern Ireland	570,000	7.8%
Total (incl. N. Ireland)	7,333,000	100%

Source: Fáilte Ireland, NITB, CSO.

Table D.2: Tourist Arrivals, in 000s (2000–2005)

	2000	2001	2002	2003	2004	2005
Britain	3,428	3,340	3,452	3,553	3,526	3,640
Mainland Europe	1,436	1,336	1,378	1,484	1,582	1,903
Germany	319	285	288	302	298	402
France	283	280	298	321	297	310
Italy	186	157	157	176	186	190
Netherlands	179	182	162	146	151	157
Belgium/Luxembourg	89	81	104	96	100	84 *
Spain	89	100	113	133	157	171
Nordics	159	129	108	124	126	98 **
Switzerland	49	38	42	51	65	54
Poland	n/a	11	13	17	39	125
Other Europe	n/a	127	141	174	224	312
North America	1,056	903	844	892	956	937
US	958	829	759	809	867	854
Canada	98	74	85	84	89	83
Rest of World	261	261	245	249	319	284
Australia/New Zealand	148	132	113	109	146	137
Japan	28	22	22	22	31	19
Other Asia	n/a	58	64	62	79	71
Africa	n/a	32	29	32	42	39
Other Overseas	n/a	12	16	21	19	19
Total Overseas	6,181	5,840	5,919	6,178	6,384	6,763
Northern Ireland	465	513	557	586	569	570
Out of State	6,646	6,353	6,476	6,764	6,953	7,333
Domestic Trips	5,478	6,307	6,452	6,657	7,001	7,173

* 2005 preliminary figures for Belgium only.

** 2005 preliminary figures for Sweden and Denmark only.

Source: Fáilte Ireland, NITB, CSO.

Note: If Northern Ireland were treated as an international market (as opposed to being classed as neither domestic nor international), then it would rank as the third largest market for the Republic.

Table D.3: European Outbound City Breaks: Ireland's Ranking by Source Market (2004)

Country of Origin	Ireland's Ranking
Britain	2
Belgium	6
Netherlands	13
France	13
Spain	14
Italy	14
Germany	18
Switzerland	19
Overall	11

Source: Fáilte Ireland.

Table D.4: Tourism Revenue in €, mn (2000–2005)

	2000	2001	2002	2003	2004	2005
Britain	1,087.7	1,210.6	1,283.3	1,319.1	1,276.1	1,274.2
Mainland Europe	727.0	814.6	866.6	885.1	930.4	1,238.6
Germany	172.0	197.2	181.5	184.3	177.4	237.6
France	119.8	161.8	185.3	147.1	158.3	176.4
Italy	90.4	111.8	110.7	120.9	119.0	124.0
Netherlands	92.2	78.8	85.4	78.1	69.4	80.1
Other Europe	252.6	265.0	303.7	354.7	406.3	620.5
North America	688.6	717.5	709.0	787.2	772.1	738.2
Other Overseas	178.4	209.0	228.7	236.4	256.3	235.9
Total Overseas	2,681.6	2,951.7	3,087.5	3,227.7	3,234.9	3,486.9
Northern Ireland	123.3	142.8	161.2	175.5	174.1	178.8
Total Out of State	2,804.9	3,094.5	3,248.7	3,403.2	3,409.0	3,665.7
Overseas Same-Day Visits	19.1	20.5	17.3	20.8	22.0	23.3
Carrier Receipts	813.0	820.0	723.0	633.0	628.0	583.0
Total Foreign Exchange Earnings	3,637.0	3,935.0	3,989.0	4,057.0	4,059.0	4,272.0
Domestic Trips	706.6	879.9	849.4	970.9	1,037.2	1,164.5
Total Tourism Revenue	4,343.6	4,814.9	4,838.4	5,027.9	5,096.2	5,436.5

Northern Ireland revenue includes expenditure on same-day visits by Northern Ireland residents.

Source: Fáilte Ireland, NITB, CSO.

Table D.5: How Overseas Tourists Spend Their Money (2005) (% Spend)

	Total	Britain	Mainland Europe	North America	Rest of World
Bed and Board	29	27	32	29	29
Other Food and Drink	35	40	34	30	31
Sightseeing/Entertainment	5	4	5	6	5
Internal Transport	9	9	9	10	8
Shopping	18	16	17	20	20
Miscellaneous	4	3	4	4	8

Source: Fáilte Ireland.

Table D.6: Summary of Total Arrivals, Total Spend and Estimated Tourist Spend per Person (2005)

	Number of Visitors (000s)	Total Spend (€, mn)	Average Spend (Euro per Person)	Ranking (Specific Countries/ Regions Only)
Britain	3,640	1,274.2	350.05	6
Mainland Europe	1,903	1,238.6	650.87	–
Germany	402	237.6	591.04	3
France	310	176.4	569.03	4
Italy	190	124.0	652.63	2
Netherlands	157	80.1	510.19	5
Other Europe	650	620.5	954.62	–
North America	937	738.2	787.83	1
Total Overseas	6,763	3,486.9	515.59	–
Northern Ireland	570	178.8	313.68	7
Total Out of State	7,333	3,665.7	499.89	–
Domestic Trips	7,173	1,164.5	162.35	–
Total	14,406	5,436.5	377.38	–

Source: Fáilte Ireland, NITB, CSO.

Table D.7: Top Markets: Rankings (2005)

	Number of Visitors	Total Spend	Average Spend
Britain	1	1	6
North America	2	2	1
Northern Ireland	3	4	7
Germany	4	3	3
France	5	5	4
Italy	6	6	2
Netherlands	7	7	5

Source: Fáilte Ireland, NITB, CSO.

Table D.8: When Overseas Tourists Arrived (2005) (%)

	Total	Britain	Mainland Europe	North America	Rest of World
Jan–Mar	18	20	16	15	15
April	8	8	8	6	6
May	9	8	9	10	9
June	10	9	11	13	12
July	12	10	14	14	12
August	12	12	12	12	13
September	9	9	8	11	11
Oct–Dec	22	23	22	19	22

Source: CSO.

Table D.9: Main Reason for Visiting Ireland (2005) (%)

	Total	Britain	Mainland Europe	North America	Rest of World
Holiday	50	46	50	66	49
VFR	31	37	24	23	35
Business	13	12	17	7	12
Other	6	6	9	4	5

Source: CSO, NITB.

Table D.10: Activities Engaged in by Visitors to Ireland (2005)

Equestrian	27,000
Golf	98,000
Cycling	43,000
Angling	56,000
Hiking/Hill Walking	280,000

Source: CSO, NITB.

Table D.11: Total Numbers of Holidaymakers to Ireland in 000s (2000–2005)

	Total	Britain	Mainland Europe	North America	Rest of World
2000	3,320	1,644	803	722	151
2001	3,140	1,623	743	626	148
2002	3,216	1,751	757	579	130
2003	3,291	1,779	772	616	124
2004	3,367	1,718	825	656	167
2005	3,365	1,662	950	614	139

Source: CSO, NITB.

Note: Holidaymakers are defined as visitors who stated that their primary purpose for visiting Ireland was a holiday.

Table D.12: Percentage of Holidaymakers on their First Trip to Ireland (2005)

	Total	Britain	Mainland Europe	North America	Rest of World
First Visit	55	38	65	68	74
Repeat	39	50	33	30	20
Irish-Born	6	11	2	1	6

Source: CSO, NITB.

Table D.13: Age of Holidaymakers to Ireland (2005) (%)

<25 years	22%
25–34 years	19%
35–44 years	19%
45+ years	41%

Source: CSO, NITB.

Table D.14: Social Class of Holidaymakers to Ireland (2005) (%)

AB – Managerial/Professional	20%
C1 – White Collar	60%
C2 – Skilled Worker	16%
DE – Unskilled Worker	4%

Source: CSO, NITB.

Table D.15: Party Composition of Holidaymakers to Ireland (2005) (%)

Alone	23%
Couple	44%
Family	16%
Other Adult Group	16%

Source: CSO, NITB.

Table D.16: Visitors from Britain to Ireland (1998–2005)

	Tourist Numbers (000s)	Expenditure (€, mn)
1998 ˙	3,199	961.7
1999	3,430	1,011.9
2000	3,428	1,087.7
2001	3,340	1,210.6
2002	3,452	1,283.3
2003	3,553	1,319.1
2004	3,526	1,276.1
2005	3,640	1,274.2
Average spent per visitor from Britain in 2005: €350.50		

Table D.17: Visitors from the US to Ireland (1998–2005)

	Tourist Numbers (000s)	Expenditure (€, mn)
1998	789	488.1
1999	890	555.1
2000	958	688.6
2001	829	717.5
2002	759	709.0
2003	809	787.2
2004	867	772.1
2005	854	738.2
Average spent per visitor from North America in 2005: €787.83		

Table D.18: Visitors from Germany to Ireland (1998–2005)

	Tourist Numbers (000s)	Expenditure (€, mn)
1998	310	156.2
1999	305	161.1
2000	319	172.0
2001	285	197.2
2002	288	181.5
2003	302	184.3
2004	298	177.4
2005	402	237.6

Average spent per visitor from Germany in 2005: €591.04

Table D.19: Visitors from France to Ireland (1998–2005)

	Tourist Numbers (000s)	Expenditure (€, mn)
1998	270	113.6
1999	275	102.3
2000	283	119.8
2001	280	161.8
2002	298	185.3
2003	321	147.1
2004	297	158.3
2005	310	176.4

Average spent per visitor from France in 2005: €569.03

Table D.20: Visitors from Italy to Ireland (1998–2005)

	Tourist Numbers (000s)	Expenditure (€, mn)
1998	141	73.2
1999	165	91.0
2000	186	90.4
2001	157	111.8
2002	157	110.7
2003	176	120.9
2004	186	98.2
2005	190	124.0

Average spent per visitor from Italy in 2005: €652.6

Table D.21: Visitors from the Netherlands to Ireland (1998–2005)

	Tourist Numbers (000s)	Expenditure (€, mn)
1998	134	54.7
1999	139	54.5
2000	179	92.2
2001	182	78.8
2002	162	85.4
2003	146	78.1
2004	151	90.3
2005	157	80.1

Average spent per visitor from the Netherlands in 2005: €510.19

Table D.22: Visitors from Northern Ireland to Ireland (1998–2005)

	Tourist Numbers (000s)	Expenditure (€, mn)
1998	530	122.5
1999	460	115.3
2000	465	123.3
2001	513	142.8
2002	557	162.2
2003	596	178.5
2004	598	183.1
2005	570	178.8

Average spent per visitor from Northern Ireland in 2005: €313.68

Bibliography

INTRODUCTION

As well as providing listings of the various sources cited and consulted in the compilation of this book, it is recommended that readers should use this bibliography to further their knowledge on the various topics discussed in the book. Much of the information is available free online. A comprehensive listing of web resources used in this book as well as suggested resources to augment the study of tourism appears in Appendix B.

BOOKS

Bradley, F., *International Marketing Strategy*, 4th edn., Essex: Prentice Hall 2002.

Byrne, G.J., *Culture and its Relationship to International Marketing (Towards an Understanding of Performance in International Marketing)*, unpublished PhD thesis, 2001.

Byrne, P., *Fuelled By Belief – The CityJet Story*, Dublin: The Liffey Press 2004.

Calder, S., *No Frills – The Truth Behind the Low-Cost Revolution In The Skies*, London: Virgin Books 2003.

Cassani, B., *Go – An Airline Adventure*, London: Time Warner Books 2003.

Cateora, P.R. and Ghauri, P.N., *International Marketing*, European edn., Berkshire: McGraw-Hill 1999.

CERT, *Tourism and Travel in Ireland*, Dublin: Gill & Macmillan 1993.

Creaton, S., *Ryanair – How a Small Irish Airline Conquered Europe*, London: Aurum Press 2004.

Culler, J., *Saussure*, London: Fontana 1976.

Dyer, G., *Advertising as Communication*, London: Routledge 1996.

Filfield, P.C., *The Effect of Cultural Values in Consumer Choice Behaviour in Western Europe and the Resulting Segmentation of the Market*, unpublished PhD thesis, Cranfield School of Management (UK) 1985.

Fiske, J., *Introduction to Communication Studies*, 2nd edn., Routledge 1990.

Freiberg, K. and Freiberg, J., *Nuts – Southwest Airlines' Crazy Recipe for Business and Personal Success*, New York: Broadway Books 1996.

Goeldner, C.R. and Brent Ritchie, J.R., *Tourism – Principles, Practices, Philosophies*, 10th edn., New Jersey: John Wiley & Sons 2006.

Gombrich, E.H., 'The Visual Image' in D.R. Olson (ed.), *Media and Symbols: The Forms of Expression, Communication and Education*, Chicago: University of Chicago Press 1974, pp. 255–8; first published in *Scientific American*, 227 (September 1971), 82–96.

Guderian, E., *Irland*, Stuttgart: Kohlhammer (Department of Foreign Affairs) 1983.

Guiney, D., *The Tourism and Travel Industry in Ireland*, Dublin: Gill & Macmillan 2002.

Holloway, J.C., *The Business of Tourism*, 4th edn., London: Pitman Publishing 1994.

Holloway, J.C. and Plant, R.V., *Marketing for Tourism*, 2nd edn., London: Pitman Publishing 1994.

Jones, Lois, *easyJet – The Story of Britain's Biggest Low-Cost Airline*, London: Aurum Press 2005.

Lasa, I.H., *The Translation of Culture-Specific Terms in Tourist Information Material*, unpublished MA thesis 1993.

Mehta, G., *Cross-Cultural Communication: A Study of the Cultural and Linguistic Representations of Ireland in Germany as a Tourist Destination*, unpublished MA thesis 2004.

Messaris, P., *Visual Persuasion: The Role of Images in Advertising*, London: Sage Publications 1997.

Newmark, P., *About Translation – Multilingual Matters*, Bristol: Longdunn Press 1991.

Rogan, D., *Marketing: An Introduction for Irish Students*, Dublin: Gill & Macmillan 2000.

Swarbrooke, J., *The Development and Management of Visitor Attractions*, Oxford: Elsevier Butterworth-Heinemann 2005.

Walsh-Heron, J. and Stevens, T., *The Management of Visitor Attractions and Events*, Prentice Hall 1990.

Weaver, D. and Lawton, L., *Tourism Management*, 3rd edn., Australia: John Wiley & Sons 2006.

Wright, A. and Linehan, M., *Ireland, Tourism and Marketing*, Dublin: Blackhall Publishing 2004.

JOURNAL ARTICLES

Lesle, D., 'Terrorism and Tourism: The Northern Ireland situation – A Look Behind the Veil of Uncertainty', *Journal of Travel Research*, 38/1 (August 1999), 37–40.

Lisella, M., 'Foreign Intelligence', *Travel Agent*, 301/12 (13 November 2000), 1.

Cope, R., 'Impact of Terrorism on Tourism', *Travel and Tourism Analyst*, August 2003.

Marvel, M., 'European Hotel Chain Expansion', *Travel and Tourism Analyst*, May 2004.

Mehta, G., 'Managing the Perceptions of Ireland as a Tourist Destination (in Germany)', (2004).

O'Connor, P., 'Online Intermediaries: Revolutionising Travel Distribution', *Travel and Tourism Analyst*, February 2003.

Page, S.J., 'E-Travel in Europe', *Travel and Tourism Analyst*, May 2004.

Poon, A., 'Where Germans Travel To', *Travel and Tourism Intelligence*, 1 (2001).

Sangster, A., 'Group Hotels', *Travel and Tourism Analyst*, February 2003.

JOURNAL ARTICLES WITH AUTHOR'S NAME UNSPECIFIED/EDITORIALS

'Bleak Summer for Tourism to Ireland', *Travel Trade Gazette UK & Ireland* (21 May 2001), 27.

'Irish tourism merger still on schedule', *Travel Weekly*, 60/61 (30 July 2001), 5.

'Ireland's Big Plans', *Travel Agent*, 305/3 (13 August 2001), 2.

'Marketing drive counters Irish tourism slump', *Travel Trade Gazette UK & Ireland* (13 August 2001), 76.

'Northern Ireland: TTI Country Reports', *Travel and Tourism Intelligence* (Autumn 2001), 75.

'Future of Travel Agents', *Travel and Tourism Analyst* (November 2001).

'Green wins Britain role on Irish board', *Travel Trade Gazette UK & Ireland* (14 January 2002), 9.

'All for one', *Travel Trade Gazette UK & Ireland* (28 January 2002), 36.

'Irish tourism companies promote best of the west', *Travel Trade Gazette UK & Ireland* (28 January 2002), 38.

NEWSPAPER ARTICLES

Anderson, P., 'Bord Fáilte and CERT consider merger', *The Irish Times*, 5 September 2001.

Boland, R., 'Wake-up call for B&Bs', *The Irish Times*, 12 April 2006.

Brennan, M., 'The céad mile fáilte falters', *The Sunday Business Post*, 23 June 2002.

Brown, J.M., 'Island unites in campaign to attract tourists', *The Financial Times*, 8 November 2001.

Brown, J.M., 'Ireland to be marketed as single tourist destination', *The Financial Times*, 8 November 2001.

Carr, A., 'Business tourism to Dublin up 26% in 2005', *The Irish Times*, 16 January 2006.

Carswell, S., 'Ryding High', *The Sunday Business Post*, 15 January 2006.

Clancy, P., 'Tourism scheme attracts 500 to north-west', *The Irish Times*, 5 January 2006.

Cleary, C., 'Temples of boom', *The Irish Times*, 25 February 2006.

Colgan, P., 'Tourists rejecting "rip-off" Ireland', *The Sunday Business Post*, 4 January 2004.

Connolly, N., 'Jurys-Doyle bids to join online booking group', *The Sunday Business Post*, 16 July 2000.

Connolly, N., 'BA takeover of Aer Lingus looks likely', *The Sunday Business Post*, 24 June 2001.

Connolly, N., 'Irish tourism to rely more on foreign staff', *The Sunday Business Post*, 7 March 2004.

Connolly, N., 'Government will secure Heathrow slots', *The Sunday Business Post*, 29 May 2005.

Connolly, N., 'Tourists desert rural Ireland', *The Sunday Business Post*, 14 August 2005.

Coonan, C., 'All the tourists in China', *The Irish Times*, 15 July 2006.

Corless, F., 'Tourism industry has nothing to smile about', *The Sunday Business Post*, 26 August 2001.

Creaton, S., 'Ryan Hotels records 20% rise in profits', *The Irish Times*, 25 September 1997.

Cullen, P. and Parsons, M., 'Tourism staff get taste of Irish culture', *The Irish Times*, 8 February 2006.

Curtin, D., 'Hotel-buying industry is steaming ahead', *The Sunday Business Post*, 9 July 2006.

de Bréadún, D., 'More than 500,000 visits by Irish to US last year', *The Irish Times*, 6 February 2006.

Deegan, G., 'Concern over east and west tourism disparity', *The Irish Times*, 11 January 2003.

Done, K., 'Ryanair presses on with new routes', *The Financial Times*, 26 September 2001.

Donohoe, M., 'New tourism authority Bill to get Dáil priority', *The Irish Times*, 4 September 2002.

Dooley, C., 'Dispute over Bord Fáilte merger', *The Irish Times*, 28 May 2003.

Dooley, C., '9 p.m. bar limit for children silly, say hoteliers', *The Irish Times*, 7 March 2005.

Duggan, J., 'Tourism body seeks €1 bn in government funds', *The Irish Times*, 1 June 2006.

Dunne, J., 'Bord Fáilte and CERT urged to amalgamate', *The Irish Times*, 6 September 2001.

Gartland, F., 'Visitors to Ireland in 2005 grew to 6.7 mn but rural tourism still in decline', *The Irish Times*, 5 January 2006.

Goodbody, W., 'New chief executive at Tourism Ireland', *The Sunday Business Post*, 22 July 2001.

Harrison, B., 'Northern tourist board takes bullish approach', *The Irish Times*, 30 August 2001.

Harrison, B., 'How to cut costs while holding appeal', *The Irish Times*, 8 November 2001.

Hayes, C., 'Ireland.ie founder has tourist market in his sights', *The Sunday Business Post*, 29 January 2006.

Healy, A., 'Target of 5% growth in visitors from abroad next year', *The Irish Times*, 2002.

Hegarty, S., 'Will the storm clouds clear?', *The Irish Times*, 5 July 2003.

Hennessy, M., 'New body to be set up to attract foreign students to Ireland', *The Irish Times*, 17 January 2006.

Hill, A., 'Wake-up call for B&Bs', *The Irish Times*, 26 March 2006.

Holmquist, K., 'Be my guest', *The Irish Times*, 22 July 2006.

Humphreys, J., 'Tourism takings rise by 21%', *The Irish Times*, 28 December 2000.

Kehoe, I., 'Fáilte Ireland appoints consultants', *The Sunday Business Post*, 11 September 2005.

Kelly, M., 'B&Bs face bleak future as tourists go bargain hunting', *The Sunday Business Post*, 24 April 2005.

Kerr, A., 'Tourists put off by pricing and airport standards', *The Irish Times*, 14 March 2006.

Kerr, A., '€5 bn spent on holidays abroad', *The Irish Times*, 16 March 2006.

Kiely, G., 'Tourists here in number but they're not travelling', *The Sunday Business Post*, 1 August 2004.

Lucey, A., 'Women targeted for west tourist work', *The Irish Times*, 16 January 2006.

Mansergh, M., 'Tourism needs the employees who are now being let go', *The Irish Times*, 21 January 2006.

McCaffrey, U., 'Bord Fáilte forecasts big losses', *The Irish Times*, 31 September 2001.

McCaffrey, U., 'Call for business tourism tax breaks', *The Irish Times*, 23 May 2006.

McDonnell, F., 'All-Ireland tourism chairman faces challenge', *The Irish Times*, 27 July 2001.

McMahon, S., 'Benchmarking for Irish tourism competitiveness', *The Sunday Business Post*, 1 June 2003.

Mitchell, S., 'Tourism Ireland spreads its net with online ads', *The Sunday Business Post*, 8 December 2002.

Mitchell, S., 'Finding Rosslare's fáilte', *The Sunday Business Post*, 20 June 2004.

Mitchell, S., 'Ireland's tourism message "confused"', *The Sunday Business Post*, 14 August 2005.

Mooney, B., 'Making reservations for your career in tourism', *The Irish Times*, 18 January 2006.

Needham, C., 'No longer a land of céad míle fáilte', *The Irish Times*, 9 February 2001.

Needham, C., 'Tough task for man redefining Irish tourism', *The Irish Times*, 29 August 2001.

Nelis, G., 'A night with knights of Glin', *The Sunday Business Post*, 3 October 2004.

Ness, F., 'Wellness reigns', *The Sunday Business Post*, 8 May 2006.

Newman, C., 'NI tourism "in tandem" with South', *The Irish Times*, 30 August 2001.

O'Brien, T., 'All-Ireland tourism body launches campaign', *The Irish Times*, 8 November 2001.

O'Dwyer, J.G., 'Sun setting on west's rural tourism industry', *The Irish Times*, 19 December 2005.

O'Mahony, C., 'Marketing Ireland in uncertain times', *The Sunday Business Post*, 30 September 2001.

O'Mahony, C., 'New tourism boss calls on low-cost airlines to help country out of crisis', *The Sunday Business Post*, 11 November 2001.

O'Mahony, C., 'Tourism Ireland defends overseas campaign', *The Sunday Business Post*, 7 July 2002.

O'Mahony, C., 'Tourist chiefs "fail to capitalise" on locally filmed hits', *The Sunday Business Post*, 4 December 2005.

Reid, L., 'Government will not intervene in Vega City', *The Irish Times*, 27 November 2003.

RTÉ, 'Ryanair July numbers climb 23%', *RTÉ News* website, 3 August 2006.

Shoesmith, C., 'Irish Ferries cancels daily route', *The Irish Times*, 25 January 2006.

Shoesmith, C., 'State's biggest annual celebration is a crock of gold for business', *The Irish Times*, 17 March 2006.

Shoesmith, C., 'Aer Lingus soars 15 per cent after takeover bid', *The Irish Times*, 6 October 2006

Shoesmith, C., 'O'Leary urges take up of Ryanair offer', *The Irish Times*, 16 December 2006

Slattery, L., 'Promoting Ireland as holiday hotspot with everlasting memories', *The Irish Times (Business This Week* supplement*)*, 1 February 2002.

Smyth, J., 'Hotels Federation calls for €31 mn US promotion fund', *The Irish Times*, 5 October 2001.

Staunton, D., 'Paddy Whackery', *The Irish Times*, 18 March 2006.

Tynan, M.M., 'O'Leary letter sparks racist row on Jordanians', *Sunday Business Post*, 27 May 2001.

Watson, P., 'Buy buy Dubai', *The Irish Times*, 25 March 2006.

NEWSPAPER ARTICLES WITH AUTHOR'S NAME UNSPECIFIED/EDITORIALS

'E-travel', *The Sunday Business Post*, 6 August 2000.

'Tourism in the North', *The Irish Times*, 20 August 2001.

'Bord Fáilte's future', *The Irish Times*, 10 September 2001.

'Serious risk to tourism', *The Irish Times*, 26 September 2001.

'Ministers join to boost cross-border tourism', *The Irish Times*, 7 November 2001.

'Marketing Ireland', *The Irish Times*, 9 November 2001.

'Tourism Ireland – new all-island tourism promotion agency in the United States launched at New York event', *PR Newswire*, 23 January 2002.

'Céad Míle Fáilte', *The Irish Times*, 28 June 2002.

'Irish Hotels Federation', *The Sunday Business Post*, 7 November 2002.

'Iraq conflict will hurt tourism, say industry experts', *The Sunday Business Post*, 2 February 2003.

'Special Report: Business Travel', *The Financial Times*, 15 November 2004.

'Tourism: The game has changed', *The Sunday Business Post*, 14 August 2005.

'Dublin turns from "craic" to culture in bid to woo tourists', *The Irish Times*, 17 January 2006.

'Biggest Irish tourism fair gets underway', *The Irish Times*, 8 May 2006.

'Martin opens first Irish tourist office in China', *The Irish Times*, 30 June 2006.

'Minister opens Tourism Ireland office in Shanghai', *Kildare Times*, 12 July 2006.

REPORTS

Bord Fáilte, *Developing Sustainable Tourism – Tourism Development Plan 1994–1999*, December 1994.

Bord Fáilte, *Tourism Development Strategy 2000–2006*, 1999.

Department of Arts, Sport and Tourism, *Operational Programme for Tourism 1994–1999 – Final Report – ESF Funded Activities*, July 2002.

Department of Arts, Sport and Tourism, *Operational Programme for Tourism 1994–1999 – Final Report – ERDF Funded Activities*. February 2003.

Department of Arts, Sport and Tourism, *Irish Tourism: Responding to Change – Interim Report of the Tourism Policy Review Group*, May 2003.

Fáilte Ireland, *New Horizons for Irish Tourism: An Agenda for Action*, 2003.
Fáilte Ireland, *Tourism Product Marketing Plans 2004*, 2004.
Fáilte Ireland, *Domestic Tourism 2004*, 2005.
Fáilte Ireland, *Regional Tourism Marketing Plans 2006*, 2005.
Fáilte Ireland, *Special Interest Tourism Plans 2005*, 2005.
Fáilte Ireland, *Summary of Activities 2005*, 2005.
Fáilte Ireland, *Visitor Attitudes Survey 2005*, 2006.
Fáilte Ireland, *Agenda*, 2006.
Fáilte Ireland, *Developing Regional Tourism 2006*, 2006.
Fáilte Ireland, *Preliminary Tourism Facts 2005*, 2006.
Fáilte Ireland, *Hotel Review 2005 – Summary*, 2006.
Government of Ireland, *Operational Programme for Tourism 1994–1999*, 1994.
IHF, *Removing Competitive Disadvantages in Tourism and Promoting Development – Submission to the Minister for Finance on Budget 2006 from the Irish Hotels Federation*, September 2005.
Implementation Group, *Establishment of New Tourism Development Authority*, April 2002.
ITIC (Irish Travel Industry Confederation), *The People & Place Programme Report*, 1999.
Minister for Arts, Sport and Tourism, *Six-Monthly Report on Developments in the EU – 1 January–30 June 2004*, 2004.
National Centre for Tourism Policy Studies, *Research Study on the Irish Self-Catering Sector*, 2005.
Travers, J., *First Progress Report of the Tourism Action Plan Implementation Group*, August 2004.
Travers, J., *Second Progress Report of the Tourism Action Plan Implementation Group*, April 2005.
Travers, J., *Third and Final Progress Report of the Tourism Action Plan Implementation Group*, March 2006.

STATISTICS

Fáilte Ireland, *Preliminary Tourism Facts 2005*, 2006.
Fáilte Ireland, *Tourism Fact Card 2000*, 2001.
Fáilte Ireland, *Tourism Fact Card 2001*, 2002.
Fáilte Ireland, *Tourism Fact Card 2002*, 2003.
Fáilte Ireland, *Tourism Fact Card 2003*, 2004.
Fáilte Ireland, *Tourism Fact Card 2004*, 2005.
Fáilte Ireland, *Tourism Barometer 2005, Wave 2*, June 2005.
Fáilte Ireland, *Markets – Australia/New Zealand 2003*, 2004.
Fáilte Ireland, *Markets – Britain 2003*, 2004.
Fáilte Ireland, *Markets – France 2003*, 2004.
Fáilte Ireland, *Markets – Germany 2003*, 2004.
Fáilte Ireland, *Markets – Italy 2003*, 2004.
Fáilte Ireland, *Markets – Netherlands 2003*, 2004.
Fáilte Ireland, *Markets – USA 2003*, 2004.
Fáilte Ireland, *Regions – Dublin 2004*, 2005.

Fáilte Ireland, *Regions – Midlands East 2004*, 2005.
Fáilte Ireland, *Regions – North West 2004*, 2005.
Fáilte Ireland, *Regions – South East 2004*, 2005.
Fáilte Ireland, *Regions – Shannon 2004*, 2005.
Fáilte Ireland, *Regions – South West 2004*, 2005.
Fáilte Ireland, *Regions – West 2004*, 2005.
Fáilte Ireland, *Guesthouses/B&Bs 2004*, 2005.
Fáilte Ireland, *Hostels 2004*, 2005.
Fáilte Ireland, *Hotels 2004*, 2005.
Fáilte Ireland, *Self-Catering 2004*, 2005.
Fáilte Ireland, *Angling 2004*, 2005
Fáilte Ireland, *Cycling 2004*, 2005.
Fáilte Ireland, *Equestrian 2004*, 2005.
Fáilte Ireland, *Gardens 2004*, 2005.
Fáilte Ireland, *Golf 2004*, 2005.
Fáilte Ireland, *Hiking/Hillwalking 2004*, 2005.
Fáilte Ireland, *Historical Cultural 2004*, 2005.
Fáilte Ireland, *Hostels 2004*, 2005.
Fáilte Ireland, *Hotels 2004*, 2005.
UNWTO, *Tourism Market Trends – 2004 Edition – World Overview and Tourism Topics*, 2004.
UNWTO, *World Tourism Barometer*, 4/2 (June 2006).
UNWTO and European Travel Commission, *MICE Outbound Tourism 2000*, 2003.

VIDEOS AND TELEVISION PROGRAMMES

Bord Fáilte, *The Island of Ireland*, Frankfurt: Grafenstein Freizeit- und Tourismus-Werbung GmbH.
Dumont Funk und Fernsehen, *On Tour Irland*, VCL Communications 2000.
Falken: *Irland*, Grünwald: Komplett-Media GmbH.
Tourism Ireland Limited, *The Current Campaign*, London: McGann-Erickson 2002.
Video Postcard from Ireland, Jersey: Channel Television.
RTÉ, 'Launch of North-South Joint Tourism Initiative – Tourism Ireland Limited', *Six-One News*, 7 November 2001.

PRESENTATIONS

Fáilte Ireland, *Roadshow Presentation – Dublin*, 2005.
Fáilte Ireland, *Roadshow Presentation – Midlands East*, 2005.
Fáilte Ireland, *Roadshow Presentation – North West*, 2005.
Fáilte Ireland, *Roadshow Presentation – Shannon*, 2005.
Fáilte Ireland, *Roadshow Presentation – South East*, 2005.
Fáilte Ireland, *Roadshow Presentation – South West*, 2005.
Fáilte Ireland, *Roadshow Presentation – West*, 2005.

Index